FIVE-FINGER
DISCOUNT

FIVE-FINGER DISCOUNT

DISCOUNT

A Crooked Family History

HELENE STAPINSKI

RANDOM HOUSE

New York

All rights reserved under International and Pan-American Copyright Conventions. Published in the United States by Random House, Inc., New York, and simultaneously in Canada by Random House of Canada Limited, Toronto.

Grateful acknowledgment is made to the following for permission to reprint previously published material:
EMI Music Publishing: Excerpt from "Marianne (All Day, All Night, Marianne) by Terry Gilkyson, Richard Dehr, and Frank Miller. Copyright © 1955, 1956 and copyright renewed 1983, 1984 by EMI Blackwood Music, Inc. All rights reserved. International copyright secured. Used by permission.
Warner Bros. Publications: Excerpt from "When Day Is Done" by B. G. DeSylva and Dr. Robert Katcher. Copyright © 1924 by Wiener Boheme Verlag. Copyright © 1926 by Warner Bros. Inc. Copyright renewed, assigned to Warner Bros. Inc. and Stephen Ballentine Music. All rights reserved. Used by permission of Warner Bros. Publications US Inc., Miami, FL 33014.
Henderson Music Co. and Fred Ahlert Music Group on behalf of Old Clover Leaf Music: Excerpt from "Bye Bye Blackbird" by Mort Dixon and Ray Henderson. Reprinted by permission of Henderson Music Co. and Fred Ahlert Music Group on behalf of Old Clover Leaf Music.

Some of the names of the author's friends and relatives have been changed to protect their privacy.

Library of Congress Cataloging-in-Publication Data
Stapinski, Helene.
Five-finger discount : a crooked family history / Helene Stapinski.—1st ed.
p.   cm.
ISBN 0-679-46306-2 (acid-free paper)
1. Criminals—New Jersey—Jersey City—Biography.   2. Stapinski family.   I. Title.
HV6785 .S73 2000
364.1'092—dc21
[B]   00-059104

Random House website address: www.atrandom.com

Printed in the United States of America on acid-free paper

2 4 6 8 9 7 5 3

First Edition

Book design by Caroline Cunningham

For Sissy and Babe

CONTENTS

CONTENTS

FIVE-FINGER
DISCOUNT

1

MAJESTIC MEMORY

The night my grandfather tried to kill us, I was five years old, the age I stopped believing in Santa Claus, started kindergarten, and made real rather than imaginary friends.

Because Grandpa was one of two grandfathers in their family, my cousins called him Grandpa Jerry. For me, he was simply Grandpa. I had only one. The other—my father's father, the Polish grandpa we called Dziadzia (pronounced *Jaja*)—was hit over the head during a burglary in his front hallway seven years before I was born and died after slipping into a coma.

Everyone in Jersey City knew Grandpa—Italian Grandpa—as Beansie, because when he was young, he stole a crate of beans from the back of a truck. Details about his life started to bubble into my consciousness during the summer of 1970, the year my memory kicked in full force. There were stories about Grandpa "going away" to Trenton for murder. Being arrested for armed robbery. Beating my mother, her sister, and her three brothers.

Grandpa was a well-known neighborhood bully and crook, though the only stolen objects I knew of firsthand were the ones he swiped while working as a security guard at the Jersey City Public Library and Museum in the late 1960s. The fact that Grandpa was able to get a city job as a security guard—through an uncle, who knew a local judge, who was connected to the mayor—says a lot about Jersey City's patronage system and general reputation. Everybody stole. It was no big deal.

My brother inherited most of the objects Grandpa took from the library and museum—the shiny, shellacked coins with Indian feathered heads; a photograph of Abraham Lincoln; small, black Indian arrowheads; a set of encyclopedias. I always wondered if Grandpa stole them book by book or had one of his friends with a car pull up to the library and help him load them in.

The only stolen object of Grandpa's that I possess is a dictionary, a Webster's Seventh New Collegiate edition, which he inscribed to my sister the year I was born: "From Grandpa. Hi Ya Paula. Year—1965." The call numbers on the spine and the blue stamp on a back page, which reads FREE PUBLIC LIBRARY JERSEY CITY, N.J., have been crossed out in blue indelible marker, his attempt to legitimize the gift. Grandpa obviously had his own interpretation of the phrase *free public library*.

Before I started school, my grandma Pauline baby-sat for me while my mother worked as a clerk at the Jersey City Division of Motor Vehicles office, three blocks away. When Grandma died in February of 1970, my mother had no one to baby-sit, so she quit her job. Though I'm sure I missed my grandma—a saintly woman with a halo of white hair and small, pretty hands—my world changed for the better. I was suddenly the center of my mother's attention. With Grandma gone, Grandpa was at the center of no one's.

Because my grandmother had stayed married to Grandpa for four decades, she died fairly young. She was only sixty. She died on Ash Wednesday, the first day of Lent. By then Grandma hated Grandpa so much that on her deathbed, with the smudge of ashes on her forehead, she made my mother promise that Grandpa wouldn't be buried on top of her when he died. She couldn't stand the thought of his remains mingling with hers.

During her lifetime, Grandma quietly threatened to poison Grandpa, but she never did. She never even got up enough courage to leave him. I couldn't understand why she stayed with him for so long. Or why she was even with him to begin with.

Maybe it was because Grandpa was so handsome. Like my mother, he had delicate features, thin lips, and olive skin. His hairless body was covered in tattoos, like a bloom of fresh blue-and-purple bruises, which he'd gotten when he was in the army, which he joined, illegally, at age fourteen. On his leg was tattooed a hula girl, which, in his lighter, happier moments Grandpa would make dance for me by rippling his calf muscle. A blue chain was tattooed around one wrist. A snake slithered up his arm, past a cross and a red-and-blue heart. On his other arm was my grandmother's name—Pauline—underneath the profile of Evelyn Nesbit, the famous girl in the red velvet swing, a popular tattoo subject in 1906. It was a sign that Grandpa adored Grandma. Though he was known to beat his children, he never laid a hand on his wife. He loved her and even had a pet name for her—Boobie.

But Grandpa's rage was so potent that it could be contagious. My aunt Mary Ann had moved to Florida just to get away from Grandpa after almost hitting him over the head with a statue of the Blessed Virgin Mary. Uncle Robby, my mother's youngest brother, was once chased by Grandpa with a broken bottle in front of his own children. Uncle Robby, pushed to the brink of insanity during one of their fights, went at him with a five iron, then smashed Grandpa's picture window.

The violent streak hadn't been passed down to my mother so much. She cursed a lot, though. Whenever she let loose a particularly nasty string of obscenities, my quiet father would yell from two rooms away, "Shut your trap." When she was going through menopause, she ripped a phone out of the wall. But that was the only time I ever saw her do something violent.

Right after Grandma died, Grandpa turned his rage on himself, since he had no one at home to terrorize anymore. He tried to kill himself three times. He jumped out the first-floor window of his apartment but did little damage. If Grandpa had lived in a high-rise, our troubles that year would have just ended there.

But Grandpa was persistent. He tried again, swallowing twenty tranquilizers. When the pills failed to do the job, he stabbed himself with a penknife. Later that spring, he was taken to Meadowview, "the crazy house," the only one of its kind in Hudson County.

Meadowview was in Secaucus, a few towns over from Jersey City. Because land was abundant there, it was not cramped like nearby Hoboken and Union City. Secaucus, destined for office parks and multiplexes in the 1980s, was still trying to live down its reputation as a pig farm in the 1970s. When I was a kid, there were jokes about Secaucus and how it smelled like manure. A joker would stretch out one arm and hand, like in a Nazi salute, and hold his nose with the other hand.

"Who am I?" he would ask. "Superman flying over Secaucus."

I didn't get it. I didn't know about the pig farms. I was convinced that people made fun of Secaucus because of the smell rising from Meadowview.

With no baby-sitter, my mother had to take me with her wherever she went—to funerals and wakes, shopping, and to visit Grandpa at Meadowview. It reeked of urine and dirty bedsheets. Legions of mentally retarded men and women and crazy people—much crazier than Grandpa—wandered the fluorescent-lit yellow hallways.

One man had the habit of twisting his wrist all the way around, then placing his hand over his skull, pressing his thumb and middle finger to his temples. The compulsive action—repeated thousands of times—left indentations in his head. I wondered if it gave him a headache and, if it did, why he kept doing it. Another floormate of Grandpa's would lift the lid off a garbage can and replace it, again and again and again. Yet another wore a turban and was known to stand up on a chair and pee onto the dinner table. Grandpa may have been crazy, but he certainly didn't belong there. Nobody belonged there. Except maybe the guy with the turban.

On my first visit to Meadowview, I learned that I actually had two relatives in residence. My father's brother Tommy had been there since 1963, but until Grandpa was institutionalized, I had never visited him. Tommy, the shame of the Stapinski clan, was now brain-damaged from years of epilepsy. Various family members had taken turns caring for him after his parents, my Polish grandparents, died. Most of the time, they had liked having him around. Uncle Tommy cleaned house better than a woman, turning the mattresses over and cleaning the bugs out of the springs. Some afternoons he even made a few bucks cleaning and waxing the cars down at the Manischewitz factory, where his brother Joe worked.

Unfortunately, Tommy was also known for his fits of rage, which always came on the heels of an epileptic seizure. He had almost killed his brother Henry, the family bookie, bending him backward over a tub and nearly breaking his back.

Once, at our house, Uncle Tommy had a seizure and, due to some especially slippery carpet, slid under my parents' bed and got stuck there. Several uncles ran to his rescue and dragged him out before he swallowed his tongue. Another time after a seizure, Uncle Tommy ran up onto the roof of his house. The cops were called, and they chased him from roof to roof until he was caught. Then there was the time he fell down the stairs and knocked his teeth out. The Stapinskis had no choice but to send Tommy "away" to Meadowview.

Whenever I saw him, timid and smiling a shy, squinty-eyed smile that looked too much like my father's, I felt like crying. I couldn't decide which was worse, visiting Uncle Tommy or not visiting him. Being at Meadowview with him was awful. But the incredible guilt and sadness of thinking of my uncle there alone was even more painful. The most heartbreaking vision of all was one that I could only imagine, one that my older sister, Paula, had witnessed as a child: Uncle Tommy standing in a doorway with a shoe-shine kit outside the downtown train station, pleading, "Shine?" over and over again at disinterested passersby. On my visits to Meadowview, I wondered if Uncle Tommy missed his job, or if he even remembered he'd had one.

For Grandpa, I felt much less sadness. What upset me most, made me cringe, was the sight of his bloody fingernails, which were chewed practically to the cuticles. Just the thought of them sent a sharp pain through my abdomen and down to my groin. I was a nail-biter myself, but there were limits.

The sight of Grandpa must have bothered my mother, too. After convincing my father it was all right, she finally signed Grandpa out of Meadowview and invited him to come and live with us in our three-bedroom apartment that summer of 1970. Meanwhile, Grandpa would search for a place of his own. Something on the ground floor.

From the second-floor kitchen window in our apartment, my mother would watch me play. She kept a close eye on me because we lived above a tavern—the Majestic—which sometimes attracted a "bad element." During the day, the Majestic was filled with harmless old drunks and corrupt City Hall politicians, who came to the tavern for lunch—soggy pot roast sandwiches with rich brown gravy or delicious pepper and egg or cheeseburgers, which seemed as big as Frisbees in my small hands.

Patrolling the corner was the Majestic's mascot and most loyal customer, a hunchback named Vince, who wore a fedora and a long raincoat. He was the bar's first customer each day, a true alcoholic, who downed his first drink in broad daylight. To help defray the cost of his beer—which he slowly sipped like tea, savoring every drop—Vince swept the cracked sidewalk outside the Majestic every few hours, then swept the gutter, pushing the cigarette butts and other litter down past the sewer grate.

My brother, Stanley, who was seven years older than I was, usually played ball with his friends across the street at City Hall Park, a concrete plaza with a few patches of dead grass. When his friends weren't around, he would join me in a game of stickball against the graffitied wall of our three-story brick building. The rest of the time I played alone, watched over by my mother and Vince.

In winter, I built snowmen with the dirty snow out front. Instead of a broom, I sometimes stuck a discarded, empty whiskey bottle in the snowman's side. My mother yelled at me for it. We weren't allowed to play with bottles, and whenever we even went near one, my mother would retell the story of the little neighborhood girl who was found standing up, dead, a broken bottle lodged in her jugular vein. Did I want the same thing to happen to me?

Some afternoons I wasn't allowed out to play at all, especially during the riots and parades that were staged outside City Hall, an imposing building with a two-story-high arched entrance and four Corinthian columns, which took up a whole city block. Guarding the entrance was a green-bronze statue, a seated woman with a helmet on her head and her right arm in the air, who I thought was a tired, miniature version of the Statue of Liberty. My mother told me that late at night, when I wasn't watching, the lady got up and danced. Maybe that was why she was sitting down during the day. Her feet obviously hurt.

We lived on the corner of Mercer and Grove Streets. My parents' bedroom window looked out onto Grove, a heavily trafficked street, and directly at City Hall and the tired lady. Our front door was on Mercer, a one-way treeless street of battered three-story brick buildings and dilapidated brownstones. The intersection was a busy one, because of City Hall, and was easy to find through the telescopic viewing machines from the top of the World Trade Center in Manhattan, where my mother took me on field trips when I was a little older. From the top of New York's tallest skyscraper, my house and Jersey City looked a lot like that statue outside City Hall—small and tired.

Living across the street from City Hall guaranteed hours of entertainment, better than watching *Kojak* and *Cannon,* because from my parents' bedroom window I could see the political action unfold.

One afternoon I made a poster, featuring the name of a political-reform mayoral candidate. I used red and blue Magic Markers, and hung the poster from my parents' bedroom window on the day Mayor Smith took his oath of office. I was on the news that night—or at least my skinny arms were, sticking out from the sides of the poster as I waved the oak tag in the wind.

One autumn, City Hall nearly burned to the ground. Along with the Tired Statue of Liberty, we sat and watched the fire department battle the flames. I bit my nails as the pump and ladders doused the building with three-story-high sprays of water. Mayor Smith, wearing a fireman's hat, ran in and out of the building, dragging soggy files into the street, his face covered in soot.

It took all day for the firefighters to extinguish the flames and a few weeks for them to rule out arson. There were reports of disgruntled workers driving off in a red car minutes after the blaze began. Those stories were either unfounded or hushed up. All we knew was that part of the green copper roof was destroyed, its metal frame poking out like a skeleton. The bronze lady was intact, though. A little wet, but undamaged.

One year my mother made us all duck for cover when bullets started to fly at the Puerto Rican Day Parade, which always ended at

City Hall. Tensions were high during the parade every summer, and no wonder, with a mix of new immigrants from the island and the third-generation Irish and Italian cops. The Puerto Ricans would wave their single-star flags, and the white Jersey City residents, forgetting they were only a couple generations removed from immigration, would yell things like "If you like it so much, why don't you go the hell back?" I remember watching one riot from my parents' bedroom window and hearing the distinct crack of a billy club hitting a hard skull. Another summer, a local anarchist threw a Molotov cocktail at the building. That time, the fire didn't catch.

Jersey City was a tough place to grow up, except I didn't know any better. I had nothing to compare it to. All I knew was that I was well fed and comfortable in our apartment. The air was filled with industrial smells that meant home. On rainy days, the sky was thick with the pungent smell of coffee manufactured by Maxwell House in Hoboken, the next town up the Hudson. On most other days, the air was dusted with scents from the Colgate-Palmolive factory just a few blocks away. Depending on the stage of manufacturing, the air either stank with the fat from which the soap was made or it hung heavy with the perfume with which it was scented. On the worst and windiest days, the city borrowed its smell from the south, from Newark's bone-rendering plant. But on its best days, Jersey City smelled of chocolate from the Van Leer cocoa factory, a five-year-old's dream come true.

The sounds of my neighborhood were as memorable as the smells. Each summer night, the Puerto Rican men on our block would drag their giant conga drums over to City Hall Park and bang throughout the night, until we fell asleep to the Latin rhythms or until my angry father called the police. "The natives are restless," he'd grumble, trying to drown out the sounds with the ball game played simultaneously on the radio and the television.

Sirens were familiar, too, and whenever one Dopplered past, we were taught to bless ourselves and say a prayer for the person on the other end of the emergency. Mixing with the sirens were the calls of the drug dealers on our street. I didn't know that it was uncommon to have guys on your corner yelling *"Tobaccos sueltos"*—"loose joints." Junkies sometimes slept on our doorstep, and I learned at an early age not to play with the hypodermic needles they left behind. One night the family was awoken by a woman having withdrawal symptoms on our doorstep. My mother called an ambulance, not the cops. That's when I learned the difference between a junkie and a dealer: The dealers were evil; the junkies were just sad.

For revenge, or maybe just for fun, I would drop my Slinky out the kitchen window, lowering it enough to graze the dealers' heads, and then yank the metal coil back up. They would reach up to see what was there, but by the time they craned their necks up toward my window, I'd be crouched down low, both me and my Slinky out of sight. Reminding the dealers that they were trafficking in front of a five-year-old's home, I would blow bubbles from that same window, letting them drift down onto the street below. The dealers would laugh and wave up at me. I waved back, or sometimes gave them the finger.

When she got frustrated enough, my mother would stick her head out the window and curse at them. "Get that shit out of my garbage cans," she once shouted to a dealer hiding his dime bags in our trash.

"Okay, lady," the dealer yelled back. "But you don't have to curse."

My teenage sister, Paula, a petite brunette voted prettiest in her high school class, suffered the most in our neighborhood. Her dating pool was extremely limited. Whenever she left the house, the dealers would make smooching sounds and catcalls. It made me so mad that I swore I'd pour pots of boiling water on their heads someday.

There were worse neighborhoods in Jersey City, my father always rationalized, and worse taverns than the Majestic. A bar just down the street from us was known for its bloody fights. I remember strolling with my mother and seeing a shirtless man covered in blood bursting out the door, screaming. He had been attacked by another man with a carving fork. What could he have done so wrong to make someone want to stab him with a carving fork? I thought of the devil, armed with a big pitchfork, and wondered if he lived in Jersey City.

An optimist like my father, I was convinced that downtown Jersey City wasn't so bad. The piers in our neighborhood may have been burnt and rotted, but at least we had a view of downtown New York from the Majestic's roof.

When my father returned from work each day at around 5 P.M., the tavern was his first stop. Some afternoons I was out front playing, climbing the pole on our corner or killing ants with shards of glass, pretending to be a mad surgeon. Daddy would kiss me hello, then disappear into the mysterious darkness that was the Majestic. An hour later, if I was still out playing, my mother would yell down to "get Daddy." Getting Daddy was one of my jobs.

In the hot summer months, getting Daddy was a pleasure, since the Majestic was ice-cold from the huge air conditioner hanging over its bar. It was even colder than our own well-air-conditioned apartment. At the Majestic, I would push open the corrugated-metal door, chilled from the inside out, and enter a cool cave of smoke and stale beer. My father usually sat on the far side of the bar, drinking a shot and a beer, so I would have to make my way around its entire U shape, passing my father's friends and various bookies along the way. They would peel dollar bills from thick wads in their pockets and hand them to me— "for ice cream," they'd say. On a good day at the Majestic, I'd make an easy ten bucks, cramming the bills into my giant Tootsie Roll bank, which we'd gotten from a family friend who worked at the nearby Tootsie Roll plant.

Daddy kept his money folded in order of denomination: singles on top, followed by fives, tens, twenties, and the occasional fifty or hundred, which slept warmly and silently in the center. The bills were bound by a thick rubber band, never a wallet. Back in 1956, Daddy's wallet had been stolen at Schneider's bar. He'd refused to carry one ever since. He kept his roll in the left-hand pocket of his sky-blue work shirt. Above the uniform pocket and his cash was his nickname, Babe, sewn in script. The nickname came from his being the youngest boy of eleven children.

I knew a secret about him that most of the men in the Majestic didn't know: Even in summer, Daddy wore long johns underneath his blue pants, because he worked in a walk-in freezer, the Union Terminal Cold Storage, the big red warehouse right beside the mouth of the Holland Tunnel. Because my father was used to the cold, we had air-conditioning in our house, a big unit blowing waves of cold air from my parents' bedroom over my father's hairy beer belly.

When my father saw me at the Majestic, he would smile, barely wide enough to reveal his missing top teeth. (Dental hygiene was never big on the Stapinski side.) When he smiled, his slanted eyes nearly closed shut and his large nose bent lower toward his top lip. His gray hair, which in later years turned white, was slicked back by a handful of Vitalis hair tonic. His laugh was high-pitched but muffled, in the wheeze family, the result of his not wanting to open his mouth too wide to reveal his gums. He also didn't talk much. But when he did, what he said was usually either wise or witty, since he'd had so much time to think through what he wanted to say. This was the opposite of my mother and me. Like Grandpa, we got way too excited over the smallest thing and let you know about it right away.

My father spoke Polish, but hardly ever around me. I pictured him having elaborate conversations in Polish with his siblings, out of earshot. The reality was that Daddy hardly ever spoke at all, in Polish or in English. His nickname for me was Helcha, a Polish version of Helen. He never cursed, unlike my mother, and his harshest insult was "you banana." When he yelled, which was very rarely, he roared, and you ran as far away as possible. His favorite animal was the elephant, which explained a lot. Slow and patient, powerful but peaceful, never forgetful. Every year he took us to the circus at Madison Square Garden, and before the Greatest Show on Earth, he would usher us underground to the menagerie to feed peanuts to the silent, friendly pachyderms, his soul mates.

He was the smartest of all his siblings, and a natural-born leader. His biggest responsibility, besides his job at the Cold Storage, was serving as president of a downtown organization called the Dudley Social and Athletic Club, so named because it was located on Dudley Street, which took its name from Jersey City's first mayor, Dudley S. Gregory.

The members of the Dudley Club, which consisted of my father's brothers and all of his best friends, ran illegal raffles, a Christmas bash, an occasional polka party, an annual dinner dance called the Dudley Dinner, a softball league, and summer bus rides to a place called Bubbling Springs, a man-made lake in western New Jersey that held mixed memories for me. Since I was the youngest, I caught only the tail end of the joyous Bubbling Springs era. But my mother regaled me with stories of the good old days, when she would bring a giant tray of macaroni and Daddy would grill lobster tails, which had fallen hot off the truck at his job at the Cold Storage. Not surprisingly, the lifeguards always spent their breaks at our picnic table.

By the time I was old enough for the Bubbling Springs bus rides, the joy had begun to run out. My most vivid memories included many of the reasons the trips were discontinued: Some kid gave a duck a cigarette and burned his bill. A poacher shot all the deer on the property. They had been tamed and fenced in for visitors to pet (along with the duck). Finally, the Dudleys were involved in a four-car pileup on the way to the lake. When they got there, the car trunk carrying all the beer was so dented that they couldn't get it open. Just when the Dudleys thought things couldn't get any worse that day, a deaf boy drowned at the lake. The trips to Bubbling Springs ended soon after that. The only thing my mother feared more than me falling on a bottle was me drowning.

Despite his Dudley accomplishments, Daddy was an underachiever, following the path of least resistance. He could have been a professional bowler, a surgeon, an accountant, or the boss at the Cold Storage, my mother said. But he never wanted the headaches that came with responsibility. The Dudley Club was about all he could handle. At one time, though, he did have the ambition to run numbers, like Uncle Henry. A guy named Chick wanted to hire him to drop off some betting slips. My mother told him in no uncertain terms—likely peppered with a string of obscenities—that no father of her children would run numbers, that she would leave him if he became a bookie. She knew the embarrassment of having a father who was constantly being arrested.

If you were from Jersey City, you were either a quick-witted crook or you sat back and blended into the ugly scenery. Otherwise, you moved out. My father was too good to be a criminal (with my mother providing an extra shot of morality) and too apathetic to move. That was why we lived where we did: the path of least resistance.

Daddy carried that concept over into his wardrobe. When he wasn't wearing his uniform, he wore white shirts with a single pocket, black or brown dress slacks, and highly polished, shiny dress shoes. Colors did not adorn his body. Colors were for women, hippies, and effeminate men. My mother did all his shopping for him.

Each night in the Majestic, Daddy would lift me onto the knee of his blue work pants so I could get a glimpse of the rows of colorful bottles behind the bar. Each one wore a tiny, brightly colored cap that looked like a little birthday hat. They made it easier to pour the drinks, Daddy told me, his breath smelling of Scotch, his work clothes heavy with smoke.

"Hi, Nicky," I'd yell to the bartender, a short, balding man with a very round head and glasses. He resembled a clay figure from an animated Christmas special on TV. If there was time before dinner, Nicky would fill me a glass of soda, with a maraschino cherry, or even let me behind the bar to clean glasses on the rounded rotating brushes inside the deep stainless-steel sink.

Each night around this time, the pay phone in the Majestic would start ringing. Wives without the convenience of living upstairs were in search of their husbands. Daddy would take my hand and with his other hand grab the bag of frozen food he'd swiped from work at the Cold Storage that day. Together, we'd walk up the two dusty flights of stairs to our apartment.

On weekend nights, Daddy would usually come home on his own, drunk, and excited to watch *The Lawrence Welk Show*. Daddy was a happy drunk. On Welk's cue—*an'-a-one-an'-a-two*—he'd sweep me up into his arms and waltz me around the living room. We'd dance until the bubbles were released from Welk's bubble machine and the chorus sang "Good night, sleep tight, and may your dreams come true."

By July 1970, my father wasn't the only relative hanging out at the Majestic. Grandpa, now living with us, hung out there too. My grandfather, an unhappy drunk, sat at one end of the bar, closest to the cold metal door, and my father sat at the other end, in his usual spot. Daddy, who seemed to get along with everyone, never got along with Grandpa. No one did.

By then, beaten down by Meadowview, Grandpa seemed humble and quiet. I rarely saw him, since he was out most of the time. His presence was more like a bad smell that lingered around the house—hard to trace, but always there. A telltale sign that he was in the house or close by were the Lucky Strike butts he left floating in the toilet, gray and pointed, with black tips. I had never seen a bullet, but I imagined that's what they'd look like.

The only time I remember Grandpa getting out of control was the night he pounded his fist on our dinner table, which my mother had inherited from Grandma when she died. Maybe because of the table, Grandpa felt right at home, comfortable enough to terrorize us. He pounded so hard that the Pepsi bottle jumped in the air.

While Grandpa lived with us, my brother, Stanley, was forced to sleep on the couch. Grandpa was given his bedroom, a back room that was always dark. I hated that room even before Grandpa arrived, and rarely went back there. Its one window looked out onto a small tar roof, where pink Spaldeen balls lost from countless games of stickball sat abandoned, covered in grease from the Majestic's grill fan. Because of the fan, my brother could never open his bedroom window. And the view of the fan and roof was so ugly, the blinds were always drawn. Every few months we would peek through the slats and glance longingly at those unused handballs out there. I hoped that someday, with a little soap and water, they would be mine to toss into the graffitied strike zone on our front wall—a giant S floating in a white square.

I wondered whether Grandpa would have done what he did that summer had he been given my sister's bedroom, a bright, sunny spot with daisy stickers on the walls and a view onto Grove Street. It probably wouldn't have made much of a difference. Grandpa was just mean, my mother said. I figured he was born that way.

He was given a key to our apartment and was told to keep the front door locked because of the junkies and dealers. But Grandpa—who had been on the wagon at Meadowview—started to drink. One night he threw up all over our bathroom. Even worse was that night after night he left the front door unlocked, the hypodermic needles—and their owners—drifting into our hallway. On rainy nights, the dealers set up shop in our vestibule.

My father decided he'd had enough. He asked Grandpa to give up his key and to ring the doorbell whenever he needed to come upstairs. Once he was buzzed in, the door would automatically lock behind him, keeping the junkies and dealers out. It was a simple and understandable request. Grandpa gave up the key, but he never forgave my father for asking for it.

One afternoon in August, one of Grandpa's sisters called my mother. I remember my mother nodding, not smiling or laughing like she usually did during phone conversations. This call didn't last long, not even long enough for my mother to sit down at the kitchen table. My aunt hadn't called to chat; she'd called to say that Grandpa had a gun and that he was threatening to kill my father.

Grandpa had often threatened to kill different members of the family, so my mother shrugged it off as just another rant. But the next night at the Majestic, with my father at the other side of the bar, Grandpa started flashing his gun. My father, having downed several beers by then, didn't see what was going on. But I can just see Grandpa, looking like a disheveled George Raft in his gangster-wanna-be fedora, his silver .22 glinting in the light from the Yankees game on the tavern TV, bragging about putting a bullet in my father's belly.

Our neighbor Ducky casually walked up to my father and asked, "What's with Beansie? He's got a piece on him."

I was upstairs, playing in the kitchen with my cousin Gerri, who was staying the night. Gerri was named after her father, my uncle Jerry, and Grandpa. Aside from the name, she had little in common with Grandpa. Gerri had no mean streak like some of us had inherited. Like Grandma, she had blue eyes and fair skin and a bright, easy smile, later straightened by braces. She was five years older than I was, but she never shooed me away like some of the other big kids in our family. My sister was eleven years older than I was, and was usually too busy dating, cheerleading, and sneaking Marlboros to spend time with a five-year-old. Gerri, my favorite cousin, didn't mind playing with me.

That night, Gerri and I were playing with our Barbies in the kitchen sink, pretending they were at the municipal pool in North Bergen, the town north of Jersey City where my cousins lived. Tap water was flowing over Ken's hairless chest when the front door opened.

It was my father, who had come upstairs to tell my mother about what Ducky had said. He knew nothing about my aunt's call. And he hadn't seen the gun and still didn't know what it was for.

My mother went to the kitchen phone and dialed the police, telling them there was a man with a gun threatening to shoot someone in the tavern. She was embarrassed to tell them it was her father and that he was coming to kill her husband. All she needed to say was the magic word—*Beansie*. The Jersey City police knew him well. Within minutes, the cops were on their way, lights flashing, siren screaming, this time growing closer and closer until the ear-piercing sound settled outside our front door. It never even occurred to me to bless myself at the sound. It was all too close.

Gerri and I took a break from our Barbie dolls to peek through the dusty venetian blinds in the kitchen. I wasn't sure what was happening, but it was very exciting. I wondered if Grandpa might shoot up at us from the street, but the police frisked him and confiscated his .22 after dragging him from his bar stool.

We watched from the window of our yellow-wallpapered kitchen as the police put Grandpa in handcuffs and shoved him into the cop car, their blue arms pushing him into the caged backseat. The next day, there was a brief story on page 3 in the local newspaper, *The Jersey Journal*. The headline read MAN SEIZED ON WAY "TO KILL 5 CHILDREN." The man was Grandpa. That last phrase was in quotation marks because Grandpa had told the police who he planned to shoot: Ma, Daddy, Paula, Stanley, and me. He'd forgotten that Gerri was sleeping over. "The police said Vena talked openly of his desire to kill his family," the story read. "He said he was despondent, he had been drinking during the morning and he had a desire to shoot someone."

Since I hadn't even started school yet, I couldn't read the newspaper account. It wasn't until years later that I found the clipping in the library. That's when the drama—or the reality of it, anyway—finally hit me, written in simple black-and-white. The memory had been clear, but it was just one of a string of family crimes and tragedies, which I thought most people experienced on a regular basis.

Over the years, in family stories told casually in passing, the anecdote had been repeated again and again until it had lost all meaning, like a word said over and over until it sounds like gibberish. I had heard a hundred times how the arresting detective, Michael Borseso, told my mother that Grandpa had the gun all ready to fire that night, that he would have kept shooting until all the bullets were gone. I imagined myself in a dramatic death scene, falling to the kitchen floor. But that wasn't how the story had ended.

I knew it all by heart, like the chorus of a familiar song: He had been just a few yards from the front door, steps from being buzzed up, a quick walk past the dust bunnies and broken tiles of the hallway that my father and I passed on our way home from the Majestic on those hot summer nights.

That night, after Detective Borseso took Grandpa away, Daddy was so upset that he drank practically a whole bottle of Dewar's. My mother wasn't as upset as he was, only because she was already numb from a lifetime of Grandpa.

He was charged with threatening life and possession of a dangerous weapon. Two days later, he was out on $500 bail, probably put up by one of his drinking buddies or one of his eleven siblings. My mother soon heard he'd gotten another gun, so for weeks she lived in fear.

She tried calling a local judge, Edward Zampella, the same guy who had gotten Grandpa the job at the library, to find out if there was anything we could do to keep him away from us. But Zampella brushed my mother off and told her not to worry. "That bastard," my mother said after she hung up. If she had offered him a cash bribe, maybe Zampella would have produced some results. He was that kind of judge. Hudson County was full of them.

So Ma worried until Grandpa was finally sentenced to twelve months in the Hudson County jail. His stay there didn't last long. To get high, Grandpa drank cough medicine, and wound up throwing up blood. He was sent to the Jersey City Medical Center, where he was tied to his bed because of his violent tendencies. When they'd had enough of him, the staff sent him to Trenton State Psychiatric, where he had a heart attack.

At some point, he went to live at my cousin Gerri's house. I remember seeing him one more time while he was living there. I was seven years old. Grandpa scared me, but in the way a muzzled attack dog scares you. I kept my distance, just in case Grandpa bit one last time. He offered me a dollar bill to try and get me to come closer. I told him to leave it on the floor, that I'd pick it up later. Once he was gone, I grabbed the dollar and crammed it into my Tootsie Roll bank.

Grandpa died the next year at Kennedy Hospital in Edison, on Christmas Day 1973. My mother went to the funeral without us.

Safely buried at Holy Name Cemetery on New Year's Eve, in a plot separate from my grandmother's, Grandpa could never bother any of us again. Not physically, anyway. But he damaged us all in different ways—emotionally, psychologically, genetically. For one of us, Grandpa opened up a door to a dark place, one much darker and colder than the Majestic or Stanley's bedroom.

In time, one of us would carry on a long family tradition, one that didn't start with Grandpa and wasn't confined to just our family. As I grew, I realized that crime was—and still is—a rich Hudson County tradition, floating from one generation to another, like a defective gene in a dirty pool.

2

LUCKY NUMBER

———————

The day I was born, my whole family hit the number.

Back then, Ma, Daddy, Stanley, and Paula hadn't yet moved to the apartment over the Majestic but lived a few blocks closer to the Hudson River. That first apartment was on Sussex Street, right across from our parish church, Our Lady of Czestochowa (OLC), the parish for all the Stapinskis.

Uncle Henry Stapinski, my father's oldest brother and the family bookie, lived just a few doors down from us, in a bachelor apartment, where he kept his "office." Henry's desk and the apartment were a complete mess. The television and radio always played simultaneously, broadcasting two different games. A pillow was kept on his hard, wooden chair for support, to protect his back, which Uncle Tommy had almost broken.

His desk was piled high with copies of *Sports Eye* newspapers, the local papers, lists of numbers, receipts, and large piles of cash in mostly small denominations. There were two phones on Henry's desk—not for efficiency, but because he was lazy. One was broken. He just never bothered to fix it.

Uncle Henry didn't spend much time in his bachelor apartment. When anyone in the neighborhood wanted to play the number, all they had to do was find Henry, loitering on some neighborhood corner, and tell him their number, which consisted of three digits. It was easy, easier than playing the Pick-6 or Pick-21. There was no waiting on line at a convenience store or filling out an SAT-like card and handing it to a man behind a deli counter.

Some people in Jersey City played the same number every day for decades, hoping the odds would finally catch up with them and reward them for their loyalty. They were the people spooked by stories of a gambler changing his number midlife and the next day that number finally hitting. Others based their bets on birthdays, anniversaries, dreams they'd had the night before, psychic predictions, addresses on doors, license-plate numbers of cars that ran into them or their family members. If it had three digits, it was up for grabs and was considered potentially lucky.

No matter how a gambler arrived at it, the number was written in Uncle Henry's small flip-up notebook. Each page was perforated down the middle, with the number and the amount wagered written on each side—one side for Henry, one side ripped out as a receipt. For obvious legal reasons, the gambler's name was left out of it. Uncle Henry would shake your hand at the end of the transaction and slip you your receipt in exchange for your money.

Playing the number was a community activity, and in my case a family affair. Nobody ever cheated you out of your winnings, and you never cheated anybody out of your losings. People paid up or else they got hurt. Uncle Henry never broke any kneecaps himself, as far as I know. Someone else took care of that.

Unlike the lottery, the daily number had a kind of dignity. It wasn't chosen from a cheesy air-generated Ping-Pong ball machine by an aspiring model/actress on a local TV station, but by cutting off the last three numbers of the total mutuel handle at the track that day. Gamblers found the number by looking in the horse-racing pages in the local paper. In Jersey City, crowds would run to the Palace drugstore each night to buy the *Daily News* as soon as it came off the truck. The number would spread through the neighborhood by flashing fingers, from corner to corner, like baseball catchers communicating secret signs. For those at home, the number would come by phone at around 7 P.M.

Ours was one of the first phones to ring, since the bookie was, after all, Uncle Henry. His call was a thrill each night, and as soon as I was old enough to walk, I would sprint to the kitchen, reach up, and grab the receiver before the first ring was even through.

Whenever he called, Uncle Henry never said hello, just in case he was being bugged. Just, "Henny. 325." Or, "Henny. 478." Always in a mumble, no matter what the number was. Before hanging up, I bellowed the number through the house for everyone to hear. It was my nightly ritual and moment in the spotlight. When my mother's boss from the DMV called to get the number, I was the one to tell him. I had no idea it was illegal. I just knew it was really important. Being the bearer of information gave me a thrill.

Back in the days before I was born, bookmaking was so popular that the bookie would come into the trash-strewn courtyard of the tenements and whistle to get the gamblers' attention. As rats hid in the bushes, housewives would lean out the back windows to toss out their coins or crumpled dollar bills. Their numbers would drift like the smell of fresh-baked bread from the warm kitchen windows, landing in the bookie's pad. The bookie would make out the slips and leave anonymous receipts in the dented hallway mailboxes. Those were the days of penny spreads, when you could bet a penny on a number boxed and straight, and win a dollar back.

In my mother's day, the local bookie was Mr. Zeller, who owned a custom dress shop and a candy store. Mr. Zeller was a gentleman and stood at the counter in the candy store, dressed in a three-piece suit, pretending to sell only old candy, Royal Crown Cola, and loose cigarettes, called loosies. All day long, customers would come in to play the number, saying, "Zellie, give me a nickel on . . ."

One day, Grandpa sent my mother around to the store to find out what the number was. She found the dapper Mr. Zeller standing with two big guys, dressed in suits just like his. "Mr. Zeller, my father wants to know what the number is," my mother politely said. Mr. Zeller almost dropped dead. The two men were FBI agents.

Unless the feds were breathing down their necks, the local police hardly ever came down on bookies. Dudley Gregory, the city's first mayor, helped institutionalize gambling in Jersey City. He was known as the Lottery Man back in the early 1800s, because of the local 50/50 raffles he held. (Just another reason for my father's Dudley Club to be named after him.) The questionable money he raised was used to build churches, schools, prisons, and roads, and no doubt to line his pockets. But it was because of Mayor Frank Hague that gambling was so ingrained in the daily life of Jersey City's residents. Hague, who ruled for the first half of the twentieth century, was one of the most corrupt politicians in the country, and certainly the most notorious in the city's history. His main income came from controlling the county's illegal gambling rings and an elaborate telephone and telegraph system for off-track betting. It was known as the Horse Bourse, and it was the Wall Street of the gambling world, the center of the horse-betting universe. Hague was its master.

A tenement would be gutted and filled with telephones and adding machines, creating a central betting system that could handle lay-off bets from around the country. In other words, if a bookie in another city didn't have the capital to cover a bet, he would call Jersey City for backing. Each neighborhood was also allowed a certain number of illegal dice and card games, in return for giving Hague a percentage of the take. A bagman from the police department was assigned to each neighborhood to collect his take from the game organizer or bookie.

With the number, the dream was to hit it big and get the hell out of Jersey City. But the odds were against you—even if you won. The odds of hitting the three digits were, mathematically, 1,000 to 1. But bookies only paid 500 to 1. So they rarely lost, unless the whole city hit the same number on the same day, as it did in 1958, the day after a commuter train fell off the bridge that linked Bayonne to Elizabethport. The five-car, two-engine Jersey Central train, a Bay Head–to–Jersey City special, was carrying a hundred passengers, among them George "Snuffy" Stirnweiss, a former New York Yankee. There would have been more people aboard had it not been a holiday—the first day of Rosh Hashanah.

The driver didn't notice that the vertical lift of the bridge, opened earlier to allow a sand boat to pass, was still open. So the train took a dive. The two diesel locomotives and first two passenger cars sank down into thirty-five feet of water, killing four crewmen and forty-four commuters, Snuffy included. One car was left dangling from the edge of the trestle for over two hours: car number 932.

When pictures of the disaster were published in the next day's newspaper, 932 was prominently displayed on the side of the car. Everyone in Hudson County played 932 that night. When the last three digits of the mutuel handle turned out to be 932, the bookies couldn't get over it. They had to pay 500 to 1 to practically every gambler in Hudson County, which included almost every man and woman who lived there. Bookie losses from the train number were $5 million countywide. Since the disaster photo appeared not only in *The Jersey Journal* but also in the New York *Daily News,* bookies in the entire metropolitan area lost upward of $50 million.

The train-wreck hit was a freak occurrence, of course. Most days, the bookies made a nice profit. Because of the crummy odds, the number couldn't make a bettor too rich. Unless a large sum of money was bet, the payout was small. People rarely had large sums of money to play with in Jersey City. If they hit, that little extra money helped, but it didn't drastically alter their lives.

There actually was such a thing as being too rich. The problem with the huge jackpots of the legal lottery was that once people hit, they weren't sure where to go or what to do with all that money. The beauty of the number was the hope, the dream. Once it became a reality, it could never live up to that fantasy of sipping tropical drinks on a boat in the Bahamas.

For instance, Ruthie, the school crossing guard at OLC, hit the lottery and became a millionaire overnight. Her life's job, crossing kids in dangerous traffic on Henderson Street as they walked to school, became an impossibility. People would laugh at her if she continued wearing that silly hat, shiny blue crossing guard coat, and white belt across her chest. So she quit. Relatives Ruthie hadn't heard from in years began to call, asking for "a loan." There were those who wanted money for an investment in a sure thing and relatives who simply wanted the cash up-front, no strings attached. How to divide it? Where to move? Would she make new friends, rich friends who would be accepting of her Jersey City accent and manners?

It was all too much for Ruthie. She died of a heart attack several weeks after hitting it big. It was not a story people wanted to hear, since it detracted from their lofty dreams and hopes of a better life. They were better off playing the number, even if it was against the law.

Uncle Henry, whose bookie career spanned three decades, went to jail only three times. It wasn't that he eluded the cops. Uncle Henry was an easy target: He was huge, weighing in at an easy 250. Watching him eat was a sporting event in my family, an amazing physical feat involving raw power and stamina. He could inhale a dozen pierogi in less than sixty seconds. And then there was what my kind Polish relatives liked to call his "lazy eye." Uncle Henry was cross-eyed.

Though the police knew that the illegal number was an integral part of the region's economy and social fabric—and were paid well to think that way—they had to do a sweep now and then to make things look good. Every few years, they arrested a bunch of bookies in Jersey City—about thirty-five in all—and sentenced them to perform community service at St. Lucy's homeless shelter, near the Holland Tunnel. On Sundays, my brother went with Daddy to visit Uncle Henry at St. Lucy's, which, for that short time, became a virtual dormitory for the local bookies. Each one had his own tiny room, but they ate meals in a common meeting room and shared a television set. After two months, they'd be back on the street running numbers.

The first time Uncle Henry was arrested wasn't for numbers but for destroying traffic tickets for friends while working in the Jersey City violations bureau. The name Stapinski appeared in the police blotter story in the local paper—the first time a Stapinski had been on the wrong side of the law. There was talk that the family name was tarnished forever. But then Henry started running numbers, and no one seemed to mind, not enough to stop placing bets with him.

Uncle Henry was, as my family would say, "a good egg." A grade-A extra-large egg, but a good egg. As homely as he was, I felt a certain affection for him. Whenever I saw him, he never failed to peel off a fiver for me. I always felt sorry for him, since he was the one who Uncle Tommy had tried to kill following one of his epileptic fits. Ironically,

Uncle Henry was the only one who still went to visit Uncle Tommy regularly. You had to love him just for that. Your retarded brother tried to break your back, and you go and visit him every week.

But Uncle Henry's soft spot for Tommy wasn't the only reason I felt a special connection to him. Uncle Henry took the bets the day I was born, scribbling my family's hopes into his little notebook, one number at a time.

When my mother was six months pregnant, she had her tea leaves read by my cousin Gerri's maternal grandmother, a psychic who lived in the housing projects in North Bergen. Mrs. McGuire told my mother she would give birth to a girl, that I would stay in the hospital ten days, and that she should write this number down: 507. Mrs. McGuire wasn't sure if it was the number of the hospital room my mother would be in or my birth weight.

After my mother went into labor, Ash Wednesday, 1965, the whole family, with the smudge of ashes on their foreheads, called Uncle Henry to place their bets. I weighed in at 5 pounds, 7 ounces—a good bet and a favorite to win. Most relatives played 507, straight and boxed. But my father's sister Terri played 057. Straight. She felt that 5 pounds, 7 ounces translated into 057, not 507. Terri, the only Stapinski sister to move out of Hudson County, liked to do things her way.

The day after I was born, my aunts and uncles ran to get the *Daily News* at the Palace drugstore. And there, on page 72, at the bottom of the Gulfstream Charts were the last three digits of the total mutuel handle: 057.

Everybody hit the number, since they'd played it straight and boxed. But Aunt Terri hit it big-time. For her 25-cent wager, she was rewarded $125, not bad by 1965 standards. To show her gratitude, Terri bought me a $65 red snowsuit with white fur trim.

Since I was so small, it took a while to grow into. At only 5 pounds, 7 ounces, I was kept in an incubator for ten days, just as Mrs. McGuire had predicted. I was skinny and sickly, but I was considered a lucky kid. By everybody except Uncle Henry, of course, who lost a small fortune.

Jersey City and I shared the same birthplace, a small coincidence, considering the city is 14.9 square miles. The Dutch West India Company acquired the first tracts of land in Jersey City, those at the edge of the Hudson River in Paulus Hook, the downtown neighborhood where OLC was and where I spent my infant and toddler years. The neighborhood, named after Michael Paulaz, a Dutch West India Company agent, was 4,400 feet from Manhattan, on the Hudson River's west bank. OLC Church, with its sturdy stone façade, was Dutch Protestant before the Polish Catholics took it over. The Dutch also built my first house, on Sussex Street.

They referred to the area as Gammontown—from the Dutch word *gemeen,* which means "abject," "abandoned," "low," or "vile." Since the neighborhood was close to the water, it was often invaded by rats. Not the most desirable place to live. Even three hundred years later, longtime residents called it Gammontown, never Paulus Hook, a name reserved for real estate brokers and historians.

From history books, I learned that Manhattan's founders bought their land from the Native Americans at a discounted price of $600, but Jersey City's Dutch waged an unnecessary battle against the same friendly tribes. Why pay when you could steal? That was Jersey City's motto. In 1643, Dutch governor William Kieft, known as William the Testy, ordered the massacre of the peaceful Lenni Lenape tribe. His attack caused all the warring tribes to band together and destroy the Hudson County colony. In the early 1700s, once the tensions with the Indians dissolved and the colony was rebuilt, settlers in Hudson County erected fences around common lands, laying claim to property that was not theirs.

During the American Revolution, Jersey City's residents sided with the British, establishing a passive Tory community that was regularly raided by both sides for food, horses, and clothing. Woollen petticoats of the Dutch women were taken and used for blankets in the long winters. When you weren't picking on someone else in Jersey City, you were the one getting picked on. It was wise to strike first, and strike fast.

Once the war was over, Hudson County became a refuge for the losers on the burgeoning American political scene. Alexander Hamilton, driven from Manhattan and from office by the Democratic Republicans, moved to Hudson in the hope of building a rival city. Jersey City, under his Federalist guidance, would become a thriving metropolis, wonderful enough to compete with the one just across the river. But before Hamilton could make his plans, he was shot and killed by Aaron Burr in a duel just a few blocks from what would later be the site of my first bachelorette apartment.

In the late 1700s, New York had a population of 60,000, but Gammontown contained an unlucky thirteen residents, who watched the important people come and go from the Grand Street ferry landing. Stagecoaches left for Philadelphia from that spot, and the ferry took everybody who was anybody over the Hudson.

Gammontown was taken over in the 1800s by an immigrant wave of Eastern Europeans, a notoriously clean people. The Stapinskis were among them. The Stapinski, or Stapienski, family (depending on who was wielding the pen when they came through Ellis Island) emigrated from the rural village of Powiat, outside the Polish city of Rzeszów, near the Ukrainian border, a dreary part of the world that must have made Jersey City look like the emerald city.

Most of my father's family lived in Gammontown, right on Sussex Street, at one time or another. There was Uncle Henry, of course, and Aunt Terri, Uncle Joe, Uncle Mickey, Uncle Tommy, who lived there before moving to Meadowview, and Aunt Stella, whom we called Cioci, Polish for "aunt," because she was the oldest and seemed the most Polish. Babci, my Polish grandmother, lived on Sussex Street as well, though I never met her. She died the month before my mother became pregnant with me. I came out looking just like her, my squinty eyes and large nose proof that Babci had been reincarnated.

By the 1960s, when I arrived, Gammontown no longer had a rat problem. It was the city's prettiest neighborhood, with rows of historic brownstones and the scent of Colgate soap in the air. With a nearly unobstructed view of the Manhattan skyline and an open feel because of its nearness to the river, Gammontown had a light, and a lightness, that was missing from the rest of Jersey City.

Warren Street, just half a block away, provided a full view of the actual Statue of Liberty, even if her back was turned to us. It seemed she couldn't stand to look at Jersey City. When kids misbehaved in school, teachers would often tell them that Miss Liberty was so mad she had turned her back on them. How's that for a guilt trip? You were so bad that you'd caused a 225-ton green copper behemoth—the symbol for hope in the New World—to turn around and ignore you.

In Gammontown, the only thing standing in the way of the Manhattan view was the Colgate factory, most famous for its giant, red-lit clock, visible from across the river. Some New Yorkers even set their watches to it. But it was backward to us. From our side, Colgate was best known for its two enclosed white steam containers, which looked like giant Q-Tips and added to the clean, fresh feeling around you. The Q-Tips were there to catch the steam released from the factory's furnace.

Because of Colgate and its giant Q-Tips, the air quality in Gammontown seemed a little better than in the rest of Jersey City. People who worked at the soap factory were the freshest-smelling residents of the city. When my brother got a job there, my mother learned the hard way not to sprinkle laundry detergent on his clothes: His shirt and pants were already so filled with soap that suds overflowed from the washing machine, like something out of an episode of *I Love Lucy*.

Noise pollution was also absent in Gammontown. Sussex Street was quiet because of the overwhelming hush of OLC Church, which was like a big quilt thrown over a block square, muffling any unpleasant sounds. I never once heard loud music blare out of car windows. Motorcycles never roared past, and drug dealers didn't loiter on its corners. The block was stuck in a time warp. Men at OLC still wore fedoras and slicked-back hair long after the fashions changed. And women, including many of my aunts, paraded around with tall, dyed bouffants, wispy and full of air, like puffs of cotton candy. The neighborhood stayed quiet and conservative because it was home to two churches: OLC was back-to-back with the Russian Orthodox church Saints Peter and Paul. Their steeples were geometric opposites. OLC's Gothic triangle didn't mix well with the onion-shaped domes of Peter and Paul. In some ways, they were a continent apart. The Russians never bothered with the Poles. And the Poles never bothered with the Russians. At least until my family came along.

Though I was much too young to realize what it was, a heaviness always hung over Saints Peter and Paul, oozing its way over OLC's copper roof and stone walls. At first I thought the bad feeling came from the unfriendly Russians who attended mass at Saints Peter and Paul. Or maybe it was from the mass itself—a three-hour ordeal that made me thank God I was Catholic. Whatever it was, that dark, mysterious cloud always threatened to ruin my sunny first impressions of Gammontown, the place where a lucky kid could at least get a glimpse of the Statue of Liberty.

3

NO SOUP FOR SUPPER

<hr>

When I was two years old, my parents moved us from our cramped Gammontown home to the more spacious apartment over the Majestic Tavern. Whenever we traveled back for church or a family gathering, I was like a pilgrim visiting the Holy Land. It wasn't just because of the clean air, the brownstones, OLC Church, or the Stapinski side of the family. Gammontown was where Grandma Pauline grew up. She was raised on the same street as Saints Peter and Paul, the church where she was baptized, her head round and new, with clean holy water poured on to cleanse any Original Sin that had settled there. Grandma was pure good, the angel to Grandpa's devil. To me, Gammontown was the fresh beginning, the Eden before the knowledge of all worldly things intruded.

Since I don't remember Grandma very well, she was never a real person to me, with a real personality. She was more of a force—or a light—in my life. No one ever spoke badly of her. She was a clean slate upon which many of the horrible family stories were written. I thought it was no coincidence that Grandma had died on an Ash Wednesday and that Ma had also had ashes on her forehead when she gave birth to me. I felt like the ashes were Grandma's silent signal that she would watch over me and make sure nothing bad ever happened. Every Ash Wednesday, we were told at OLC that ashes were associated with purification. They looked like dirt, but they were sprinkled on the altar in a ritual to clean the church. They were also a reminder that we were simply dust. And to dust we would return, like Grandma had. God used the same dust to mix with water to make the clay to make Adam, the first man, whose name meant "Earth." Ashes weren't the end, the priest said, but a fresh, new beginning.

In those first pictures implanted somehow in my brain, Grandma, her hair white and soft, holds me close to her. She baby-sat for me in the two-bedroom apartment on Sussex Street, which was too small to contain three rambunctious children. I imagine myself rubbing up against her as a toddler, trying to inhale her goodness and take it with me when we moved over the Majestic. Her goodness would brace me for the evil of Grandpa to come.

I thought Stanley and Paula were luckier than I was because they had grown up in Gammontown, with real memories of Grandma. I remembered isolated moments, abbreviated and colorful like dreams, which were recorded before full memory kicked in. Grandma taught me to play cards—games like War, Go Fish, and, for when I was without her, Solitaire. The thing I remember best is that Grandma never got mad and never yelled, even when I sliced open one of her vinyl kitchen chairs with a toy plastic saw.

Stanley and Paula remembered what Grandma's house smelled like, its walls infused with the aroma of the sauce she cooked for Grandpa and the chicken soup, with soft carrots and broad noodles, that she made for their children and grandchildren. I settled for the pleasant smells in my mother's kitchen, the recipes having been passed down over time.

My brother and sister told me stories about how on snow days they could build igloos in the middle of Sussex Street, since there was hardly any traffic. The snow stayed white, with no car exhaust and very few footprints to ruin it. Gammontown seemed like paradise to me. By age three, living over the Majestic, I was already nostalgic for the good old days, for the place where I had learned to take my first steps. When

I dreamed of home, I dreamed of Gammontown, not the Majestic. Grandma had been raised there, with books on the shelves, a sturdy brownstone roof over her head, and pots boiling on the stove. Before I was even old enough to reason, I wondered why she would marry a guy like Grandpa. How and why had good and evil collided?

I got my answer in a parable that sounded too bad to be true, like most of my family's history.

Grandma's mother, my great-grandmother Irene, was the illegitimate daughter of a Russian Orthodox priest and a Hungarian cleaning lady, a crime in itself in most social circles. She was a beautiful woman, with a shock of black hair, a smooth complexion, and a love for dancing— all passed down to my mother, who is named after her.

We have no photographs of Irene Kaminsky, only my mother's face and the stories handed down, like genetic code, over the past century. My grandmother did have a picture of her mother. It hung on the wall of the living room, but Grandpa, in one of his fits of rage, took it down and destroyed it by sticking his foot through it.

Because Irene was called Gypsy by her friends and family, I pictured her with hoop earrings and a tambourine decorated with colored ribbons. She was filled with Hungarian blood, energy, and life. If anyone could eventually escape from Jersey City, Irene could. She was pure fire and spirit.

Because of her poor social standing, Irene came to the United States in 1893, promised to a man named Peter. It was the year after Ellis Island opened its doors. The Statue of Liberty was new, shining bright in the harbor, causing a distraction from the dense Manhattan skyline. As Irene sailed into the harbor, she likely rushed onto the deck from steerage to get a glimpse of that skyline. Office buildings had only just begun to scrape the sky in Manhattan. The steel skeleton–framed Manhattan Life building was going up, not far from the Tower and World buildings on Park Row.

The skyline was noticeably smaller, a prepubescent version of the one I would come to know from the riverbank of New Jersey. But the city was amazing, young, and vital, just like fifteen-year-old Irene. With all the excitement of seeing New York, Irene probably never noticed Jersey City creeping up on her, a dwarfed, dirty industrial afterthought, like a midget with soot on its face.

Irene never really made it to New York. She probably visited. But she settled in Jersey City, the railroad link for the rest of the country. Immigrants would initially land at Ellis Island, but they would continue their journey into the New World from Jersey City. Two thirds of all Ellis Island immigrants—an estimated 8 million—passed through the Central Railroad of New Jersey terminal, pulling up into one of three wooden ferry slips. From the time its first terminal was built in 1864, Jersey City was the departure point for hundreds of thousands of Poles headed to Chicago, Norwegians with cousins in Minnesota, and truly adventurous souls on their way to the wilds of California and the Pacific Northwest. All aboard in Jersey City.

The crowds passing through, past my relatives, were so thick that the wooden station was rebuilt with red brick in 1889 and expanded in 1914, its tall, pointed tower and large white clock almost as much a beacon as the round domes of Ellis Island. By the turn of the century, the terminal handled between 30,000 and 50,000 arrivals each day, coordinating 128 ferry runs with 300 trains. Thousands upon thousands visited the waiting room that is Jersey City, just long enough to catch a train to a better life.

Some lingered awhile longer—resting on their baggage, or maybe moving into town while a generation passed. It's not uncommon for people, particularly on the East Coast, to have a relative who once lived in Jersey City. Like a modern-day Mesopotamia, it was a beginning for many people. But eventually they got it together and moved on.

Amid the thick black smoke and screeching, oily locomotives, the crowds of immigrants were herded through the north baggage tunnel of the three-story station to tracks 1 and 2, set aside especially for them. The powers-that-be made sure the passengers from steerage did not mingle with the first-class ticket buyers inside the French château–style headhouse, complete with a chandeliered restaurant, a newsstand, bar, post office, and barbershop.

Whether you had the luxury of the metal starbursts and iron balconies of the station proper or the cramped view of the baggage tunnel's wooden ceiling, the view of the railroad tracks at the other end was the same for everyone: a dozen shining steel paths headed westward, with a shed supported by a forest of Corinthian columns.

Of the hundreds of trains that left from those tracks—from the Central lines and the B&O and the Reading—a handful were local. With the New York skyline at their back, some immigrants took the train to Bayonne or to the Jersey shore. Some rode trains just a stop or two away to prettier parts of Jersey City, to the West Side Avenue station, the Greenville station, Communipaw, Jackson Avenue, or Arlington Avenue.

Irene didn't even get that far. She hopped a trolley to Gammontown. I imagine her being so tired from the boat ride that she simply gave up in Jersey City and surrendered to Peter, her mail-order husband. Perhaps she had schemed to board a train going farther west, but he was there waiting for her at the station.

Peter was not a pretty sight. He was an albino, with hair so blond it was white and eyes so light blue they were nearly colorless. He was shorter than she was, five-foot-two to her five-foot-four. Looks weren't everything, of course. But Peter wasn't even kind. He was wealthy—at least by Jersey City standards—but he was a cheap bastard.

Irene grudgingly put her bags down on that Gammontown soil and called it home.

Wherever she looked, east toward the tiara of the New York skyline or west toward that great big bulge she couldn't conquer, Irene probably felt a little cheated. I know I would have. Jersey City was—and is—an ugly place.

Other industrial towns nearby had their bright spots. Paterson, founded by Alexander Hamilton before he caught that piece of lead, had its falls. The 77-foot-high, 280-foot-wide waterfall laid claim to being the second-largest, by volume, east of the Mississippi. So it wasn't the largest, but it was easy on your eyes while you worked yourself to death in a silk mill.

When Irene arrived downtown, there were acres of rail yards, littered vacant lots plagued with sickly weeds, and miles of dirty streets, which back then were clogged not with cars but with piles of horse manure. The local pencil factories and canneries were just beginning to belch the black smoke that would scar the city's buildings and residents—my family—for life. There were no waterfalls. No tall buildings. Coming to America through downtown Jersey City was like entering a big, beautiful restaurant through the service entrance. You passed the garbage and the stockroom along the way. You were ignored, and if you were lucky, you got to sneak a few scraps from the kitchen before your shift was through.

Even the city's name contained no poetry, no mystery to be unraveled. There were no Indian cadences, as in *Weehawken* or *Hoboken*. The name was the butt of a joke, worse than the punch line "Jersey" alone, with the image of urban squalor added on, like insult to injury.

Jersey. City. As simple and as ugly as that.

Those who, like my great-grandparents, came to the Hudson's west bank did not settle in Jersey City. They settled *for* Jersey City. They were settlers of a different kind, the kind who always feel cheated, because they settled for less.

In Irene's case, she settled for Peter, a Russian albino a decade older than she was. He had emigrated just six years earlier from Galicia, a place that was in either Poland or Austria, depending on what year you looked at a map. By language and religion, the family was Russian. Irene had no siblings. Except for her husband, she was alone in Jersey City—a strange and ugly land. Perhaps not as ugly as Galicia, but a tough place nonetheless.

Gammontown lived up to its nasty Dutch name. The railroads—with control of the legislature—filled in beyond the shoreline, extending the city out to the water's edge. The fill, comprised mostly of New York's garbage, started New Jersey's long and continuing reputation for smelling bad.

By then, Hudson County had its first convicted politician—William Bumstead, a builder and member of the board of aldermen. A list of indictments had come down in the Bumstead Ring scandal in the 1870s, but only the alderman was found guilty of tipping off a realtor about land to be purchased for a Jersey City reservoir, lending the guy money to buy it, then reselling it to the city for a profit. Soon after, city treasurer Alexander Hamilton (no relation) ran away to Mexico with $87,000 in bonds. Then, after the 1889 election, sixty-six election officials were convicted when seven thousand phony ballots surfaced. But they were all eventually pardoned and given new political jobs.

An even bigger scandal broke four years after Irene arrived. One of the nation's biggest jury-riggers had been making frequent visits to the Hudson County prosecutor's office until, finally, two officials were indicted. They were charged with taking bribes to let prisoners go free. Not surprisingly, the case ended in a hung jury.

In this less-than-perfect place she called home, Irene bore six children—three boys and three girls—two of whom, William and Mariana, died of cholera while they were still infants. After Mariana died, Irene had no more children. My grandmother Pauline, the youngest, stayed the youngest. Grandma was named after Peter's much kinder twin brother, Paul, who lived with the family on and off for several years, traveling between the Old Country and Jersey City at least three times in steerage. In 1913, he arrived with $25 in his pocket. The rest of his money was hidden in the soles of his shoes.

When I was young, I thought their church, Saints Peter and Paul, was named after Great-Grandpa and his twin. With brown hair and blue eyes, Paul was more handsome than his fraternal twin, and taller, meeting Irene's gaze at five-foot-four. Unlike Peter, Paul couldn't read or write, but he had lots of spunk. Some say he left Jersey City and returned to Russia to fight in the revolution. Another family story has him moving to Pennsylvania.

I often wonder if Irene slept with Paul in those last hours before he left for St. Petersburg—or Pittsburgh—to conceive my grandmother. Paul's name—not Peter's—has been carried through the generations, to my sister, Paula, and to her son, Paul. We have no Peters in our family.

The Kaminskys were well-off for a Jersey City family, since Peter owned their house and the attached row of brownstones on Grand Street. Irene thrived in the Gammontown soil, making the best of what she had. She kept a garden in the backyard, behind a high wooden fence that separated her from the neighbors. Each day she would shovel horse manure from the cobblestone street out front to use as fertilizer. It embarrassed my grandmother. But Irene didn't care who saw her shoveling shit. She kept an immaculately clean house. Because of the soap dust filtering out of the Colgate factory, housewives in Gammontown only had to add water to their rags to clean their windows. I can see Irene sticking her proud, bun-topped head outside her sparkling windows, breathing in that fresh, sanitized breeze, or the stench coming from the waterfront fill, depending which way the air was blowing that day. From the front of the house, she could watch the kids gather across the street at the Whittier House, an extra-wide brownstone that had been converted into a boys' club. From the rear window, Irene could glimpse her flowers, the small shed near the back fence, and, farther in the distance, the Morris Canal basin.

Along the canal, flat-bottomed boats carried coal from the anthracite mines of Phillipsburg, Pennsylvania, to homes and factories in New York City, bypassing Jersey City residents. Once the canal was closed and the railroads took over, local kids often raided the coal cars and took as much as they could cart away.

To Irene, the coal canal was likely a pretty sight from high up, a bit of country in an industrial area. But up close it was polluted. When kids went swimming in the canal, they came out looking as if they'd been dipped in tar.

Irene's son Sam swam in the Morris Canal as a child. While diving into the shallow waterway one afternoon, he got his head stuck in the mud and muck at its bottom. He was an excellent swimmer, but when he didn't come up for air after a minute or so, his friends jumped in and rescued him. Sam went home shaken, his hair a dark, cruddy mess. He probably got a beating from his mother. Or, more likely, his father. Peter was strict, sometimes to a fault. When his son John was arrested for some minor infraction years later, Peter left him in jail overnight. Uncle John cried and carried on but supposedly learned his lesson.

Whenever the potential for mischief arose, Irene and Peter were there, waving fists at their young sons and keeping them in line. On a Sunday morning in the summer of 1916, a Jersey City pier storing munitions headed for the European Allies caught fire, causing an explosion that rocked the metropolitan area for twenty-five miles around. The Black Tom explosion occurred at 2:10 A.M.; the city was sure of it, since the force of the blast stopped the clock atop the *Jersey Journal* building.

When it blew, Black Tom was the single most dramatic event in my family's history up until that moment. The blast was so strong that babies were thrown from their cribs and patients at St. Francis Hospital were knocked clear out of bed. The stage doors on the Majestic Theatre, down the street from the tavern, were pulled off their hinges. Yelling that the world was coming to an end, mothers, their babies in their arms, ran into the middle of city streets. Crowds of people whose homes had caved in gathered on the grass at City Hall Park and camped out all night around the tired statue. Inside, politicians inspected the cracks in the walls and the damaged floors and worried that City Hall might collapse, too. The blast broke hundreds of stained-glass windows in the city's churches, their images of Jesus and Mary falling into shimmering piles of red and blue glass. Shop windows came crashing down in a crystal hail.

In the early-morning blackness, hundreds of Poles from the neighborhood swarmed outside the wooden doors of OLC Church, trying to push their way in. But the doors were locked tight. The crowd grew hysterical until a brawny Polish guy—possibly one of my relatives—busted the door down. The parishioners rushed in and got down on their knees and started praying.

When their own house shook, my teenage uncles Sam and John jumped out of bed and pulled on their pants. They had no plans to go to Saints Peter and Paul and pray. They had some window-shopping to do. With the city's store windows gone, looters were out in force. Sam and John planned to join them. But Peter stopped his sons from meeting their hoodlum friends.

Neighborhood looting was kept under control, not so much by parents or police, whose billy clubs were knocked out of their hands by the force of the blast, but by the merchants. They made a run on hardware stores and lumberyards and nailed boards and wire netting across the gaping shop windows as soon as they could.

Only one looting incident was reported, and it didn't involve my family. Two hours after the blast, a young man carrying two typewriters was spotted by a cop on the beat near City Hall. "This is a kind of strange hour for a young literary man to be meandering around with his typewriters," said *The Jersey Journal,* getting inside the cop's head. When the cop asked him where he got the typewriters, the kid was "so disconcerted by the effects of the explosion that he couldn't remember," the paper said.

The young poet was escorted to the police station, which received a call five hours later from the receptionist at Jersey City Typewriter Exchange. Two typewriters were missing. The young poet was booked and fingerprinted.

The typewriters weren't the only things missing after the explosion. When they looked down Warren Street, residents thought the Statue of Liberty was gone, swiped by the blast. *The Jersey Journal* received calls all that night from people worried that she lay at the bottom of the Hudson, the target of German sabotage. Not to worry, the editors said. The dynamos lighting the statue were simply cut off, leaving the Lady standing in the dark. Her gown and skin were pockmarked with some shrapnel, but she was still there.

It wasn't until later that morning, after the sun rose, that the Lady reappeared. In the midmorning haze, many of the neighborhood kids went down to the Black Tom pier, where a thick cloud of smoke still hovered. They dove into the water naked, searching for souvenir shells. I imagine Uncle Sam was still too traumatized by the Morris Canal incident to participate. Maybe Peter locked his kids in the house, mistakenly thinking it would be safe inside 173 Grand Street.

Because 173 Grand was so near the canal and the river, the high water table would cause floods in the basement. Water filled the crawl space and would burst through the bricks. Neighbors called it a "tumultuous house." One plumber, who sidelined as a psychic, asked years later what on earth had happened there. He wasn't just talking about the water table. He claimed to have seen a spirit pass next door into the neighbors' basement. "Did someone die here?" he asked.

You could take or leave the psychic melodrama. But while doing construction on the house, the new owners ripped down the original backyard shed and found a human skull inside. Maybe it was an aborted baby or a lover of Irene's.

Despite his wealth and his good job as a railroad freight handler, Peter felt he didn't deserve Irene. By the 1920s, she spoke at least three languages—Polish, Russian, and English—and was a popular, independent woman who ran card games in the house and an employment agency in the basement, in addition to her job at a pencil factory.

Peter grew more and more jealous. Self-confident and headstrong, Irene often refused to have sex with him. To try and keep her in line, Peter beat Irene every now and then, just as he did the children. Wife battering was not uncommon in the 1920s. But one unseasonably warm autumn day—November 2, 1922—the mercury hitting 61 degrees, Irene refused to make Peter soup. Irene probably laughed at her husband, telling him, "It's much too warm for soup, you stupid albino bastard." Maybe she was too busy, with all her jobs, and told him to make it himself.

Peter and Irene got into one of their usual arguments. My grandmother, Pauline, only twelve years old, and her sister Helen, fifteen, were home that night and heard their mother's screams from the kitchen. They thought nothing of it, since their parents fought all the time. But that night was worse than other nights; Peter beat Irene viciously.

Despite severe head injuries, Irene continued her "housewifely duties," according to a story in *The Jersey Journal* the next day. I guess that means she gave in to Peter's demands—groggily filled a pot with water, threw in a few carrots and a chicken, then boiled some egg noodles before lying down and bleeding onto her bedroom pillow.

That morning, with their father at work, the girls found their mother unconscious in bed. My aunt Helen heard the death rattle in her mother's throat, threw open the carved, wooden front doors, leapt onto the wide stoop, down its nine stone steps, and out onto Grand Street, screaming to anyone who would listen that her father had killed her mother. A neighbor, Mrs. Phillips, calmed the hysterical girls and had Irene taken to the city hospital. She was pronounced dead at the age of forty-four.

Noticing a bruise on her head, a doctor notified police, who launched an investigation. Peter denied hitting Irene. But according to the second-to-last line in the news story, "The daughters say that it was no unusual thing for their father to beat their mother."

NO SOUP FOR SUPPER, SAY HE STRUCK WIFE FATAL BLOW was the

headline on November 3, 1922. My great-grandfather was charged with murder, but a week and a half later was acquitted. The family says that he paid off the corrupt Jersey City police officials and that because of his high profile as a landowner and railroad employee, he was let go. The charges were dropped.

Had my great-grandmother Irene died in any other city, or at another time in the city's history, my family might have given Peter the benefit of the doubt and said that, well, maybe he was innocent. But it was 1922, when Mayor Frank Hague was at the height of his long and powerful reign. Police corruption and cover-ups were so widespread that the FBI stopped accepting crime statistics from the Hague machine, because they were so unreliable. Nineteen twenty-two was also the year Hague was made New Jersey's national Democratic committeeman. And the year he started building the hospital maternity wing named after his mother, Margaret.

Peter was released in time for Irene's wake, which was held on the parlor floor of the brownstone. As far as we know, Irene was not buried in the backyard shed. Helen, emotionally wrecked, missed the funeral. Her father, probably haunted by her accusations, sent her away to a youth house for troubled children. That left Grandma Pauline alone with her murderous father. Her brothers were grown men by then, with wives and troubled homes of their own. For four years Grandma lived with her father in that brownstone, until he died, leaving her orphaned. Paul, her namesake, never came back to adopt her. I imagine her sitting in the front-parlor window, waiting for her handsome Russian uncle to come and rescue her on a white horse. But the family said he'd heard of the scandal and was too embarrassed to return.

Grandma inherited money from her father's real estate holdings, but at the age of sixteen, she failed to invest it wisely. She went to live with her brother John and his wife in Brooklyn for a few months. But she wound up back in Jersey City. Without her mother to give her guidance or her father to discipline her, Grandma started dating a good-looking Italian kid who hung out at the boys' club across the street.

His nickname was Beansie.

4

OFF THE TRUCK

After Grandma died at what I considered the incredibly old age of sixty, I began asking my mother how old she was every few hours. Forty, she would say. Same as last time you asked. She questioned the pediatrician about it. The doctor said I was afraid Ma was going to go next—that she'd go from forty to sixty in a flash. And then die, like Grandma.

With Grandma gone, my mother attempted to enroll me in nursery school. Armed with my plastic Banana Splits lunch box, I went bravely into the playroom of Holy Rosary. The program was run by a nun so old that she barely had the energy to walk, never mind work a room of preschoolers. She tried in vain to get us to take long naps on the little cots she provided. And when that didn't work, she left us in front of a black-and-white television set. My schoolmates and I sat staring at the screen, watching Popeye scroll by. The nun didn't know how to fix the horizontal hold.

I missed my grandmother and the excitement at City Hall and was insulted that my parents would deposit me in such a boring place. To escape, I thought up a clever lie, the first lie of my life. I told my mother that the horrible nun was giving us vitamins. My mother was convinced she was drugging us to get us to sleep on the tiny cots, and immediately removed me from Holy Rosary.

My mother rarely left me with Stanley or Paula—not because she didn't trust them, but because she didn't want to burden them. Because her father was in jail and her mother was always working, she had been forced to watch her brothers and sister as a child. The only one she didn't have to keep an eye on was her older brother, Sonny, who kept an eye on her. But Sonny died when he was only fourteen, killed in a truck accident that left Ma the oldest in her family.

She knew how much she resented those long days of being the little grown-up, having to tell her siblings what to do. And she didn't want Stanley and Paula to have to go through the same thing with me. Besides, one of the few times my brother did watch me, we got into trouble. It wasn't his fault. I take full responsibility, though I think I blamed it on him at the time.

Stanley was my first hero, and my scapegoat, protecting me at all costs. He was skinny and dark-haired like me, but had hazel eyes and a crooked, uncertain smile that I would later inherit from years of living in Jersey City. It was part smirk, part fear of letting anyone catch you smile, and it shows up in decades of family photos.

While my mother was at work at the DMV, Stanley and I played a game of soccer. I kicked the hard plastic ball, the kind sold in large bins at the ShopRite supermarket, and hit the living room light fixture, a glass bowl hanging a few inches from the ceiling. It didn't break right away, but it came falling down toward the round coffee table in the middle of the room. It smashed into hundreds of pieces, creating a glass minefield all around us. We carefully tiptoed to the kitchen and called my mother to break the bad news. She came running home, more worried we were hurt than mad at us. Ma quit her job soon after that.

On the days indoors with Ma, I would place my father's dusty polka 45's on my Close 'N Play phonograph and fly through the rooms to the clarinet and accordion until I was exhausted. It sometimes took all day. When I needed a rest, I'd listen to my favorite 45, an old Jerry Lewis song that went, "Put something on the bar besides your elbow. Something like an old ten-dollar bill . . . They can't ring up your elbow in the till." When the song was over, I'd lift the needle and place it back at the beginning. I thought Jerry Lewis was hysterical, though I'm sure my mother couldn't stand to hear that whining, off-key voice sing the same stupid song over and over again.

But Ma never complained about the noise. Neither did our upstairs neighbor, Ducky, the guy who had tipped us off to Grandpa's plan to shoot us. Ducky often let me play with his Siberian husky, Keno, named after his master's favorite casino board game. Like Ducky, the drunks downstairs never complained about my noise, either. I was allowed to sing Jerry Lewis songs and run free in our three-bedroom apartment above the Majestic.

Depending on the season, Stanley and I would play Nerf football, basketball, or baseball, the home-run zone the space behind my father's vinyl recliner. After the incident with the light fixture, plastic balls were no longer allowed. And soccer season was eternally suspended.

One summer, Stanley and I ate dozens of Popsicles and used the sticks to build a miniature of the Twin Towers of the World Trade Center, which were growing at a much faster rate than I was. Stanley and I watched it rise floor by floor from across the river. First the steel girders were laid down, one atop the other. Then the vertical holes were filled in with concrete, metal, and glass.

Every day I would beg Stanley to play house, and he would grudgingly agree. "Pretend I'm your husband and I'm at home sick," he'd say, turning on the television and lying down on the couch, smiling that crooked smile.

To pass the time between my favorite TV shows and the City Hall excitement, my mother would read to me. My favorite book was a children's biography of Christopher Columbus, which she read in a mock Italian accent, imitating her own grandmother. She would improvise passages: "And then, his-a mama said, 'Christopher, whatsamatta for you? You don't like-a my meatballs?'" My mother and her siblings all had a sense of humor, which was how they survived Grandpa all those years.

When things were calm outside, I would go downstairs and place my feet in the stream of cool hydrant water that flowed down Mercer Street. The hydrant was turned on by the Puerto Rican kids down the block. I envied them, because their parents let them play out in the street on those hot summer days, letting them run in and out of the hydrant's spray. I could see them in the distance doing their awkward hydrant dances, arms flailing, bare feet kicking. Beyond the high, cold spray, and a block or two past the low-rise homes and boarded-up city buildings, stood a few trees. I wondered if that's where "the country" was and if someday I might be able to walk there. For the time being, I was confined to the curb, the small brook washing over my tanned feet, my only entertainment an occasional cigarette butt or a much-needed Popsicle stick floating past.

I had seen the dark side of playing in the street, so I knew my mother was right to confine me to the curb. Every summer, souped-up Chevys and Caddys without mufflers sped past, and each year kids were run down. Parents had petitioned for a traffic light at the corner of Mercer and Grove, but because the poor neighborhood had no pull at nearby City Hall, a traffic light was never installed.

At a very early age, I got used to the drill. The screech of tires was followed by a thud and a scream, my mother's signal to run downstairs with blankets and bandages. The smaller the kid was, the more likely it was that he would die, because his head would be about even with the car grille.

To get me out of the neighborhood, my parents took me everywhere with them. Some parents in Jersey City just left their kids at home while they went to work. Once in a while, there'd be a story in the paper about a kid discovered handcuffed to a radiator while his parents went out on the town. Most mothers stayed at home with their kids, ignoring them and providing very little entertainment. But I was constantly amused. My parents held me close, but they rarely sheltered me.

Daddy liked taking me to the movies, particularly to Journal Square, to the Loew's or Stanley Theatres, the only bright spots in that part of the city. Journal Square was a mini-Calcutta, filled with crippled pencil sellers in wheelchairs, midgets who hawked the evening *Jersey Journal*, deranged people with growths and tumors, and mumblers who walked the streets talking to themselves. Chief among the mumblers was a defrocked priest who still wore his frock and paced up and down the sidewalk delivering private sermons.

The deformed and disabled liked to congregate on Journal Square. One woman had a goiter on her neck the size of a baby's head. There was a bowlegged dwarf with an underbite named Helenka, who always wore a housedress. The local guys would tease Helenka by picking her up by the ankles and shaking her. Back in the old days, there was a man with no legs who came around begging on a little board with skate wheels, singing songs like "My Time Is Your Time" through a megaphone. He had a beautiful voice. People would lean out their windows and throw down two or three cents wrapped in a small piece of paper torn from *The Jersey Journal*.

Wandering the streets was a grown-up mongoloid named Rachel. She wore several dresses and coats but would take the top layers off to turn rope for the kids in the street, her strong, long arm throwing the jump rope into a high arc. There was also a guy who would step up onto the curb and then back down, over and over again, then march in place. He was probably a war veteran, but no one ever got up the courage to question him. Sometimes out-of-towners unfamiliar with the curb guy would wind up walking behind him and get stuck at the curb until they realized he was crazy and that they should walk around him.

Because of the Journal Square bus and PATH station, the area also attracted the homeless, who back then were called bums. My favorite was a woman named Mary, who never spoke but always ran around in a rush, dressed in a raincoat and worn black loafers. I wondered where she was off to in such a hurry.

The Loew's—mispronounced *Low-ees*—was just about the only pretty thing left on Journal Square and was as magical to a five-year-old as visiting Disney World. More than pretty, the Loew's was beautiful. Or as Jersey Citizens pronounced it, *beauty-ful*.

The place was ornate and over the top, with a huge white, lighted marquee, a tall tower, and a clock that featured St. George slaying the dragon. The façade was made of textured terra-cotta blocks, encrusted with dirt from years of Journal Square traffic pollution. What made the Loew's beauty-ful were the fantasies and, later, the memories everyone attached to it.

Once in the lobby, I would let go of Daddy's hand and run up the red-carpeted stairs. Not bothering to hold on to the bronze railing and the lion's-head banisters, I'd head straight to the red velvet–trimmed balcony, where I would stand overlooking the rococo lobby and wave to my adoring fans, Daddy in particular. He would wave back, smiling his toothless smile. There were golden mosaic tile alcoves and red-and-gold tapestries along the walls. The ladies' room had a marble mantelpiece and four big, mirrored vanities, which made me feel like a movie star. Daddy would wait for me outside the bathroom near the shell-shaped blue-tiled fountain, where goldfish swam. Hanging over everything was a Czechoslovakian-crystal chandelier that cost $60,000 back in 1929, the year the theater was built, just a month before the stock market crash.

Whatever decade it was, when you went to the Loew's, you felt special. It inspired you, unlike any other place in Jersey City. It was where a young guy named Sinatra took his date to see Bing Crosby sing in 1933 and decided he could do better than that. And better than Hudson County.

It was where a giant Wonder Morton organ piped out *Phantom of the Opera*–like chords that rattled your insides and made you think God lived inside the theater.

In 1960, with John F. Kennedy on his way to visit Journal Square during his campaign, local politicians held a rally outside the theater. The loudspeakers and music were so loud that they bled into the theater. The manager asked them to turn it down, to preserve the quiet inside and the illusion that the theatergoers were royalty. When the Democrats refused to turn down the volume, the manager threatened to shut down the marquee that night—which would have left JFK in darkness. The young Democrats bowed to the Loew's and piped down.

One of its architects commented that the Loew's was "where the rich rub elbows with the poor, and we are the better for it." Even in the 1970s, when vandalism on Journal Square was at all-time high, graffiti never touched its walls. Young vandals knew the theater was special.

As if to make up for all the ugliness in Jersey City, Journal Square had two movie palaces. The Stanley Theatre, which I used to think was named after my brother, was a block away and was almost as gaudy as the Loew's. Built in 1928, it had a vestibule made of Italian marble and stained glass and lighted by a colorful chandelier hung with crystal fruit baubles. In the main lobby hung a Grand Crystal chandelier taken from the old Waldorf-Astoria, which was knocked down to make way for the Empire State Building. The chandelier was 13 feet high and 10 feet wide and shimmered with 144 lights and 4,500 pieces of crystal.

The ceiling was painted sky blue, with wisps of white cloud sailing across. Brass rails ran along the staircases, and at the top hung small lanterns. A woollen shepherd tapestry, an antelope mosaic, and a tiled fountain with a lion spitting water decorated the upstairs lobby. The Stanley, with its stylized animals, was as close as Jersey City came to having its own zoo.

My favorite part about it, though, was the auditorium. The huge room held 4,300 people and was decorated like a Venetian courtyard, with painted urns and flowers. There were no real flowers in Jersey City. Spring was marked not by the first tulip or crocus but by the first floater, or dead body, to wash ashore in the Hudson River, its arrival always recorded in *The Jersey Journal.*

At the Stanley, terra-cotta buildings with red-tile roofs surrounded you, and the Rialto bridge stretched over the wide screen in front of you. The only dead bodies inside the Stanley were the ones that turned up on its extra-wide movie screen.

Overhead, stars twinkled and clouds actually floated past, thanks to the Stanley's mysterious cloud machine. Because of its ceiling and because it was named after my brother, the Stanley was my favorite place in Jersey City, and for years, my favorite place on earth, long before I knew there was an actual place called Venice or real courtyards with flowers and stars.

My mother saw her first movie at the Stanley when she was twelve years old, with her brother Sonny. When he noticed the stars, he got scared and told her they had to get home. "Sissy," he said. "It's late. Look. It's already dark out. Mama's gonna be mad." It was always a shock, even twenty-five years later, to emerge from the Stanley and be greeted by daylight and the reality that was Jersey City.

To escape reality, my parents had gone to the Stanley on hundreds of dates, the most memorable in 1953, when they went to see *The Moon Is Blue,* an Otto Preminger film starring William Holden and David Niven.

The movie wasn't very racy, but the dialogue included the words *virgin, sex,* and *tramp.* Local priests objected to the theater showing it, but the Stanley's management showed it anyway. My parents, who hadn't heard yet of the controversy, sat upstairs in the loge, where they always sat, so that my father could smoke and my mother could watch the stars twinkle and the clouds drift. Each in their own way, they waited for the movie to begin. But it never did.

The house lights came up and an announcement was made that everyone in the theater had to leave: *The Moon Is Blue* was no longer being shown. My parents left their seats and walked down the long, grand staircase in the lobby, that Waldorf chandelier blazing overhead. Like Norma Desmond in *Sunset Boulevard,* my mother slowly descended, with newsreel cameras and photographers' flashbulbs going off at the foot of the stairs. It turned out that Jersey City's public safety commissioner, Bernard Berry, had had the theater's manager arrested. It was big news, making national headlines. Once he became mayor, Berry continued to boycott the Stanley, banning the movie *Blackboard Jungle.* Berry and Jersey City became synonymous with small-town, narrow-minded thinking. It was already considered too corrupt a place to be thought of as puritanical.

———

While still a preschooler, I could never tell the difference between a trip to Journal Square and a trip to Manhattan. From downtown Jersey City, we had to take the underground PATH train—called the Hudson Tubes—to both places. There were trips to Macy's in New York, where Mom would let me play with the toys and ride the bicycles around the showroom floor, and excursions to the Battery, the place where the boat left for the Statue of Liberty. We would feed Cracker Jacks to the pigeons and watch the tourists line up for ferry tickets. Mom gave me dimes for the viewing machines in the park, which were meant for looking at the statue and Ellis Island. But I would focus my sights on Jersey City, searching for the Majestic and for Vince sweeping the gutter. In the summer, we'd go to Greenwich Village, to check out the hippies in Washington Square Park or the annual outdoor art exhibit.

But more fun, and more frequent, were the trips to the funeral parlor. My mother attended hundreds of funerals with me in tow.

To my mother, there was no concept more depressing than dying and having no one come to view your body. Funerals were my first lesson in what-goes-around-comes-around. If there were three or four people at a wake, it was obvious the person in the casket had not made many friends and had not gone out of his or her way to help others. The more people at the wake, the kinder the person was in life. It was a true, and final, test of character.

Heaven wasn't so much the goal after death. A crowded funeral parlor was.

Since my mother had lots of friends and knew practically everybody in the city because of the DMV, she attended everyone's wake. My grandmother's wake is the first one I can remember, though not the first I attended. Grandma was dressed in a powder blue gown that matched her eyes, which were now forever closed, and rosary beads were weaved between her fingers. I was so blasé, I leaned my coloring book on the kneeler in front of the casket and broke out the Crayolas. Dead bodies didn't faze me in the least. As a preschooler, I was an expert in public grief.

At other families' wakes, I knew the right moment to approach the relatives of the deceased, when to cut off conversation and kneel in front of the coffin, how long to pretend to pray and gaze longingly at the stiff inside, and how much the mass cards and flower arrangements cost. By the time my best friend's grandmother died, I was a pro. Still a child, I took Liz's freckled hand and bravely escorted her up to the casket, the stuffed body inside and the gardenias surrounding it. My mother was so proud.

Wakes were important, because that's where many of the family stories were retold. Funeral masses were better than wakes, because they were followed by the burial and a full meal at a local restaurant. The burial was key, because it guaranteed a romp on some of the only green grass in the county. There were trees and grass and freshly cut flowers thrown on the coffin at Holy Name Cemetery, signs of nature I was otherwise deprived of. It made no sense to me that the dead got all the green space in Jersey City. They certainly couldn't enjoy it.

While the casket was lowered into the freshly dug grave, I was off running and jumping on the grass between the other, older graves. I never stepped directly on them, avoiding them like I sometimes avoided stepping on the cracks in the sidewalk. Ma said stepping on a grave was sacrilegious.

The reward for attending the burial was the meal afterward. If the deceased was a close enough relative, we'd get to ride in a limo to the cemetery and restaurant. Otherwise, we'd have to bum a ride off someone in the funeral procession. Ma didn't drive; neither did Daddy or their parents or most of the Stapinskis. For forty-one years, my father got a ride to work from a friend. He and my mother took a bus to her senior prom. In the snow. (She graduated in the winter semester.)

After a burial, we'd hitch a ride with an old friend of my mother's to a place like the Hi Hat, a big banquet hall in Bayonne, the town to the south of Jersey City, where some of my Polish cousins lived. The Hi Hat specialized in funeral meals. A good funeral meal was something you never passed up.

Eating was the most important form of entertainment in my family— better than the movies, better than polka music. We were taught at a very young age never to waste food or turn your nose up at it or disrespect it in any way. I cringed when I saw other kids in nursery school throw their peanut butter and jelly sandwiches in the garbage or, worse, throw them at each other.

It was a sin to throw God's food on the floor. Though our family had plenty of food, we treated each supper as if it might be our last. Both my parents were born during the Depression, so they never took basic things like food or heating oil for granted.

As a child, my mother and her brothers and sister stole K rations from the Armour yards and coal from the railroads to keep warm. Always on the lookout for "the bull"—the railroad detective—they would steal loads of the dark black fuel and drop it down to their accomplices stationed under the trestles. My father and his brothers did the same. Well, most of them.

My uncle Eddie, Daddy's brother, didn't like to get his hands dirty and usually stayed away from the shoots, the coal cars down on the tracks. But on one occasion, Daddy and his brothers brought Uncle Eddie along to be their lookout. "You stay here," they said to Eddie, "and watch for the bull." But they never told Eddie that *bull* was slang for "detective." So there Uncle Eddie stood with a big red wagon, waiting for a bull to come running down the tracks.

It wasn't such a dumb mistake. The rails were often filled with cattle and other animals, mooing on their way to slaughter at the Armour stockyards. My mother and her friends saw a dead lamb one morning in the street, which had fallen from a train car stopped on the Seventh Street trestle. Another time, a bull actually got loose. My mother was wearing a red coat that day, and ducked into a hallway to avoid the charge.

So it was no surprise when one of Uncle Eddie's brothers yelled, "Cheese it! The bull!"—code for "Get going! The cops are coming!"— and Eddie hung around to get a glimpse of the animal. Wildlife was rare in Jersey City, save for the doomed livestock, a few pigeons, rats, and the ornamentation at the Stanley. A chance to see a bull charging down the railroad tracks would not be missed by young Eddie.

But there was no bull. Just the railroad detective, who caught Eddie red-handed with the red wagon. "Who sent you here?" the cop demanded. Not knowing what to answer, Eddie stupidly said, "My mother."

Eddie was escorted to the police precinct for a good scare, then home in a big car. He was sure he was being taken to jail. He probably would have been better off. The police reprimanded Babci, and after they left, she reprimanded Eddie, giving him a beating like he'd never known. His brothers never took him to the shoots again.

Poor epileptic Uncle Tommy even got in on the action and was caught stealing oranges at a fruit-and-vegetable stand in the neighborhood. The police brought him home and yelled at Babci again for not keeping a better eye on Tommy. Daddy got into trouble, because Tommy was usually his responsibility. Uncle Tommy was held back in school two years so that he and Daddy would be in the same class. That way Daddy could keep an eye on him. It was like asking one inmate to keep an eye on another.

Stealing food outright from stores and delis was never condoned— not when my father was little and not when I was growing up. But my father, a Teamster, fed us with the merchandise that fell off the truck at work. At the Union Terminal Cold Storage he was a warehouse checker, which meant he had to make sure everything they said was on the truck got into the warehouse, and vice versa. There were meat and fish trucks on their way to butcher shops and fish stores, sausage that was delivered to the feasts in Little Italy, and more exotic food—like snake, venison, and bear—on its way to the swankiest restaurants in Manhattan. Everything stopped at Daddy's place before going on to Tavern on the Green and Sparks.

At least once a week, a crate of Steak-umms or prepackaged Chicken Cordon Bleu would fall off the refrigerated truck and into our own freezer at home. Mom insisted Daddy never stole a morsel, that the boxes were gifts from the truck drivers for whom he did favors. As if it was theirs to give away.

Thanks to the drivers who Daddy let cut in line to unload their hauls, we always had a big bag of frozen french fries on hand for late-night snacks. Daddy would come home half-crocked from the Majestic and cook them up for us in a pot of oil, the flames licking the ceiling.

My mother resourcefully used everything he brought home, which usually came in large quantities originally intended for restaurant delivery: A big box of clams was made into a big pot of clam chowder. A huge hunk of Muenster cheese was melted over macaroni. A giant bag of oranges was sliced up and placed on a ham Daddy had brought home a few days earlier. Our family never once bought a turkey for Thanksgiving. It was part of the unofficial Teamsters' benefits package: major medical, dental, and swag—the extra box that just happened to fall off the back of the truck.

Because of my father's daily packages, tied in brown paper and carried under his arm, I was the only kid on my block who knew how to peel a lobster tail from its curled shell and who could tell the difference between a sirloin and filet mignon. For a while, I thought lobster and steak were staples in all working-class homes. But my father knew it was special. When the timing was precise and the right boxes fell off the truck at the right moment, my father would treat us all to surf and turf, with a shrimp-cocktail appetizer served on a bed of iceberg lettuce to start. His cocktail sauce was a sinus-searing light pink mixture of six parts fresh horseradish to one part ketchup. My mother wasn't allowed to cook the lobster or steak. That was Daddy's job. He would place the orange-black shells in the broiler with love, and join the lemon and butter in a small saucepan. With tenderness, he would trim the fat from the steaks, leaving just enough gristle to give the meat its sweet, juicy flavor. My mother complained that my father had missed another of his many callings: He should have been a butcher. He handled that meat more gently than he handled her. The steaks—the love of his life—were then grilled to perfection.

It was because of meals like these that my cousins were always sleeping over at our house. Gerri started having a weight problem because of my father's hot roast beef sandwiches. My father loved Gerri, because she had such a good appetite. And she loved him. Uncle Babe's cooking was always the best in the family, she said, even better than my mother's sauce or my aunt Millie's meatballs. And each day we destroyed the evidence, our insides digesting the buttery fingerprints Daddy left.

There was no money saved for college, since most of my father's cash went to Uncle Henry and to Nicky, in the Majestic, for gambling and booze. But we always had plenty of food. And we always had a block of dry ice that Daddy would bring home from work on Halloween to place in a bowl of water to make bubble and smoke for my astonished party guests. We couldn't go trick-or-treating, since the neighborhood was dangerous, so my mother invited all the kids over to bob for apples.

Thanks to Daddy, I was never at a loss when ordering in a fancy restaurant. Whenever he hit the number, Daddy would don his suit and star-sapphire pinkie ring and take us all out to eat. He loved food so much that he couldn't confine himself to the kitchen. It was at places like the King's Court, a Jersey City restaurant with its own coat of arms, and the Top of the Meadows, a swellegant spot atop the North Bergen Holiday Inn, with a view of the swampy meadowlands, that my father and I learned lessons in fine dining.

By the age of six, I knew the menus by heart, the difference between a scallop and scrod, between Chateaubriand and porterhouse, the maître d' and the waiter, all thanks to Daddy. Because he brought home high-quality frozen cakes, the kind restaurants use, I could tell whether a restaurant had a bakery on the premises or not. I could identify the culprits: seemingly homemade but actually mass-produced wheels of cheesecake, or Black Forest chocolate cake that we had in our freezer at home.

Sara Lee cupcakes were a favorite commodity at Daddy's warehouse, and they sat piled high atop our refrigerator, each box missing its chocolate cupcake first, its strawberry next, the coconut and lemon left for desperate midnight raids. Sometimes you'd have to search through six boxes before getting to the cupcake you wanted, hidden at the bottom.

Whenever there was a parish event at Our Lady of Czestochowa— a card party or a Chinese auction—my father provided the dessert free of charge. And any Pepperidge Farm chocolate layer cakes that were left over, the Polish nuns took back to the convent with them. As far as I know, they were never charged with receiving stolen property. Like us, the nuns ate the evidence.

At one card party, a woman named Lillian tried to steal the cake that was left over, stashing it under the table. "Imagine the nerve?" my mother complained. Stealing stolen chocolate cake from the mouths of nuns? Lillian was destined for the fires of hell.

Bake sales at school were easy for my mother, even though she didn't know how to bake. She would simply show up with an armful of Daddy's swag from the Cold Storage. That cake was the first to go at the sale, before Mrs. Romanski's cupcakes or my aunt Julie's cream puffs. It wasn't exactly in the bake-sale spirit of things, but this was Jersey City. Swag was just part of everyday life.

Swag wasn't the same thing as out-and-out stealing. It was an unwritten rule in Jersey City—and all of Hudson County—that you could take as much merchandise as you could carry from your job. The politicians skimmed off the top, so why shouldn't the little people?

As far as I know, my father never got into trouble for taking all that cake and lobster. His hauls paled in comparison to the other stuff going on at the Union Terminal. In the 1970s, vast numbers of canned hams started to disappear from the warehouse. It turned out that a night crew was pulling a truck up during the lobster shift (which I thought was named for the lobster crates that came in around midnight) and piling on the canned hams. One night, when they were almost caught, the crew threw the canned hams in the freezer to hide them. Canned hams are never frozen, merely refrigerated. So when the bosses found dozens of canned hams in the wrong place, they launched an investigation. Fingerprints were lifted from the frozen hams and about twenty-five guys were collared.

Things got worse over time. A new foreman affiliated with the Gambino crime family was brought in, because the Bonanno family was hijacking trucks. As long as the swag didn't exceed daily needs, bosses in Jersey City looked the other way when employees walked away with a paper bag or two of merchandise. Some companies even gave the merchandise away in small quantities, to discourage grand theft. Excessive greed was to be avoided. In 1943, for instance, three men were arrested for stealing $23,000 in toothpaste from Colgate. For months, they had been pulling a truck up to one of the loading docks and taking boxes of the stuff, selling it as part of a fencing ring in New York City. As long as you stayed modest, you were safe.

When I was growing up, because we had friends and relatives at Colgate, we were never in need of toothpaste or toothbrushes. It was ironic that the Polish side of the family, which lived closest to Colgate, always had such bad teeth. Our Colgate connection also provided us with a steady stream of shaving cream and soap. We had all the Irish Spring we needed. When a new product line debuted, like the Colgate pump, we were the first in the state to try it.

Though he was the biggest swagster in our family, Daddy was certainly not alone. When she was in high school, my mother worked at the General Pencil factory. Half her class seemed to work in the same building. Her job was to polish—or paint—the pencils yellow in the second-floor "dip room." The more important your job, the higher the floor you worked on. Downstairs, black workers were busy putting lead in the pencils, exposing themselves to lead poisoning. Erasers were placed on the pencils on the third floor. So the pencils my mother and her classmates stole for school never had erasers on them. It made her a more careful person, never able to erase her mistakes.

My mother and her friends would also go down to the Old Gold cigarette factory and yell up to their friends working inside, who would throw down loosies. Old Gold was my mother's first smoke.

All the books on our shelves were swag, either from Grandpa from the *free* public library or from my aunt Mary Ann, who worked at the American Book Binding Company. They weren't crummy little paperbacks or galley proofs. These were serious hardcover books, which, over the years, grew into an impressive library.

The first book I ever read—*A Mystery for Meg,* a sort of Nancy Drew knockoff—came free of charge from Aunt Mary Ann. My adolescent fantasies ran wild thanks to the collection of Daphne du Maurier novels that she brought home. Like Rebecca, I pined for Manderley. My favorites, though, were the leather- and clothbound series of half-size classics. Aunt Mary Ann transported them in her oversize girdle, worn intentionally to place the whole collection—nineteen books in all—around her midriff. When a coworker jokingly grabbed Aunt Mary Ann one afternoon and swung her around, he commented that she'd gained a little weight.

I loved to flip through the books and smell their yellowing pages, thinking that Aunt Mary Ann had taken them just for me. *The Collector's Edition Book of Quotations* and *The Pocket Book of Greek Art,* with photos of statues missing their arms, were my favorites from that series. I looked at those pictures for hours and wondered if someone had stolen the arms. What could they want with arms?

Aunt Mary Ann didn't limit her talents to books alone. While working at the Jersey City Medical Center, where she landed a job sterilizing instruments for the operating room, Aunt Mary Ann brought home the occasional unnecessary tool. We had a stainless-steel funnel, which my mother used for cooking, and a surgical clamp, which helped us change the channel on a small black-and-white TV long after the knob had fallen off.

Aunt Mary Ann was my idol—not only because she loved books, but because she was the first person in my mother's family to move far away, to the wilds of Miami. We visited her there three times when I was a child, and just a taste of life outside Jersey City—the coconuts and palm trees, the white sand and surf—made me dizzy with happiness. Back in New Jersey, I took to wearing suntan lotion just so I could smell like Florida, and Aunt Mary Ann.

My new favorite 45 immediately became a Harry Belafonte calypso number called "Marianne." Jerry Lewis was knocked off the charts.

The song went something like this: "All day, all night, Marianne. Down by the seashore sifting sand. All the little children join in the band." I believed it was written for my aunt. And I loved her deeply, though I hardly knew her.

All I knew was that Aunt Mary Ann was everything my mother was not: bleached-blond, sarcastic, and cynical. For years she swore she'd never get married, and even when she did, at the old age of thirty-six, she stayed independent and sexy. She never had kids, and she wore a purple velvet bikini even after she married Uncle Ray. Their apartment had modern orange furniture. They were cool.

Just the mention of her name conjured thoughts of the mystical. Whenever my mother cursed, she would shout, "Jesus, Mary, and Joseph," which I misheard as "Jesus, Mary ANN, Joseph." I thought Aunt Mary Ann was a member of the Holy Family. The outlaw member.

Moving out of Jersey City didn't destroy Aunt Mary Ann's talent for swag. She was the family's only test case that showed swag was in your bones, not a viral infection floating through the Hudson County air. As a dental hygienist in Dade County, Florida, Aunt Mary Ann compiled an impressive stockpile of toothbrushes and dental floss in her pantry at home. We even had a small chrome dental mirror, which kept me occupied for hours as I checked my incoming molars.

Aunt Mary Ann rarely stole for herself. Like Robin Hood, whom I had seen at the Loew's in an animated Disney film, Aunt Mary Ann selflessly took from the rich to give to us. There was the story about the lamp on the wall in a fancy restaurant in Florida that someone had admired during dinner. Aunt Mary Ann unscrewed it and placed it in her large pocketbook. She was brave, ballsy, and wonderful. She was the outsider. And in a campaign to be more like her, I began to swipe restaurant ashtrays, smudging my rigid, childish concept of good and evil.

5

THE MACHINE

For as long as I can remember, the time after supper was reserved for reading in our house. Whether we ate lobster tails or macaroni and cheese, we'd retire to the living room afterward and unfold a newspaper or crack open one of the books Aunt Mary Ann had brought home in her girdle. Daddy brought a pile of newspapers home with him every night folded under his arm, next to the frozen food of the day.

Reading time was one of the few times my parents ignored me, their faces buried deep in the *New York Post,* the *Daily News, The Jersey Journal,* and the other local paper, the *Hudson Dispatch.* Before I could even read, I looked at those headlines and traced the letters with my fingers. It seemed that every day the local papers carried a story about some politician under investigation or accused of wrongdoing. I assumed all cities were filled with such sleazy city workers.

In Jersey City, the dirt ran deep. Corruption was so ingrained over the decades that adults thought, as I did, that every place was the same and that you couldn't escape it—that you might as well vote for the person who could help you or your relatives get a job on the city payroll.

Though there was no escape, there was a reason the world—our world—was the way it was. The reason was Hague.

I can't remember the first time I heard his name mentioned. For kids in Jersey City, it was a syllable—like *God* or *Ma*—that had always been in our vocabulary.

Hague. Omnipotent and ever-present.

He ruled for three decades—from 1917 to 1947—though his control and influence bled over into later years. Dozens of county politicians who came after Hague used him as a model for robbing their cities blind. Beating suspects like Grandpa to a pulp, taking kickbacks, doling out no-show jobs to political supporters, getting the votes of the dead and buried, demanding tribute money—it was all synonymous with the name Hague. Though he wasn't the first crooked politician to come out of Jersey City—and certainly not the last—Hague raised corruption to an art form.

Like Grandpa, Frank Hague was born in the Horseshoe section of downtown, so named because the Republican-controlled state legislature tried to cram all the Democratic voters into one U-shaped assembly district in 1871. Grandpa was born on Bay Street, on a block that's still one of the shabbiest in the city; Hague was born on Cork Row, an Irish enclave located where the approach to the Holland Tunnel is now.

Both Hague and Grandpa were afraid of germs. Growing up in squalor will do that to a person. Grandpa spent his early years in a seedy tenement called the Bay View. There was no bay, and not much of a view. Hague was raised in a tenement called the Ark, because it seemed adrift on a large pool of smelly water that often collected outside its wooden door after a heavy rain.

Hague, like Grandpa, was the fourth child in a large family. Their mothers were strong and domineering. Their fathers were quiet working-class guys: Hague's father was a watchman at the Beehive Bank; Grandpa's father was a barber.

Both Hague and Grandpa left school in their early teens. Grandpa quit when he was thirteen; he was in third grade. By then he already had a few tattoos, and sat with his sleeves rolled up beside children half his size. When his teacher saw the tattoos, she covered her mouth and exclaimed, "Oh, you poor child!" Grandpa probably told her to go to hell.

Hague was expelled at fourteen from grade six, too early to learn proper grammar, a problem which made him an easy target in national circles—especially after he delivered a speech or testified before an investigative committee.

On paper, he and Grandpa were physical opposites. Hague was a tall Irish redhead, and Grandpa a short, dark Italian. But there was something about their stern faces, bald heads, and hand gestures that linked them in my mind. I had never seen Hague in action, but I had seen pictures, particularly one in which he's banging his fist, just like Grandpa did on our kitchen table.

I liked to think of Hague and Grandpa as opposite sides of the same stolen coin. They both had an aversion to physical labor. My grandfather refused to hold down a job and would go to great lengths to find money from other sources—other people's pockets. He once took a train to Indiana, then a cab to his son Robby's military base, just to ask him for a loan. Grandpa had no other business in Indiana.

Hague was a bit more inventive when it came to finding cash. He had only to work one menial labor job—on the Erie railroad, as a boilermaker—to know that the blue-collar life was not for him. While he was a teenager, Hague managed a Brooklyn boxer named Joseph Craig. Soon after, he entered the world of politics.

In 1896, a local saloonkeeper named Ned Kenny, known as the Mayor of Cork Row, gave Hague $75 to run for constable in the second ward. Hague parlayed that job into deputy sheriff, then precinct leader, ward leader, and custodian at City Hall—a job that helped him develop his talent for patronage: There was always room for one more maintenance man on the payroll.

One of the things Hague liked most about politics was dressing for the job. Like Grandpa, Hague appreciated fine clothes. Grandpa had his fedora cleaned and blocked once a week and made his kids get down on their hands and knees to spit-shine his shoes. Grandpa often urged his son, a clerk at Zampella's clothing store, to steal merchandise for him.

Hague, even with his $100-a-month job as ward constable, could buy his own tailor-made double-breasted suits and derby hats, his pearl-headed stickpins and silk underwear, and his high, white Belmont collars, which he wore to keep drafts away from his throat. He was deathly afraid of drafts. One legendary story had an eight-year-old Hague nailing shut all the windows in his house to keep out those nasty breezes. Later in life, he would keep the windows of his limousine rolled up to the top, even on the hottest days, though every now and then he'd have his driver pull over so that he could roll the windows down and lead his entourage in breathing exercises. The first thing Hague did when he awoke in the morning was take his own pulse.

Because he was such a stickler for hygiene, Hague kept an office—used as his main office—at the state-of-the-art, multimillion-dollar hospital he built.

Grandpa didn't have the pull to build institutions, but he did wash his feet three times a day, a textbook example of obsessive-compulsive behavior.

Before he became mayor, Hague staked his claim as commissioner of the Department of Public Safety, heading up the city's police and fire departments. His goal was to abolish police drunkenness and extortion, and through a series of trials, he cleaned up the force. "Jersey City," he declared ungrammatically, "is the most moralest city in America."

He created an elite squad of plainclothes police known as zeppelins, or zepps, who were there to do his bidding. They came down on anyone loitering, causing trouble, or bad-mouthing Hague. Through his zepps, Hague established a strong police presence that he would use for his own devices when he was elected mayor four years later.

Because of Hague, Jersey City became a safe place, with a cop on every corner—unless, of course, you rankled the cops or the powers-that-be. Then it was an unsafe place and you got your head broken, sometimes in several places. "I am the law," Hague once said. And he was. He created his own rules. One story had it that Hague's zepps killed a tavern owner, then let the man's widow run the tavern, just to shut her up, even though it was illegal for women to work behind the bar.

But if you could point to one single event that made Hague what he was, this was the one: The story illustrated the hatred between the Irish and the Italians, who had banded together against the Puerto Ricans and blacks in Jersey City by the time I was born. But back when Grandpa was coming of age, the Italians were considered to be the scum of the city. They were the bad guys in Hague's moral universe, a place where nobody but he and his Irish friends prospered.

During Holy Week in 1916, while residents of other cities were busy Easter-egg rolling and bonnet shopping, Jersey Citizens were embroiled in a murder mystery. The victim was the son of Ned Kenny, the Mayor of Cork Row, the man who had given Hague his start in politics.

On Good Friday, twenty-six-year-old Frank Kenny and his new wife were strolling along West Side Avenue on their way home from church at St. Aloysius, the same parish where I would attend high school years later. The West Side was below Journal Square, on a slope near the meadowlands, part of the Greenville ward. The West Side overlooked Newark Bay, so polluted with spilled oil, it was brown. I mistook the bay once for a large parcel of undeveloped land. Back in 1916, before it became nasty-looking, people with money lived in Greenville, in big, beautiful houses not yet ruined by aluminum siding.

On that Good Friday, Kenny went into a bakery on Union Street for a bag of rolls, and for some reason, left his wife standing outside. Maybe he wanted to surprise her with an especially large coffee cake or a dozen hot cross buns—who knows?

While she waited for her husband, Mrs. Kenny was accosted by an Italian immigrant. Witnesses later said they noticed the Italian guy catcalling as women went by. In Mrs. Kenny, he chose the wrong cat. And the wrong call.

"Hello, chicken," he said to her. *Chicken* was a term of endearment back then, maybe a precursor to the more modern but just as annoying *chick*. Or maybe Mrs. Kenny simply looked like a chicken. Insulted, and in an effort to avoid the Italian, Mrs. Kenny walked quickly down the street toward her house, the creep following close behind.

When Frank Kenny came out of the bakery, he saw his beloved chicken and the Italian up ahead and ran to catch up with them. Kenny insisted that the man apologize to his wife and, depending on whose version of events you believe, probably used a few choice racial slurs to get his point across.

The pro-Kenny version was the tame "You apologize to my wife or I'll turn you inside out." Nice dialogue, but highly unlikely in Jersey City, where practically everybody had a dirty mouth, even my mother.

The Italian said Kenny called him a dago and a wop and then smashed him in the face. Either way, provoked or not, the Italian pulled a revolver from his breast pocket and shot Kenny, point-blank, in the chest. With a bullet to the heart, Kenny died on the spot, right outside his house, the rolls still warm in their bag.

The murderer escaped into the meadowlands, losing his hat, a dark-blue felt number with a green velvet band and the name of the hat store written inside. Jersey City police, under the direction of commissioner Frank Hague, traced the hat to twenty-nine-year-old Michael Rombolo, a strikebreaker at the Ryerson steel plant.

The search for Kenny's killer began, with mobs of angry Irishmen shaking down every Italian who fit Rombolo's description: five-foot-six, 130 pounds, with a stubby black mustache and a big diamond ring on the second finger of his left hand. Every Italian in Jersey City fit that description, even some of the women.

Italo-Irish relations reached an all-time low. Suddenly, the Irish who ruled the city had a very good reason to hate the Italians, not that they really needed one. They were in charge, so they could hate whomever they pleased. Their plan, once they caught the murderer, was to string him up from the nearest telegraph pole. The police began a systematic "cleanup" of the Italian and Polish sections of the city, raiding saloons and conducting random searches, harassing as many immigrants as they could find.

A week after the murder, Hague and his henchmen traced Rombolo to a boardinghouse in Newark. Hague said he found the man in a local grocery store. As soon as he saw Hague, Rombolo ran out the back door, almost into the arms of a waiting Newark detective. But Rombolo made a break for it, sprinting down an alley to a playground two blocks away. Hague was close behind.

Rombolo hid behind a public rest room, but Hague came around the other end of the building to find him crouched down on one knee, his gun drawn, waiting for Hague to come into view. Hague jumped on top of Rombolo's back and wrestled him to the pavement. During the struggle, Rombolo slipped his revolver into his coat pocket. But a Newark detective frisked him while Hague held him down, pulling out the revolver and a knife.

Italians from the neighborhood poured out into the street to watch the drama, and to try and get in between Hague and his waiting car. Hague half carried and half dragged Rombolo to the car, knocking the other Italians out of the way. All the while, Rombolo threatened to kill him.

Hague drove Rombolo back to Jersey City in his own car to prove he was the one who had made the collar. The soon-to-be-mayor was greeted by a crowd of zepps and Jersey Citizens, including twenty-three-year-old John V. Kenny, the young brother of the murder victim.

When they arrived at police headquarters, Hague asked John V. if he wanted to take a few potshots at his brother's killer. When John declined, Hague did the honors, swinging his polished shoe back and smashing Rombolo in the ribs. Rombolo confessed to the murder later that night and was eventually sentenced to the electric chair.

That night, the Friday after Easter, *The Jersey Journal* wrote a glowing editorial about the commissioner of public safety, pushing the start button on the Hague machine.

It was partly due to Hague's success that my grandfather was such a failure. Beansie could never get a break under the Hague regime because his name, like Rombolo's, ended in a vowel. Even when he cooperated, he got screwed. Once, the local cops asked Grandpa to round up some gamblers for a floating crap game. The plan was that the cops would raid the game, then take all the money and give Grandpa a cut. But when the raid was over, the cops left Grandpa empty-handed. They threatened to arrest him if he complained.

Because he was not a yes-man, Grandpa was arrested and beaten down time and again. When the police captain shouted, "Round up the usual suspects," Grandpa was always on his list. I wouldn't be surprised if he was hauled in for a lineup in the Kenny murder. Grandpa was only nine years old at the time, but he got off to a bad start early in life.

Grandpa was hit by an ice truck when he was a kid. The accident apparently knocked something loose in his head. "Pazzo," my relatives would say, making circles near their ears. My mother was convinced Grandpa's problem was that he was once locked in the closet when he was a kid. He was extremely claustrophobic and couldn't stand to even ride on a train through a tunnel. Some nights he woke up in bed screaming, my grandmother consoling him in the darkness. We weren't sure what had happened to Grandpa early in life, but whatever it was, Hague only made it worse.

When one of his brothers did something wrong, Grandpa was often arrested for it, because they all looked so much alike. In the 1940s, my uncle Bicky broke a guy's nose at the Sunflower diner for picking on their brother Frankie. That night, the cops were out looking for Beansie.

Like Grandpa, Hague was a bully and would think nothing of hauling off and punching you in the nose. One of the most famous stories about him was the time he called for an ambulance in the middle of the night and, when the driver got there late, the mayor lost his temper. While the man was explaining that it had taken him a while to get dressed, Hague punched him in the face.

"Justice at the end of a nightstick" was one of Hague's favorite slogans. And Grandpa's head, already damaged, was often on the other end of that stick.

Grandma had pictures of Grandpa with welts on his back from one of many rubber-hose beatings by Hague or his henchmen. They said they were going to do something about it, but then they threw the pictures away. You couldn't beat the machine. But it could beat you— whenever it liked.

The Irish ran the city, through a group of neighborhood wards and committeemen and -women, who were usually based out of local saloons. When I was growing up, the city was divided into six wards, a term that always reminded me of Meadowview: Wards were for crazy people.

In my family's case, it would be convenient to say the criminal insanity trickled down from the top, from Hague to Grandpa and to later generations. But considering our track record, that's just not true. It's more complicated.

What Hague and his criminal progeny did was establish a climate for the crimes and immoral acts my family committed. A justification. Because if the Boss was doing it, how illegal could it really be? It was more than just okay to steal; it was your birthright. It was all right to beat people up, since Hague's zepps did it all the time. That's just the way it was. Nobody could change it. Nobody.

Though he had ties to mobsters Longie Zwillman and Willie Moretti, Hague allowed no boss but himself to operate on his streets. Even the powerful Dutch Schultz, who liked to travel to Newark every night to play cards, had to get permission from the Boss to come through Jersey City. One night, after coming through the Holland Tunnel, Schultz was stopped by Hague's zepps, who were always on the lookout for troublemakers and those who didn't belong. Because Schultz hadn't gotten Hague's permission to pass through his little fiefdom, he was arrested for vagrancy.

In 1920, a group of Princeton students traveled to Jersey City to help ensure a fair election. They were met by a dozen Jersey City men—with names like Mud Miller and Piggie Wilbough—who kicked the shit out of them and sent them crying, with concussions, back to their ivy-covered walls. The incident led to the first full state investigation of Hague, which led nowhere because of the many judges and high-level politicians he had placed throughout the state. His greatest coup was appointing his son, Frank, Jr., who didn't have a law degree, to the Court of Errors and Appeals, the highest court in New Jersey.

During political campaigns, Hague's zepps took control of the streets. Jersey City, even when I was growing up, was still known for its political rallies and bonfires. Kids would beat each other up in school yards over which candidate their parents planned to vote for. Back in Hague's day, parades were held at night, with supporters carrying signs and oil-lit torches, not unlike the angry villagers in *Frankenstein*. Speeches were made from soapboxes and the backs of trucks, with clowns like Muggsy Haskins entertaining the crowd until the mayor arrived. Muggsy, with a bright red nose, matching tie, beat-up hat, and white suit, was abruptly knocked off the platform when Hague got there.

When a vote didn't go his way, Hague would have the paper ballots thrown into the river. At certain locations, Hague would hire "sluggers"—

groups of bat-wielding men, who would chase opponents away from the polls. Once, an eight-year-old girl was accidentally hit in the head by one of the sluggers and killed.

When voting machines were finally introduced, Hague taught his committeemen and -women a trick to ensure that the residents voted for the right man. One of those women was Beansie's sister Katie. Taught by Hague, the master, Aunt Katie would place ashes on the lever for the correct candidate and then shake the hand of the voter when he stepped from the voting booth. Katie needed only to look down at her hands to see if the person had voted for the right candidate. Depending on the outcome, either a pat on the back or a swift kick in the ass followed.

Hague knew at all times what was happening on his streets. Phones were tapped, mail was opened, and spies lurked at Bickford's, a popular Journal Square cafeteria. And, always, the traitors were punished. His critics would find their right to vote revoked or their tax assessments raised, and if they were especially feisty, they'd be beaten and then arrested for "sarcastic criticism of superiors."

Though many of its reporters were kept on Hague's payroll, *The Jersey Journal* would occasionally launch an attack on the mayor. In the early 1920s, when the paper criticized Hague's payroll-padding, its tax assessment was raised by $175,000. *Journal* delivery boys were found in violation of child labor laws, and Journal Square was renamed Veterans' Square, although the new name never stuck. Movie houses were bullied by City Hall into pulling their ads from the paper. Word on the street was: "If you want to know what movies are playing, call Mayor Hague."

Intimidation was not the only key to Hague's success. Making certain people feel like they were part of the machine also had a lot to do with it. Aunt Katie was one of those people. Carefully building his support one favor at a time, Hague worked his way up through the county political structure, using the railroads and big business as a foil and identifying with the working-class voters. It didn't take a lot to make people happy, especially during the Depression. In 1933 alone, Hague's people delivered more than fifteen thousand Christmas baskets to hungry families. A job here, a job there. Only Hague could get away with creating titles like "supervisor of sinks" and "foreman of vacuum cleaners" for friends. Even the clergy got in on the action: More than fifty priests, rabbis, and ministers were on the city payroll.

But the favors were returned. Through his deputy mayor, John "Needlenose" Malone, Hague collected his tribute. Each worker was required to turn over 3 percent of his or her salary to the Boss each month on what was called Rice Pudding Day.

In addition to their tribute, Jersey City residents paid the highest taxes in the nation—for very little in return. Streets were safe, but they were dirty and filled with potholes; open horse-drawn wagons still collected garbage long after trucks became the norm in other cities; gaslights lit the street corners years after Thomas Edison made his discovery. The sewer system was in rough shape, rats were rampant, public schools were in poor condition and overcrowded (but there were few complaints, since those with the power sent their kids to Catholic school), and there were no after-school recreational programs—despite the large Recreation Department payroll.

And no one complained, because practically everyone was guilty: There were policemen who were paid $8,000 to sing in the police quartet, two county-jail organists, workers in the City Clerk's office who were paid daily to repair the ballot boxes, and a special inspector of kosher meats.

Though his own salary was only $6,500 a year, Hague owned a $125,000 summer mansion on the Jersey shore, in what was called "the millionaires' colony"; a luxurious fourteen-room Jersey City duplex apartment; a place on Park Avenue; a villa in Biscayne Bay, Florida; and he spent the rest of his time vacationing in Paris.

When questioned about his finances, Hague told the authorities to mind their own effin' business. And because he made it a policy never to put anything in writing, his padded payrolls and kickback schemes could never be traced. It helped that Hague had practically everyone in his pocket.

Hague controlled not only Jersey City and its residents; as vice-chairman of the Democratic National Committee, he pulled in the vote for Franklin D. Roosevelt as his point man in the Northeast. In August 1932, Hague bused in over 100,000 Hudson County residents to Sea Girt, New Jersey—providing a free box lunch and a day "down the shore." It was one of the largest outdoor political rallies ever held. In Hudson County alone, Hague brought in 184,000 votes for FDR that year.

Roosevelt was warned about Hague's corrupt tactics and told by aides that the man was "a son of a bitch."

"Yeah, but he's our son of a bitch," replied FDR.

The relationship was a give-and-take. In return for Hague's loyalty, Roosevelt poured $47 million of WPA money into Hudson County. For Roosevelt Stadium alone, $3 million was given to the city. The playing field for the minor-league Jersey Giants was built in tribute to Hague's friend in Washington, next to a site that contained a million tons of toxic waste. Each season, Hague was there, ready to throw out the first ball. Guaranteed to be in the stands was his legion of no-show city workers—all required to purchase Giants' tickets. Hague loved sports, particularly baseball, and one of his favorite sayings was "Play ball with me and I'll make you rich."

Roosevelt often made a pilgrimage to Jersey City when an event was important enough to Hague. In 1936, for instance, the president laid the cornerstone of the Medical Building of the Jersey City Medical Center. My mother was there that day with the rest of the kids in her kindergarten class, waving a little American flag as Roosevelt drove by in an open car.

The Medical Center was a wonder. I was born there, as were my mother and most Jersey City residents, pulled kicking and screaming from their mothers and into the city. The Margaret Hague maternity hospital was one of seven Medical Center buildings that were the only distinguishable features of the city's skyline.

The hospital's stepped Art Deco buildings climbed into the overcast sky like some ancient stone ziggurat that an alien culture had plopped down on the Hudson River's western shore. The Medical Center looked lonely and abandoned from a distance. And up close, its twenty-three stories didn't fit in with the surrounding low-lying, dilapidated buildings.

The Medical Center was not just an architectural wonder but a Democratic one. The $30 million complex was Hague's experiment with socialized medicine, and for a while, the experiment worked. Medical Center surgeons saved my uncle Jerry's leg after an attack dog nearly chewed it off. Grandma was treated there for cervical cancer by one of the best gynecologists in the metropolitan area. She even got a job there, in the nursing school's dining room in Murdoch Hall.

But by the time I was born, the Medical Center was growing shabby and was headed for bankruptcy. The city was no longer known for its first-rate hospitals. When teenagers learned to drive in Jersey City, part of the instruction was to keep driving if you had an accident inside the Holland Tunnel so that you could pull up to a good hospital on the New York side.

The Medical Center's woes were often blamed on the politicians who came after Hague. But the truth was, Hague was partially responsible for the hospital's decline. Though the Medical Center did offer free services to the poor, it also offered those same services to people who had the money to pay. It was bad business. In Hague's day, there were so many no-show jobs at the hospital that the patient-to-staff ratio was said to be one to one. Janitors outnumbered nurses. Patient costs were double those at private hospitals. A French chef cooked all the staff meals.

Though the hospital and city finances were a mess, Hague was so powerful as to be beyond reproach. It wasn't until 1937—the year after FDR's visit—that Hague took things too far. That fall, forty members of the Committee on Industrial Organizations (CIO) came to Jersey City to hand out flyers and copies of the Bill of Rights. Thirteen members were arrested; the others were put on the ferry back to New York.

The following winter, *Life* magazine ran a seven-page spread on the Hague machine's union-busting activities, calling the mayor a dictator and comparing him to Hitler, saying he lacked the Führer's imagination and "rabble-rousing eloquence." Though the magazine was banned on Jersey City's streets, "Haguetown" became the laughingstock of the nation.

The CIO successfully sued, forcing Hague to take the stand for three days—ample time for him to put his ass-kicking foot in his ungrammatical mouth and denounce democracy. At one point, the mayor proposed deporting all of the country's rabble-rousers. Communists, he said, should be sent back to Europe where they came from. If the rabble-rousers were born here? "We ought to establish a camp in Alaska there and house them there away from the American people."

Roosevelt was embarrassed. And, eventually, so were Jersey City's residents. It was the first time they realized that the rest of the world wasn't quite like home. This was no land of the free. And what was this Bill of Rights everyone was talking about?

It wasn't long before Jersey City's young men found themselves defending democracy, sitting in foxholes with guys who teased them about their city's dictator, exposed in the pages of *Life*.

By the mid-1940s, Hague was losing his grip, because young veterans like Uncle Bicky had seen and experienced other places, and had walked down the Champs-Elysées. Even war-ravaged and blown to bits, most places were a lot better off. And a hell of a lot prettier. More important, the Depression, which had helped Hague keep his grip on poor and hungry Jersey Citizens, was finally over. Political reform seemed like it might be in the cards.

Sensing his loosening hold, Hague made one last indirect grasp at power, resigning midterm in 1947 and passing the mayoralty to his nephew, Frank Hague Eggers, a stubby man with none of his uncle's charisma. Though the resignation was made with great fanfare, including aerial bombs and a brass band, Hague planned to run the city by proxy, away from the heat. His exit was purely theatrical.

Resentful that Hague would choose a relative over a loyal soldier like himself, one popular ward leader began mounting a campaign to unseat Eggers. The ward leader was John V. Kenny, son of the Mayor of Cork Row and brother of Frank Kenny, whose murder had helped cement Hague's popularity with voters.

John V. Kenny had stood at Hague's side the night Rombolo was hauled into the precinct. That night, John V. had refused to kick a man when he was down. But since then John had grown up a bit. Like Aunt Katie, Grandpa, and most people in Jersey City, John V. had learned from the master.

6

CHECK YOUR
COAT AND HAT

The summer after I graduated from kindergarten, Jersey City's mayor was convicted and thrown out of office. By first grade at Our Lady of Czestochowa, I knew how to spell *indictment* and *subpoena*—two tricky vocabulary words for a six-year-old. I also knew how to spell *Czestochowa,* an even bigger feat. Pronouncing it was hard enough. Grandpa jokingly called it "Our Lady of Check-Your-Coat-and-Hat."

In 1971, while I was learning to write, Mayor Thomas Whelan and eleven other local politicians were part of the biggest corruption case in Hudson County history. Known as the Hudson Twelve, they were charged with taking $3.5 million in kickbacks for county construction contracts.

To teach us right from wrong, all the nuns at OLC would have needed to do was tell us about Whelan and his buddies. Every moral lesson we needed to know was right there in front of us: Thou shalt not steal. Thou shalt not bear false witness against thy neighbor. Thou shalt not covet thy neighbor's goods. Instead, the lessons we learned at OLC came from an occasional film strip on the life of Jesus or about the evils of drugs, two things that seemed to have no bearing on my life at age six. Every so often an overweight, dim-witted Jersey City cop called Officer Friendly would come to class and try and teach us about right and wrong. "Cross at the green, not in between," he said. "Cross at the red and you'll be dead." By first grade, I knew that life on Jersey City's streets was much more complicated than that.

I found it strange that no one mentioned Mayor Whelan at school or at church. He was never held up as a poor example of human conduct. The waterfront was nasty and abandoned and the parks were filled with garbage and broken glass because of politicians like Whelan. That's what they should have taught us—I could have related to that. But maybe Officer Friendly and the teachers were Whelan supporters.

One teacher did sit us down in front of the television to watch the Watergate hearings, though. Not that she understood what was going on. She never explained it to us. She just told us it was a historic moment. Really, it was a moment for her to ignore us and file her nails.

OLC functioned in its own bubble, stuck somewhere in the late 1950s or early 1960s, with bored housewives working more as babysitters than as teachers. The school was out of touch with the world around it. At OLC, there was an alarming number of boys with crewcuts, whose parents couldn't face the fact that it was the 1970s.

A cultural revolution was passing our parish by, and no one wanted to know about it. The Equal Rights Amendment was evil, one nun told us. Why would we want to share bathrooms with men? she shouted at us girls. For years I thought equal rights for women meant the right to use a urinal.

I had no idea that society at large, and even Catholic churches throughout the county and the country, were undergoing great changes. Girls were allowed to be altar "boys," and women deacons were even handing out Communion. One friend went to a church where they celebrated a folk mass, with guitars, tambourines, and songs written in the twentieth century.

At OLC, all the songs in church were played by an immaculate man named Matty, who knew a few chords on the organ and sang in a nasal monotone, like a fifteenth-century monk with a bad head cold. To imitate Matty, you had to hold your nose, then spit out the lyrics in one long gasp, chanting more than singing, one syllable a note higher than the others: Glory-be-to-the-father-and-TO-the-son-and-to-the-holy-SPIIIIrit. As-it-was-in-the-beginning-is-now-and-ever-SHALL-be. World-without-end-A-men." That was considered singing at OLC. We didn't have a real musical director, because Matty came cheap. He worked for nothing.

I longed for a folk mass. *Godspell* was my favorite Broadway cast album. And in my heart of hearts, I knew Jesus was a groovy guy who wouldn't mind long hair, rainbow suspenders, and the ERA. Jesus, from what I could tell, was a revolutionary.

I knew that even He would be bored by the sermons at OLC. Never once did I follow a sermon all the way through during a mass. At first I thought it was my fault, that I was intrinsically bad or that my powers of concentration were flawed. But then I attended mass at nearby St. Peter's and realized it was just our priests who were incredibly dull. They never bothered to write down interesting lessons drawn from everyday life that the parishioners could relate to. They'd just get up there and wing it. I wasn't sure if the parishioners stopped listening first or the priests stopped trying to make them listen first. Daddy stood at the back of church during mass so that when the priest got up to talk, he could sneak out and have a smoke. I wished I could go with him.

If OLC taught me one thing, it was that nothing was sacred in Jersey City, not even church. The truth was that most of the priests in my parish needed to hear a sermon themselves. At OLC, one oversexed priest chased my mother around the rectory one afternoon when she went in to buy a mass card for a funeral.

There were tales of Father Piasecki, whom we called Father Grab-It-All. Piasecki often took weekend trips to his house in Pennsylvania with the rectory housekeeper, Wanda, who always wore a plush fur coat, a gift from the generous pastor. My sister once asked my mother if Wanda was the pastor's wife. When Piasecki retired, letters were sent to parishioners asking them to come to his farewell party. People mailed him empty wallets and ripped-up dollar bills. Only the ass-kissers attended the gala.

At a very young age, I discovered that our parish was hardly hallowed ground.

Father Ziggy, who had emigrated from Poland, seemed more pious than the other priests. But then again, how would we know? He spoke no English. Ziggy came to our school once a month to hear our confessions in the children's library. Ziggy and I sat on folding chairs, facing each other. No screen, no kneeler. With his face turned and his eyes averted, Ziggy would listen and nod his head as my sins poured out past the Nancy Drew mysteries and Encyclopedia Britannica.

Father Ziggy had no idea what I was saying. No matter what I confessed—whether I told him I had disobeyed my parents or I confessed to killing Archduke Ferdinand—the penance was still the same, delivered in broken English: "One Our Father, two Hail Marys." It was the only English Ziggy knew.

Every Friday during Lent we got into a double-file line and were marched four blocks over to the parish church to go to confession there and to recite the Stations of the Cross, fourteen vignettes that traced Jesus' last, horrible day on earth: from being sentenced before Pilate to meeting the Good Samaritan along the road to being crucified. The stations were like a Top Ten countdown: Jesus' greatest hits. We followed along with the graphic depictions along the church walls.

Easter was considered the holiest time of the year, even holier than Christmas. It was so holy that you had to do penance for forty days before it, to cleanse your soul in preparation. It all started on Ash Wednesday, when you were expected to give something up for Lent. Some people only went to church on Ash Wednesday and then, a few weeks later, on Palm Sunday, the two days of the year they got something for free. The pastor called them A&P Catholics—for *ashes* and *palms*. I thought maybe OLC should hand out little gifts every week, then maybe more people would come, like on bat day at Yankee Stadium.

Mass could be painful. On Holy Thursday, three days before Easter Sunday, a High Mass was held in the evening. The mass was penance enough for the entire year. We had to wear our blue-and-white-checked school uniforms and beanies. It was bad enough we had to wear them day in and day out. Wearing them at night was especially humiliating. The worst part, though, was parading around the church carrying ten-pound lily pots. The lilies would poke me in the eye, blocking my vision. If I was really unlucky, yellow dusty pollen from inside the flowers would get in my eyes or in my nose. I couldn't rub it out, since I was, after all, holding a ten-pound pot of lilies. By the last processional round, with my eyes and nose running, that pot grew mighty heavy. I tripped countless times at Holy Thursday mass but, miraculously, never fell.

The best part of the mass was when the priest pretended to be Jesus and washed the feet of a dozen pre-chosen male parishioners, who were seated on folding chairs up on the altar, playing the part of the Apostles. We watched in awe as the guys took their black shiny shoes off and rolled down their dress socks and Father Pastor, as we redundantly called him, actually washed their feet in a basin. The point of it all was to show that no man was better than another. But to us kids, there was a perverse excitement in seeing the naked feet of men from the neighborhood. In church no less. On the altar.

Every Holy Thursday—and at most Sunday masses, really—a crazy Polish lady in a babushka would get up and pray loudly to the statues in church. She would yell and gesticulate and make me really nervous, mostly because I feared the stone statues would come to life and yell back at her. One Holy Thursday, Father Pastor just couldn't take her ranting and raving anymore, and right in the middle of mass he stopped his boring sermon, turned to her, and yelled, "Shaddup." Everyone in church had always wanted to say it but couldn't get up the nerve.

On Holy Saturday, the day before Easter, my family would go to the church basement to have our Easter food blessed. There was a mound of butter shaped like a big Easter egg, which my father sculpted each year by rolling a pound of butter around in a bowl for a half hour or so. He placed a fuzzy sprig of parsley on top for garnish. Surrounding the butter on the fancy crystal plate was a ring of fresh kielbasa. Easter eggs that I had colored were placed around the outside of the kielbasa, beside a shot glass full of salt. On another plate was the babka, a soft and airy cakelike bread that I was always tempted to rest my head on, like a pillow, while we waited for the priest to finish his blessing.

Father Pastor would throw holy water on the food and on us, usually hitting me in the eye with a drop or two. Then we'd carefully carry the plate back home to our refrigerator, opening the door every now and then to peek longingly at the kielbasa until we could eat it the next day. It was so garlicky that it made everything in the fridge smell like it, even long after Easter was over.

Though the nuns and priests did their best to ruin my concept of religion, it was always beautiful inside OLC, with its tall stained-glass windows and Gothic glass-and-wrought-iron light fixtures strung from black chains. The most striking feature was the huge wooden crucifix above the altar, upon which a suffering, bleeding, life-size Christ was nailed. More than any parable or film strip, that cross convinced me what a great guy Jesus was. He looked so miserable up there. And He was doing it all for me. He would even wash my feet if I asked Him to.

As I gazed up at the cross, ignoring Father Pastor's sermon, I remembered what the nuns said: Jesus died for my sins. My sins didn't seem bad enough for anyone to die over, though. I never could understand how Jesus' dying wiped my slate clean, but I was grateful to Him. If only the nuns could follow His selfless example. For them, fear and intimidation were synonymous with "morality."

When something was stolen in the classroom, like the time Shawn swiped Anthony's race car after show-and-tell in second grade, the nuns resorted to Nazi tactics and would punish us all to try and rout out the perpetrator. Our principal hit everyone in my class with a paddle in the hopes that someone would rat out the evildoer or—far less likely—that the evildoer would confess.

It never worked. The evildoers would continue to do evil, unpunished. The girl who stole my pencil case in kindergarten wound up getting a job in city government.

Like the priests, the nuns were often on the wrong side of the moral lessons they were trying to teach us. They set a good example of what not to do to your friends and neighbors. Sister Isabelle was by far the most sinister. She told us in second grade that Noah's Ark had recently been found, which signaled that the end of the world was coming. It was prophesied, she said, that once the Ark was found, the end was near. She told us—we're talking seven-year-olds—that the Russians had a button they could push which would destroy us all. Any day now, she said.

I sat awake at night biting my nails, waiting to be blown up.

Sister Isabelle's greatest crime, though, was terrorizing my best friend, Liz, the only girl in school whose parents were divorced. Sister Isabelle embarrassed Liz in front of the whole class, singling her out and declaring divorce was a sin. As if it were Liz's fault that her parents had split up.

Every day at OLC crimes were committed, but none that the administration could be charged with. One teacher smoked in the classroom and swore us all to silence. Her bad habit was to be our little secret, she said. In third grade, Miss Linda, who wore miniskirts to show the eight-year-old boys what to expect in a few years, filled two blackboards with homework assignments one afternoon because, she said, we were bad. We copied it down, crying all the while, not knowing how we'd ever get all that work done in one night. As the dismissal bell rang, Miss Linda yelled, "April Fool!" She laughed as we all whimpered out of class, trying to catch our breath from crying so hard.

Instead of showing us Jesus film strips, our fourth-grade teacher, Mr. C., pulled down the shades and showed us slides of his honeymoon, complete with his wife sprawled out on a hotel bed. For science class, he had us melt chocolate eggs and crayons on a hot plate, then feed each other fish food.

In a burst of creativity, Mr. C. decided to prove how terrible it would be to be blind. He paired us off and blindfolded one person in each pair, then had the seeing-eye student lead the blind kid around the school. It was all fun and games until someone led her partner down a flight of stairs. The "blind" kid nearly lost an eye.

Though I had a great deal of fun, I learned absolutely nothing in fourth grade.

Thanks to two or three good teachers, I somehow learned to read and write. Geography was not considered an important subject: Jersey City was all you needed to know.

My favorite class was gym, because my brother was the teacher. He tended bar at the Majestic most nights, but he still had his afternoons free. He took the gym job to make a few extra bucks. Stanley lasted only one year, but I was so proud of him. He came to class in sweats and sneakers and made us do relay races and play actual games. OLC had no sports teams or after-school programs. But when Stanley arrived, he had us compete for the Presidential Physical Fitness Awards, a national program to try and slim down America's fast-food-gorged youth, which involved a series of sit-ups, pull-ups, and wind sprints.

Even when Stanley gave up the gig and got a job sweeping bubbles off the roof at Colgate, gym was still my favorite class. It was the one hour of the day when we were allowed to run without getting yelled at. I longed to roam free, and even considered running away from home. But I could never do that to my mother. I liked her too much to worry her.

Gym was held in Victory Hall, which was divided into Upper and Lower Victory Hall. Upper Victory Hall had a big stage and was mostly used for our lame school "productions" on the priests' feast days. We never put on plays or shows. OLC had no activities of any kind. On the afternoon of the given day—which fell on the feast day of the saint that the priest was named after—we were simply dragged onstage, class by class, to sing ditties like "Old MacDonald" or "The Wheels on the Bus." Parents were never invited. It was all for the amusement of the priests and nuns.

Victory Hall was connected to OLC via the boys' bathroom. To get to Victory Hall, teachers had to either drag the schoolchildren outside and around the corner, an undertaking that involved putting coats and hats on each kid, or simply escort them through the boys' bathroom. The teachers always took the easy way out. Whenever my schoolmates and I took the shortcut to Victory Hall, we made sure to hold our breath to avoid smelling the overwhelming stench coming from the urinals. The teacher would yell a warning before traipsing through with us, just in case a boy was still at the urinal doing his business. Inevitably, there was one boy who was still taking a piss, or at least pulling up his fly. The teacher told us girls to close our eyes, but I usually peeked, in the hopes of seeing what the big deal was. The urinals fascinated me, since they were the key to equal rights for women.

Lower Victory Hall was graced with a netless basketball hoop but little else. In the years before and after Stanley's short stint, our gym instructor was Sophie, the kindhearted but physically unfit cleaning lady. Sophie was the all-around school Mrs. Fix-It. When someone threw up, it was Sophie who came by with the sawdust to sprinkle over the mess. It was Sophie who heated our soft pretzels in the ovens of Lower Victory Hall for recess break, Sophie who, if you gave her a few bucks in the morning before classes began, ran out and got you pizza for lunch. Sophie was the pizza connection and everyone's stand-in mom. For gym class, the principal simply handed her a whistle. Sophie was not trained in physical-fitness education, so she just let us run wild and scream for a full hour or sometimes threw a dodge ball our way to let us fight it out.

The best gym activity was pretending to work in the old ticket booth and coat-check room located between Upper and Lower Victory Halls. Though they provided hours of entertainment, I wondered what the ticket counter and coat-check room were for, exactly. Certainly no one was purchasing tickets to Father Pastor's feast-day celebration.

Digging through my mother's dresser drawers one rainy afternoon, I realized the ticket and coat-check facilities were left over from the days when Victory Hall, like Jersey City, was a much more important place. In its prime, Victory Hall had been ground zero for the Polish community, a place for polka dances and parties, where group pictures were taken of the whole crowd, hundreds of people decked out in fancy dresses and suits, sitting at long tables. I found a few of those big black-and-white photos among my mother's things and spent hours searching out Ma, Daddy, and all my Polish relatives. The focus was deep, so even the tiny heads at the back of Victory Hall were clear, their features recognizable.

The two-tiered Victory Hall was where my parents' wedding reception was held and where the Dudley Club held many a polka night. During one of those dances, in 1949, John V. Kenny made a campaign stop on his hand-shaking/baby-kissing rounds to unseat Frank Hague Eggers. Kenny's campaign was called the Freedom Ticket and worked off the momentum of World War II. Wherever they went, his supporters flashed the V made popular by Winston Churchill. V for victory and for John V.

Victory Hall was an obvious campaign stop for John V.

Though Kenny was an Irishman through and through, he was concerned with pleasing all the ethnic groups in Jersey City. He wanted the Poles—a strong Jersey City voting block—on his side. And the night he visited my father's Dudley polka dance at Victory Hall, he got them.

It was a warm spring night. A polka band was playing downstairs behind the basketball hoop, and an American band was on the stage upstairs. There were two bars—one set up on a long card table on the upper level and one built-in wooden bar on the lower level, complete with stainless-steel sinks and brushes, just like in the Majestic. So many people attended the dances at Victory Hall back then that they worried the upper floor would cave in and the revelers would come crashing down on the lower-floor dancers.

Kenny, dressed in a dark suit, his graying hair slicked back, walked into Upper Victory Hall, the crowd swarming around him, the air close with cigarette smoke and the musty smell of tap beer. Word must have traveled upstairs quicker than Kenny himself, past the coat-check room and ticket booth, because when he made that grand entrance, the American band was already playing his campaign song, "Now Is the Hour."

"Now is the hour when we must say good-bye," the song went, a direct jab at Hague.

Since this was indeed a dance, Kenny decided to get out on the floor. He probably wasn't a very good polka dancer, being Irish and all. The American band was much more his speed. And they were playing his song.

Of the hundreds of women in the crowd, my mother was the one Kenny grabbed and swept onto the dance floor for a waltz. Kenny, who was only slightly taller than my mother, picked her because she was petite and pretty. Little did Kenny know that she was a great dancer, too. It was the Russian blood in her veins, Great-Grandma Irene's. Russians were great dancers, I thought, because they had to move around a lot to stay warm in the old country.

My mother was happiest when she danced. She could do it all: the polka, the jitterbug, the lindy hop, the Montclair. She even made the hokeypokey look graceful. Whenever she was out there, she glowed, and could make any guy look good on the dance floor. She could lead without letting on and embarrassing the guy. When my father danced with her, he barely had to shuffle his feet. My energetic mother twirled and bounced enough for the both of them.

So Kenny had picked the right woman. She and Kenny spun around, my mother's dress twirling in the humid Victory Hall air and making short, unattractive Kenny look like Gene Kelly, graceful and handsome and the center of attention. The other women looked on in awe as my mother enjoyed several minutes of local fame. Everyone loved Kenny. And she was the one to dance with him. The only one.

My father, never a jealous man, was so proud of his beautiful girl: This was his dance, and that was Jersey City's future mayor dancing with his girl. He sipped his Scotch and flashed a wide, white smile. It was 1949, so he hadn't yet lost his front teeth.

After the Victory Hall dance, every piece of the campaign puzzle fell into place for Kenny. The candidates were made to draw for their positions on the ballot. Eggers and his running mates drew the coveted first four spots. Kenny drew spots seven to eleven, but brilliantly used the numbers to his advantage. Every gambler and bookie in Jersey City could identify with the 7–11 craps reference. "A natural," was Kenny's slogan. The numbers were an omen and Kenny's secret sign that illegal gambling would not only be tolerated under his administration but that it would flourish.

Kenny had been a ward leader for thirty-five years and knew the inner workings of the system. Some say he had been planning his attack on Hague since 1929. It took him two decades to get up the gumption. In 1936, Hague got wind of Kenny's plot to overthrow the local government, called him down to the mayor's office, punched him in the face, and then made him pledge publicly, "All I am and all I ever will be, I owe to my dear friend Frank Hague."

But by 1949, everyone was sick and tired of being beaten down by Hague, even Aunt Katie. She became one of Kenny's biggest supporters. When Hague came downtown to campaign for his nephew, Katie made sure he was not greeted warmly. While delivering a speech outside P.S. 37, Hague was pelted with rotten eggs and fruit. "Get them little dirty bastards," he screamed into the microphone, pointing at the kids who threw the bombs. Even at Hague's beloved Roosevelt Stadium, Kenny stole the show: Planes trailing his campaign banners buzzed overhead.

Kenny took out full-page ads in *The Jersey Journal,* confidently declaring, "The cynics, the shrug-the-shoulders crowd said it couldn't be done. But it looks as though Kenny will make a killing. A vote for the Freedom Ticket is a vote for Liberty."

In another ad, he warned voters, "It's your last chance to save Jersey City."

The Hague camp knew it was all over the night they and Kenny simultaneously converged on Journal Square for their respective campaign stops. Kenny held a large labor parade on May Day, five days before the election, which wound from Greenville down Bergen Avenue and ended on Journal Square—an impressive place in the 1940s. It hadn't yet become the mini-Calcutta I would come to know. In 1949, it was—like Victory Hall and Kenny—in its prime, a place that songs were written about. The big band hit "Jersey Bounce" proclaimed: "It started on Journal Square. The memory lingers there." The Square even had its own radio station, WAAT, which broadcast as far as the nation's capital. The signal was so strong that a crazy guy from Baltimore who once heard his first name mentioned in a WAAT program got mad and took a bus all the way to Jersey City, where he busted into the studio and tried to stab a singer who was on the air.

Despite the occasional outbreak of violence there, the Journal Square my parents remember is where you took your date on a Saturday night. My mother's first date was on the Square, at age fifteen, at the Spa, a hamburger joint near the Stanley Theatre. She went out with a teenager named Junior Bellino, who got her home past curfew to find my beast of a grandfather waiting angrily on the stoop for them. It was their one and only date.

When my father came along, he took my mother to crowded Journal Square spots like the Art Deco China Clipper restaurant, a curved building on the corner near the Loew's, with a small fleet of airplanes on its sign; the Canton Tea Garden, where red-jacketed Chinese waiters served steaming plates of chow mein to couples snuggled in red booths; Oyster Bay, a place that covered its tables with tablecloths, even for lunch; and Robinson's Steakhouse, which made the best cocktails in town and where my great-uncle Sam—Pauline's brother—always hung out, Scotch in hand. He was the uncle who'd gotten his head stuck in the Morris Canal.

Teachers took kids on field trips to the Square in the 1940s. My mother remembers going there during World War II to visit a Japanese midget suicide submarine, which had been captured at Pearl Harbor and taken on a national tour to encourage the sale of war bonds. The kids were made to crawl inside, where they met a wax Japanese sailor face-to-face. My mother almost had a heart attack.

It was a time when Journal Square was never quiet and never empty, a time when people took first the trolleys and then the Hudson Tubes from downtown to pay their utility bills in person. Before the discount stores and sleazy motels invaded, the Square was known for Russell Lou's beauty parlor, Cara Carson's boutique, the Glove Shop, Five Corners Bakery, and State Gown, a high-class dress shop made famous when a man pumped a bunch of bullets into his girlfriend there.

The burgers at Bickford's cafeteria, where Hague's spies often took notes of overheard enemy conversation, competed with the ice cream sodas at Liss's drugstore and the crispy hot dogs at the new Boulevard Drinks, its pink neon installed that same year, 1949.

The night of the Kenny parade, thousands came out and gathered at the grandstand even though it threatened to rain. Banners were waved. Traffic was stopped. Speeches were made. A bricklayer took the microphone and yelled, "Let it rain! This crowd is going to stay here no matter how hard it rains." The crowd thundered back its approval.

Dozens of cops patrolled on horseback, and the Hudson Boulevard police, dressed, like the Gestapo, with chaps, high boots, and helmets, waved their clubs to keep the mob in check. Nearby, a hook and ladder truck was set up so newspaper photographers could get their shots. Just a few hundred feet away, the Hague/Eggers ticket held its gathering at the Hotel Plaza, a classy place where my godparents spent their honeymoon night, sipping drinks at the Montmartre piano lounge downstairs. But the crowd on Journal Square wasn't there for the Eggers meeting. On their way out into the street, Hague's people knew they would be defeated. Commissioner Arthur Potterton took one look at the Kenny mob and smirked. He knew right then that the Hague machine was about to be traded in for a new model.

Kenny, with a big nose, big ears, and bad teeth, was a man of the people. Unlike Hague, Kenny always blended in with the crowd. While Hague was still riding around in limos with bodyguards, Kenny used the Hudson Tubes and broken-down cars to get where he was going. Some say it had nothing to do with modesty, that Kenny was just a tightwad. Even after he made millions, he would eat at the cafeteria and tip the busboy only a quarter for carrying his tray to his table.

Kenny's "Ragamuffin Army" followed his thrifty cue. The 'Forty-niners, as they came to be known that fateful year, wore knitted ties, mackinaws, and mismatched jackets and pants. They were a colorful bunch—and fit right in with the riffraff of Jersey City. One Kenny sidekick, a guy named Barney Doyle, matched Yogi Berra in his propensity for dumb witticisms. He once criticized a mayoral candidate as being so stupid that he couldn't be a lifeguard in a car wash. He said that his own team could run with five parking meters and win the election, that Judas Iscariot was the patron saint of all politicians, and that his political club's slogan was the same as the word on the back of a vegetable truck: *produce.* The inflection was all wrong, but somehow Barney was always right-on, in a Jersey City sort of way.

On May 10, 1949, Kenny was swept into office, winning eleven of the twelve wards in the city and beating Eggers by 22,200 votes. To celebrate, men stood ten deep at bars like Casey's, a pub around the corner from the Hotel Plaza, where a big floral arrangement declared KENNY IN MAY. Everyone with a car got in it and drove through the city, honking the horn and picking up friends along the way, my relatives included. They moved in a long line, headlights beaming, through Journal Square, past a woman on a sound truck who repeated over and over again, "You're free. You're free. The people of Jersey City are free." A Greyhound from out of town pulled up. People on the bus looked out their windows, very confused. What the hell was going on here?

My mother was downtown, sitting on a stoop with her best friend, Ann, who was nine months pregnant and ready to burst. They got caught up in the rowdy crowds as they marched by on Grove Street, streaming down toward City Hall. One group of guys went by carrying a gray coffin with a sign that read HERE LIES THE REMAINS OF THE HAGUE MACHINE, 36 YEARS OF AGE. In a photo taken that night, my mother is in the left-hand corner of the frame, wearing a white turban on her head, smiling up at the coffin.

My uncle Robby, just thirteen at the time, rode his bicycle down to City Hall, JVK written in chalk on the back of his jacket. To him and the other poor kids in Jersey City, Kenny was a hero, like Joe DiMaggio.

He and his friends arrived at City Hall before all the ballots were counted, hoping to cop some free soda or ice cream. But there wasn't any. The crowd at City Hall was mostly adults, and they were too excited to even think about eating or drinking. Some danced on the roofs of cars or on the grass at City Hall in front of the tired statue, music blaring from the sound trucks. One policeman stood on the City Hall balcony waving a broom. Inside, the coffin drifted overhead upon a sea of bodies.

In another photograph that captured the moment, a somber-looking girl sits alone in the background at City Hall, away from the mob, to the right of the coffin sign. That's my aunt Mary Ann, looking blankly off into the distance. A kid with big ears and a wide smile lights up the foreground of another picture. That's Uncle Robby. When he saw the coffin go by, Robby got scared, thinking Hague's body was in it. Ever since his brother, Sonny, had fallen off the truck and died, Robby had been afraid of coffins. Now, he got down on his knees, crawled out of the crowd, and ran all the way home.

In one more black-and-white snapshot taken that night, the most posed of the bunch, another family member smiles for the camera. Grandpa, all decked out in a freshly blocked fedora and suit and tie, is one of two men holding a sign that reads UNDER NEW MANAGEMENT. A crowd of seven men and boys are gathered around them and the plate-glass door to the mayor's office, flashing the two-fingered V signal.

For victory. For John V.

Grandpa must have been overjoyed, but his face, the only one in the picture that is cast in dark shadow, betrays only a slight grin. Everyone else looks grim or surprised, worried that Hague might walk out any second and punch him in the nose—or, worse yet, see the picture the next day in *The Jersey Journal* and have him hunted down and killed.

Despite their disbelief that Hague was truly out, Jersey Citizens partied until dawn. One 'Forty-niner played taps outside Eggers's home at 3 A.M. There were rallies in the street, from Greenville down to the Horseshoe.

"Let us bid farewell to fear," said Kenny in his victory speech. "Let us say good-bye to corruption. Let us walk forward now as free men and women."

Because of Kenny, an investigation was finally launched into Hague's three-decades-long rule. Needlenose Malone—not Hague—was indicted on charges of corruption, and pleaded guilty after thousands of city workers signed affidavits attesting to Rice Pudding Day. Malone, not a well man, was given a suspended sentence. Eventually, Hague was informally exiled from New Jersey. If he stepped within its borders, he would be served with a subpoena. Traveling back to Jersey City five years later for the wake of his nephew, Hague was handed a subpoena by a deputy sheriff. Hague threw the subpoena to the ground and ignored it, but from then on stayed the hell out of Jersey City, funerals and all.

Some say that in his last days, he had trouble sleeping in his Park Avenue apartment, plagued by thoughts of all the families he'd damaged. Now and then he would call old friends in Jersey City and have them check on the survivors of breadwinners he had crippled or killed. My family never got a call.

Hague died, without apology, in 1956, on New Year's Day; Grandpa died seventeen years later on Christmas Day.

———

Though he had promised reform, John V. Kenny simply carried on where Hague left off. Patronage flourished. When Barney Doyle was appointed county superintendent of weights and measures, Gene Scanlon, a reporter from *The Jersey Journal,* called him for an interview. At the end of their chat, Scanlon threw him a giant softball.

"How many ounces are in a pound?" he asked Barney.

"How the hell do I know?" snapped Barney. "I just got the job."

Like Hague before him, Kenny also encouraged illegal betting. He loved the horses and spent all his free time at the track. Legend had it that the Turnpike extension in downtown Jersey City was built to accommodate Kenny's frequent trips to Monmouth Park, the racetrack on the Jersey shore.

One of Kenny's best friends was the notorious bookie Newsboy Moriarty, who, with his fortune, bought a new altar for St. Michael's Church—Kenny's parish. Moriarty was a former newspaper hawker who never wrote down a bet: because of his photographic memory, he kept it all in his head. Since there were no records, it was difficult for the police to arrest him, even though he always had large wads of cash—upward of $7,000—in his pockets. Newsboy, who ran a $10 million operation, did some time in jail, but it was a small price to pay for being a millionaire—tax-free. When the cops chased him, he would throw money at them. It was guaranteed to slow down the pursuit.

Newsboy was a rich man, but he never boasted. He drove an old car that had cost him around three hundred dollars, wore tattered clothes, and always ate sandwiches, never fancy sit-down dinners. He lived with his two unmarried sisters in an old brownstone. He dated a girl from Newark for years, and every night, though he had the money to buy a fleet of stretch limos, he put her on a bus back home.

In the early 1960s, the Mafia started to infringe on Newsboy's territory. The inside story goes that New York Mob boss Crazy Joe Gallo was given the okay to run the numbers racket in Jersey City and that Newsboy was ready to make a stink. The two were to meet at the Harmony Bar in downtown Jersey City's Italian Village section, a known hangout for the local mobsters.

Kenny's chief of police had Newsboy picked up from the streets before he could meet Gallo and start trouble. To get even with Kenny, Newsboy started a rumor that some of Kenny's payoff money was hidden in a car trunk in a West Side garage. Since most of it was earmarked for Kenny, it was no loss to Newsboy when two carpenters found the $2.4 million inside an abandoned 1947 Plymouth sedan. Stacks of the money disappeared, and once Newsboy claimed the rest, a big chunk of it went to the IRS. It was Newsboy's revenge for Kenny letting the Mob in on his turf.

Kenny had no choice, though. He was already in too deep, and well known down on the waterfront, where he had controlled the 6-for-5 shylock business before becoming mayor. Longie Zwillman had put up $350,000 in street money for Kenny to pay off voters. In that very first election, Kenny paid fifteen dollars a vote to Hague's five.

In 1952, Kenny double-crossed a gangster named Mo Manna and was hospitalized for pneumonia and phlebitis, according to the papers. Word on the street was that the Mob had given Kenny a bullet in the ass.

To make peace with Kenny, the Mob put Mo's son, young Anthony "Bobby" Manna, at the mayor's disposal. If somebody in the city needed fixing, Bobby would take care of it.

That same year, Kenny was called to testify before the Waterfront Commission, and denied having ties to the Mob. The commissioners knew he was lying, had proof, and threatened him with a perjury charge. A week later, he made a public announcement saying his testimony was a lie. Kenny stepped down as mayor, but he remained the unofficial boss of Hudson County. It wasn't until 1971, the year I started first grade, that Kenny finally lost his power, sentenced with Mayor Whelan in the Hudson Twelve case.

7

LUCKY STRIKE

Great-Aunt Katie was Grandpa's sister, a tough, gray-haired woman who kept a handgun in her dining room sideboard and smoked unfiltered Lucky Strikes. She said it was the filters that gave you cancer. Every day, to go with her cigarettes, Aunt Katie drank a shot of Canadian Club. She said it cleared her lungs and kept her going.

For my mother, Aunt Katie was a replacement for Grandma, even though she wasn't anything like her. Katie was squat and muscular, with short hair that made her look like a little man. Grandma had always worn dresses. Aunt Katie always wore pants.

She was the only woman I knew who really knew how to gamble. When Aunt Katie went to Atlantic City, she didn't play the slot machines like the other old ladies. She shot craps—and had to stand on a box to reach the pit, because she was so short. Many a night, after a big win, the casino sent her home in a limo. Whenever she went to Florida to visit one of her sisters, Aunt Katie was sure to lay some bets at the dog track.

I loved spending time at Aunt Katie's house, especially in her backyard. It was the same house where she and Grandpa and their ten other siblings had lived. It was my grandparents' first address together, the place where Pauline's water broke when she was pregnant with my mother.

While Aunt Katie and my mother drank coffee, I played with Katie's dog, Buddy, who was so smart that he knew how to open the door from the hallway. Katie treated him like a human, and often sang the old war tune "My Buddy" to him. "Nights are long since you went away. I dream about you all through the day. My buddy. My buddy." His ears would perk up and he would place a soft paw in her lap.

From Katie's backyard, where Buddy's doghouse stood, I could hear the bells of St. Mary's ringing nearby. The St. Mary's neighborhood, back when Grandpa and Aunt Katie were young, was still an Irish neighborhood, a bad place for a bunch of Italian kids to be raised. Because of her name, many people thought Katie was Irish, so she fared a little better than Grandpa had.

St. Mary's was the church where Grandma Pauline converted to Catholicism from the Russian Orthodox religion in which she was raised. Aunt Katie backed her, getting Grandma in touch with the priest and helping her study for each of the sacraments. Aunt Katie was there when Grandma was rebaptized, when she received First Holy Communion and Confirmation, and on the day she remarried Grandpa. Grandma and Grandpa were remarried in St. Mary's so that the marriage would be recognized by the Church and Grandma could receive Holy Communion every week.

It always astonished me that Grandma married Grandpa not once but twice.

During the ceremony, which was held in the parish rectory, Grandpa had a claustrophobic fit. He could never stand tight spaces, and I guess the chapel and the thought of getting remarried made him want to run. Grandma should have let him.

Because Aunt Katie had been so good to Grandma, my mother loved her. So did I. When I cried, Aunt Katie made me laugh by telling me that the water from my tears was making my eyes shrink. I had squinty eyes to begin with, and the thought of them growing even smaller made me stop crying.

Aunt Katie knew I hated being short like she was, so she told me that someday she would buy a racehorse and, since I was so tiny, I would be its jockey. I looked forward to those days at the track and imagined myself in photo finishes, my family raking in big bucks from lucky bets on me and my trusty steed.

The horse never did materialize, but Aunt Katie provided other distractions. She could throw a mean fastball in the backyard, or imitate a crowing rooster—that is until Uncle Al, her longshoreman husband, came home. As soon as Uncle Al came in the door, he would order Aunt Katie around. But she would make funny faces behind his back and "yes him to death," as she called it.

Uncle Al's face looked like one of the faces on the Indian-head coins that Grandpa had stolen from the library. He was Polish, but he looked just like an Indian chief. Though he wasn't as crazy as Grandpa, he could be just as mean. He was stubborn, too, and insisted that Aunt Katie buy Tip Top bread. "Tip Top bread makes Tip Top toast," he said without a hint of humor in his voice, as if he were a staff sergeant. Since Tip Top was expensive, Aunt Katie would buy regular A&P bread and put it in a leftover Tip Top bag. Uncle Al never knew the difference. Aunt Katie was very resourceful.

If Uncle Al lost his temper, he could go into a frenzy and break all the kitchen furniture. Aunt Katie always had a new kitchen set. When he was drunk, Al could be as abusive as Grandpa. But Aunt Katie knew how to handle Al. She was much smarter than he was.

After Uncle Al came in stinking drunk one night and terrorized her, Aunt Katie got an idea. "I'll fix him," she said. While Al snored, she smoked four cigars and a half pack of Lucky Strikes and left the stubs in ashtrays on the table. She sloppily spilled some Canadian Club into glasses, took a few swigs, and left the glasses sitting half empty. She dealt a round of playing cards and tossed some furniture around. Then she went to bed.

When Al got up the next morning, his head pounding with a hangover, he found Katie sitting at the table crying. She was a good actress.

"What's all this?" he asked.

"What do you mean?" Aunt Katie sobbed. "Don't you remember?" Uncle Al looked at her blankly.

"Last night you and your fucking friends wrecked the joint with your poker game," she said, waving her stubby arm. "Look at this mess. They were cursing and drinking and smoking. One of your buddies even made a play for me." She cried a little harder, to show how traumatized she was by the near-rape experience.

Uncle Al was horrified at his and his friends' behavior, and even more horrified that he couldn't remember a minute of it. That day, he went to St. Mary's and took a pledge never to drink again. He kept his promise for two long years.

Aunt Katie could handle anyone and anything that came her way. She once explained what to do in case a rabid dog tried to attack me. "Take your coat off and wrap it around your arm, like this," she said, winding an imaginary coat around her forearm. "Then stick your arm out so the bastard goes to bite it. When he jumps up, you give him a swift kick in the balls." I never got a chance to use the rabid-dog defense, but it was good information to have in downtown Jersey City, where an occasional pack of wild dogs would roam into my part of the neighborhood.

Katie was full of life lessons. But best of all, she could tell a funny story—like the one about the time she was cutting her toenails and one of them flew into her sister Eva's eye. You had to hear Aunt Katie tell it.

It was Aunt Katie who told us about our Italian ancestors, about my great-great-grandmother Vita, the life-giver of the Italian-American line. Vita—Beansie's grandmother—was married to a man named Francesco, who got involved in a fight during a card game in Bernalde, a town in the district of Matera, a lawless, godforsaken corner of southern Italy. Somehow, maybe in defense, maybe because of the temper that I inherited decades later, Vita killed the man. At least that's what Aunt Katie said.

Perhaps Vita stabbed the cardplayer and twisted the knife a bit before pulling it out, or maybe she hit him over the head with a very heavy saucepan. Maybe the whole story was a fable. But Vita did escape to the United States around 1897, taking with her the last name of her lawyer or lover. The stolen last name was Vena. In Italian, the name means "vein," as in the vein that runs through your arm, or through your family history. Figuratively, *vena* can also mean a talent or gift passed down from generation to generation. In our case, a talent for making trouble. The scandal was a blessing in disguise and a good excuse to leave Matera, which was well known for its violent card games and bandits, its chalky landscape, its cave dwellers, its pagans, witches, poverty, and malaria, its frescoes depicting original sin, and its Via del Riscattoò—"Street of Vengeance." If Jersey City was hell, it was only the first circle. Ancient Matera was the core of hell, from which my ancestors—Vita and her children—barely escaped.

Vita left her husband behind and traveled by ship, in steerage, with her three young sons. One was lost in transit. Maybe while Vita was gaping at the Statue of Liberty in awe, looking away from her boys, her little son slipped away, stolen by a black-market adoption ring or child-labor slave trader. Perhaps he fell overboard, greedily sucked in by the waves.

Between the missing son, the homicide, and the escape from Italy, Vita was a wreck by the time she arrived at the Jersey City railroad terminal. Like my Russian great-grandmother, Irene, who had arrived four years earlier, Vita put down her bags and gave up in Jersey City. The Statue of Liberty pedestal may have read, "Give me your tired, your poor," but if Jersey City had had a statue in the harbor, it would have said, "Give me your completely exhausted, completely broken, completely hopeless and weak, who have no train fare to go any farther." Vita lived to a ripe old age, but in keeping with the family's flair for drama, she didn't die of natural causes, naturally. She was accidentally killed while walking down the street when a mischief-making neighborhood kid hit her in the head with a rock-filled sock on Halloween night.

Vita's two remaining sons were named Leonardo and Valente. My great-grandfather Leonard—Beansie and Katie's father—grew up to be a barber, and opened his shop right across the street from Hague's headquarters at City Hall, only three doors from the Majestic Tavern. Leonard was a small man with a full moon of a face. He was so good and clean that you could smell his fresh barbershop scent when he walked past you. Opening the barbershop so close to City Hall was a brilliant move, since it guaranteed a steady clientele, including Hague and all his cronies. The shop was in a basement, a few steps down from the rotating red-and-white barber pole.

From his perch on a bench in City Hall Park, Grandpa could look straight inside and watch his father cut infamous heads. They sat in a row of old-fashioned chrome-and-leather barber chairs—state-of-the-art at the time—their dishonest faces thrown back at them in the bank of mirrors along the wall.

It was Leonard's difficult job to make them look clean and fresh, to comb over their souls with hair tonic and shaving cream. Combs floated in antiseptic jars. Shaving brushes and straight-edged razors lay out like a surgeon's tools. Each regular had his own shaving mug sitting on the shelf. Business was so good that Leonard even hired a female manicurist, who kept the politicians' hands soft and their nails clean and trimmed.

Though the politicians were his main clientele, Leonard served the working men of Jersey City, too, whose hands were callused and dirty. One afternoon, just as a local man was stepping up to the chair, Hague came strolling into the shop.

"Leo, I'm in a rush," he barked. "I need a fast shave."

"Mayor, I understand," said Leonard, bowing his head and pointing his scissors. "But this man is next. He's been waiting."

Leonard was lucky Hague didn't haul off and punch him in the nose. Instead, the mayor grabbed his shaving mug, left, and never returned.

Though he was the best barber in the neighborhood, with a thriving business, Leonard never taught his sons to cut heads. Maybe they refused. Grandpa preferred to hang around across the street. And his older brother Frankie worked nearby, right outside City Hall.

Frankie would stand in plain view of his righteous father and swindle young lovers. He'd stop those who had come to get married—and who didn't know the system—on the City Hall steps and tell them not to pay the exorbitant City Hall prices for a marriage certificate.

"Come with me," Uncle Frankie would say, then lead them to the dining room of an associate, where they'd meet a "judge"—another criminal, who had stolen a judge's robe and marriage seal. Sometimes, if the couple was more religious, Frankie would take them up to Union City, to one of the cathedral chapels. Charging them a discounted price—twenty-five dollars for a normal affair; a hundred for one with singing and flowers—Uncle Frankie would have the couple "married."

Dozens, if not hundreds or thousands, of marriages in Jersey City are fakes because of my uncle Frankie. Even one of our Vena cousins from Brooklyn fell for Frankie's scam and lived for years, unknowingly, in unholy matrimony.

Frankie was simply no good. Aunt Katie said that he would often take his girlfriends to Holy Name Cemetery to have sex with them on the graves or beside the bones in the mausoleums. Aunt Katie made excuses for Frankie, like she did for Grandpa, saying that when he was a boy, Frankie had suffered a terrible trauma, worse than getting hit by an ice truck. The house caught fire and Frankie, in an effort to save his little brother, dragged the baby carriage out of the burning building, but he stumbled and dropped the carriage down the stoop. The baby died. And Frankie was never the same. He drank for years, and was given the nickname Clearwater.

Urged by his father to get a real job, Frankie became the cashier at the Majestic Theatre. It was just a few doors down from the tavern, the barbershop, and my childhood home and was a nationally known vaudeville theater that attracted such acts as Bing Crosby and Mae West. By the time I came around, the Majestic Theatre was long closed, boarded up, and at the center of a restoration battle. For most residents, the Majestic was a small slice of beauty and proud history still left standing in Jersey City. It seemed a shame to knock it down.

But I knew a little too much of its history. The Majestic's former manager, Charles Suozza, testified at one of the many Hague inquiries that the mayor regularly shook him down for $100 "to keep from being bothered."

Uncle Frankie's Majestic job didn't last long. After a while, word spread and couples would come looking for the marriage broker at the Majestic. But that wasn't the reason Frankie lost his job. He lost it because he plotted with some friends to rob the theater of its large cash box and safe. Frankie stashed the $3,800 in advance. Then his friends stuck a gun in his face to make it look like a real burglary. A few days later, the scam was uncovered and Frankie and his friends were arrested. The story ran on the front page of *The Jersey Journal* on October 30, 1923: SAY MAJESTIC CASHIER STAGED HOLD-UP. It embarrassed poor Leonard.

Frankie was not much better than Beansie. He was just more

crafty. When Hague was rounding up the usual suspects, Frankie high-tailed it home and hid out for a few days. If the cops cornered Frankie, he would bullshit his way out of a beating. "Officer," he would lie. "I went to the doctor yesterday and he told me I have a very bad heart condition."

Grandpa, even if he hadn't committed the crime, spit in the cops' faces. That was the crucial difference between the brothers. That, and Frankie's organized marriage scam. Grandpa was more of a freelance criminal, committing crimes whenever the opportunity arose.

Without his two eldest sons to help him in the barbershop, Leonard turned to his daughter Katie. She had a steady hand and, as a young girl, helped her father shave the customers. She was so skilled with a razor that many of the men requested her when they came in the ringing door. Although she was not the prettiest, Aunt Katie was the smartest and spunkiest and the favorite girl in the family. It was in the barbershop that Katie learned the tricks of the trade—not just cutting hair, but working the political machine.

Katie was so charming that New Jersey governor A. Harry Moore asked Leonard if he and his wife could adopt her. "Leo," said the child-less Moore. "You got so many children. Why don't you give us one?" He knew there were eleven other mouths for Leonard to feed, so he would be willing to take this one—this special one—off his hands.

Leonard was flattered by the offer and told the story to everyone who walked into the shop. But he loved Katie too much to give her away. Katie stayed close. Little did Leonard know that when he wasn't looking, Katie would steal change from the barbershop to shoot dice with the guys on the corner.

Each week, Leonard gave Katie two dollars for each child in the family, which she was to put away in the bank. When cleaning the closet one day, her mother came across Katie's coat, which held in its pocket all the bank deposit slips. The money had never been deposited.

There was also the time Katie got up onstage at school and recited a poem she claimed to have written. Everyone clapped and cheered except one of her sisters, who knew Katie had plagiarized the poem. But she didn't rat her out. She loved Katie too much. Everyone did.

When she wasn't stealing words or money, Katie was watching out for her younger brothers and sisters—a role that prepared her for her job as a neighborhood committeewoman for Hague. When her little brother fell in with the neighborhood gang and started to play hooky, Aunt Katie went to the ice cream shack where the gang leader hung out and beat the living shit out of him. She was only twelve. And the boy, probably around the same age, was forever disgraced for being beaten up by a girl.

With the money from his barbershop, Leonard bought a home for his family in the neighborhood where all his Irish customers lived. My grandfather and his siblings were the only Italians in the St. Mary's neighborhood, and were often ridiculed and beaten for being dirty guineas. Beansie, who had serious problems with authority to begin with, had to fight his way through life. Had he lived in the Italian Village, just a few blocks north, he probably wouldn't have developed such a complex. He probably would have become a full-fledged gangster, not a two-bit criminal.

Katie was smart, and would never be outdone by the "Irish bastards." As a little girl, at Christmastime Katie watched with envy as a neighbor held her new baby doll up to the windowpane. But Aunt Katie thought fast and did the girl one better. She ran inside and grabbed her little sister Tessie, still a baby, and held her up for show. The little girl sulked away, jealous that Katie had a real baby.

In 1931, at the age of twenty-two, Katie became a committeewoman. Jersey City's population was then at its peak, around 316,000, and through her father's barbershop Katie had met all the right people, the players and the dealers.

Katie's territory consisted of two city blocks, from First to Third and from Henderson to Grove, and included eight hundred voters. She was so in tune with her constituents that she could tell on Election Day how many votes the Republicans would get—usually as few as three or four. She eventually became the first-ward women's Democratic leader. Her district usually won six to one.

The committeeman or -woman was the point person you went to see when you had a problem in the neighborhood—any kind of problem: a problem with your landlord, a noisy neighbor, you name it. Katie, big sister to the whole neighborhood, knew all the judges and department heads. If a kid had trouble and it didn't involve a gun or drugs, Katie was his get-out-of-jail-free card.

Like the time my uncle Robby accidentally ran over a traffic cop's toe in a borrowed '37 Chevy the week after he got his license. The cop pulled him out of the car through the driver's side window, roughed him up, then drove the car, with Robby as his captive, down to the Seventh Street precinct house, where he planned to book him. Robby was smart enough not to mention that his father was Beansie. But he did mention that he was Katie's nephew. She was called down to vouch for him, and Robby was set free.

Aunt Katie was always looking out for the family. Had she not been such an insider, Grandpa would have wound up like Michael Rombolo, the Italian guy who got the chair for killing an Irishman. When her mother got sick, Aunt Katie took a hospital bed from the Medical Center. I'm not sure if she rolled it out in one piece or took it bit by bit—headboard, mattress, box spring, and frame. My great-grandmother Concetta died in that luxurious bed, courtesy of the Medical Center, but in the comfort of home. Since the bed was returned after Concetta died, the family likes to say it was a loaner.

If you needed a job, Katie would hook you up with the ward leader, who in turn would put you in touch with the mayor's office. If you were new to the neighborhood, it was Katie's job to help you move in, then get you registered to vote as soon as possible.

Katie and the ward leaders were the foot soldiers of the Hague administration. And Katie was one of the best, serving for over three decades. Though she had spent only two years in high school, she understood the political machinery and the voters better than anyone. Her mentor, a committeeman named Joe Fay, who lived next door, told Katie, "Always do a favor for the people, but never let them know how you did it. Because once they know that, they don't need you anymore."

Katie made everyone feel she was their best friend. She once gave—rather than loaned—her big, new broiler pan to a new neighbor. Around the holidays, she would go door-to-door to the Newark Avenue shopkeepers and schmooze them into donating turkeys for the baskets for the city's needy. In one year alone, she sold five thousand books of 50/50 chances for a St. Mary's fund-raiser.

At her city job in the Complaint Department at City Hall, she never condescended, but almost unconsciously, she could change her voice or accent to match yours and make you feel completely at ease. And Aunt Katie loved to sing, particularly a little ditty she wrote about Jersey City: "They called it Paulus Hook in sixteen hundred and four. A little piece of heaven along the Hudson shore." At the St. Mary's CYO dances, painted in blackface, Katie entertained the crowd with "Ol' Black Joe" and "Bye Bye Blackbird."

If she had been a man, she would have someday been mayor. But the idea of equal rights—urinals and all—was decades away. Instead of becoming mayor, Aunt Katie got married to Uncle Al and gave birth to two sons. But as a woman, she pushed the boundaries. During the war, she read a leaflet that encouraged women to "work, not wait, for victory" and took a job as a riveter at the Continental Can Company, building P-47 Thunderbolt fighter planes. Aunt Katie earned seventy-five dollars a week, starting at dawn and working late into the afternoon. When a jealous male worker started throwing rocks at the female riveters, Aunt Katie and her coworkers made sure he got his— a beating and his walking papers.

Between her jobs—at Continental and as a committeewoman— Aunt Katie found time to invent a few gadgets. One in particular, a clothespin dispenser, received a patent but never caught on.

Aunt Katie's greatest invention, though, was Aunt Katie. She was constantly reinventing herself, and never lived in the past, as most Jersey City old-timers did. When Kenny ran for office, Katie followed her intuition and became one of his 'Forty-niners. Then, when an Italian from the neighborhood named Thomas Gangemi decided to run for mayor in the late 1950s, Katie threw her three decades of experience and power behind him.

In her heart, Aunt Katie hated the Irish as much as Grandpa did. She never forgot that her parish, the very Irish St. Mary's, had given her a hard time about joining the Rosary Society because she was Italian, that they had even tried to deny Italians Holy Communion in the old days.

For years, Aunt Katie held it all in, waiting for just the right moment to strike.

8

STRAW KATIE

An Italian mayoral candidate was Katie's best revenge. For the time being, anyway. I imagine that for Jersey City, an Italian running for mayor was equal to the excitement Polish people felt when John Paul II was made pope. About fucking time, they all said. What took you so long?

Thomas Gangemi was known as the Watermelon King because of his fruit-vending business downtown. He was better looking than your average Jersey City Joe, and taller than most downtown Italians. But good looks could only take you so far in such an ugly place. Gangemi's poor grammar and street-tough background scored him points with the voters. They liked his "dese," "dem," and "dose" vocabulary. It didn't matter that he'd been accused of being a no-show on Hague's payroll or that he'd been responsible for the county's unwise purchase of pricey marble-topped (Italian, no doubt) office furniture, said to cost more than President Eisenhower's.

The Italians loved him, including Aunt Katie.

In 1961, with her help, Gangemi was elected mayor. But he only served two years. The thing that got him into office—his Italian roots—also got him thrown out.

As part of a public relations stunt in 1963, Gangemi was to travel to Italy to escort a man named Christopher Columbus—a direct descendant—back to Jersey City to march in the annual Columbus Day parade with him. The parade was a big deal, with the city's entire Italian community gathering on Journal Square at the tall, bronze Christopher Columbus statue and marching up Hudson Boulevard, soon to be renamed Kennedy Boulevard.

With the first Italian mayor ever, accompanied by a man named Christopher Columbus, the Italians were sure to whip themselves into a frenzy. It was their chance to thumb their noses at the Irish politicians who had run the city for decades. But the plan went to hell when Gangemi applied for a passport to go to Italy and the U.S. Immigration and Naturalization Service discovered he was not an American citizen. Which meant that he could not hold office.

Before the story broke, and before his staff even knew what was happening, Gangemi checked himself into Columbia-Presbyterian Hospital in Manhattan, claiming he didn't feel well. To throw *The Jersey Journal* off the trail, the paper's editor was immediately appointed Jersey City's ambassador to Italy and sent to the old country in Gangemi's place. Flying first class on Alitalia, with a seat next to Cardinal Spellman, the editor was to meet Christopher Columbus and escort him to the parade. Gangemi, meanwhile, hid under the hospital covers.

When *The Jersey Journal* city desk found out about Gangemi's passport troubles, they called the Rome airport, just as the editor's plane was landing. He left Columbus in Genoa and took the next flight home. Columbus traveled alone to Jersey City. Though Gangemi was no longer mayor, he was still chairman of the Columbus Day Committee. He donned his morning suit and marched alongside Columbus anyway.

Some people, particularly the city's Italians, think Gangemi was set up, that Kenny knew for years about Gangemi's illegal status, and kept that card in his pocket for a time when he would need to play it. Gangemi's supporters went so far as to say that Bobby Kennedy had had something to do with his downfall—that because of Gangemi's Italian roots, the attorney general assumed he was connected to the Mob and had it in for him.

Whether the passport fiasco happened accidentally or not, the fact was Gangemi could not hold office. The rush for a new mayor was on. Gangemi was promised that his son, Buddy, would get the nod. But at the last minute the city council elected Thomas Whelan, a handsome World War II veteran, six feet tall, two hundred pounds, with blue eyes and a lovely wife. He was another in a long line of Irish mayors whose strong-arm tactics echoed those of Hague's zepps of the 1940s.

During the racial unrest of the 1960s, Whelan gained favor with the predominantly white community by playing on residents' fears. There had already been riots in Rochester, Harlem, and Brooklyn; the violence was creeping closer and closer to home.

Whelan saw his opening. After one small skirmish in August 1964, with just a few black people arguing on the street, the police were sent in. Rumors spread that a young black woman had been hit with a blackjack. A rock was thrown, then a bottle, leading to a series of arrests and an announcement by Whelan: "We will not tolerate anarchy in the city by any person or any group of people." Wink-wink. To make the black politicians happy, Whelan threw in a quote from Abraham Lincoln. "Law without enforcement is only good advice."

Police cars rolled into the black neighborhoods, with cops holding shotguns through their windows, aimed at the crowds in the street. Old-timers liked to say that Whelan "kept the blacks in their place." That's why the people loved him.

While Whelan was striking his tough-guy pose, Gangemi was busy learning about George Washington and memorizing the Pledge of Allegiance. He finally became a citizen and then launched an attack against Whelan in the 1965 election.

Whelan's team circulated a picture of Gangemi talking to a black politician with the catchy kicker *What are these two guys whispering about?* Jersey Citizens, with the "riots" and Gangemi's nickname Watermelon King echoing in their racist brains, fell for it.

Well, most Jersey Citizens. Aunt Katie turned her back on both Gangemi and Whelan. She had her own secret weapon. Despite her long list of accomplishments, Katie was still a woman, and as a woman, her main job was raising her boys, Mike and Chubby. She poured all her political knowledge into her older son, Mike, a naturally smart kid, whom she sent to college and to Harvard Law School. If Katie couldn't be mayor, then maybe Mike could be. Like any parent who isn't able to attain her own dreams, Aunt Katie put her hopes into her child. Having her son run against the machine cost her her job at the Complaint Department at City Hall. But she thought that with Mike in office, everything she had done and worked for would pay off—the years in the barbershop, as a committeewoman, district leader, good neighbor, and entertainer. None of it would go to waste.

I always wondered if Aunt Katie, in her effort to anoint Mike the chosen one, paid too little attention to her younger son, Chubby. From the time he was five years old, his parents told him he would be a longshoreman like his father. And when he grew up, Chubby became one. Even though he was muscular and looked like a boxer, Chubby was a sweet and gentle guy, very soft-spoken. I liked Chubby. He had been in the army, but there was something fragile about him.

When I was a kid, Chubby got beaten up by the Jersey City cops for a traffic violation. The morning after, my mother was on her way to work when she bumped into Aunt Katie, who was headed to court, carrying Chubby's bloody sweatshirt as evidence of police brutality. Maybe Chubby's burly appearance was the reason the cops had hit him so hard. Or maybe it was Aunt Katie's politics. But the cops had been relentless, kicking him in the head and knocking something loose. The family won a large settlement against the police, but it didn't help much. After the beating, Chubby was never the same. He eventually killed himself with a shotgun.

Resourceful to a fault, Aunt Katie sold the gun.

Mike made his first bid for mayor during the 1965 election, while Chubby was still alive and well. Chubby helped him campaign. Everyone in the family did, even my mother. She went over to Aunt Katie's and helped stuff envelopes. I was just a baby, sleeping on a bed in the next room.

Mike was the first college graduate I ever knew—never mind Harvard graduate or law-school graduate. In Jersey City, people were actively illiterate and proudly went around saying things like "I never read a book in my life." They boasted that they had managed to get so far without reading a single page. I wanted to say, Well, good for you, you idiot. Look where you are. You're still in Jersey City.

I looked up to Mike, because he was smart and because he admitted that he read books. He spoke to me like my parents did—like I was a person and not a stupid little kid. He showed me his Norman Rockwell prints and talked to me about the novels he'd read and the films he'd seen. It was called interesting conversation. Most people I knew talked about sports scores, the good old days, and the veal parmigiano they just ate and the agita it was giving them. Or they gossiped about yet another neighbor with a tumor. It got old after a while. For me and a lot of other people, Mike was a breath of fresh air in the polluted sky of Jersey City.

Mike was born on the same day as Hank Aaron, the man who had broken Babe Ruth's home run record. He was the first of a new generation, a new wave of politicians in Jersey City who could finally tear down the old order and dismantle the political machine.

Mike had inherited Katie's brains but, unfortunately, not her warmth. He looked as smart as he was, with horn-rimmed glasses and soft hands. Though he did have a Jersey City accent, Mike spoke to everyone in the same direct, lawyerly way. Even me.

I admired him for his large vocabulary and his ability to use mnemonic devices to remember everything. Katie had prepped Mike well—maybe too well—sending him to St. Peter's Prep, the best school in the county. To give him a worldview, she encouraged him to take a Fulbright scholarship to Italy, where he studied the effect of economics on political change. At Harvard Law, he often won debates against fellow student Michael Dukakis. Ruth Bader Ginsburg and Antonin Scalia were also classmates. Roscoe Pound lived in the same hotel in Cambridge as Mike, and though he wasn't a poet like his brother Ezra, he was capable of interesting conversation.

After graduation, Mike considered staying in Cambridge, where people could understand what he was talking about. But Hudson County called out like a sickly uncle. And Mike came to the rescue.

Though he understood the city and state tax system better than anybody, his knowledge was unappreciated by the unsophisticated residents and politicians. In an effort to explain the tax situation to the voters, Mike tried comparing taxes to a poker game, explaining that everyone had to throw in their fair share of money and that Jersey Citizens were being hustled by the dealers.

He tried to explain, to make them understand—in the simplest terms—that Jersey City residents paid one of the highest residential property tax rates in the country ($113 per $1,000), that the once great Medical Center was now operating at a $5 million deficit, that unless an honest mayor was elected, the city would become, "as one Harvard sociologist has already predicted, the first total slum city in the United States."

Mike's biggest fault was a belief in the American system of democracy in such a corrupt place. In a newspaper article that appeared in 1965, Mike naively declared, "I have great faith in the common sense and basic fairness of American people—that's why I have a chance to win." Common sense was abundant in Jersey City. Without an education, common sense was all you had to go on. We called it street smarts. But fairness? In Jersey City? That was something else altogether.

Before the election, Gangemi summoned Mike, telling him he should drop out of the race, that he wanted Mike's help on *his* campaign. Mike tried to explain his theories about high finance but got nowhere. Unable to convince Mike to bow out, Gangemi used the only strategy he could think of: "You should support me because I danced at your mother's wedding." Jersey City logic. Common sense.

But Gangemi got nowhere, and started to get frustrated. "What do you wanna run for? You're gonna waste your money," he told Mike. Gangemi was so confident Mike was wasting his time, he bet him $25,000 he couldn't get two thousand votes. But Mike was more confident. He took the bet and raised it to $30,000. The two made a date the following Monday for Mike to drop off the certified check. When Mike showed up, Gangemi's secretary said he was at a wake. Gangemi never placed the bet.

Whelan wanted Mike out of the way as much as Gangemi did, especially since Mike drew the coveted A1 position on the ballot. One night a Whelan operative came to see Mike. "I heard you're doing well," he said. He congratulated Mike. Then he promptly offered him a $50,000 bribe to get out of the way.

"Joe, that's real nice," said Mike, "but I'm gonna stay in it." Mike, who had been practicing law in Manhattan for the past few years, didn't need the cash. What he needed was the political exposure. He had no illusions that he would win the election. He just wanted to make a name for the next time around. Mike had a long-term strategy.

During that 1965 election, bookies were making bets that Whelan would get more votes than all the other candidates combined. Big bets. Hundred-dollar bets. Mike's father, Uncle Al, was tempted to lay down some cash. "Down the piers, they're betting," Uncle Al told his son. "It sounds like a good bet."

But Mike knew better. To build his political base, Mike was campaigning door-to-door, with the help of only twelve political-science students from local St. Peter's College. "You got nice credentials," the voters told him, "but we're voting for Whelan." Mike knew Whelan would win big-time and told his father not to bet, that the bookies were right.

When the election was over, Whelan got 57,000 votes. Mike got a healthy 10,000 votes. And the rest of the candidates got 45,000. The smart-money bookies won the bet. But it was close.

To prepare himself for the next mayoral election, Mike organized an independent legislative ticket in 1967, including four senatorial candidates, eight assemblymen, and three freeholders who ran against Kenny, still the county boss. Mike financed the ticket himself but decided not to run. He had his eye on the 1969 mayoral race. He knew you could only run so many times and lose before they write you up as a perpetual loser. But Mike's ego got in the way. His friends talked him into joining the ticket as a senatorial candidate. With help from the family, Mike's ticket gained momentum. Our cousin Sonny from Brooklyn knew a printer who made campaign cards. Aunt Katie called in all her favors. Things were rolling.

The Democrats won, but Mike's ticket had a good showing, with 20,000 votes in the county. The Republican party, by contrast, got only 12,000 votes. The editor of *The Jersey Journal* called Mike and told him he should become a Republican.

In 1969, Mike ran for mayor a second time, with Whelan and Gangemi his main opponents again. In a *Jersey Journal* article published that

May, Mike, still the political idealist, quoted Alexander Hamilton: " 'Someday the great American city will rise on the west bank of the Hudson,' " he said. "Alexander Hamilton meant Jersey City and he knew what he was talking about."

Unfortunately, most voters didn't know what the hell Mike was talking about. In one campaign ad, he shot way over their heads, using terms like *confiscatory* and *tax ratables*. He called for "the elimination of nonproductive jobs and the ending of the use of the city payroll for rewarding political hacks." A few too many political hacks made up the voter base. The ad simply translated as "Mike will take away your no-show job." It didn't matter that *The New York Times* had called Mike "a refreshing new voice in the morass of Hudson County politics." No one in Jersey City read *The New York Times*. Few knew the definition of *morass*.

Mike opened a political club on Journal Square, choosing ten reform candidates as the nucleus for his movement. One day Grandpa walked into the club, thinking it would be an old-fashioned ward club, with guys in fedoras smoking cigars, offering bribes over the phone, and collecting street money to try and get the vote out. By then, the committeeman system Hague had built was in tatters. Worried that history would repeat itself, a paranoid John V. Kenny started dismantling the system, afraid of getting stabbed in the back by a "loyal soldier."

Full of violent energy, Grandpa was ready to roll up his sleeves and help Mike campaign. But Grandpa was still lost in the era of ward leaders and bat-wielding sluggers. When Grandpa saw all the college kids hard at work, clean and scrubbed, with glasses rather than fedoras, he realized it wasn't his place. He wished Mike good luck, shook his hand, and walked out. It was an oddly graceful and humble moment. I could almost feel sorry for Grandpa, if I didn't know what a bastard he was.

Mike lost again in 1969. But in 1970 he was given another chance when Whelan, Kenny, and the rest of the Hudson Twelve were indicted. By then, Kenny, the man of the people, was spending winters in Florida and summers at the Jersey shore, as Hague had before him.

Two of the Hudson Twelve became government witnesses. The

others either pleaded out or were convicted in federal court. The trials were as colorful as expected. One former county Democratic chairman testified against Whelan, admitting that the mayor, so nervous about being exposed, had given him $50,000 in cash to bribe a witness in the case. The chairman had hidden the money in a trash can in his basement. The prosecutor wheeled the can into the courtroom and revealed the $50,000 hidden inside.

During another trial, the blind treasurer of the Mosquito Commission, wearing dark glasses and tripping on his way into court, testified that city exterminators embezzled money by simply placing illegal checks in front of him to sign—sight unseen, naturally. His testimony gave new meaning to the phrase "rob the city blind."

Over the years, former mayor Kenny stole as much money as he could get his hands on. He had fooled the people into thinking he was one of them. But once again, Jersey Citizens got screwed. When they found out that Kenny had reneged on his promise to make Jersey City a better place, the disappointment was so overwhelming that many residents abandoned the city for good. The population took a sharp nosedive, from around 300,000 at Kenny's election in 1949 to 260,000 in 1970. People left in droves. Except for my family, of course. We stayed behind.

If ever there was a time for a reform candidate, it was the early 1970s. It seemed everyone and his mother was running for office. Mike was one of eighteen candidates.

To save the city, Mike knew that the waterfront had to be developed. He campaigned on the tax issue again, but this time emphasized that a shortage of commercial space in Manhattan would bring companies across the river and build up Jersey City's tax base.

Mike's father and brother were longshoremen, after all, so Mike knew the potential down at the docks. He called the waterfront the eighth wonder of the world, the passageway to the West. He claimed to have private bankers from New York behind him, men who could raise millions to build up the waterfront. But by the time the election rolled around in 1971, Mike's ten handpicked supporters decided not to support him, since he had run twice before. They decided to back the president of his political club instead, another young, nerdy-looking man with horn-rimmed glasses. Paul Jordan, a doctor who had never run for mayor before, won the election. He became known as the man who opened the city's first methadone clinic—a wonderful addition to beautiful downtown Jersey City.

Mike blamed himself for his downfall. He should have hugged more babies. Should have been warmer. But it's hard to be warm and fuzzy when talking about tax reform and development. Maybe he should have played up his mixed ancestry. A young journalist had once told him he was the only Pole with an Irish-sounding name who spoke Italian and looked like a Jew. She told Mike to marry a Puerto Rican girl with a black father "and you'll have all your bases covered."

But Mike's biggest blunder occurred in 1970, when Whelan called Mike's house and said he wanted to meet to talk about taxes, finance, and economics. Mike was excited that Whelan was finally going to listen to his ideas. "Christ," said the still wide-eyed, horn-rimmed Mike. "This is good. This is what I've been trying to get the son of a bitch to do since 1965, to understand this issue."

Whelan came down to the basement at 222 First Street, the same basement where I played with Buddy the dog, the very same basement where Aunt Katie kept her .22. Whelan and Mike talked for about two hours, during which time a reporter from the *Hudson Dispatch* showed up. Before Whelan left, a photographer took a picture of the two of them chatting.

Here he was fighting against corruption, and Mike winds up in a picture next to Whelan, the most recent incarnation of Jersey City political evil. In Mike's own home, no less. Now it looked like Mike was looking for a county job, or at least aligning himself with the forces of darkness. It never occurred to the voters that Mike was just trying to get his point across. No one in Jersey City ever had a point to get across, so how could they understand?

During Paul Jordan's campaign, copies of that newspaper photo were sent to 100,000 people, almost every voter in the city. It ruined Mike's chances of ever being elected.

Though I don't remember the campaign itself, I remember Mike's campaign party, on Mischief Night, October 30, 1971. The car we drove in—my sister's boyfriend's car—was pelted with eggs.

My mother had never let us out on Mischief Night, since bad kids from the neighborhood would hit you with flour-filled socks. Or eggs. Or worse. So it was a thrill to be out, to see firsthand what really went on. The sidewalks were slippery and yellow with egg yolks and the streets were nearly empty, since everyone knew to take cover. We drove past gang after gang of rowdy boys hurling eggs at our car. The windshield wipers couldn't do much. They smeared the egg whites and eggshells and made the view worse, but we somehow arrived safely at the party at the Polish Home on Liberty Avenue.

It was in full swing. Red, white, and blue bunting hung from a stage, upon which a band was playing popular songs that were no longer so popular. People were dressed up, even Aunt Katie. She had on a dress and a faux straw hat made of white Styrofoam, with a red, white, and blue band. The real hats—the straw kind—were called straw katies. I asked Ma if they were named after Aunt Katie. Maybe, she said, laughing. Maybe they were.

Aunt Katie was also wearing her partial dentures, so I knew this was really a special occasion. Whenever she wore the false teeth, which was rarely, Aunt Katie looked a little scary—not like herself, but like somebody else's aunt or like that horse she kept promising me. The teeth looked too big for her mouth.

I had just gotten my first pair of eyeglasses, so it all seemed very clear to me. Things had been pretty blurry before, but until I got my glasses, I had no idea about the details I'd been missing.

That night, coincidentally, was the same night my sister lost a contact lens. It's strange, the facts that cling to your brain at that age, when you can see things clearly and starkly. While we searched around on our knees for Paula's lens in the lobby, Aunt Katie was onstage singing "Bye Bye Blackbird." The election wasn't over yet. But everyone knew it was over for Mike. They had all gotten the picture of him and Whelan in the mail.

I had never seen Aunt Katie cry, but tonight she couldn't make it through the song without her voice cracking. She had bet everything she had, even Chubby's future, on a sure thing—her fortunate son Mike. The years with Hague, Kenny, and Gangemi—they were all just a dress rehearsal for her son's ascension to mayor of Jersey City.

"Pack up all my cares and woe, here I go, singing low, bye bye, blackbird," Aunt Katie sang as we made our way from the lobby to our table. "Where somebody waits for me. Sugar sweet, so is she, bye bye blackbird." Cousin Chubby, big and burly and just a few years away from suicide, stumbled up onstage with a bouquet of two dozen red roses for his mother, as if she were the one running for office. "Where somebody else can understand me," she sang. "Oh, what hard luck stories they all hand me."

By the time Aunt Katie was through, we were all in tears—Chubby, Mike, Uncle Al, Paula, Ma, me. Even Paula's boyfriend was misty. I wasn't sure what I was crying about as I took my new glasses off to wipe my eyes. But I knew that whatever it was, it was very sad, since even Great-Aunt Katie was sobbing.

9

PENNIES FROM HEAVEN

———

Even though she never got a driver's license, Ma got a job at the Division of Motor Vehicles in 1964, just before she became pregnant with me. She worked right through the pregnancy, her belly protruding under the counter while she typed. I liked it under there, she told me, soothed by the noise of the electric typewriter. It was the first time my mother had worked since having gotten married back in 1952. She loved the DMV because, like Aunt Katie, she liked helping people with their problems. Working also gave Ma a sense of independence.

Though she had to quit when Grandma died, Ma got her job back after I went to school in 1970. The office was just a block from home and from City Hall, and the hours were flexible. A few years later, my sister got a job at the DMV to pay for her night classes in college, and Ma was promoted to head clerk.

My mother had known the DMV agent, Frank, for thirty years, ever since his days as a teenage salesman behind the candy counter at the Capitol Theatre downtown. Frank looked like Van Johnson. I knew Van Johnson from the song-and-dance number he did on *I Love Lucy*, the one where he and Lucy sing, "I like New York in June, how about you?" Sometimes I imagined Frank and my mother dancing and singing that song, trading lines and wisecracks. But then I'd remember Daddy and feel bad for thinking it.

All the DMV offices were state offices, but each was like a franchise, with a private agent, like Frank, running the place. Since it was government-controlled, the DMV was almost like a political appointment. You had to be somebody to be the agent. And Frank was somebody. He had a long political history. His uncle had been Mayor Kenny's closest adviser. Frank had been a city councilman but had a political falling-out in the late 1960s because he didn't get along with Mayor Whelan.

Now that Whelan was going to jail, Frank was planning his own political comeback. Bumper stickers and pens bearing his name circulated throughout the city.

Frank was a favorite to win because, like Aunt Katie and Ma, he was always doing good things for people. Favors, my mother called them. Frank was so kindhearted that he even did Grandpa a favor and gave him a job, back before he tried to shoot us. Ironically, it was Grandpa's job to make sure that people stayed in line. On busy days, he would walk up and down and straighten the DMV line, pushing people around. It was his dream job.

Frank had a way of making you feel special. He once told me he needed to buy a present for his niece, and asked me to accompany him and my mother to the toy store to pick something out. I was honored he would put such trust in my taste. After careful consideration, I chose a Baby Thumbelina doll, which I had secretly wanted. I would never admit it to anyone, being a tomboy. But I knew Frank's niece would love it.

I hadn't realized that my seventh birthday was just a few days away and that Frank had had me pick the doll out for myself. I wasn't yet suspicious of everyone's motives. Only most people's.

Later that week, when Frank handed me the present, everything clicked. I knew what it was before I unwrapped it, but I felt that strange new sensation called surprise: feeling both happy and duped at the same time. I knew Frank's lie had been a good lie. There were good lies and bad lies. It wasn't always so easy to tell the difference.

Frank was a dream boss. He offered big bonuses and understood our working mother's busy schedule. If one of us had a fever, forcing Ma to stay home, Frank never complained. And he never docked her pay. To most people, the DMV was a nightmare of long, messy lines and nasty civil servants. But to me, it was a refuge. The building had twelve gray steps that led down to a wonderful place: a backyard. Frank convinced the "girls" at the DMV to let us kids play back there after school. For the first time in my life, I came close to having a normal childhood, with backyard clubhouses and lemonade stands.

The DMV backyard was better than Aunt Katie's backyard, because there were other kids to play with. Buddy the dog was smart, but he couldn't play army or help me climb a tree. This new yard was my paradise: There was grass—a twenty-foot stretch of it to the back fence, where a large tree bloomed. To the right were a small white shed and a white wall made of cinder blocks, ideal for scaling. To the left was a small chain-link fence, through which you could see clear through to the other backyards.

My playmates included Joe Wendolowski and his older brother, Frankie, whose mother, Angie, worked with Ma. Joe, who was the same age as I was, never took off his baseball cap. He was my first crush. All the girls in our class were in love with him.

Ronnie Pawlak, my mother's coworker who rented an apartment above the DMV, unloaded her young son, Adam, in the yard as well. He became the first man in my life, the first boy I ever kissed during a game of Spin the Bottle.

Other local kids soon joined us. The Puerto Rican kids whose house abutted the DMV heard the laughter and merriment and climbed the fence to join me and my growing harem. A boy named Eggy and, occasionally his little sister, Iliana, the only other girl in the backyard day-care crowd, became regulars.

My mother's good friend Jane Liana, who lived just around the corner and worked as the sales manager at the Rainbow Shop, a women's clothing store on dilapidated Newark Avenue, brought her son, Alfred, to the backyard. Alfred was one of my best friends. We took baths together in our bathing suits at my house.

Alfred was the kindest boy I knew. Once when we were out with my mother on a trip to the Battery, she bought us both helium balloons. I lost mine. Alfred, who felt bad, selflessly let his balloon float away too. We watched both of them trail off together in the direction of the World Trade Center. (Years later, when my boyfriend and I broke up a week before the junior prom, Alfred proved his mettle once again and came as my date.)

Having been raised with an older brother, it didn't faze me that I was surrounded mostly by boys in the backyard. Together, using the tools from the white shed, we built clubhouses made from wood stolen from the next yard over. Eggy was the bravest, and would climb the tree to venture over the high back wooden fence to retrieve old doors, chicken wire, and planks studded with rusty nails. Beneath that tree, with its trunk as a foundation wall, the clubhouse would rise as we sawed and hammered away. Once it was built we'd hold a meeting. Frankie was president, since he was the oldest. I was vice-president, since I was bossiest. Alfred was treasurer, and Adam was sergeant at arms.

Each night, after our club meeting was over and our mothers punched out for the day, Kelsey, the building janitor, would tear our clubhouse down. Kelsey was a stickler for order. Once Grandpa went to jail, it was Kelsey's job to straighten the moblike crowds of DMV customers gathered in the waiting room each morning. He did a better job than Grandpa.

Kelsey never told us he was the one who knocked the clubhouses down, and he never stood in the way of our building a new one. But he scowled and shook his head every time new construction began. So the game continued, week in and week out. We'd construct architectural masterpieces only to have them torn asunder while we were home eating supper.

Between contracting jobs, we played other games, usually war games or hide-and-seek, squatting in the cool shade of the shed, under the stairs, or in the tall tree. On rainy days, Ma brought me inside, where I sat at the counter and typed drivers' permits or poems.

One hot summer day in the yard, during a challenging game of combat, all the boys took off their shirts. Since I was sweating just as much as they were, I followed their lead. They all laughed as I stood there, toy gun in hand, bare-chested and flat as the rest of them. I ran inside, crying to my mother. She stopped what she was doing, rounded up the boys, and yelled at them for making fun of me. She then knelt down and told me, ever so gently, to put my shirt back on. I was not happy about it, but when my mother asked you to do something, you just did it. She always had a good reason.

Most days in the DMV yard passed without incident. Though there was the one time the kids and I greased the gray stairs with soap in the hopes that a particularly scary car dealer would come out and slip down the stairs. His name was Louie and he walked with crutches because he had the gout. We figured that when he fell, the change in his pockets would scatter and we would be rich. Fortunately, we were found out by Kelsey, who mopped up the slippery trap before Louie had a chance to break his neck.

There was also the day Eggy robbed Alfred's catcher's mitt and painted it with black shoe polish to disguise it. But we all knew it was Alfred's. Jane visited the backyard, retrieved her son's glove, and gave Eggy hell. He never stole again, as far as we knew.

One afternoon, bored by the clubhouse, we built a lemonade stand, which was patronized by car dealers, who our mothers guilt-tripped into visiting the backyard. Car dealers came into the office regularly to register new fleets of Cadillacs, Pontiacs, Oldsmobiles, and Lincolns. They were given special treatment by being taken off the long DMV line—the least they could do was buy some lemonade. Each of them came back and peeled off a few bills, then told us to drink the lemonade ourselves. With no output and a steady customer base, we made over a hundred dollars' profit in a day.

Our other form of income came from Frank. Every week, after balancing the books and closing out the machines, Frank would assemble us kids in the front waiting area of the office, take all the accumulated change—mostly pennies and nickels—and toss it into the air. Frank, a redheaded Irish tenor, sang "Pennies from Heaven" while we screamed and scrambled for our take, stuffing our pockets until they overflowed.

Because of Frank, the staff at the Montgomery Street DMV was the happiest around. Drivers from across the county went out of their way to go there because of the unusual, smiling clerks. For Ma and the rest of the girls, boring clerical work became a comedy with Frank in attendance.

The customers provided the punch lines, unintentionally.

My sister once asked a customer if he had a lien on his car. "No," the man answered, "but it tilts a little to the left."

When filling out a permit application, one old lady failed to fill in the box for SEX. When asked why, she blushed and whispered, "My husband's been dead for a long time."

Our mothers often helped illiterate drivers fill out their paperwork, particularly local Gypsies, who claimed to have forgotten their glasses at home. At other DMV offices, the staff would ridicule people who couldn't read and send them away without helping them. But not on Montgomery Street.

"Darling, sweetheart," the Gypsies would say. "Can you read this for me?" My mother always obliged, never condescending, never laughing out loud. While helping a foreigner fill out his paperwork once, my mother asked how many doors his car had. It was part of the usual description—either you had a two-door or a four-door.

"Three," the man answered.

"Three?" my mother asked.

"One fall off," he replied in broken English. Ma somehow kept a straight face.

My mother was often tipped for her kindness and patience, virtues she'd developed while raising three kids. One customer showered her with compliments, telling her she typed so fast she should be the secretary for the president of the United States.

Ma could have made big bucks by filling out phony paperwork for some dealers, who would offer a one-hundred-dollar cash bribe to fix an odometer reading, change the year on a car, or conceal the fact that a car had been in a flood. Ma never accepted out-and-out bribes. She didn't want to embarrass us by being arrested. But she was not above accepting perfectly legal though slightly unethical presents from dealers, who appreciated being taken off the long line. For Christmas, there were dresses, large bottles of perfume, and gallons of Johnny Walker Red. Free lunches and snacks were abundant: Corned-beef sandwiches or hot dogs that would grow cold on busy afternoons.

Amid all this goodwill, it never occurred to us—at least not to the backyard gang—that something was really wrong. But it was only a matter of time before the truth about the DMV came out.

It was noon on a cool day in late September 1972 and my mother, as usual, was at school to pick me up for lunch. I was a finicky eater, and the sight of other children in the OLC cafeteria chewing deviled ham with their mouths open made me sick. Ma and I usually went home for lunch, but on special occasions we would venture to the Greek diner across the street, where I'd have a cheeseburger or chicken soup with orzo.

On this particular autumn day, my mother showed up with Angie and my sister, who joined us for lunch at the Greeks'. "What are you doing here?" I asked Paula and Angie, as they slid into a booth with us. "Who's running the DMV?"

My mother explained that in the morning, when she went to work, the state police were waiting at the front door. Frank had been shot in the head during a robbery. He was still alive, in stable condition, she said. But Ma, Paula, and Angie looked nervous and upset, and talked about stuff I couldn't really follow, about detectives and car titles and money. My mind was drifting.

Would Frank be a vegetable like those people in a coma? What if my friends and I had been there when the robbers had come in? What if they had come into the backyard and taken us hostage? This was by far the most exciting thing to happen since Grandpa had tried to kill us.

That night, I read the rest of the story in *The Jersey Journal*. Right there, on the front page, was a picture of Frank. Under his picture and name, it said, "Shot in head." It was weird seeing someone I knew so well on page 1 with something so dramatic written underneath. Even Grandpa had never made the front page.

I wondered if Frank was going to die. Most of the stiffs I'd seen at the funeral parlor had been distant relatives or old friends of Ma's. I considered Frank one of my friends. I didn't want to have to go to his funeral. I really liked him.

I read the story over and over, or at least the words I understood, and learned that right before 9 A.M., Frank had called the police and said simply, "I have a problem." When the cops arrived, Frank answered the door in a "semiconscious state" (I wasn't sure what that meant), his head bleeding from a bullet wound behind his left ear. There was also a bullet hole in the office wall. Two customers had been standing outside when the shooting occurred, waiting for the office to open. They told the police they hadn't seen anyone suspicious entering or leaving. I wondered if the bad guys had escaped through the backyard.

When my mother and the other girls arrived for work that morning, detectives had them step into the office, past the yellow police tape and over the barely dried blood on the carpet. The cash drawer was open, and money and paperwork were scattered everywhere. Thinking that an illegal-car ring had robbed the DMV, the detectives asked my mother and the other girls to count the titles and permits, which were numbered. But the papers were all there. In the meantime, Frank was admitted to the Medical Center, where doctors removed two .32-caliber bullets from his head after four hours of surgery.

The next day, with Frank's blood cleaned from the rug, the DMV opened for business as usual. My mother had to go in early to open the door, since Frank was still in the hospital. While the police searched for clues to the crime, Ma and the other girls worked the counter. We played in the backyard, lost in games of Red Rover and One-Two-Three Red Light, forgetting, for the time being, all about Frank's terrible head wound.

There were people who were being paid to think about it, though. Detective Michael Borseso, the same detective who had arrested Grandpa when he came to shoot us, noticed that Frank was a southpaw and that the wound was on the left side of Frank's head. Two days after the shooting, Borseso got Frank to confess from his hospital bed that there had been no robbery, that he had shot himself—that he even shot one round into the office wall to make it look like a robbery. Frank told Borseso exactly where to find the gun.

The detective came up behind my mother while she was typing a license renewal that afternoon. "Don't move," he said, bending down and reaching between her feet into the space under the counter.

There, under my mother, beneath the floorboards in a secret hiding place, was a .32-caliber revolver.

Frank's gun.

Frank was "despondent over domestic and financial difficulties," the front-page story the next day said. Now that they mentioned it, my sister did notice that Frank had been a bit off lately. He had come to work recently wearing four wristwatches. His hair was a mess. Paula figured he was having a nervous breakdown, but since he was the boss, she couldn't really ask him about it. We, in the backyard, had seen none of Frank's unusual behavior. The closest we came to noticing any financial problems was a slowdown on the "Pennies from Heaven" routine.

Frank survived, since the gun he had used was an antique. Even the bullets were old—they failed to penetrate his skull, lodging just below his skin line. When the bleeding wouldn't stop, Frank stumbled over to the counter, hid the gun, then called the police. It was one thing to die instantly from a gunshot wound. It was another to bleed to death slowly in the waiting area while customers stood outside, banging on the door to be let in for license plates.

I guess dying slowly like that gave Frank some time to think about things, like the fact that he didn't really want to die after all.

Charges weren't filed against Frank for four years, until the feds could rack up a list of sixty-one counts of conspiracy, misapplication of bank funds, and submitting false credit statements on loan applications. Frank had been borrowing money from the DMV drawer and replacing it with money from loans he acquired illegally. Along with a banker friend, he was accused of scamming more than $100,000.

This, I realized, was the bad kind of lying, the kind you went to jail for. It was the kind of lying the mayor had gone away for. Frank faced a maximum of 227 years in prison. I imagined him with long white hair, a long white beard, and long fingernails, like Methuselah in the Bible, standing there all hunched over as the jail guard finally creaked open his cell door.

Frank paid back the money somehow, pleaded guilty to one count, and received just five years probation. I was glad he didn't have to spend 227 years in jail.

His real punishment was that he lost the agency. My mother broke the bad news to me over lunch at the Greeks', telling me the office would have to move to a new location. They would have a new boss.

What would happen to the backyard? I asked. To the tree and to the grass? And to our clubhouse? What would become of Kelsey? Would he move with us? My mother shrugged and smiled and said not to worry, that things would work out. But I had my doubts.

The DMV office was moved up to Journal Square, and a man named Saul Farber became the new agent. He owned a parking lot, a gas station, and a car wash. The DMV was to be the jewel in the crown of his automotive empire. Saul was the kind of outsider the state was looking for after the Frank fiasco: a Jew from outside Hudson County, with no Democratic-machine connections and no Jersey City accent.

I knew Saul was certainly no Frank. The nuns had made me unduly suspicious of Jewish people. There was that story Sister Isabelle had told of God striking down a man named Saul as he rode through Damascus on his horse. "Saul, Saul, why have you forsaken me?" God asked him. I felt like asking Saul the same question.

The DMV girls—like God in the biblical version—grew to love Saul. I refused to speak to him for two years—not because he was Jewish, but because I was sure he'd disappoint me, too.

In a way, he already had. Saul had no backyard, no tree, no space for a clubhouse or for my friends. All Saul could offer was some blacktop and the car wash, where it only rained cold water. Never pennies. Not even once.

10

BAD BOY

Along with the other DMV mothers, Ma was one of the troublemakers at OLC. At PTA meetings she, Angie, Jane, and my aunt Julie, on my father's side, were the only mothers who got up and protested the piddling injustices that were done to us at the hands of the Felician Sisters.

My mother and her friends were tough. Ma would have liked to have wrestled with an idiotic nun or administrator on the floor of the church hall during those PTA meetings. But she kept her cool. There were arguments over favoritism at the school, when some kids were left to stand outside in the cold on winter mornings before the bell rang (i.e., me and most of the students) while other kids got to sit inside the warm school (i.e., the fat Polish kids whose mothers worked in the administration). My mother argued that we should all be allowed inside.

Ma never let anyone push her or her kids around. She even yelled at the checkout girl at ShopRite when she bounced our cantaloupe into the bag. It embarrassed me, but I learned from my mother to stand up for myself, and to dislike careless and unfair people. There were quite a few of them living in Jersey City.

Because I was preoccupied with being like Aunt Mary Ann, I didn't realize that my mother was a rebel. There was a lot of Beansie in her. She refused to work Bingo, even though it would have reduced the price of my school tuition. All the mothers were expected to wait tables once a month at Bingo. But my mother and her friends couldn't stand the game or the women with their beehives and long cigarettes, flicking their ashes into lipstick-stained cardboard coffee cups and calling out for new cards in the dingy school basement.

I felt that Ma didn't belong at OLC. Unlike most of the other mothers, she and her crew didn't wear housedresses and curlers when they came to pick us up after school. Some mothers didn't bother to pick their kids up at all even though Jersey City was not a place where you wanted your ten-year-old to walk home alone. My mother, always there at dismissal, made me proud with her pretty clothes and her freshly combed hair, which was never done up in a bouffant. She had normal hair, like me. She hated the beauty parlor and never had a hairdo, even in the hairdo-crazed 1960s.

Every day we'd eat lunch together at home or at the Greek diner. Most mothers at OLC didn't care what their kids ate for lunch. Their lunch boxes were dirty and rusty, with sour milk and old, discarded breadcrusts. One kid came to class with a sandwich of Marshmallow Fluff and liverwurst. Together. Just the thought of it made me want to vomit.

I ate leftover spaghetti or chicken soup, side by side with Daddy, who also came home for lunch, dressed in his blue work uniform. We would watch *The Don Ho Show* together. They were happy afternoons; Daddy got to thaw out for an hour away from the walk-in freezer at work, and I had a full hour away from the clutches of the evil nuns, who seemed to grow meaner as time went by.

In a desperate bid for respect, the nuns trained us to rise when one of their fellow stormtroopers entered the room. As soon as the door cracked open, we shot up from our desks and recited, "Good morning, [insert name of evil nun here]." The first time our new principal, Sister Mary Grace, entered our classroom, we only got as far as "Good mor—."

She cut us off, yelling, "Sit down before I knock ya down." We didn't doubt for a minute that she would punch each and every one of our scared little faces.

Sister Grace was much worse than Sister Isabelle. She bore a strong resemblance to the actor Robert Shaw, particularly in his role as Quint in the movie *Jaws*. One of her front teeth was filled with silver. Or gold. I never got close enough to find out. Behind her back, we called her Orca—a reference to another killer-fish film. The whale's black-and-white body resembled Sister Grace's black-and-white habit. And she was just as fat.

One spring, during graduation practice at OLC Church, one of the boys mouthed off while Sister Grace's back was turned. When the instigator failed to present himself, she resorted to the usual Nazi tactics, punishing the group to rout out the evildoer. The class would stay after school until she got a confession. Of course, it didn't work. I started to think that maybe the nuns didn't expect results, that maybe they simply liked punishing us. I hadn't yet heard the word *sadist,* but the day I learned its definition—a person who takes an abnormal delight in cruelty—a picture of Sister Grace popped into my head.

When the evildoer failed to step forward, Sister Grace threatened to cancel graduation. The girls were in tears. They had all bought their white graduation dresses. The corsages were already ordered. My cousin Stephen, my aunt Julie's son, stepped up and took the blame. He wasn't the guilty party, but he bravely offered himself up so the rest of the class wouldn't suffer. It was an incredibly noble moment for a fourteen-year-old boy. But soon Sister Grace figured out that Stephen wasn't the true instigator. She called him stupid and slapped him across the face. He stood there, unflinching. He didn't even blink. Stephen was the most stoic kid I knew.

The next day, when Aunt Julie got wind of the story, she took off from work at the Beehive Bank and came marching to school, ready to rip Sister Grace's head off. When Julie walked through the big wooden front doors, the principal was at the top of the stairs, waving her big, beefy hand. "Come on, come on," Sister Grace taunted. "I know you want to fight." I can just see her metal tooth glinting in the hallway lights.

Julie stormed up the stairs and gave it to her good. "How would you like to get hit across the mouth?" she asked Sister Grace. Sophie, the gym teacher, stood behind Sister Grace with her fist clenched, mocking the nun and encouraging Julie to peel one off. But Julie kept her composure. She walked away, and never spoke to Sister Grace again. I wished Julie had knocked her sparkly tooth out. But Julie knew, as Ma did, that she was better than all that.

Aunt Julie was too good for OLC and for Jersey City. She had almost escaped once. As a testament that you couldn't run away, the story of my aunt Julie was often invoked in OLC circles. Julie was the pioneer on my father's side of the family, like Aunt Mary Ann was on my mother's side. In the 1970s, she had gone to Arizona with her husband, John, and her son, Stephen.

John looked different from most of my uncles. While most wore white shirts and dress slacks, he was always decked out in jeans, western shirts, and cowboy boots. All he needed was a horse. But as I already knew, you couldn't keep a horse in Jersey City. Uncle John yearned for the wide open spaces. And Julie was madly in love with him. We all were. Even my father, a very quiet guy, liked talking to John. He was different, in a place that didn't encourage individuality. He played drums in a jazz band. Julie was different, too. Unlike everyone she knew, she didn't have her first child until she was thirty-seven. In Hudson County, she and John were practically freaks. But in a good way.

When Stephen was three years old, Julie and John loaded him and their belongings into a camper and drove out west. John found work as a carpenter and, later, as a manager of a sign shop in Chandler, Arizona, while Aunt Julie helped out in a small hotel. She loved Arizona—the beauty of it, the independence that comes with being anonymous in a new town, the freedom of not knowing every person who walks down the street.

Not that you personally knew every man, woman, and child who walked down the street in Jersey City. But you knew them well enough, could immediately see down into their dusty souls. You knew they had eaten hot dogs at Boulevard Drinks, had gone to the matinees at the Loew's, had relatives who worked for either the Parks Department or Public Works and had paid that 85-cent toll on the New Jersey Turnpike a few too many times. You knew what their wardrobe looked like, what their dates looked like, and the kinds of teachers they had—what they had learned or, more important, what they had failed to learn at a place like OLC.

Julie's feeling of freedom was fueled by the knowledge that there was a better, bigger world out there, past the gray skies and dirty gutters of downtown, around the weed-infested corners of Hudson County, and beyond the entire joke of a state. That feeling came from not being afraid to go away. And stay there. And live there.

It didn't last long for Julie.

Uncle Henry called our house one night. It was later than his usual numbers call. When I answered the phone, I was surprised to hear his voice on the other end asking for Daddy. He rarely made social calls.

We knew something was wrong when, after a few minutes, Daddy pulled up a kitchen chair and sat down. They were not gabbers, he and Uncle Henry. And this call was lasting quite a while. We gathered around Daddy and watched his frown grow deeper than usual. He nodded his head slowly, his forehead wrinkling like a strip of bacon, and he murmured, "uh-huh, uh-huh," signaling Uncle Henry to continue whatever the hell he was saying on the other end. The suspense was too much.

Between nods, Daddy said, "It's John. There was an accident."

That afternoon, John had gone pistol shooting in the desert with his boss and the boss's brother. Julie went to a flea market with a friend. After shooting practice, the guys locked their guns in the boss's jeep and went to hear a musician friend play at a local bar. As they drank their final beer, some words were exchanged with an army sergeant seated at the bar. Or something John and his friends said was overheard. It's unclear. But the sergeant angrily walked out of the bar.

John left a little later, and while walking to the jeep, he was almost run over by the sergeant's car. John knocked on the guy's window to yell at him. The sergeant rolled the window down, put a 9mm German Luger to John's chest, and pulled the trigger. As John fell into his boss's arms, the guys thought he was fooling around, that he couldn't possibly be shot.

The shooter sped off toward the Mexican border, but he got nervous and returned when the cops started searching for him. He told the police he'd merely tried to scare John, that he hadn't meant any harm.

That night, Julie called Uncle Henry, since he was the oldest in the family. And Uncle Henry had called Daddy.

As he hung up the phone, Daddy put his head down and gripped the kitchen chair for support. "John is dead," he said without looking up. I think he was crying and didn't want us to see. The bullet had hit John's main artery.

At an inquest a few days later, the killer said he had been listening to John and his friends' conversation and thought their insults were directed toward him, that he was being harassed. He was never charged with the shooting. Julie blames his eighteen-year record in the service and says that the government whitewashed the whole affair.

The other mothers at OLC glommed on to Julie's tragedy as a lesson in hubris. "She thinks who she is," was an all-too-familiar refrain. According to them, it didn't pay to leave, to think you were better than everybody else. Sooner or later you'd find yourself right back in Jersey City, sorry you ever left. John went all that way, they said, just to get shot. He could have done that right here on Jackson Avenue.

Julie didn't want to come back but, like Ma, she didn't drive. And in Arizona you had to have a car. A driver's license was one of the basic requirements for escape.

She had bragged about the fresh, dry air of Arizona and its wide open spaces, but Julie found herself back in smelly old Jersey City, getting a bouffant like my other aunts. The problem with leaving was that if you ever did have to come back, the place looked even uglier than it had before you left.

I was glad Julie came back to Jersey City, because Stephen was my favorite cousin on the Polish side. We goofed around a lot. Once, we put toothpicks in Aunt Julie's hair. They stood up like antennae. Aunt Julie didn't even know they were there, since her hair was so high off her scalp.

Stephen and I saw *Star Wars* together. For us, seeing that movie was like the day JFK got shot. Everyone we knew remembered exactly where it had happened and who they were with at the time. Daddy came with us to see it, but he stood in the back of the theater through most of the movie and smoked. He preferred movies about real things and real people. Science fiction was not for him. "Garbage," he said, scowling.

But Stephen and I loved *Star Wars*. We even had fake light sabers, which we used to clobber each other over the head. I liked boys better than girls, because they didn't cry when you hit them over the head. They were more fun. Hitting each other, climbing poles and trees—when you could find one in Jersey City—was much more entertaining than playing with dolls.

I calculated that I had no fewer than ten cousins at OLC at one time, all from Daddy's side of the family, most of them boys: Stephen, George, Mark, Andrew, Victor, Phillip, Scott, Melissa, and two Michaels.

Our cousin George once told Stephen that if he ever needed anyone beaten up, he would do it for him, since Stephen no longer had a father. Not having a father could be a problem in a tough place like Jersey City. And George knew about it firsthand.

George always seemed much older than the rest of us, as if he thought that shooting bottle caps or playing TV tag were pointless, silly exercises. He participated, but reluctantly.

He was a distant—fourth—cousin and we weren't particularly close. If you saw him on the street, George would look just like any other kid. He was polite, always said thank-you, and always put his toys away at the end of the day if he came to play at your house. He was short, and blended into the background with dark hair and thick glasses. People called them Barney Google glasses, after a cartoon that used to run in the Sunday funnies.

To me, Stephen, and the other kids, there was something unusual about George. Behind those glasses, he had a light in his brown eyes that was missing from most of the other kids' eyes. George seemed smarter, or wiser. You would think that it was just his glasses that made him look wiser. But there were other kids at OLC with glasses—like me—and we didn't have that same George quality. There was a vibe hovering around him, as if the air around his body were charged. More than anyone I knew, George had that crooked, reluctant Jersey City smile.

I knew why. And it wasn't just that he had no father.

We all knew George's story, though we never talked to him about it. It was just another of the many hard-luck Stapinski tales. On a foggy night after Valentine's Day 1971, when George was just four years old, he woke his mother up in the middle of the night because he had to pee. Mary Ann, a cousin on my father's side, groggily took him out into their hallway, to the building's communal bathroom. On the way, they saw George's father standing in the doorway. He looked like he was standing on his tippy toes. In the dark, it seemed as if he were staring at them.

"What's the matter?" Mary Ann asked him. When he didn't answer, she asked again. But then she realized that he was hanging from the doorway by a belt around his neck. She nervously let George pee, then hurried him out of the hallway.

George's father had been a heroin addict, so it was just a matter of time before something bad happened to him. His death was listed as a suicide. Some people, like George's mother, thought he had been murdered. Either way, George no longer had a father.

Having Grandpa try and shoot us was pretty dramatic, but seeing your father dead like that was something else. Even Stephen had been spared the details of his father's death. I tried to imagine what it would be like to see Daddy hanging in a doorway by his black leather belt, the one with the cracks and the metal buckle. The thought was so terrible that I pushed it from my mind and tried never to think it again.

George supposedly didn't remember the incident. But I knew that first memories were the ones that stuck, that they were the memories that struck hardest, even if we didn't want them to. I wanted to talk to George about his father, and to tell him about Grandpa, but George wasn't very approachable.

The kids treated him differently because of what he had seen. We were in awe of him, or afraid of him, or maybe afraid for him. George's story was the only lesson we needed that you shouldn't do heroin. Forget the OLC film strips and the lectures from Officer Friendly. We had cold, hard facts.

Though he said he didn't remember the tragedy, you could tell that George carried it around with him, like heavy luggage. It weighed him down and made him mad. Sometimes it made him do bad things. Like the time he and his friends picked a fight with me and my friends after school. I remember George cursing us out. He was the first boy ever to do such a thing, and the shock of it set me off. I told him off right on the spot that he should leave us alone and that he was a disgusting pig. George just smiled that crooked smile. He gave me a knowing look filled with sexual innuendo—too mature for a twelve-year-old kid.

George scared me, because the thought flitted across my young mind that he was a distant cousin, the most dangerous of my Polish cousins, and that it would probably be legal for me to kiss him. There was something exciting about the danger that lurked beneath George's skin—something mysterious, sad, and smart. He was the class bad boy. And as the bad boy, he possessed that special quality that made you want to run with him but then save his soul at the end of the day.

For the first time, I realized that bad boys were much more interesting than good boys. For the first time, in my first flash of wisdom, I understood finally why Grandma had fallen for Grandpa.

11

GONE AWAY

All my knowledge of Grandpa came from family stories, repeated over and over again until I knew them by heart. Though wakes and funerals provided an unending chorus, the best place to hear a Grandpa story was at my cousin Gerri's house in North Bergen. The township was never anything to write home about, but its ugliness paled in comparison to Jersey City's. As did its reputation.

North Bergen was shaped like a semiautomatic handgun. But people felt it wasn't half as tough as Jersey City, Hudson's largest city and the county seat. When we visited North Bergen, kids would step back an inch when they heard where I came from, as if I were carrying a .44 in my back pocket. I didn't mind, really. Being from Jersey City made me feel taller.

There were no brownstones in North Bergen, mostly wood-frame or brick houses built on incredibly steep hills. Some houses were on such an incline that North Bergenites couldn't get reception from their antennae, since they faced the meadowlands and not New York City, where the signals were sent out from the Empire State Building.

I always considered North Bergen the suburbs, because it had hills and trees. But the towns of Secaucus and Kearny and Harrison—connected to Jersey City by a street called Fish House Road—were even more suburb-like. Its residents were often embarrassed to be associated with the rest of Hudson County.

On my trips to New York and to Hudson County's other towns, I started to piece together a map of my world in my head. If I surgically removed Kearny, Secaucus, and Harrison, which protruded from the western edge of Hudson County like polyps on a cancerous host, I was left with a strip of land floating between the polluted Hackensack River, Newark Bay, and the Hudson River. This strip of land, which consisted of Jersey City, Bayonne, Hoboken, Union City, West New York, Weehawken, Guttenberg, and North Bergen, lay directly across from Manhattan.

The strip resembled a wrench or some other blunt object aimed at the back of New Jersey's head. To me, the state looked like the bust of a hunched-over little man wearing a fez. He was in profile, and had an overbite and a big nose, which pointed toward the rest of America. He was giving New York the cold shoulder because New York thought it was so great. Which it was. I wanted to live there someday. Eventually, all my Hudson County reference points would have to do with Manhattan.

If I waded into the Hudson from downtown Jersey City, swam less than a mile, and didn't die from the undertow or PCBs, I would be in New York City's financial district. If I looked at the city from Hamilton Park in Weehawken, I had a perfect sight line down Forty-sixth Street, straight to the horizon. Or if I took a dive from Frank Sinatra Drive in Hoboken, I could doggie-paddle over to the Empire State Building. New York was so close that I worried its skyscrapers would fall and hit my house if there was ever an earthquake. I should be so lucky.

People thought places like North Bergen and Bayonne were a step up from Jersey City. To visit my cousins who lived in those towns, we had to take a bus or get a ride down Kennedy Boulevard, originally called Hudson Boulevard. The boulevard was the county's main artery, filled with plastic flag–fringed car dealerships and low-lying bowling alleys.

Most of the other towns along the boulevard were populated by former Jersey Citizens who had moved on to two-family, aluminum-sided homes with driveways and bathroom mat–size backyards. In some ways, those other towns were worse off than Jersey City. People there were lulled into a false sense of security. They had toxic waste, just like us. Sometimes even more.

Their mayors were no better, either. In 1970, Mayor John Armellino of West New York was found guilty of taking bribes to protect illegal gambling; U.S. representative Neil Gallagher of Bayonne, once a potential candidate for vice-president of the United States, pleaded guilty to income tax evasion. Then in 1976, Guttenberg mayor Herman Klein resigned when prosecutors threatened a case concerning his no-show county job. Klein was reelected a few years later, demonstrating the forgiving nature of no-show city workers.

That same year, North Bergen mayor Angelo Sarubbi was convicted of taking bribes from a contractor. But North Bergen's most notorious character was town clerk Joey Mocco. Prosecutors were constantly accusing Mocco of all sorts of things. He was indicted and arrested on charges of embezzlement and fixing votes in favor of his brother, mayor Peter Mocco, but was never convicted. Eventually, Joey got twenty years for bribery, official misconduct, and illegal dumping. When he was sentenced, the judge told him, "You plundered and pillaged your town and treated it as a fiefdom as if you were a medieval lord."

Parts of North Bergen looked better than Jersey City, but the danger was there, lurking just below the surface. Kids in those satellite towns were lost in some kind of netherworld—not urban and not suburban, but the worst of both worlds. North Bergen kids wore concert T-shirts, faded Lee jeans with patches of the Rolling Stones tongue on their butts, and lots of suede and brown corduroy. They wore their hair long in the back and short in the front, as if they lived in white-trash Middle America. They hardly ever visited New York. For some reason, Manhattan seemed farther away from places like North Bergen and Bayonne than it did from Jersey City. But the rest of America seemed closer, with its pickup trucks and country music.

In Jersey City, kids listened to R&B and disco and dressed up when they went out. They were better groomed, in general, with shorter, cleaner haircuts. In the other towns, kids were more racist, since they were exposed to very few blacks or Puerto Ricans. Even in Union City, which had the biggest population of Cubans north of Miami, people were racist. The Cubans, many of them formerly doctors and businessmen in their own country, looked down on other Latinos.

Jersey City wasn't exactly enlightened, but at least we had black and Puerto Rican friends and neighbors. We knew they were the same as we were. My brother's best friend was a black kid named Jay, who taught him how to dance the robot, which he did, very well, at the high school Ebony Club dances. Stanley was the only white guy in attendance, and was voted best dancer in the class of '75. His nickname was Brother Kielbas, as in kielbasa.

The African Americans lived mostly in the Bergen-Lafayette ward, made up of beautiful Victorian mansions next to burned-out and abandoned buildings and drug dens. The neighborhood had once been an elite shopping district, but white flight had left the area with a few liquor stores and check-cashing joints, a white-owned cheap-furniture store, and little else.

Kids in Bayonne and North Bergen were afraid of black people, so they called them names, something my mother forbade. I remember one of my cousins choosing sides for a game of freeze tag once and singing, "Eenie meenie miny mo, catch a nigger by the toe." I couldn't believe she said the *n* word. We always said "catch a *tiger* by the toe." She must have picked it up from the kids in her neighborhood.

One other crucial difference was that kids in towns like North Bergen attended public school. Jersey City's public schools were so bad that only the poorest of the poor went to them. Any parent who could scrape together the money sent her kid to Catholic school. Even Protestants and Muslims. It was a flawed system that we had inherited from the days of Hague.

Catholic schools like OLC were lame, but public schools were much worse—even in Hudson County's other towns. In public high schools, there were fistfights and drugs for sale in the hallways, as well as apathetic, tenured teachers who couldn't care less if you showed up for class. The nuns were bad, but at least they instilled discipline. That was my mother's rationalization for subjecting us to Sister Grace. The only good thing about public school was that you could wear your own clothes every day.

Though we had junkies and dealers on our corner, it seemed there were more drug-addicted hippie teens in North Bergen High School. It was the only place in Hudson County where I had heard of kids doing LSD. There was the urban legend about the girl who tripped out at White Castle in North Bergen after eating a mini-burger laced with the drug. She danced on the tables and scared everyone out of the restaurant. There was something wild and scary about North Bergen. I loved going there, and whenever I could, I'd convince my mother to let me sleep over at my Italian cousins' house.

Whenever I visited Gerri and her siblings, we didn't have to get up early on Sunday to go to church. My cousins only went to mass on special occasions, which seemed like a great idea to me.

In North Bergen, I was allowed to play in the street, especially the many dead-end streets. I liked dead ends, because there was less traffic zipping past. It was on one of those streets that Gerri taught me to ride a bike without training wheels. There were fewer cars, not to mention an abundance of hills and rocks, on which we'd climb in the summer and slide down on cardboard boxes in the snow of winter.

Whenever I was there, I felt a certain freedom that I didn't get at home. I felt more grown-up. When I slept over, we made Aunt Millie breakfast in bed. My cousins and I would get up before she did, perc a pot of coffee, poach two eggs, and make triangles of white toast. It was a special treat for me, since my mother never let me near the stove for fear I would set my hair on fire.

Aunt Millie worked nights, as a career waitress, so during the day she usually slept. My uncle Jerry liked to tease her about snoring so hard that when she inhaled, the curtains would blow off the windows and the ships would come in from the harbor. Uncle Jerry was the family comedian. To make a living, though, he drove a bus. I thought he might get on his bus one day and keep driving and never come back to North Bergen. He longed to leave Hudson County, and did so whenever he could. He visited Aunt Mary Ann more than anyone else in the family. When he didn't have time to go to Florida, he'd drive to the airport and watch the planes take off for foreign destinations, places he wanted to fly to. He could do almost any accent—Russian, Greek, whatever. And he could imitate all of the Muppets. So could my uncle Robby, the family storyteller. When he and Uncle Jerry got together, we were entertained for hours.

At Gerri's house, over Aunt Millie's famous meatballs, Uncle Jerry told the story about Grandpa forcing Mom and Aunt Mary Ann to go get a block of ice from the iceman when they were little. The ice weighed more than they did, but they managed to carry it up the stairs. Or most of the stairs. Just as they got it up to the top of the long flight, the ice slipped out of the pan and bounced down, step after step. Whenever Uncle Jerry told that story, I watched that block of ice slip and bounce, step by step by step in my mind's eye, eternally falling as Grandpa came running out like a maniac, cursing them, then grabbed the ice under his arm and took it upstairs himself. Every time Uncle Jerry told the story, we laughed and laughed, imagining Ma and Aunt Mary Ann as skinny little kids.

There was also the story about Grandpa's ridiculous visit to Uncle Robby's army base in Indiana when he went to borrow some cash. And the story of Grandpa taking the settlement money after a flying bowling pin hit Uncle Jerry in the nose while he was working as a pin boy to help support the family. Uncle Jerry's nose was still crooked after twenty years.

When Uncle Jerry and Uncle Robby told the stories, they seemed funny, not tragic. Living in poverty and having rats run under your bed seemed comical when they talked about it. Their sense of humor had helped them survive it. That and the fact that the family was so close. Getting together to talk and joke about the bad times helped a lot. It was their therapy. My family didn't believe in psychiatrists, and never had the money for them, even if they wanted to believe in them.

While they were telling stories about the bad old days, the one about Grandpa trying to shoot us would sometimes come up. My cousin Gerri said she couldn't remember that night. I thought it was strange, since Gerri was a few years older than I was. How could she not remember? Maybe she was like George, with the awful memory clinging somewhere back there in her brain like a big tumor, pushing, pushing. But Gerri didn't seem to be haunted like George. She was an optimist, and remembered the good things about visiting our house: the hot roast beef sandwiches my father made, the lobster tails, french fries, and Sara Lee cupcakes.

Gerri was everybody's favorite cousin. My sister, Paula, was Gerri's sponsor for her Holy Confirmation, so they had their own special bond. Even Daddy loved Gerri, since she had such a good appetite. He and my mother were Gerri's stand-in godparents. Her real godmother was a friend of Aunt Millie's who'd forgotten about Gerri and never sent her cards on her birthday. Ma adopted Gerri and always sent her a birthday card with money inside.

I felt close to Gerri, because our birthdays were just three days apart. I tried not to remember that Grandpa's birthday was only a day before mine. I didn't want any special bonds with him. Not after hearing all about him. But I never tired of the stories, Christmas after Christmas, family wedding after family funeral, until the family soul was recycled and we got together again for a baptism.

My brother would grin his crooked grin. My cousins Susan and David, the same age as I was, and the youngest in their families, too, would sit with me and giggle. Gerri smiled her big, toothy smile, her eyes sparkly blue like Grandma's. Unlike me, she had an open face, without shadows or doubt, and a great laugh, which flowed clear and clean like the spring water we had to buy whenever a water main broke.

When we got a little older, the family get-togethers and storytelling sessions were often held at my sister's house. Paula was the oldest girl cousin in both the Italian and Polish families, so she became the natural hostess when she moved out and got her own place. Paula married a banker from Hoboken named Basil, and traded in her difficult-to-pronounce three-syllable Polish name for an even more difficult to pronounce four-syllable Italian name. She had a baby, whom she named Paul, after herself and Grandma and her favorite Beatle, Paul McCartney.

Paula and Basil would have the whole clan to their modern highrise apartment three blocks from the Majestic. They lived in the newly built Gregory Apartments, named after the first mayor, Dudley S. Gregory. Cousin Mike helped the city secure the financing for the three buildings' construction.

My best friend, Liz, lived in the Gregory building across the street from Paula, and when I slept over at my sister's house, Liz and I would wave to each other while talking on the phone. It was from Paula's seventh-floor apartment, high above the crowded buildings, that I watched the sun set for the first time, the sky smeared with the vibrant reds and purples that only serious air pollution could provide. It was at Paula's apartment that I tasted, for the first time, Kraft Macaroni & Cheese and Chef Boyardee ravioli in a can—two things Daddy didn't have at the Cold Storage. In her own way, my sister rebelled.

When Gerri, the next girl in line, came of age, she got her own apartment, too, in North Bergen. Gerri had a family get-together every Christmas, putting out a big spread of cold cuts and beer and wine. I looked forward to it every year. I looked up to Paula and Gerri and hoped someday I could have family parties at my apartment. I imagined what my bachelorette pad in New York would be like—with bean-bag chairs and plastic beads hanging from the doorways and a view of the tall buildings surrounding me. I couldn't wait. Everyone would come to my luxurious apartment to tell their funny stories. Even Aunt Mary Ann.

She came from Florida to my sister's house a few times. I remember one time, everyone was gathered together, each with a big plate of antipasto on their lap: roasted red peppers, provolone cheese, salami rolled like little fleshy cigars. Cousin Susan always liked the black olives, and would place one on each finger and then eat them one at a time.

As the stories were told, I watched Aunt Mary Ann's face. I figured that she, my favorite aunt, would outdo my uncles with her hilarious memories. But the ice story and the Indiana story didn't make her laugh at all. Aunt Mary Ann didn't say a word. She looked like that picture of her the night Kenny won—there but not there, her mind floating somewhere off in the distance, somewhere you didn't want to go.

After that night, I found that the stories about Grandpa didn't seem as funny anymore. All of sudden I saw them through Aunt Mary Ann's eyes. The older I got, the more I blamed Grandma for staying with Grandpa and subjecting her children to a life of torture. I could understand how Grandma wound up meeting Grandpa and why she thought he was attractive, being the bad boy and all. But why had she married him? If you looked at Grandpa's arrest record and listened to the stories, without the laugh track, you could see what a terrible person he was.

Aunt Mary Ann was right. It wasn't funny at all.

In the early days of their marriage Grandpa didn't need to work, because of Grandma. With her three siblings, she'd inherited the row of brownstones on Grand Street when her father died. Her siblings did well for themselves with their inheritance and with their lives.

Her brother John had some problems early on, when his wife and baby both died while she was in labor, because of a tubular pregnancy. But Uncle John persevered. He became a Wall Street stockbroker, married a member of the Daughters of the American Revolution, and settled in Brooklyn, first on Dean Street, where Grandma had lived with him for a little while as a teenager, and then in Flatbush. We visited him there about once a year, usually around Easter. It was always an adventure. My cousins and I would pile into Uncle Jerry's car and ride, squished, through the Brooklyn-Battery Tunnel. Susan got in the car with dog-doo on her shoe one time, and we threatened to throw her out the window. We were just kidding, but she cried all the way to Brooklyn.

Uncle John's wife, Aunt Frances, looked like George Washington and had an impressive collection of Revolution-era antiques. Uncle John collected rocks, which was much more impressive to a kid. Every time we went there, Aunt Frances cooked lamb, another food that Daddy never brought home from the Cold Storage. I liked it, but it made Paula gag. So I ate her portion. I was always sad to leave Uncle John's house when night fell. Though he had had a traumatic childhood, he managed to make himself a happy home.

Uncle Sam, the one who got his head stuck in the Morris Canal, had a wobbly start in life as well. His daughter, Rose, died of pneumonia when she was two years old. Then his wife left him for a cop whose beat was Journal Square. But Sam, like John, bounced back. He remarried and became a professional bowler, then managed a bowling alley over the Canton Tea Garden. He retired, like most of the city's elders, to Miami. We saw him whenever we went to visit Aunt Mary Ann. Sam's swimming days were over, but he taught me how to fish in a canal near his house.

Even troubled Aunt Helen, the one who discovered her Russian mother dead in bed, made a better life. After getting out of the youth house, she became a flapper, got a job at Lord & Taylor, and met a Puerto Rican strawberry-shortcake baker from Lindy's in New York. Aunt Helen and Uncle Jesús retired to Puerto Rico. On a visit to our house once, Jesús was fed lobster and french fries by my father and was sent home with a Butterball turkey so large that it was still frozen when their plane landed in San Juan.

Grandma didn't manage her inheritance, or her life, quite as well as her siblings did. She let Grandpa handle the finances. He pissed it all away, gambling, drinking, and taking a vacation to Canada, of all places. By himself. He could have at least gone to Italy or somewhere romantic. But Canada? Within a year, Grandma's money was gone. Grandpa even hocked the wedding ring he had given Grandma, forcing her to go to Woolworth's and buy a cheap replacement.

Using pop psychology, I figured Grandma married him because he was a brute like her father, the Russian wife-basher. Grandma was continuing the cycle. Grandpa beat his children regularly—when he wasn't in prison, anyway.

Even Grandpa's sisters couldn't understand why Grandma stuck around, and they repeatedly tried to get her to leave him. After one of his violent binges, one of his sisters went to Grandma and begged her to pack her bags. "Get dressed, get lost," my aunt whispered. "Get the boat to China. Anything. Just get going." Instead of leaving, Grandma had a fight with Grandpa and wound up telling him what his sister had said. When Grandpa saw his sister, he attacked her, wrapping his hands around her throat, yelling, "Why the fuck are you telling my wife to leave me?"

Grandpa could not—or simply would not—hold down a job to support his wife and five children. He tried working as a union deliverer for the *New York Sun,* a good gig during the Depression. But a life of crime appealed to him most. When Grandma needed milk, Grandpa would go out and come back immediately with three or four bottles, having robbed them from the doorsteps of the neighbors. The only time he ever put food on the table was the night he came home, drunk, with fruit that he'd stolen from a local vendor. It wasn't a lovely fruit basket. It was a big, stinking freight box full of rotten oranges, which were probably headed for the garbage anyway.

Grandpa would steal whatever he could lay his hands on. His conscience knew no bounds. One afternoon, the local Jewish door-to-door salesman came to collect on a statue of the Blessed Mother that my grandmother had purchased. Grandma was paying for the statue on time, a quarter a week. The statue of the Virgin, dressed in blue, with her arms outstretched, was about two feet tall and encased in a bubble of glass, like a bell jar.

Not only did he refuse to pay, but Grandpa threw the salesman down a long flight of stairs, the same one where my mother and Aunt Mary Ann dropped the block of ice. The salesman never returned. But Grandma got to keep the holy statue, free of charge. My mother inherited it when Grandma died, and whenever I helped Ma clean the house, it was my job to dust its rounded globe. I never opened the glass bubble, but I peered at the saint safe inside. Though it would be a poetic story, it was not the same statue my aunt Mary Ann tried to beat Grandpa with years later.

Thanks to Uncle Al, Grandpa landed a job as a stevedore down at the Linden Avenue docks, stenciling names of places he would never visit onto wooden boxes destined for the high seas. He stole the long, chrome stencil guns and brought them home, thinking he was doing the family a favor. He quit the job because, he said, it was too easy. But there may have been more to it than that. Grandpa got into a fight with a fellow member of the International Longshoremen's Association while eating with his brother Bicky at Nedick's diner in the Grove Street PATH station. While Grandpa was eating a hot dog, a dock worker named Joseph Wykoff hit him in the forehead with a portable coffee urn. But Grandpa retaliated.

The next day, my mother was waiting for a train at the PATH station when she overheard some guy say to a cop, "Hey, what happened to the pay phone?"

"Oh, fucking Beansie pulled it off the wall and beat some guy in the head with it." Everybody knew Beansie. And it was just another one of his tantrums. My mother slinked away, but later that day she read all about the fight in *The Jersey Journal*.

This time, Grandpa was the victim for a change. All the detectives in the city were on the lookout for Wykoff, whom the papers described as a "dock character" and "an ally of Frank 'Biffo' DeLorenzo." Ma wasn't sure who Biffo was, but with a friend named Biffo, Wykoff had to be bad. When he hit Grandpa with the urn, Wykoff was already under indictment for breaking-and-entering and possession of burglar tools and was out on $15,000 bail for possession of a dangerous weapon.

After getting stitches at the Medical Center, Grandpa talked to the cops about Wykoff, and was released. But early the next morning, Grandpa was picked up for his own disorderly-person's charge. When questioned about Wykoff, he changed his story from the day before and said he got hurt when he fell and hit his head on the curb. Who knows why he changed his story. Maybe Grandpa was afraid Biffo and Wykoff would strangle him for ratting. Or maybe the bad guys felt they had to stick together, like all those criminals on *Batman*.

In 1935 Grandpa was arrested at least four times. His first victim, Gabriel Gurman, worked at a butcher shop and was cleaning up the blood and bones one March evening when Grandpa and a friend came through the door. At first they asked Gurman for five cents, which he gladly handed over, in the hopes they'd leave him alone. But then, always the overachiever, Grandpa asked for ten cents more. Gurman, starting to get nervous now, gave Grandpa the ten cents.

Sensing the butcher's weakness and unwillingness to fight, Grandpa snatched a large butcher knife from the countertop while his friend stood lookout in the doorway. Grandpa held the knife over Gurman's head while he riffled through the poor guy's pockets with his free hand. He came up with $32, and ran. Maybe some cop on the beat noticed the robbers burst out from the butcher-shop door, or maybe Gurman screamed for help. After a short foot chase through the downtown streets, the cops cornered Grandpa.

While out on bail two months later, Grandpa was arrested again for assault and battery. His crimes often overlapped, one on top of the other, like a deck of cards when you fan it out during a magic trick: Pick a crime, any crime.

When he wasn't out stealing, Grandpa was out drinking and fighting. Most nights, after a bout, his kids could hear him coming, weaving down the street and growling like a mad dog. He would often come home smelling of booze and covered in blood, and would then pass out on the kitchen floor, leaving his kids to drag him into the living room, where he'd sleep it off night after night.

From the next room, the family could hear Grandpa sing himself to sleep. There was no radio, since he had hocked it to play the horses. A cappella, Grandpa would sing an old Bing Crosby tune: "When day is done and shadows fall and twilight's due, my lonely heart keeps sinking with the sun. Although I miss your tender kiss the whole night through, I miss you most of all when day is done." Grandpa liked "When Day Is Done" so much that he once recorded it at a booth in Coney Island, dedicating it to Grandma. "Hey, Boobie, this is for you," the record began. (Years later, after Grandpa died, my mother and her brothers found the haunting recording and burned it.)

Grandpa's worst binges were always around Easter. Maybe because the moon was guaranteed to be full—since Easter Sunday is based on the Paschal full moon—Grandpa always lost his mind during Holy Week. One Good Friday, Judge Zampella refused to lock Grandpa up after he broke every piece of furniture in the house. Grandpa was a Catholic, the judge reasoned, and it was Holy Week. My aunt Mary Ann cursed the judge over his Jersey City logic and was almost locked up herself. The rest of the kids kept their mouths shut.

The morning after a particularly harsh fight, Grandpa would send one of them to the Palace drugstore for three or four sticks of eye makeup to cover his black eyes. He would sit in front of the mirror and blend the different shades until they were perfect.

Grandpa was incredibly vain, and blamed baldness for ruining his life. His hair started coming out at age twenty-six, and by the time he was twenty-eight, he was pretty bald. Not completely bald, but close. Whenever his son Robby combed his own thick black hair in front of the mirror, Grandpa flew into a jealous rage and threatened to kill him.

To give his skin a healthy glow, Grandpa liked to sunbathe on the roof, reading a detective magazine or smoking marijuana to pass the time. When he wanted, Grandpa could be handsome and even charming. But those times were rare. He was usually covered in scabs and bruises, cursing out everyone around him.

One of his favorite objects was his gun—a .45, which he kept in a strongbox without a lock, stowed away on the top shelf of the kitchen closet. We're not sure if he ever used it to kill anyone. Or if he simply preferred his bare hands.

In August 1935, Grandpa was arrested for atrocious assault and battery, the crime that would seal his reputation as a murderer. Though it was by far his most serious crime, it was the one we knew the least about. The complainant's last name was Craig, from Brooklyn. I often wondered if he was related to Joseph Craig, the boxer Hague had managed years before. But there were no stories written about it in *The Jersey Journal,* and the records were sketchy. My mother tried to find out more about the crime after Grandpa died, but the county worker in charge of such documents said that the only records kept were those filed under homicide. And this wasn't quite a homicide. Back in the 1930s, without a dead body, atrocious assault was the highest charge the cops could bring.

Ma suspected that the records were on file somewhere but that the clerk was just too lazy to look them up. The ancient files were kept inside Murdoch Hall, the old Medical Center building where Grandma had worked back in the 1940s. Because of a broken window, a family of pigeons flew inside one of the file rooms and took up residence. Many of the criminal records were covered in bird droppings and were ruined. Others simply sat there, yellowing and decaying. If they still existed, Grandpa's files lay buried beneath a ton of long-forgotten murders and homicides, file upon file, box upon box, row after row, and room after room of other families' crimes, tragedies, and sorrows.

All we had to go on were our own family stories. Aunt Katie said that during a campaign rally for Hague, a riot broke out. Craig was clubbed in the mayhem, and Grandpa was framed for the attack. Craig eventually died, but too late for the cops to charge Grandpa with murder. Knowing Hague, it's not a stretch to think that Grandpa was framed. Especially if Craig was related to the boxer Hague had managed.

But then again, Grandpa was a man who, a few decades later, would plot to murder his own children and grandchildren. It seems as if Grandpa could have willingly beaten Craig to death. He would probably even have enjoyed it.

While out on bail a month later, Grandpa was arrested again, for breaking-and-entering and larceny. He pleaded not guilty to all his charges but was sentenced to seven years for the assault on Craig. In 1935, Grandpa went away—not to the country or overseas, but away. In Jersey City, when someone mentions that a relative has "gone away," it means they've gone to jail or to the crazy house in Secaucus. Jersey Citizens, though they'd have you believe they've seen it all, were never enthusiastic travelers.

Grandpa went not to Atlantic City or Miami, two popular destinations for the most adventurous Jersey Citizens, but to Trenton State Prison. With time off for good behavior, he spent five years in the "Big House," the state penitentiary, where the electric chair was kept.

They were wonderful years for my mother and her brothers and sister—Beansie-free years. But the times he had hit them, knocked them down the stairs, stuck a live Christmas tree into the coal-burning stove, balls and all, and almost burned the kitchen down, were still fresh in their young minds.

And it wasn't long before Grandpa was back from Trenton State, re-creating all those precious family moments. My mother was sitting outside her house the day he was sprung, and she saw him come down the street. She was only nine years old, but she recognized him right away. Grandpa bent down and kissed her, then walked inside, where Grandma was curling her hair, getting ready for his big entrance. When she saw him, she dropped the curling iron on the floor and was swept up in his embrace. They hugged and kissed like in a movie. It was the worst day of my mother's life.

Soon Grandpa was assaulting them again. He beat my uncle Sonny up so bad that he threatened to kill Grandpa someday. When my uncle Robby asked to go play in the pumps on a hot summer day, Grandpa filled the tub up with ice-cold water and viciously threw him in it. Then, when my mother had her hair up in a towel and was drinking a glass of milk, Grandpa unleashed this particularly obscene string of compliments: "What are you drinking milk for, you Hindu dying-looking fucking pimple-faced cocksucker? You'll get more pimples on your fucking face."

Ironically, my mother always had beautiful skin, just like her father.

With a monster like that for a husband, Grandma should have packed up the kids and left. But she couldn't leave Grandpa. She was afraid. Not for herself, but for her children. Grandpa told her that if she left, he would track her down and kill the kids. That was why Grandma stayed.

Though he scared them, hurt them, and threatened to murder them, Grandpa embarrassed his children more than anything. The other kids in the neighborhood called Uncle Jerry, Uncle Sonny, and Uncle Robby jailbirds, beat them up, and wouldn't let them play ball with them in the lot. All because of Grandpa.

My mother didn't have to worry about stickball, but she had her own problems. She once woke up for school and found a half-dozen restaurant sugar shakers on the kitchen table.

"Where'd they come from, Mama?" she asked.

"Your father brought them home in his coat last night," Grandma answered, shaking her head and wringing her small, white hands. "He was drunk."

The next day, my mother and her girlfriends walked uptown to go swimming at Dickinson High School, the neoclassical Parthenon-like structure that's visible from the New Jersey Turnpike approach to the Holland Tunnel. Like the Art Deco Medical Center, Dickinson's elaborate architecture seemed somehow misplaced in Jersey City. The high school looked lost up there on its hill, like a crisp, new dollar bill you found lying in the gutter.

After swimming at Dickinson, my mother and her friends walked down the long hill, their hair drying in the warm sun. Along the way, they stopped for hamburgers and coffee at the local Greek diner. The owner, Poly, brought them their order, but when they asked for sugar, he threw up his hands.

"Some sonofabitchin' drunk came in last night and stole all our sugar," he yelled. My mother cringed and almost slid under the Formica counter.

She was actually relieved when Grandpa wound up behind bars again, out of their lives once more. It didn't take long. While the rest of the country was at war, Grandpa was arrested and went away again in October 1943 for robbing a guy named Stanley Miniski, of Northport, Long Island, of three hundred dollars and a watch and chain after the two had been out drinking together in a saloon.

This time the crime made the paper, with the headline FATHER OF FIVE SENT TO PRISON. According to the story, Grandma passed out in the courtroom, but not before shouting, "Whatever is to become of my five children?" As if Beansie were a positive role model and great provider. The kids could surely steal their own bottles of milk, smelly oranges, stencil guns, and shakers of sugar.

If only the government had had the foresight to ship Grandpa off to Germany, he could have terrorized the enemy rather than his family. But he was too old for the service and had too many children. Instead, he was sentenced to three-to-seven. He was in prison barely a month when he was let out again, bound in handcuffs and shackles and accompanied by prison guards, taken from his cell just long enough to attend the funeral of his son.

12

FALLING STAR

Sonny was my eternally adolescent uncle. There were times, as I approached my own adolescence, when I tried to imagine him as a grown man who had made something of his life, left something behind, or at least spawned his own children. I imagined birthday cards coming in the mail from Uncle Sonny with twenty bucks inside, just like the ones my other aunts and uncles sent each year.

I knew Uncle Sonny's story well, so well that I felt I knew him. Sometimes it was like he was still alive, since the older I got, the more I learned about him. Every year, on April 10, his birthday, Ma went to church, even the years it didn't fall on Easter Sunday or during Holy Week. It was like she was going to visit him. Like he was waiting for her in one of the church pews.

My mother and Sonny were a year and six days apart and looked exactly alike, so much so that some people thought they were twins. Uncle Sonny didn't like to eat, not that there was ever much to eat in their house. My mother was always hungry, always felt an emptiness in her stomach, so when Uncle Sonny hid his vegetables under his plate, my mother would eat them for him. They had a good thing going.

Grandma was the provider in the family, with help from Sonny, the oldest of the five. Because he was the oldest, Uncle Sonny was very serious. He worked for the local butcher delivering meat to downtown brownstones and tenements and gave all the money he earned to Grandma so she could provide an unsteady diet of lentils and stale Italian bread. While Grandma worked at a local luncheonette, my mother cleaned the house and took care of the younger children—Mary Ann, Robby, and Jerry, whom they used to call Junior, since he was named after Grandpa.

Uncle Sonny's story starts on a Tuesday night in 1944, when he was fourteen. It had been a hot week in August, with temperatures bubbling over a hundred degrees. It was too hot to sit in the house at night, so the whole family, and everyone in the neighborhood, was out on their stoops. While they were sitting there, Grandma argued with Sonny about what he was doing the next day, his day off. He had plans to work on his clubhouse, in an empty lot on First Street, with his friends. But Grandma wanted him to go to the movies instead. As they argued, a shooting star streaked across the sky. The kids were excited. But Grandma said that whenever you saw a falling star, it meant that someone was going to die.

The next morning, Sonny stubbornly left the house to meet his friends. Before he slammed the door, he turned and looked at his brothers and sisters seated at the wooden kitchen table. My mother got a good look at him before he stormed out, like a slow-motion part in the movies she saw at the Stanley Theatre: his jet-black hair, straight like hers, covered in a sailor hat that he'd borrowed from his brother Junior, striped polo shirt over a skinny seventy-five-pound body, black sneakers, and baggy jeans bulging with swimming trunks underneath. Sonny wore the trunks in case he and his buddies decided to go swimming down by the docks later that day. It was that kind of day, so hot it makes you want to do something stupid, like swim in the dirty Hudson.

Grandma went to work at the luncheonette and told my mother to meet her there when she was done cleaning the house. If her boss wasn't looking, Grandma could serve my seventy-pound mother a bowl of soup or a ham sandwich, and maybe even give her some food to take home to the others, who were now out playing in the vacant, garbage-strewn lot next door.

That afternoon, while finishing her chores, my mother happened to look out the window and notice a green-and-white police car, the old kind, with running boards and rounded hood popular in gangster movies from the 1930s. Because of the Depression, the war, and Hague's stolen tax money, new police cars hadn't been bought in years.

A cop in a dark blue uniform, the badge above his heart glinting in the high summer sun, walked over to the neighbors' stoop across the street. A group of kids soon gathered around and began looking up at my mother in the window. Her first thought was that Grandpa had broken out of jail. The cop looked up at the window and yelled to her, "Is your mother home?"

"No," she answered. "She's at work."

"Well, tell her to come to the police station after work," he said, walking back to his car.

After he pulled away, Annie, Grandma's best friend, called to my mother to come downstairs. When she got to the bottom of the rickety staircase, Annie was standing in the vestibule, closing the door gently behind her. She placed her hand on my mother's bony shoulder and said, "Junior's been killed by a truck."

"My little brother," my mother thought as a small bomb exploded in her brain. She couldn't speak. She remembered the shooting star from the night before.

As my mother stood there in the vestibule, dumbstruck, Annie went to find Bill Barrett, a boarder in her house who was one of the few people on Second Street who owned a car. She called Aunt Katie, who lived around the corner. With my despondent mother, they all gathered in Annie's kitchen and tried to work out a strategy for telling Grandma the bad news. Suddenly, the door opened and Junior walked in. Since he was supposed to be dead, they all flinched when they saw him. For a second, my mother thought it was Junior's ghost.

"Junior," my aunt Katie yelled. "What the fuck are you doing here? You're supposed to be dead." The hopeful thought that maybe this was another family's burden flashed in their heads. But my mother knew what was happening. She remembered the sailor hat. She knew it was Sonny who was dead. The cops simply had the wrong name, she told Aunt Katie.

Knowing Sonny was the firstborn, the police had thought he was named after his father, and therefore a Junior, the name stitched inside the cap. The cap Sonny had borrowed from Junior.

With the *new* news, the knowledge that Sonny was dead, Annie, Katie, Bill, and my mother climbed into Bill's car and headed for Montgomery Street, to the luncheonette.

"Sonny's been hurt," Annie hedged when she saw my grandmother behind the counter. "You better come home." On the short ride, less than a mile, Grandma wrung her hands, and my mother placed her skinny arm around her shoulders.

When they got home, Aunt Katie knelt before Grandma, who sat in a kitchen chair. Katie laid her hands on Grandma's hands and said slowly, "There's nothing you can do. Sonny is dead."

Grandma heard a sound like leaves falling inside her head. Then she fainted and fell off the kitchen chair.

At the morgue, they wouldn't let Grandma see Sonny, because his chest had been crushed in the accident. But she knew it was her son. She was told he was wearing swimming trunks beneath his pants.

Sonny's best friend, Vinnie Antoniack, later told my mother what had happened. Sonny and his friends were on their way to the Gypsum Company at the edge of town to try and scam some shingles from the dumping ground for the roof of their clubhouse. Sonny was pulling a wagon, so the trip was slow. Diadato DiTorio, a local truck driver, saw the boys and offered them a ride on the running board. I imagine them as the cast of *East Side Kids*—dirty, dressed in baggy clothes, always in black and white, jumping onto the running board of the truck. When they jumped off a few minutes later, Vinnie noticed that Sonny wasn't with them.

"Where's Sonny?" Vinnie asked the other boys. He looked down the street and saw the frail body of his friend lying in the gutter. Vinnie ran over and knelt down, shouting, "What happened?" to his friend. When he lifted Sonny's head for an answer, blood gushed out instead.

Diadato was taken into custody while the cops investigated. They determined that Sonny accidentally fell from the truck and was dragged underneath it when his wagon got caught in the wheels. Grandma didn't press charges. Friends encouraged her to sue, but Diadato had five small children of his own. His knowing he had killed her oldest son was punishment enough, Grandma said.

Grandma's hair began to turn white that night, and would be completely white by winter. Her four remaining children climbed into bed with her like kittens, and stayed up throughout the night crying.

It was standing room only at the Introcaso Funeral Home the next night. Sonny was small for his age, but he was a smart kid, the smartest on the block, and everyone liked him. The front-page story in *The Jersey Journal* that day told about the clubhouse and the kids' new plan to name it after Sonny—the Sonny Vena Victory Club. They would place a photo of Sonny inside as a tribute.

Sonny's popularity and the front-page news brought people who didn't even know Sonny to the funeral parlor. Italian relatives wailed in the heat of the room, the smell of the embalming chemicals smothered by so many bouquets of flowers. Instead of giving Grandma gardenias, Aunt Katie had gotten Uncle Al to collect money from the other longshoremen down at the docks. Though it was a beautiful gesture, Uncle Al gave Grandma only half of the collection. He and Katie kept the other half.

As soon as he died, stories of the supernatural started to attach themselves to Uncle Sonny. At the wake, people said he had once seen Jesus' face in the sky and pointed it out to everyone else, and that the *Hudson Dispatch* had snapped a picture of it and printed it in the paper the next day.

Aunt Katie said that when Sonny was little, he had carved his initials into the hot, black tar on Second Street. While he was bending over, a bee flew over his head and buzzed around three times. Years later, after Sonny died, cousin Chubby went back to the very same spot, took his knife, and cleaned out Sonny's carved initials. A bee flew over his head and buzzed around three times. It was Sonny's way of marking Chubby, of letting him know he was waiting for him in heaven and that it wasn't so bad up there.

At Sonny's wake, my mother stayed far away from the coffin, because the body inside didn't resemble her brother. The way she could tell it was really Sonny was by looking at his hands. Those were the hands she knew, their fingernails chewed and bloody, like Grandpa's. Ma didn't understand why the women were saying things like "He looks so good. So peaceful." To her, Sonny looked dead.

In the next room lay a man who had died of a heart attack. His widow was screaming loudly and singing sad songs that seeped through the thin walls. My mother was afraid to stay in the room with Sonny, but because of the sounds outside, she was even more afraid to leave. She wouldn't even go to the bathroom.

When the wake was almost through, one more guest arrived. It was Grandpa, chained in handcuffs, escorted by prison guards. He cried, tears sliding down his reddened face as he hobbled over to the coffin that held his son's crushed body. The guards let one hand free from the cuffs so Grandpa could stroke Sonny's cheek. My mother had no love for her father, but she felt sorry for him, like she would feel sorry for any stranger who sees his dead son for the first time. Some friends of Grandma's were angry to see him there. Who was he to cry? Never around to feed those kids. How could he even show his face?

At Holy Name Cemetery, where most of my relatives were buried and where Uncle Frankie met his lovers, Sonny's grave lay under an old apple tree, littered with decaying apples. There was no tombstone, since Grandma didn't have the money. A house brick marked the grave. My mother and the other children tossed small handfuls of apple-scented soil into Sonny's grave as his coffin was lowered.

After the funeral, Grandma and her four remaining children went to Annie's house for ham, rye bread, and potato salad. Grandma never returned to her job at the luncheonette, because it reminded her too much of Sonny. When he was old enough, Uncle Jerry got two jobs to help feed the family—setting up pins at a local bowling alley by night and delivering newspapers by day.

Grandma was never the same after 1944. Sonny had been her favorite, though his birth was the source of most of her life's pain. It was because of Sonny that Grandma had had to marry Grandpa. Until I was an adolescent, I hadn't realized that Grandma married Grandpa because she was pregnant. People had said that Grandma "got into trouble." I thought that simply meant she had met Grandpa.

For me, Grandma was no longer so pure. She was finally human. More important, Grandma had a good excuse for marrying Grandpa.

My mother, to retain Grandma's saintly image, insisted that she had been the victim of a splash pregnancy. That would make Sonny the blessed child of an immaculate conception, which would make his untimely death more meaningful than it actually was. He was the sacrificial lamb of Second Street, the savior who died too soon.

To make themselves feel better, the family concocted a reason for why Sonny died so young: Had he lived to be an adult, he would have eventually killed Grandpa, and the sin of patricide would have been an even greater tragedy than Sonny's birth or death. God took him while he was still innocent. But I always thought it would have been a good thing if Sonny had killed Grandpa. Years of pain and suffering could have been avoided.

A sadness, like Sonny's ghost, stayed with my mother and her siblings in that Second Street apartment for years, until Grandpa came home from Trenton and replaced the sadness with terror. Aunt Mary Ann got enough money together to eventually buy Sonny a tombstone. It infuriated Grandpa, because he wanted the money for himself.

But Grandpa could never lay another hand on Sonny. With a front-page story above the fold all about him, a victory club in his name, and local sainthood granted forever, Sonny was probably better off dead.

Had Sonny lived, he very well may have killed Grandpa. Or maybe Grandpa would have killed him. Or maybe—worse—Uncle Sonny would have lived a mediocre life, working himself to death in a factory or getting beaten up by the cops like Chubby. Instead, Sonny was as prized and as safe as that Virgin Mary behind the glass bubble, canonized and finally above it all.

Almost a half century later, I decided to check out Uncle Sonny's story for myself, to relive his posthumous, adolescent moment of glory. I walked over to the library on Jersey Avenue, in a huge limestone building, the same library where Sonny and my mother had done their homework together, the same library where I had researched school papers, the same place Grandpa had worked as a security guard in the 1960s, before he tried to shoot us.

Remembering all the objects Grandpa had stolen from there, I nervously took the worn marble stairs to the second-floor reference room two at a time, worried that someone might notice a resemblance and demand I return the encyclopedias and Indian arrowheads. I could have taken the elevator, but it had been one of Grandpa's jobs to run the elevator when he worked there. It gave off bad vibes. I thought that in a final fit of rage Grandpa might send me hurtling down to the basement to an early death.

The 1944 reel of microfilm was thick, dark, and shiny and felt good in my hand, so heavy with all the stories from that year, with the story of Uncle Sonny. The machine was not easy to operate. I wound the film through the take-up reel and figured out which buttons to push. I sped through winter, January stories passing in a blur, stories of grieving families whose sons were killed in the war, picture after picture of young heroes in uniform. That blurred into spring ads for Easter clothes and hats. And then there was summer. In search of August 10, the day after Sonny died, I sped past the steamy months of June and July, with their baseball stories and weather reports. When I hit August, I slowed down, using my fingers to turn the thick reel. I didn't want to miss it.

August 7 . . . August 8 . . . my head and eyes hurting from the blurred microfilm, the focus off enough to be annoying. I felt a little nauseated, both from the moving images and the anxiety of getting closer. I found August 9, and then the last page, the editorial page. . . . And then, there, on August 10 . . .

A big black hole where the lead story should have been.

There was a left-hand column story on FDR, a tear, and then nothing. Where was Sonny? Before I even finished asking myself, I knew the answer. I knew what had happened. I knew that Grandpa had torn the story out while working in the library years ago. It felt as if his hand had reached from the grave, through the soil at Holy Name Cemetery, and ripped the clipping right from under my eyes.

I felt a pain, a dull ache in my chest, the pain my mother must have felt whenever her father did something horrible. The pain Aunt Mary Ann still felt, even years later. I'd heard those bad stories about Grandpa so many times, I thought I'd become numb to them. But this was a new one. I felt like Grandpa had whacked me in the gut. My hands shook as I fingered the reel and tried to figure out what to do next. But what could I do? Like Grandma, Ma, and her siblings years ago, I was helpless. I wanted to point to the screen and scream, yell out, tell the people sitting on either side of me what was missing. That Grandpa had stolen it. But no one would understand.

I couldn't even complain to the librarian. I knew who had stolen this story, this evidence, and I was too embarrassed to even mention it. The story was Sonny's only glory, his fifteen inches of fame in the local paper, and the family's only printed news story without an arrest attached to it. Grandpa had wiped it out, in one swift tear. It was Grandpa's final, posthumous act of stupidity and violence. His sucker punch in the face of family history.

I did the only thing I could do. I pressed the rewind button and watched the microfilm go whizzing back in time. Summer turned to spring turned to winter and the new year, 1944.

13

THE HEIGHTS

When my sister was pregnant with her second baby in 1980, she decided to move out of the Gregory and out of downtown altogether. Paula had been the first in our family to drive a car and the first girl to go to college. Now she was the first to buy a house. We moved with her—Ma, Daddy, and I into the first floor, Paula and her family upstairs. Stanley took the basement apartment. Cousin Mike, the lawyer, did the closing on the house, as a favor to Paula. It helped having a lawyer in the family.

The house was a mother/daughter two-family yellow brick on a street called Summit Avenue—as if we'd reached a mountaintop or some other high point in our lives. We had, in a way, thanks to Paula. Summit Avenue was part of the Heights, the northernmost ward of Jersey City. Since it was mostly populated by German Americans and other fair-skinned residents, it was known as Little Johannesburg. The area was also populated by lots of mosquitoes because of the nearby meadows and reservoir. One of the biggest parks in the Heights was called Mosquito Park.

Paula's house was a fixer-upper, but it was beautiful. Out front was a big porch, surrounded by a pretty, black wrought-iron gate with loops and swirls. There was a huge hallway and a wide staircase with a sloping wooden banister that ended on a landing lit by an oval stained-glass window. The floors were polished parquet, with swastika-like patterns around the borders of each room. The bottom half of the walls were covered in embossed antique leather.

Paula even got a dog to go with the house. His name was Marty, and he was a golden retriever. He was the only dog in Jersey City who was fed steak on a regular basis. I had always wanted a dog, but our apartment above the Majestic had been too small. When I was really little, I wanted a dog so badly that I pretended to be one for a few weeks, crawling around on all fours and drinking water from a wooden salad bowl. My favorite TV show had been the exercise program with Jack La Lanne, because at the end of the show, Jack brought out his German shepherd, who looked just like Buddy. By the time we got Marty, I was fifteen, too old to enjoy him. I had better things to do than play with a dog. I had new friends to make in my new neighborhood.

The move to the Heights was a major change for all of us, but it was most traumatic for Daddy. Since he didn't drive, he had no way of getting downtown to the Majestic. He couldn't place his bets with Uncle Henry, who also didn't drive, so I had to buy Daddy a Pick-It lottery ticket every day. I think he was too ashamed to do it himself. The Pick-It was for old ladies. The number was what guys played.

But the legal lottery was becoming more and more popular. Hardly anybody played the number anymore. As overzealous prosecutors tried to make names for themselves, illegal gambling became more and more taboo. In 1984, Uncle Henry was fined $5,000 and sentenced to five years in jail. Not St. Lucy's, but jail. Fortunately, he was allowed to serve his time in the Hudson County Jail Annex, a much less dangerous prison in Secaucus. That way he could visit Uncle Tommy on weekends at nearby Meadowview.

Each day, I would buy Daddy a lottery ticket and leave it on his clock radio at night when I came home from gallivanting, as my mother liked to call it. Without the Majestic downstairs, Daddy stopped drinking, except for special occasions. I knew what a loss moving away from the tavern was for him. At the turn of the century, when Dziadzia arrived in Jersey City, he and practically every one of his brothers had opened his own tavern. The Stapinskis were tavern owners by trade. And tavern lovers by nature. During Prohibition, Dziadzia made home brew to keep his downtown business afloat. One night in 1927, while Dziadzia was out, Babci had to tend bar. She was pregnant with Uncle Tommy at the time. That night, an Elliot Ness wanna-be wandered in and noticed the bottles without labels on the shelves. The tavern was raided, and Babci was so upset that she fainted and fell to the floor. Dziadzia was taken to the Seventh Street precinct and arrested for bootlegging.

That autumn, when Uncle Tommy was born, he began having spells. He had epilepsy, the doctors said, and Babci blamed herself. She thought that if she hadn't fallen down on the night of the raid, maybe her baby would have been born healthy.

Because of the home brew, Dziadzia's tavern was closed down, and he paid a fine. Because of the Tommy tragedy, he never opened another bar, but he continued to patronize the family's other Gammontown establishments. The night Dziadzia was attacked and hit on the head, he was on his way home from one of those neighborhood bars, Wozniak's on Morris Street.

In a way, I was glad Daddy didn't find a bar in our new neighborhood. Tripping up the stairs on the way home from the Majestic was one thing. But I didn't want him wandering around outside getting hit on the head like Dziadzia. For the first time in my life, I worried about Daddy. I didn't like the feeling. I was happier when it was the other way around, and Daddy was worrying about me. But I couldn't help it. Daddy needed looking after.

While walking out on the porch one day, he stepped on a nail. By the time he showed it to us weeks later, red streaks were running up his leg. He went to the hospital, and our incompetent family doctor almost killed him by giving him a glucose-water drip. Daddy, it turned out, was a diabetic, which was why he didn't feel the nail in his foot and why the sore on his foot hadn't healed. It was a no-brainer.

Daddy almost lost his leg but got away easy, with only four toes amputated. He had to wear special orthopedic shoes. Standing on the platform at the Cold Storage wasn't so easy for him anymore. But he had no choice. My mother had lost her job when the DMV office closed, its latest agent involved in yet another scandal, this one involving stolen sales-tax money.

Ma blamed Daddy's diabetes on all the Sara Lee cake he had brought home over the years. But there was more to it than that. Drinking for forty years hadn't helped. Neither had smoking. So Daddy stopped smoking, cold turkey. He left his last pack of Marlboros on the mantelpiece in the new house, a trophy of his accomplishment. With all his free, sober time, he liked to sit out on the porch and watch the unfamiliar faces go by. Now and then he'd throw a tennis ball down the stoop for Marty to run after.

I knew virtually nothing about the Heights. But I soon discovered that the local kids were like the kids in nearby North Bergen: into suede, corduroy, long hair, hard drugs, and kegs of beer. By my sixteenth birthday, I was wearing peasant blouses and Lee jeans, complete with a patch of the Rolling Stones tongue. I was also smoking pot and drinking under the gazebo at Mosquito Park. I didn't consider smoking pot a crime, since I rationalized that drugs should be legalized. And drinking? I was just picking up where Daddy had left off.

Compared to my friends and boyfriends, I was a goody two-shoes. The kids in the Heights had more money than the kids I'd grown up with downtown, so they had more disposable income to spend on mescaline and LSD. My downtown friends had been happy with a pint of malt liquor and a loose joint.

Crimes in the Heights were committed out of boredom, not need. A guy I went out with for four weeks in 1982 turned out to be an ex-con who had stolen money from the safe at the Foodtown supermarket. Another boyfriend was regularly beaten up by the local cops for being a druggie and all-around troublemaker. My serious high school boyfriend, whom I took to the senior prom, was a cousin of Bobby Manna, the mobster who had befriended Mayor Kenny. I didn't know it until my mother interrogated my boyfriend one day to find out who exactly her baby was dating.

For the first time, Ma really started to get on my nerves. I had to carry mouthwash with me so that she wouldn't smell the smoke or beer on my breath when I walked in the door. She forced me to lie to her constantly about where I was going and who I was going with. It was for her own peace of mind that I failed to tell her about the ride my friends and I got to the Cars concert in the back of a shag-carpeted van with five stoned guys we didn't even know. Or the time I went camping with my friends—but had to sleep alone in a tent with my boyfriend. Or the many Saturday afternoons I spent smoking pot and hanging out at Washington Square Park in Greenwich Village.

My friends' parents weren't as strict as Ma. Why couldn't she be more like them? Whenever I hung out "down the tracks"—near the old railroad cut on the West Side—I had to sleep over at my friend Gretchen's house. There was always a bonfire at the tracks. One stoned girl set her long, blond hair on fire while dancing around it. I never got that close. But the smoke left me smelling like I'd just gone out to fight a blaze with Engine Company Number 9. Gretchen's mother didn't notice the smell. Either her nose was stuffed or, more likely, she was a complete idiot. My mother would have been all over me if I'd come home smelling like that. After a night down the tracks, I'd sleep at Gretchen's, then wash my clothes before going home.

My friend Tammy did mescaline right in her own bedroom. She even convinced her parents to get her a Mustang, which we'd drag-race down at Caven Point, near where the Black Tom explosion had happened years ago. We'd drive over a hundred miles an hour on the concrete pier, Jimi Hendrix blasting from Tammy's state-of-the-art speakers, Budweiser nips clamped and sloshing between our knees. The only reason we didn't crash and burn was that Ma was home saying her rosary.

The greatest thing about becoming a teenager was learning to drive. A whole canon of fifties songs was written about it, but I thought I was the first teenager ever to feel liberated by a steering wheel and a motor. I realized that greener pastures actually existed within driving distance. Going on vacation was one thing, but getting in a car and just going somewhere, anywhere, wherever I wanted, was truly exhilarating. With my friends, I drove to Garrett Mountain out near Paterson or went camping on weekends at the Delaware Water Gap. I drove past farms in western Jersey and beach towns in south Jersey.

To get out of town, you had to be subjected to the worst possible strip of pavement. It was as if the city planners had saved the absolute worst street for last. Tonnelle Avenue (pronounced *TON-lee*) was filled with chemical plants built next to toxic-waste sites, jug handles, auto-paint shops, sex-video stores, a place called Hubcap World, and the occasional hooker motel. If you drove fast enough, it all sped past your window in an unrecognizable blur. There was no sidewalk on Tonnelle Avenue. It was built for cars and tractor trailers, as if humans were not driving them. It was the outer fringe of a place that was already edgy, the puss-filled nodule on a rotted limb. But once you got past Tonnelle, you were out, headed to somewhere green, away from the decaying buildings, burnt piers, and dirty streets.

While out gallivanting, I realized that the Heights wasn't all that different from downtown. Most of my new friends' families lived on swag, just like we did. Donna, a girl who lived around the corner, sobbed one Christmas night after showing us the three dozen sweaters—mostly velour—that her father had given her. We couldn't understand what the problem was. A few of the sweaters were ugly, with orange and green velvety stripes, but for the most part it was a nice haul. Donna would never have to wear the same sweater twice.

Between sobs, Donna explained what the problem was. "He didn't buy any of this," she sniffled, waving her arm over her bed, desk, and carpet, where the offensive sweaters lay. "What kind of gift is that?" It had never occurred to me to complain about the merchandise that fell off the truck. Maybe it wasn't always what you would have picked out had you been able to do some proper shopping. And maybe it didn't always provide for the perfect gift. But swag was part of everyday life.

And then it hit me. Christmas was not every day. Swag and Christmas did not mix. Wrapping it up and giving swag as a present was unacceptable. It was tacky, and much more morally wrong than swag itself. A girl would rather get Fruit of the Loom underwear and socks—a typical Hudson County Christmas present—than swag. It just wasn't done.

Then again, Donna's father was connected. He wasn't in the Mob, but it seemed he could have been pretty close to it. She was lucky he was even alive to give her presents. Besides, Donna wasn't exactly a saint herself. Many an afternoon we would wind up at the local drugstore, Donna shoving cosmetics into her faded Lee jeans. I was always terrified of shoplifting. Swiping ashtrays was one thing—restaurants expected you to steal them. I figured it was free advertising for them. But shoplifting was illegal, something you could go to jail for, the Hudson County Jail, the house of horrors where Grandpa had spent several years of his life.

My friend Nina had shoplifted a few times from the downtown Woolworth's. Eventually, an old clerk in the store saw her and told her mother, an apathetic woman who was known for taking other people's chicken bones home from parish affairs. "For the dog," she claimed. But who ever heard of giving your dog chicken bones? My mother felt sorry for her and said she probably made soup from them. My mother—who kept her eye on everyone and everything—let me know that she knew that the Woolworth's clerk knew about Nina. It was an indirect warning. But I would never shoplift, mostly because I never could let my mother down like that.

What made me even more uncomfortable than going "shopping" with Donna and Nina was going to church with my friend Molly. Her father would give her the family envelope to place in the collection basket each week. Every Sunday, Molly would steal the money and deposit the empty envelope in the basket. It made my stomach turn, but not out of fear of God or guilt about the Catholic Church. By then, I was developing into a smart-ass teenage agnostic who believed the Church was a corrupt, sexist, homophobic multimillion-dollar tax-free business. My fear stemmed from knowing that someday Molly would be found out.

At the end of the season, when the church bulletin listed how much each family had donated that year, there was a big fat zero next to Molly's family's name. Her father, unlike Nina's mother, was not so apathetic. He was apoplectic. Molly was grounded for much of sophomore year.

I stole. But in a socially acceptable way. When I was old enough, I carried on my father's tradition of coming home after work with a brown paper package under my arm. My first job was as an ice cream scooper at Carvel on Journal Square. The place was at a very bad intersection, across the street from a White Castle hamburger joint, which back then was a hangout for the neighborhood bums. I kept waiting for somebody to trip out on acid there, like at the North Bergen franchise. It never happened, though lots of other shit went down at the White Castle—which we nicknamed White Casket. When you got hungry enough, you might take your life into your hands and venture over to the Casket, where you were guaranteed to see at least one person sprawled out on the tile floor.

By comparison, Carvel was clean and wholesome, filled mostly with young kids and ice cream-a-holics, who were weird but usually not dangerous. The Vanilla Fudge Man, who came in every night and purchased one pint of hand-scooped vanilla fudge, was in his sixties, wore a stocking cap and a shy smile, and probably lived nearby with his elderly mother. Except for his trips to Carvel, he was likely a shut-in. But he was harmless. The Cherry Vanilla Man was another story. He was younger, and liked to flirt with me and my teenage coworkers. One night, when my friend Michelle wouldn't respond to his advances, he got a little crazy and hurled his cup of cherry vanilla ice cream at her.

I had my own run-in with a local Sikh, who bought a sheet cake one Saturday afternoon. As a service, we would squeeze a birthday greeting or some other celebratory message onto your cake with sugared gel, free of charge. The man in the turban handed me a long note in his native language and insisted that I copy the entire paragraph onto the ice cream cake, verbatim. I tried, but screwed up, which sent the man into a rage. Maybe I wound up cursing his mother on her ninety-fifth birthday. But what did I know? He left, without the cake, screaming a slew of foreign curses at me. I was left to scrape the squiggles off the sheet cake for recycling. Nothing at Carvel got wasted. Almost nothing.

One time, I got stoned before going to work. I tripped out—not as badly as the girl at the North Bergen White Castle did, but it felt just as bad inside my head. I remember washing aluminum cake molds in the industrial-size sink in the back of the store and thinking that I had become a robot. I could see myself washing and washing, removed from the action. I washed mold after mold after mold after mold. (There were only five shapes, from which all Carvel cakes were fashioned: round, rectangular, log, Cookie Puss/leprechaun/Abe Lincoln/pilgrim, and Fudgie the Whale/Santa/Elf/guitar/tennis racket/ghost.)

Minutes dragged on like hours, and after a while I started to worry that maybe I was dead and this was purgatory, washing mold after mold in the back room of Carvel. I freaked myself out so badly that I wanted to go yelling and screaming from the store, hurling Fudgie the Whale molds onto Kennedy Boulevard. But I somehow managed to stay calm. Once I came down, I swore I'd never smoke pot again. At least not at work. It was too dangerous.

There was a robbery at Carvel once, on my day off. A scooper named Chloe was working with the owner, a little Paul Simon looka-like. When the robber came in, the owner was in the bathroom, reading the paper on the bowl. Chloe was forced to sit on a tub of ice cream inside the walk-in freezer while the guy emptied the cash register. She was shaken up, and almost quit. Especially when the owner emerged from the john too late and scolded her for giving up the cash.

He was my first lesson in hating the boss. The owner was not from Hudson County. He owned a Mercedes and commuted from the suburbs each day. He was so stingy when mixing his tubs of ice cream that customers dubbed the rum raisin "rum raisinless." His chocolate chip mint was so light on chips and mint flavoring that people thought it was lime sherbet. We were taught to make parfaits the tight-ass way: brush a little syrup around the inside of the cup, then fill it with ice cream. From the outside, it looked like the syrup was swirled throughout.

He taught us the "S" method of scooping ice cream, something he was probably taught at Carvel College. The S motion was designed to place as little ice cream in the scooper as possible, filling the center of the scoop with air. The ball of ice cream—light as Styrofoam—often fell off its cone perch with one lick. The licker, usually a small child, would scream until his parents bought him a new ice cream cone. Customers got one for the price of two.

On a regular basis, our boss ignored Carvel College rules, using unsanctioned Disney characters and drawing copyrighted Smurfs onto sheet cakes. But his worst offense was making obscene ice cream cakes for bachelor and bachelorette parties. On at least one occasion, he made a cake shaped like a penis. He used the log-cake mold but had to improvise the rest. While sculpting the cake, he ran back and forth to the bathroom every few minutes to check on his still life. And never once did he wash his hands. When he was done with his masterpiece—covered in flesh-tone peach ice cream, with colored coconut for pubic hair—he told us he was leaving early. He left us with the cake—and the dirty work. We were barely sixteen years old, the age when you're most easily embarrassed, left to face the man who came to pick up the penis.

We were horrified to find that he was black. Peach ice cream was out of the question. My friends and I poured chocolate shell over the shaft, which hardened on impact. It was a brilliant Carvel move, something they didn't teach at Carvel College.

When the owner wasn't there, my friends and I took our revenge. We dug deep into the tubs and gave kids their fair share of ice cream. Then every night, before mopping and closing up the store, I would call home and take my family's order.

Paul, my little nephew, always asked for a cup of chocolate ice cream with chocolate syrup, chocolate crunch, and chocolate sprinkles on top. My mother and sister loved the ice cream sandwiches, called Flying Saucers, and my brother, a hot fudge sundae. Basil, my brother-in-law, liked vanilla fudge in a cup. And for Lauren, the baby, I brought home a small cup of soft vanilla. On special occasions, I'd swipe a Cookie Puss cake. I always brought my father a plastic container of Thinny-Thin, the sugar-free ice cream, because of his diabetes. But I would have loved to have brought him a big banana split every night, dripping with wet walnuts, fudge, and whipped cream, with a cherry on top. The Great Provider deserved more than a Thinny-Thin and a Pick-It ticket at the end of the day.

With a large paper bag in my arms, just like the kind Daddy used to carry, I'd walk in the door each night. Until one night the owner staked us out from the White Casket. The next day, my friends and I were fired for stealing merchandise.

I was outraged. How dare he fire us? He was lucky we didn't report him to phlegm-throated founder Tom Carvel for all his franchise and copyright infractions. But it was probably for the best that we were let go. With all that free ice cream, my nephew was entering what would later become known as his chubby phase. My brother was sprouting love handles. And I was starting to grow hips.

14

THROUGH THE TUNNEL

I made a break for it after high school, escaping to New York University, commuting every day on the PATH train. Greenwich Village was only a few miles away, but it may as well have been in another solar system.

At first I was intimidated by the other students. I sat at the back of the classroom most of that first semester, trying to hide. Every time I opened my mouth, I was embarrassed by my accent. I was convinced everyone was smarter than I was, that I didn't belong there, and that one day the dean of the School of Arts and Sciences would discover my existence, find out about all the criminals in my family, and have me escorted from campus.

NYU was the first school I'd attended where the students and teachers were not like me: Catholic, working-class, heterosexual, and jaded from years of living in Hudson County. There was a woman at my work-study job who was a lesbian and a girl in my Italian class who, ironically, wore a flowered housedress and had dyed blue hair. It was bright blue, not the old-lady bouffant-blue that I was used to. It was a whole new world.

Everyone at NYU thought I was Jewish, not because of my last name, but because of the cases of "free" Manischewitz matzo and macaroons that one of my uncles would send from his job at the Jersey City plant for me and my college friends.

Catholic, Jewish. It didn't matter. I wasn't even sure I still believed in God. Heaven and hell were definitely out—concepts that society had created to keep all the workers in line. I had come to NYU believing in heaven and hell. But it was all called into question during freshman year on the afternoon I overheard a conversation the girl with the blue hair was having in my Italian class. She was ridiculing a TV show she had seen the night before in which real people gave their accounts of "going to the light" and "traveling through the tunnel." Everyone was laughing with Blue Hair about it. And I suddenly felt stupid and naive. I had always assumed that there was life after death. No one I knew had ever questioned it. The afterlife was a given, like toxic waste, political corruption, and bodies washing up in spring.

But by sophomore year I nearly forgot all that existed. I found a boyfriend who played acoustic guitar. I was busy going to art films or to classic black-and-white movies that stood the test of time. I realized Hudson County was often used as a backdrop for corruption. Directors making movies about beautiful places never chose it as a setting, but both Elia Kazan and Woody Allen had used Hudson as a grim set—in *On the Waterfront* and *Broadway Danny Rose*. Sid and Nancy, in the movie version, lived out their seedy punk existence on Hudson's grungy streets.

I spent less and less time on those streets. I went to fewer family functions, and stopped going to mass on Sunday. I crashed most nights at a Ukrainian friend's $90-a-month rent-controlled railroad flat in the East Village. It was next door to a row of Indian restaurants, and at night the smell of curry would waft up into Lana's bedroom. It was a new smell for me.

In the East Village, there were still mumblers and rejects, two-bit criminals and crazy people. I just wasn't related to any of them.

To channel the temper I had inherited from Grandpa, I took up playing the drums and writing articles for the school paper. I found a new newspaper, the *Village Voice*, which I bought religiously every week on Tuesday nights. I didn't read *The Jersey Journal* anymore. The stories in the *Voice* were long and complicated and got me riled up—but in a different way. When the drums and the writing weren't enough of a release, I went to Washington, D.C., to march against the evil Republicans. There were marches for abortion rights, housing rights, and arms reduction.

I was starting to develop a social conscience and was especially pleased with myself. I read Plato and Aristotle and suddenly despised people who voted for someone because of what they could do for them personally. I even got mad at a Hudson County friend when he voted for a candidate because the guy got his mother a job. I found it despicable. Nobody in Hudson County cared about the common good, just what they could scam for themselves.

Plato talked about the cave and how the unenlightened, short-sighted people inside the cave were so busy watching shadows of themselves on the cave wall that they couldn't see the light outside. It all made perfect sense to me. Hudson County was the cave. Every time I commuted back home through the Tubes, I felt like I had to duck my head back under.

But I had no right to feel so self-righteous. What convinced me was another family story. Normally, it would have been thrown on top of the growing heap of family tragedies and dramas I heard retold every few weeks. But this one was different. No one in the Stapinski family had mentioned it before. When I heard it repeated a few times, it was not by my relatives. The story sounded like something out of the pages of the *Village Voice*. It had been written about in Jersey City history books and social critiques of the Hague years. The town historian had used it to describe the city's corrupt ways, but I hadn't known that it involved a relative. That it involved my last name.

I remember the afternoon the city's history and my family's history dovetailed. It was like finding two matching cards in a game of Go Fish. I should have recognized it sooner, but until sophomore year, I hadn't bothered to turn the right cards over. Daddy never talked about his family. But one day Ma mentioned the story in passing. And that's when I put the two tales together. Suddenly. Finally.

In 1934, Andrew Stapienski, a cousin of Dziadzia's, had a run-in with the police. Though most of the family had settled downtown, Uncle Andrew and his wife, Kunegunda, ran a tavern on Pacific Avenue in the city's Lafayette section, a more upscale neighborhood. Their main customers were recent Polish immigrants whose wives had stayed behind in the old country. They would come to Kunegunda for a home-cooked meal or to rent a room upstairs.

Kunegunda was a shrewd woman, not your typical steerage slob. Even her name was special. In Poland, to have that name was an honor. It was considered high-class. Her namesake, Cunegund, a Bavarian empress around the turn of the first century, was elevated to sainthood around 1200. Her feast day, March 3, was, coincidentally, the same day as Grandpa's birthday.

Kunegunda had a head for business and didn't simply rent rooms and feed her hungry Polish brethren out of the goodness of her heart. When food and drink tabs grew too large to settle, Kunegunda accepted parcels of land outside the city as payment. By 1934, a year after Prohibition was repealed, the Stapienskis had a pretty good thing going. The beer was flowing, and so was the cash.

When Andrew and Kunegunda's son announced he was going to be married, the Stapienskis took it upon themselves to throw the party. Young John was engaged to a Jersey City girl named Anna Lukachyk, who was, rumor has it, already with child. No matter. This was to be a weekend of dancing and drinking, shotgun or no shotgun. The day before the wedding, on a busy Friday afternoon in June, the sky threatening thundershowers, the family was busy with last-minute preparations.

Having been to many a Stapinski wedding, I'm sure the polka band was on tap, as was the beer. The clarinet and accordion were no doubt in tune, ready to dance across pages and pages of sheet music. I can imagine Kunegunda running around in an apron, grinding the meat for the kielbasa, stirring pots of sauerkraut, and folding piles of pierogi. And, of course, bottling the hooch for the Saturday celebration.

Around 11 A.M. on Friday, detectives from the city's Bureau of Liquor Control raided the tavern on an anonymous tip that the Stapienskis were distilling their own whiskey. Detectives Leon Wilzewski and Michael Noonan and a lieutenant demanded that Uncle Andrew show them the booze in the basement. When Uncle Andrew refused, he was beaten.

He was arrested for liquor-law violations and hauled into the station house, along with the evidence—a five-gallon jug of brown liquid, a two-gallon jug of alcohol, a copper funnel, a capping machine, and a quart bottle of spirits.

Twelve hours later, while out on bail and trying to finish his chores in time for the impending wedding, Uncle Andrew was rushed to the hospital. When he was brought into the Medical Center, still very much alive and in pain, Uncle Andrew was placed under anesthesia. He soon stopped breathing and was given oxygen and adrenaline. Doctors tried massaging his heart. But Uncle Andrew was gone, dead from abdominal injuries.

The death made the front page of *The Jersey Journal*: POLICE BEATING BLAMED AS MAN DIES. FAMILY SAYS FATHER WAS BLACKJACKED. POLICE ATTEMPT TO SUPPRESS NEWS.

Somehow, amid the murder and scandal that weekend, the family went ahead with the wedding on Sunday. The rationale was that all the food was already made. What could they do? They drowned their sorrows in kielbasa and what was left of the liquor. The Stapinskis—myself included—have always had a good appetite. Funerals were never an excuse for not eating and drinking; they were just another reason to indulge.

As Uncle Andrew's long funeral procession made its way down Sussex Street toward OLC the following Tuesday, police headquarters became the scene of the investigation. The papers said he was killed over just two gallons of liquor, that bruises under his arms were six by three inches, and that his lips had been cut. It looked like a clear case of police brutality.

The police denied any involvement in Uncle Andrew's death, of course. The chief claimed to have seen him in the station house after the arrest and said, "He made no complaint." I wondered if Uncle Andrew was even conscious at the time. It was hard to complain when you were passed out on the station-house floor.

The medical examiner was right on board with the cops. "The case is closed as far as we're concerned," he said. The official cause of death was "incipient peritonitis following rupture of the intestine and precipitated by syncope due to cardiac dilation and myocardic degeneration."

They claimed that Uncle Andrew fainted because of heart problems. While lifting a heavy beer barrel, they said, he passed out and hit the sharp corner of a metal tub, busting his own gut. But as much as police hoped, the story wouldn't die quite as easily as Uncle Andrew had. The papers milked it for days. Finally, on July 3, an inquest was held. A former judge, Robert Carey, represented the family. He started the proceedings with a dramatic flair.

"A serious crime has or has not been committed," he said, rising to his feet. "If it has, we are here to see justice is done."

Carey was cut off by the assistant prosecutor, who said speeches were not in order. But Carey continued in typical Jersey City fashion, misquoting Shakespeare.

"There is something wrong in Denmark," Carey told the jurors, who probably had no idea what he was talking about. Carey then, thankfully, stalked out of the courtroom and let the real drama unfold.

The first witness was Kunegunda, who testified in broken but defiant English that it was impossible for her healthy forty-six-year-old husband to just up and die. "He never was sick," she testified. "He was a healthy man, God help me.

"He get beat. First detectives come up my house," she said, glancing over at Noonan. "Lieutenant and other guy grabbed him behind arms . . . hit him with fist on chin. Another used first fist, then club." That all happened before they dragged Andrew downstairs.

Andrew's daughter Nellie said that she heard him yell from the cellar, "You have no right to use that blackjack on me."

"Show me where the stuff is," Detective Noonan yelled, punching Andrew twice in the gut.

Noonan and his boys testified that Uncle Andrew had resisted arrest and that they got into a scuffle. They denied using the blackjacks.

"Stop lying!" John, the newlywed, yelled from the back of the courtroom.

Despite four hours of evidence from eyewitnesses at the bar and from among the family, the jury ruled in fifteen minutes, just before 1 A.M., that the cops weren't lying, that they were innocent.

In the follow-up story the next day, the police were quoted as saying that Uncle Andrew must have hurt himself after being arrested, that it was impossible for him to receive an intestinal rupture in the morning, then carry ice, lift a two-hundred-pound keg of beer, and drive an automobile before complaining of pain at 6 P.M. The police didn't know my Polish relatives. They were workhorses. "Strong like bull," we always joked. And when a party was at stake, well, they were known to go to superhuman lengths for a good time.

The Stapinskis never relied on hired help or caterers. Affairs were always run the old-fashioned way, everybody selflessly pitching in and lifting, decorating, and cooking until they nearly collapsed. For my mother's wedding, sixty-one-year-old Babci cooked for a week, rolling stuffed cabbage, cooking huge vats of sauerkraut, and mixing frighteningly large bowls of potato salad.

Despite the jury and police findings, everyone was convinced the cops had killed Uncle Andrew, particularly Kunegunda and the Polish-American community. On July 5, fueled by the patriotic fervor of Independence Day and The Jersey Journal's sensational headlines, three thousand Poles held a protest rally, with Kunegunda, their sad widow, among them. They demanded that a civil-rights committee be appointed to investigate the death and to suspend the police officers involved. Uncle Andrew wasn't the first Pole to be beaten by Hague's zepps. And the Polish community—with no representation in Hague's cabinet—wasn't going to take it anymore.

The rally was held at the Polish American Community Center and made the front page of the paper: POLISH-AMERICANS DEMAND STAPINSKI DEATH PROBE. Another rally was scheduled for Monday, July 9, at Victory Hall.

It was time for Kunegunda—the queen of the family—to shine. It was her moment in the spotlight, to demand justice for her martyred husband. But if you look at the next week's papers, the story disappears, its space filled by other controversies and untimely deaths. There's a story headlined RADICALS DEFY JERSEY CITY POLICE. But these are different radicals, not the Poles at Victory Hall. The news involves striking furniture workers picketing Hague's antipicketing rule. In another front-page story that week, a priest is reported to have died in the chapel at Meadowview while kneeling on the altar.

The follow-up Stapienski story is nowhere to be found—not that week or the next. There's no story about a Victory Hall rally. There are no Polish crowds demanding justice. The furor ends with no explanation. None in print, anyway.

The story that wasn't reported—one that became part of Jersey City legend—was that Kunegunda cut a deal with Hague: She was allowed to keep the tavern at a time when women weren't even allowed to drink in taverns. Kunegunda shut her trap and bellied up to the other side of the bar, continuing the Jersey City tradition of keeping your sights as low as they could possibly go. She didn't reserve the cowardice just for herself. Kunegunda spread it around, like a nasty rumor that no one particularly wanted to hear. She forbade anyone in the family to attend the rallies. Kunegunda quashed the uprising.

The Polish Americans had their martyr. What they needed was a hero. But Kunegunda wasn't up to the challenge. Or she was just too pragmatic, tricked by those shadows on the cave wall.

"You can't bring him back," she was overhead saying of dead Uncle Andrew. "I got a living to make."

As my relatives like to say, Kunegunda "had a finger in it." She made a pretty penny from her husband's well-publicized death, having been told by the cops or Hague—or both—to keep quiet.

Realizing I was related to the city's infamous female barkeep did more than embarrass me. I was ashamed. No one at NYU knew about her, but I did and that was enough. Her story was worse than all the crime stories in my family, because of Kunegunda's squandered potential. It seemed that Grandpa never really had a chance. And my Russian great-grandpa was always a bastard. But Kunegunda could have been a hero. She really blew it. Now she was a pathetic, selfish footnote in the sad history of Jersey City.

At NYU, I continued to write scathing articles for the campus paper and to march on Washington, but my heart was no longer in it. I was humbled. I had no right to feel self-righteous, not with relatives like Kunegunda. I felt like I had to get away from Jersey City, and from my history.

I figured that education was my key to escape. I soaked up as much information as I could, majoring in journalism and taking extra credits each semester. I took a music class called "The Art of Listening," then smoked pot and for the first time heard—really heard—Bob Dylan's lyrics and the Beatles' harmonies. I became a walking college-student cliché.

I took a summer class reading the great modern philosophers, and came to the obvious conclusion that life was meaningless. The following semester, I took an extra two-credit class on Kafka, which sent me on a two-month binge of muttering that life was not meaningless but that its meaning was ambiguous. For a fleeting moment, I even understood what the giant cockroach was all about.

When I got over that phase, I took "Observational Astronomy" and climbed to the top of the highest building at NYU every week to observe the few stars one could see through the lights and haze of the city. I loved it so much that I minored in astronomy. Through a telescope, I glimpsed the craters of the moon, the rings of Saturn, and seasonal meteor showers. Falling stars were a regular annual occurrence, scientifically mapped and charted. They were not harbingers of death, like Grandma had said the night before Sonny died.

Using my astronomy text as a guide, I drove up a dark stretch of the Palisades Parkway and pulled over to the side of the road. Lying on the warm car hood, the engine clicking underneath my back, I waited and watched the Perseid meteors shoot past. Right on schedule.

I knew that the farther I got from Jersey City, the less angry I became. In senior year, just when I thought I should sign up for a trip on the space shuttle, it exploded.

I settled on a trip to Europe.

For my college graduation, my family got together and threw me a typical Stapinski bash in the OLC Church hall, lugging giant trays of pierogi and kielbasa and sauerkraut. I made enough money at the party to get to Italy. And back, if I wanted.

That summer, I got as far as Siena as part of the study-abroad program. I visited Venice and walked in courtyards right out of the Stanley Theatre. I visited the real Rialto bridge. I visited St. Peter's in Rome and understood why people liked being Catholic: It was all so sturdy, old, and official.

More important, I did my own laundry for the first time and hung it from the roof of the fifteenth-century building where I was living. I loved the smell of the wet clothes and the way the warm sun made them look so white and clean. One afternoon, while walking in the town of Assisi, I got that feeling of freedom and unbridled joy that Aunt Julie had told me about. It was as if a heavy appliance, like an air conditioner, had suddenly been removed from my back, as if my eyes were wider now that cool air had been pumped into my lungs and brain. I felt as if I'd awoken from a deep sleep that I didn't know I had fallen into. Or was it a sleep I had always been in, one that came with being born in the Margaret Hague maternity wing? In Siena, I lived in a monastery for a few days and thought, amid the cypress trees and medieval frescoes, that in a world so big and so beautiful, there was absolutely no reason to live in a place as ugly as Jersey City.

When I got back home, I could suddenly see how ugly it really was. I felt like I had the day I got my first pair of glasses: Everything was suddenly clear. I hated Jersey City so much I could taste it—bitter and rotten, like the flavor left in my mouth after a particularly bad frat party hangover.

Ironically, as a journalism major, I met all kinds of enthusiastic students whose dream it was to cover crime and corruption, students who wound up getting jobs in places like Jersey City. There was even a campus band at NYU called Urban Blight, a name I never found the least bit amusing. If you'd actually grown up in it, urban blight wasn't hip, and wasn't funny. These people thought the Pulaski Skyway was cool. They'd grown up in bland suburbia and yearned for the grittiness of places like Hudson County.

I longed to escape. Permanently.

I set out to find a job in a whole other city, a whole other state. Maybe even a whole other country. On the bulletin board in the Journalism Department there was a sign advertising openings at *The Sacramento Bee,* and though I'd never been to California, I was sure I'd love it: sunshine instead of industrial-gray skies; sparkling beaches instead of contaminated riverfronts.

If not California, then I'd head to the thoroughly scrubbed Midwest. Or maybe the fresh, pine-scented Northwest. Or maybe I'd fly off to London and rent a flat. The world seemed limitless. And I was only twenty-two.

But that autumn, on the night of the Orionid meteor shower, another Stapinski tragedy occurred, the worst one yet.

Daddy died.

15

TEN PLAGUES

We had been to the hospital with Daddy several times in the recent past—what with his near-gangrene experience and the complications from his diabetes. So on October 22, 1987, when Daddy woke up early in the morning and had trouble breathing, it meant just another trip to the hospital.

I got into the ambulance with Ma and sat next to Daddy on the stretcher. He was wearing an oxygen mask and his face was very pale. But his eyes were open and he was breathing all right. Though he was suffering congestive heart failure, the paramedics didn't seem too worried. He was only fifty-nine, after all. They stopped at red lights and drove slowly through Jersey City's streets. No siren necessary. I should have made them run all the lights and head straight for the Holland Tunnel, to a hospital on the New York side.

When we got to St. Francis Hospital in downtown Jersey City, there was no doctor in the emergency room. While Ma and I waited in the long, dim hallway, the code-red light began flashing and nurses started to run back and forth. Still, no doctor arrived. Before I knew it, my mother was fainting onto the waiting room floor while I tried to pull her up by her armpits and tell her that Daddy would be okay. But she saw the nurse's face before I did. And understood. My father had been right here minutes earlier and now the nurse was telling us that he was gone.

I thought she meant they had transferred him somewhere, to another floor or to another room. But in a terrible moment of recognition I figured that my mother was on the floor for a reason.

The nurse meant Daddy was dead. That was what she meant by "gone." He was gone for good. "No longer with us," she added for clarity.

I couldn't cry, since I had to finish picking Ma up off the floor, make sure she didn't collapse again, get her seated in a safe place, and then call Stanley and Paula from the pay phone. I dialed without thinking and delivered the bad news as if it weren't happening to us. I felt like I had that day I got stoned at Carvel, watching my body perform various tasks from afar, listening to words leave my mouth without even knowing that I was speaking.

When I hung up the phone, the nurse asked me if I wanted to see my father. I didn't really want to, but I had read somewhere that seeing a loved one's dead body helped with closure. I had never had closure, had never been wide open enough to need closure, and wasn't sure if I needed it now. But I nodded and drifted into the curtained emergency room alone.

When I saw Daddy there on the gurney, I still couldn't cry. I was too confused. I had seen dozens, if not hundreds, of dead people at all those wakes but had never really thought much about them. I realized now they had been all made up, in fancy clothes and pancake makeup, with cotton in their mouths to keep their cheeks from sinking. They looked more like big dolls than dead people.

From movies, we're taught to think that when people first die— before the cotton and makeup—they look like they're just sleeping or, at worst, unconscious. But that wasn't true at all. Daddy didn't look like he was sleeping or knocked cold. He looked dead. Gone. No longer with us, just like the nurse said. The blood was drained from his face, and his mouth was wide open—something Daddy never allowed to happen, even when he was asleep.

I was confused, because I knew this dead man. I loved him. But this was not him. Daddy had been right here minutes earlier, and now, now that he was dead, he was inexplicably gone. In a flash. Just like that. This body was here, but Daddy was missing. Where had he run off to?

I looked nervously around the emergency room, then up above me, thinking I might see Daddy hovering there, smiling down with that toothless grin of his. But all I could see was the harsh fluorescent light buzzing overhead. I thought about Blue Hair from my Italian class laughing and saying so confidently that there was no such thing as life after death. I wished she were here right now so that I could punch her in the mouth. Fuck you, I thought, shaking my head. Fuck you.

———

Though I wasn't sure exactly where Daddy had run off to, his body was taken to the Bromirski Funeral Home on Warren Street, the street where you could get a good glimpse of the Statue of Liberty. My mother, the lover of wakes and funerals, had Daddy laid out for three whole days. She didn't want to part with him, and since she was closer to a nervous breakdown than I was, I didn't argue with her.

But it was torture. For three days and three nights I had to sit in the front row of the funeral parlor and stare at Daddy's body while people came and went. They said things like "Oh, he looks so good. So peaceful." No, I wanted to say, he looks dead. Can't you see? He's dead. It's not even him, really.

I know there was a burial at Holy Cross Cemetery in North Arlington, out near where Daddy's sister Terri lived, and a Hi Hat funeral dinner afterward. I don't remember it. But I do remember thinking about Daddy being put into the ground. And I remember wondering whether he would be cold down there all alone now that winter was coming, even though I knew, really knew, and tried to convince myself that I knew, that the body wasn't really him anyway. That he was gone.

I remember being comforted by the cemetery's green grass and trees, which were in the peak of autumn, their leaves dying in vibrant orange and yellow. When I was a kid, skipping around the graves and past the lines of tombstones, I thought that all that nature was wasted on dead people. But now I knew better. The pretty grass and trees and flowers were not for the dead but for the survivors. I wanted to lie down in a pile of crunchy leaves and stay there for a few days.

When we got home, after everything was over, Marty, the dog, looked really depressed, as if he knew Daddy wasn't coming home again. I was depressed, too, though I still hadn't cried. I was exhausted from three days of smiling at my father's friends and relatives. I couldn't wait to go to sleep. I gave Marty a pat and looked over at the clock radio to see what time it was. And there, on top of the radio, was the lottery ticket that I had brought home for my father the night he died. He hadn't seen it, and now he never would.

That's when I started crying, and couldn't stop. I cried in giant heaves, like when I was little, like the times Aunt Katie told me my eyes would shrink. I tried to catch my breath, but the tears kept coming, in waves. I cried for hours, the autumn afternoon turning to night, the stars coming out over our Summit Avenue porch. Between sobs, I took the Pick-It ticket off the clock radio, smashed it into a ball, then threw it away in the kitchen garbage. I didn't even bother to check it against the winning lottery numbers.

Now that Daddy was gone, I couldn't really move out. My plans for westward expansion were over. Stanley had gotten married a year earlier and soon had his first child, Nicole. My sister was busy with her own family. That left me to worry full-time about my mother.

Ma not only fell into a depression; she had to have major gallbladder surgery. She was sure she was going to go next to meet Daddy in the great beyond. It was my job to make sure she didn't. For years, she had scraped together tuition money, raised the cash to send me to Italy, and protected me from a life of crime. I loved my mother. She never asked me to stay. But I felt that sticking around was the least I could do.

Most of all, I was afraid to leave her. I wasn't just afraid that she would die. I was afraid of my own life for the first time. Just when I thought I had it all figured out, life came up from behind and kicked me right in the ass. I had seen death and tragedy and sorrow—our family had so much of it—but it always seemed to be whirling around me, never really touching me. Daddy dying left me stunned for the first time in my life.

Some fortunate nights, I even forgot he was gone. Waking up in the early morning, I thought I could still hear him shuffling in the kitchen, sneaking a coconut cupcake or some Sara Lee cheesecake. But then the reality would hit me that I would never see him again, and Daddy would die all over again for me, my soul curling back up into a ball and weighing me down in bed like a heavy stone.

I was stuck in Hudson County for the rest of my life, too crippled to limp away. The farthest I could crawl was Weehawken, where a friend and I rented a crummy, steamy attic apartment. Though I moved in on Independence Day, I felt no spine tingles of freedom. My street corner was almost as bad as the Majestic corner I'd grown up on. There was even a group of guys who played conga drums across the street in summer. I didn't feel a bit nostalgic.

Since I wasn't going anywhere, I completely surrendered and took a job at *The Jersey Journal*. People in Jersey City always made fun of the paper. They called it a rag and joked that the proofreaders were blind.

The office was housed in an old five-story building on Journal Square, one that I had passed thousands of times in my life. I had never once dreamed of working there. On top of the building stood the unlucky thirteen battered red letters that spelled out the paper's name. The bottom two floors were reserved for the press, which made the building shudder at night. To get to the newsroom, I had to take the elevator to the third floor. I could see that it had once been state-of-the-art, with its big silver buttons and turquoise walls. But that was sometime back in the 1960s.

After the short elevator ride back in time, I stepped out into an even deeper time warp. I had to walk down an eerily quiet, shaftlike hallway devoid of color. Everything was dingy off-white and brown, with a few old gray filing cabinets thrown in for variety. Though it wasn't dirty, *The Jersey Journal*'s office seemed dusty, as if the newsprint from the press seeped through the floorboards into the rest of the building. It was hard to breathe.

In the long hallway, there were wooden doors with windows of frosted glass, with company names stenciled on them, like something out of a movie from the 1940s. I expected to see the name Sam Spade stenciled on one. Instead, at the very end of the absurdly long hallway, I found a door that said KNEWSROOM. Some joker had drawn a K in front of NEWSROOM.

As soon as I walked through that door and into the windowless knewsroom, I knew I wasn't like the other young reporters who were sitting at their computers, busy writing the day's stories. They were all just passing through on their way to somewhere else, like the Jersey City coal cars and freight trains whose contents were destined for fancy homes in New York. The other reporters were Columbia Journalism School graduates or people from Ohio or Colorado who thought that Hudson County was an exciting place to work. I had arrived by default.

My desk was right near the front door, so I could run out if I ever got up the gumption to leave. But I had a feeling I never would. I had walked the long shaft of the hallway, and now I was trapped.

The knewsroom was divided into two camps: the newcomers and the old-timers. I wasn't sure which camp I fit into. Sometimes both; usually neither. I looked like a newcomer, but I felt like one of the old-timers. The new reporters called them B&Rs, for *born and raised*. When the young reporters used phrases like that in front of me, it was as if I were an undercover agent. *I* was born and raised, I wanted to shout at them. But was I bragging or complaining?

One B&R had lumps all over his body. There was the mumbling copy editor, who barked like a dog, and the narcoleptic, who would fall asleep at his desk while typing; the guy with the perpetual neck brace; the reporter with a truss who hadn't had a byline since 1968, on a byline strike for a cause long forgotten; the guy who resembled a cadaver—he'd just forgotten to lie down; the reporter who chewed on his tongue when he talked to you; and the sixty-year-old night editor with the mohawk, who wore leather and chains.

They all scared me until I got to know them better. Eccentrics like them were slowly being edged out by smart-asses like me who had studied journalism in school. But we had a lot to learn.

I was hired as the new police reporter, replacing a guy who went on to work for the mayor's office. In days of yore, he would have simply taken on both jobs, with the editor's blessing. But things were changing. The year before I arrived, the new editor, Steve Newhouse, fired a reporter for being on the city payroll. *The Jersey Journal* wasn't *The New York Times,* but it had its standards.

Each day, it was my job to cover crime, fires, and all the other breaking bad news in Hudson County. I was a very busy person, since there was always an abundance of bad news. As the police reporter, it was my job to interview people on the worst day of their lives. The police beat was like an extended hell week—the job the editors gave new recruits to see if they could take it. If you survived the Jersey City police, you could survive anything.

Every morning, I called the precincts to see how many horrible things had happened overnight. One morning, a cop picked a fight with me over the phone about a story someone else had written. I fought right back and called him an asshole before hanging up on him. George Latanzio, my city editor, had to field the cop's complaint minutes later. When he finished calming the desk sergeant, George hung up politely and walked over to my desk. He was not smiling.

"Next time you have a fight with a cop," he instructed, "hang up first, then call him an asshole." George smiled.

To check up on my phone leads, every afternoon I drove around to all the precincts and read the police blotters. At the downtown precinct, there was a desk sergeant who liked to give me a hard time. I tried to pretend he didn't bother me.

"Anything happen today?" I would ask, day after day, in as chipper a mood as I could dredge up from my shrinking, defeated soul.

"There was a rape," he said one day as some of the other officers looked on. "Why don't you come in the back and I'll tell you about it?"

I took a deep breath. I had had it with this guy.

"You dirty old man," I said, loud enough so the others would hear. "What makes you think anybody would even look at you twice, never mind touch you, you pervert?" The other cops applauded and laughed. I bowed and walked out.

I put on a tough show. But day after day, whether I was on the street chasing down a story or at my desk in the claustrophobic knewsroom, I felt like I was drowning. When I was out reporting, I bumped into guys from grammar school who were now cops, whose faces I never wanted to see again, but whose hairlines I watched slowly recede week after week. I knew some streets so intimately, I could tell you where the cracks were and how many gum marks pocked the sidewalk.

Every time I referred to the paper, I had to catch myself and edit my words before they left my crooked lips. The other young reporters called the paper the *Journal,* a pretentious name that was usually reserved for *The Wall Street Journal.* When I was around them, I did the same thing. But like everyone born and raised in Jersey City, I wanted to call the paper the *Jersey.* I pronounced it with an accent, dropping the *r* just enough to betray that I was from this awful place. Some old-timers actually called it the *Joisey.* They were the same people who called the toilet the *terlit* and the refrigerator the *frigidaire* or the *icebox.*

What you called the paper was an easy test to see who was from here and who, luckily, was not. *Jersey* or *Journal?* I was very conflicted. The paper was, in spirit, the *Jersey.* It contained all that was wrong with Jersey City, wrapped up in a nice little ink-stained package that could be read well within an hour. Most readers thumbed right past the stories we wrote and headed straight to the obituaries, to see which of their friends and enemies had died.

Writing obituaries was the only job more depressing than mine. Each day, the poor guy with that job had to write one feature to lead the page, to try to make one dead person's sad life sound interesting. The obit writer, Wendell, didn't come in until 4 P.M., and for the first couple of hours he would use a desk in the back of the knewsroom, in the Lifestyles section of the paper. We called that section Life and Death. When I left after deadline, at around 7 P.M., Wendell would come and work at my desk at the front of the knewsroom. On my way out, I could hear him making the phone rounds, calling all the funeral parlors in the county, including Bromirski's.

We often covered the same dead people in our stories, but since we worked different shifts, we barely waved at each other. The first conversation we ever had was about a story that came to be known as the Knife-Toss Murder. While writing the victim's obituary, Wendell realized that the guy was only twenty-nine years old. He asked the funeral director what had happened.

"You better talk to the cops," the funeral director told him.

Since I was the police reporter, Wendell asked me about it. I had just written the news story, so I gladly filled him in. A couple of guys in a Bayonne tavern were sitting on their stools, taking turns tossing a knife at a balloon floating above the bar to see if they could pop it, when the knife bounced off a glass hanging over the bar and landed in one guy's neck, puncturing his jugular vein. He died within seconds as his buddies helplessly watched. The prosecutor indicted the friend who had tossed the knife, as if seeing his buddy bleed to death wasn't punishment enough.

It was a terrible story, but it was fascinating in a gruesome sort of way. I spoke animatedly about it, waving my arms and talking with my hands, like I always did, trying to describe how it all happened, the angle at which the knife came flying down, and how stupid and sense-less the whole thing was. And how stupid and senseless the prosecutor was.

That's how Wendell and I met. After the Knife-Toss Murder, when-ever Wendell came to sit at my desk at the end of my shift, we would chat about that day's horror stories. One afternoon, Wendell came in a little early and we went on our first date, to Boulevard Drinks. The hot dogs and Journal Square were all new to him.

The Square was just as nasty as it had been when I was growing up. Maybe even worse. The bums were replaced by what everyone now re-ferred to as the homeless. I wondered what had happened to Mary, the woman with the dirty raincoat. Had she gotten to wherever it was she was hurrying off to? The midgets selling the newspaper had disap-peared. But they were replaced by a woman who looked like the Fat Lady at the circus, and a parade of misfits like characters out of a Fellini film. The crippled pencil seller was still there, as were the vast army of freaks with growths and tumors and the mumblers who walked around arguing with themselves. I was sure I was destined to become one of them.

To try and avoid my sad fate, I got out of town as much as I possi-bly could, taking my first paid vacation to Miami. It was the first time

I'd gone alone to Aunt Mary Ann's. I thought the visit might give us a chance to bond and compare our many similarities—how I was skeptical about marriage and cynical about everything else, how I wanted to escape from Jersey City like she had so long ago. But before I got the chance to tell her, Aunt Mary Ann told me that I was just like my mother when she was in her early twenties. She couldn't believe how much I looked like her, sounded like her, and acted like her. Ma had even wanted to be a reporter at one time.

I'd had no idea. Like most kids, I selfishly assumed that my mother had no ambition before she had me. I figured she liked Jersey City. But maybe she was stuck here because of us. It wasn't easy to pack up and run with three kids.

I came back to *The Jersey Journal* a bit wiser and with a deep tan. But it soon faded. On my next vacation, I took a road trip along the West Coast with Wendell, my new boyfriend. The following fall we took a trip to Paris. Those vacations didn't last nearly as long as I would have liked. The following Monday, we'd end up back in the dusty knewsroom.

Wendell, who loved newspapers, didn't mind *The Jersey Journal* half as much as I did, and he almost convinced me I was lucky to work there. He got me to watch the press run, its clanging, inky parts miraculously belching out our words and bylines in a continuous blur. For about fifteen minutes, I was happy to be at the paper. But I hated Jersey City too much.

Around this time, strangely enough, Hudson County started to look a little better, around the edges anyway. While I had been at NYU, the brownstones on Mercer Street were restored as gentrification replaced urban blight. In the late 1980s, Jersey City had become a bedroom community, after years of being a toilet (pronounced *ter-lit*). I wasn't sure which made me more angry, yuppies or drug dealers.

The waterfront's burnt-out piers were being magically transformed into prime real estate for back-office space. New glass office towers were erected in Jersey City and Weehawken. Sidewalk cafés bloomed in Hoboken. Parks were built along the Hudson River. A mall was even constructed near the Holland Tunnel, in a development called Newport. In an effort to separate themselves from Jersey City, though, the developers asked for their own Zip code and tried to leave Jersey City out of their address altogether. They tried to say the mall was in Newport City, a fictional place. I was outraged, and suddenly felt protective of Jersey City.

But Jersey City's planning board, bribes or no bribes, wouldn't let that one slip past. Newport would take advantage of the city's tax abatements, so it sure as hell would keep the name Jersey City in its address. And be proud of it.

Working as a reporter, I knew a little too much of what was going on behind the scenes. I wished I could just sit back and enjoy the new waterfront walkways, cafés, marinas, and boutiques along with most of the other Jersey Citizens. But some people were suffering because of the development, and I felt more comfortable suffering along with them. It was my nature.

In 1989, the Colgate factory was closed to make room for a new development project, devastating a large part of the downtown worker population—Stanley included. He had worked there for nine years and was forced to leave his job as a warehouseman. I was assigned to cover a worker résumé-writing meeting. I wanted to interview the president of Colgate so I could punch him out. How could I be objective when my brother was getting canned?

The counselors on hand were encouraging the workers to relocate to Kansas City, to the Colgate plant there, where several of Stanley's friends got replacement jobs. But Stanley stayed and got a job in a machine shop in Rutherford. Good thing. A year after they relocated, his friends were laid off and left jobless in Kansas City, a strange new land, where they had just taken out mortgages on new houses.

It was another lesson in why you should never move away. You'd just wind up back in Jersey City, defeated.

Aside from the factory closings, I tried to convince myself it was generally a good thing that the waterfront was finally being developed after years of languishing under the control of corrupt politicians and rich railroad companies. But I knew that in typical Hudson County fashion, shortcuts were being taken, not to mention bribes and kickbacks.

When Newport Mall was built, construction crews forgot to bait for rats, so an army of rodents invaded downtown—just like in Gammontown's heyday. A pack of rats ran past the candy counter in one of the mall department stores one afternoon. Then a small boy was bitten while sitting on the toilet in his own home, in the mall neighborhood. The rat had come up through the pipes and into his bowl. Firefighters visited nearby St. Anthony's High School, where Paula worked as a teacher, to make sure the nuns had all their toilet seats covered.

The Newport rats were only the first round of development woes. While Hudson's politicians turned their heads, buildings were constructed on top of and next to contaminated land left over from Jersey City's industrial glory days. But people were so used to hearing about toxic waste that they simply shrugged. If they weren't dead by now, they were probably immune, they thought. Everytime I looked at Hudson County's rising skyline, its blue and green gleaming buildings growing taller each day, all I could think of were the dirty deals the politicians were making.

I wound up uncovering stories about the toxic waste that lay beneath lots I had played in as a kid. I had memories of playing bartender in one of those lots, pouring dirt—now known to be contaminated— into a Coke bottle while my brother played baseball a few yards away.

Cancer-causing chromium was buried all over Hudson County, left behind by three companies that produced chemicals for paint, ceramics, and ink. Sodium dichromate, their main product, was used for the ink on money. Gammontown was one of the few neighborhoods in the city that contained no chromium, simply because the adjoining brownstones there, crowded together with no empty lots in between, were built long before the city starting burying tons of the industrial slag.

But the downtown school where Hague had been hit by an egg back in 1949 was built next to a chromium dump. The Liberty Science Center, a showcase for the entire East Coast, visited by 850,000 kids, teachers, and parents each year, was built on top of a contaminated parcel of land owned by the state. Before construction, the site was covered over with clean soil and deemed safe by the state Department of Environmental Protection.

I wrote stories about chromium found under the drive-in where Stanley had taken his dates, under the Gregory Apartments, where my best friend, Liz, had lived. Chromium stalactites dripped from the ceiling of the newly renovated Newport PATH station, where I had waited for trains to NYU. A friend and fellow reporter, Dan Rosenfeld, collected some of the crud in a jar and had it tested. He found that the chromium levels were dangerously high. The DEP did its own test and pronounced the station safe.

I covered the chromium stories as if I were on a mission. Which I was.

Objectivity was never an issue.

I remember having an argument with the flack for a Society Hill development project planned for the old Roosevelt Stadium site, next door to the biggest chromium site in the city, where a million tons of waste lay buried and covered over. The flack accused me of having a chip on my shoulder. I wanted to dig up the contaminated dirt and shove it down his throat. That Beansie temper was rising. And the more I learned, the angrier I became.

Some friends and I, frustrated that the DEP would never get anything done, banded together and formed a guerrilla group called Chromium Underground. We stenciled the name at unmarked tainted sites using spray paint the color of chromium slag—fluorescent green. We made flyers designed like PATH newsletters and handed them to commuters outside the cruddy train station.

One night, during one of our spray-paint runs, an off-duty cop on his way home from the precinct stopped his car, pulled out his badge, and asked us what the hell we thought we were doing. We weren't your typical graffiti artists but three smug white women in our twenties.

When I saw his badge, all I could think was how much a conflict of interest this was for me, how *The Jersey Journal* would fire me when they found out I was spray-painting messages at night about subjects I was writing about during the day.

"Officer," I said, trying to sound respectful. "There's chromium buried on this lot and we just wanted people to know that it's here, so . . ."

"I know all about chromium," the cop said, waving at me to shorten the speech. "I'm an environmentalist too." He looked around at the empty streets. "Just hurry up, before somebody else sees you."

He pulled his Pontiac Firebird out onto Grand Street, and left us standing there, spray paint in hand, in disbelief. "Nice cop," I said, ashamed at myself for thinking that was an oxymoron.

Since I had such a problem with authority, objectivity, and keeping my opinions to myself, the wise editors at *The Jersey Journal* gave me my own weekly column. I could pick my subject matter from a wide variety of everyday scandals and then complain about it as much as I liked. As long as it all fit inside nineteen inches.

It was a lucky break, since continuing to cover crime would have been a major conflict of interest. To get back on her feet, my mother had applied for a job as a file clerk in the prosecutor's office. When she went for the interview, she was asked about her relationship to the criminals in the family. A background check was part of the usual procedure for the prosecutor's staff. They asked Ma if she was related to Beansie. Was Henry Stapinski her husband? Satisfied with her answers, the investigators hired my mother. It was her first non-DMV job in more than twenty years. .

After a few months, the prosecutor's biggest fear wasn't whether Ma would tip off any criminals during an investigation but whether she was tipping off her daughter at *The Jersey Journal*. I kept my distance, though, with my new beat. Ma had been through enough. I didn't want her to lose her job because of me.

I chose my subjects—and my causes—carefully. The Loew's Theatre, my childhood refuge, was in danger of being torn down. The thought of a wrecking ball bashing through its coffered ceilings and golden-tiled alcoves made me feel woozy. So I covered that story. Hartz Mountain Industries—makers of dog collars and the corporate parks that had replaced Secaucus's pig farms—wanted to replace the theater with an office building. The theater had closed in 1983 after showing its final unlucky movie, the last installment of *Friday the 13th*.

I attended more than a dozen planning-board meetings, where the fate of the theater was being decided. Jersey City's few political activists—Joe Duffy, Ted Conrad, and Colin Egan—organized a preservation committee to save the Loew's. It was because of people like them, who were still fighting the good fight, that Jersey City had any bright spots left.

While at the paper, I got to know Ted well. He was an architect and lived in a plantation-style house in the Heights, overlooking the Hudson River. His home was filled with architectural models he had built over the years and refurbished antique car seats from the 1950s and 1960s that he had mounted and which he used as love seats. He was tall and lumbering and often wore a cap over his white hair and suspenders to hold up his drooping pants. Ted drove a banana yellow Cadillac and loved to take me out to lunch, where he would fill me in on the latest worthy cause. He lectured me in his gravelly voice and begged me never to leave Jersey City.

Joe Duffy was the physical opposite of Ted. He was a small, nervous ball of energy, with glasses and a combed-over strand of hair that fell in his face when he became agitated. He walked very quickly and carried around a huge stack of documents and newspaper clippings. Joe always seemed flustered, but he was on the ball and got right to the point.

Joe and Ted made sure that every planning-board meeting was packed with people like me, with fond memories of the Loew's.

The Stanley Theatre had been saved by Jehovah's Witnesses, who had turned it into a Kingdom Hall. It was one of life's ironies that the Stanley, the theater that had showcased a naughty Bill Holden and the rabble-rousing music of Bill Haley and the Comets, wound up in the hands of evangelical Christians. Working their way into heaven with each brush stroke and swipe of a rag, the Jehovah's Witnesses shined the copper outside, refurbished the cloud-covered ceiling inside, and painted clothes on naked cherubs and classical figures. But at least they had managed to save the theater from the wrecking ball, something Ted, Colin, and Joe were trying desperately to do with the Loew's.

Ted had successfully saved the old domed Hudson County courthouse, a palatial marble masterpiece, with a rotunda painted in the high classical style, with angels and signs of the zodiac floating in delicate colors above.

Two other activists, Morris Pesin and Audrey Zapp, had saved the historic railroad terminal, through which Vita and Irene had passed a century ago. While everyone was focused on preserving Ellis Island, Audrey and Morris knew that the railroad terminal was sacred ground, too. If not for them, the terminal would be a pile of rubble at the water's edge.

Some buildings were beyond saving, like the old Margaret Hague maternity hospital. It sat abandoned on Clifton Place, sad and haunted looking, its windows broken and doors boarded up, not a newborn baby in sight. The rest of the Medical Center was in rough shape as well. In 1982, the public hospital went bankrupt. Since then, the new, private owners had been trying desperately to find a location for a new state-of-the-art facility. Meanwhile, asbestos was found. Concrete was eroding. Then, in 1991, a brick fell from one of the buildings, totaling a car below. Roofs leaked, floors sagged, and walls cracked. The building's boilers were so antiquated that hospital workers had to make their own replacement parts. Since there were only a few elevators, patients on their way to surgery would often ride up with hospital visitors. Hague's grand Art Deco masterpiece was obsolete. But there were other structures in Jersey City that were worse.

In 1990, *The Jersey Journal* staff covered the closing of the sixty-four-year-old Hudson County jailhouse, one of the most overcrowded and decrepit in the nation, where inmates were beaten to death and a fire had killed seven prisoners. Inmates were always trying to escape. You really couldn't blame them. Three of them succeeded one night, tying bedsheets together and dropping down from the fourth floor onto heavily trafficked Pavonia Avenue, right next door to the courthouse, where my mother and all the judges worked.

Some days I felt like one of those prisoners, waiting for the warden to turn his head so that I could leap out the window on my bedsheets. I was the only reporter, I realized, whose relatives had spent considerable time inside the jail. My mother had waved up to Grandpa from Pavonia Avenue when she was a child. He had waved back from behind bars.

No one complained when the jail was finally destroyed—least of all me and my family, who were happy to see a bit of our criminal history crumble.

The building that brought me—and the city—the most grief, though, was the Union Terminal Cold Storage, where Daddy had worked, the big red building at the mouth of the Holland Tunnel that I saw every time I drove to New York. The building was still standing, but it had closed soon after my father died, its big refrigerator switch flipped to OFF. The abandoned building reminded me of more innocent times: eating stolen lobster tails that Daddy cooked and slathered in butter and lemon; cases of shrimp and steaks; the dry ice for our Halloween parties.

The city's board of health closed the warehouse down after ammonia leaked from a faulty cooling system and sickened some of the toll collectors. They vomited and had to be evacuated. But when the building was closed, someone forgot to remove the 10 million pounds of frozen food inside. Oozing calamari and decaying frog's legs were finally hauled out in the sweltering month of August. Special chemicals were spread to cover up the odor.

The smell lived on. For nearly two years, the wretched stench of rotten fish was the first thing that hit you when you got anywhere near the Holland Tunnel. The approach ramp was unbearable. It was worse than the Newark bone-rendering smell on a bad day—much worse— and forced drivers to close their windows when the wind blew the wrong way. I thought the odor wafted over from the river, from a large pile of dead fish murdered by the PCBs in the water.

Even worse than the smell were the flies and rats that invaded the tunnel toll booths like the ten plagues that had invaded biblical Egypt. It wasn't long before some unlucky son of a bitch discovered the origin of the smell and the flies: One last freezer full of thawed fish had been left inside the building and thousands of bloated, foot-long rats had eaten themselves to death. Food poisoning, experts said.

It turned out the one locker had not been emptied because a three-foot ice floe had frozen outside its door. The ice was no challenge for the rats. An army of them gnawed through that, and then the six-inch layer of insulation around the locker, to get to the rotting treasure inside. Men in moon suits were called in to clean up the mess. They made the front page of *The Jersey Journal*. I tried to imagine what their job was like.

I wasn't sure there was such a thing as heaven. But now I knew there was a hell.

The story ran for several days, with follow-ups about the president of the cold-storage company, who was arrested, spent the night in jail, and was released on a half-million dollars' bail. To get sprung, he had to put up his house—in suburban New Milford, not smelly old Jersey City. The charges against him were dropped after he agreed to pay for the cleanup and the $10,000 extermination bill to get rid of the last of the living rats.

It was one of the worst stories I'd ever heard. But it aptly described Jersey City—the incompetence, the neglect, the extreme ugliness—so close yet so far from wondrous New York City, threatening to wipe out even the tiniest fond memories I had of home.

I was glad Daddy wasn't alive to read about it.

16

ON TRIAL

For most of *The Jersey Journal*'s reporters, covering City Hall was like going to the circus for the first time: The death-defying acts and walks on the high wire were too amazing to be believed. There were clowns and midgets and even a ring master.

I felt too old and jaded for the circus. I had been to the menagerie, after all, with Daddy. I had smelled the lions and tigers up close and had fed peanuts to the elephants. By the time I started working at the paper, I had witnessed quite a bit from that Majestic apartment seat, high above the ring.

Still, I knew that the current mayor, a good man and a dapper dresser named Anthony Cucci, made sensational headlines only once while in office—after visiting Jersey City's sister city, Cuzco, Peru. (Jersey City had sister cities in places like Korea, Italy, the Philippines, China, and India, to reflect its cultural diversity. Because of a growing Peruvian population, Cuzco was chosen as the latest sibling.) While Cucci was there, visiting with Cuzco's mayor, their train derailed. Both the mayors' wives were killed. Though the deaths were first blamed on the Shining Path guerrilla group, it was later learned that the train's driver was simply drunk.

Cucci's tragedy was cited as yet another example of why you should never leave the confines of Hudson County.

To get into office, Cucci had beaten Gerald McCann, who had been mayor from 1981 to 1985. The two had been allies and were so close that people called them McCucci. But they were now sworn enemies.

McCann was a throwback to the old days of Democratic machine rule. He was the 1980s version, with a designer suit and an interest in a Florida savings-and-loan. When he ran against Cucci in 1985, off-duty cops, illegally carrying guns, were positioned at the polls, set to challenge black and Latino voters who came to cast their ballots. More than 1,400 would-be voters sued McCann, claiming that he had cheated them of their right to vote. McCann settled his case, paying out half a million dollars in damages.

After he beat McCann, Cucci scheduled his swearing-in ceremony for midnight, in a rush to get into office as quickly as possible. McCann was on a rampage, forcing people to resign at the last minute and filling city board seats with political appointments. Right after Cucci took his midnight oath at City Hall, a bomb scare sent him and his aides running from the building and out onto Grove Street. When Cucci returned early the next morning, the mayor's complex was a stinking mess: desks and chairs were overturned; rugs were soaked with urine and human feces; glue had been squirted into the locks of most of the office doors. A locksmith was called in.

A file cabinet was missing; Cucci could tell by the imprint left in the piss-stained carpet. There was talk that documents had been shredded, but no one could prove it. The mess was cleaned up, but for months Cucci was reminded of the McCann regime by a big urine stain that remained. Cucci finally got new rugs.

McCann denied relieving himself in the mayor's office. But everyone blamed him and his cronies. He was a class act.

I had never met Hague or Kenny, but I imagined that McCann was cut from the same dirty cloth. He never really looked at you when he spoke to you. His eyes had a busy, nervous jump to them, almost like a rabbit's. They always seemed to be scoping out the rest of the room, darting over your head, past your shoulder—even when he was the one doing the talking. Before he became a politician, McCann had been an accountant. His fingers, and the rest of his mind and body, seemed to be twitching with nervous energy, adding up imaginary figures from big scores he hadn't yet made.

McCann's voice was in the whine family. He rarely conversed. He told you what he had to say in a condescending drone, as if you were an idiot. You always felt as if you were wasting his time, like he had somewhere he had to be and something really important he had to do. He made me, and everyone I knew, feel very uneasy.

What made us most uneasy was that McCann ran again in the 1989 election. Nine other candidates ran against him, including my cousin Mike, who was giving it one more go-around, running on his tax platform. The city's home owners were facing a revaluation of their property, evening out the chips in the poker game that Mike had tried to explain decades ago. People in the Heights and downtown, whose taxes had been unfairly low for years, were now getting hit with huge bills to make up for lower taxes in other neighborhoods. They had to ante up.

As much as Mike tried to lead the reval bandwagon, it was too late for him. Waterfront development, his baby, had already grown up in Jersey City. Telling people "I told you so" when their tax bills came in the mail wasn't enough to get him elected. Mike had other solutions, but as usual, his complicated economics included state tax reform and shot way over everybody's head.

I covered the 1989 election but kept my distance from Mike's ticket. I figured it was a conflict of interest to write about him. Besides, I couldn't even understand what he was talking about half the time. I was assigned to follow one of the front-runners, a black guy who made it into a runoff election with McCann. Glenn Cunningham was a former cop, a decent, honest man who had been a city councilman for years.

He didn't stand a chance.

At one political debate, Cunningham questioned McCann about his lavish lifestyle. McCann lived in Jersey City's most exclusive waterfront development, Port Liberte, which was so close to Lady Liberty that McCann could stick his head out his window and practically kiss her ass. It was a gated community built along canals that separated one cluster of pastel-colored homes from another, which gave it the nick-name Venice on the Hudson. It even had its own private ferry to Man-hattan. Since he had enough money to live in a place like that, everyone at *The Jersey Journal* suspected that McCann was somehow on the take.

When Cunningham suggested that McCann was up to no good, the audience at the mayoral debate applauded McCann, not Cun-ningham, and shouted "good for him." Why shouldn't McCann steal money and live in Port Liberte if he could? It was only natural. He should take what he could get while the gettin' was good. It was be-cause of people like them that McCann was elected to a second term.

At first I thought the only explanation for McCann's victory was that voters, overwhelmed by the number of choices, went with the most familiar Irish face, that there was no way a black man was going to get into office. I blamed racism. But now I think their decision was even more stupid than that: Jersey City's voters missed being abused. It didn't feel like home without a criminal in office.

Midway through his second term, Mayor McCann was charged with defrauding money through a scheme that involved a failed Florida savings-and-loan. He was indicted for mail fraud, bank fraud, tax eva-sion, making false statements to the IRS, and failure to file his taxes. The day he was indicted, McCann called a press conference and hurled excuses, his face growing red and his forehead dripping with sweat. He blamed the Republican party, which, he said, was out to get Democrats like himself so they could cover up the crimes of the Bush family. He blamed Attorney General Dick Thornburgh for using the indictment to boost his Senate run in Pennsylvania.

McCann, playing by the dirty Jersey City rules, didn't simply pro-claim his innocence. He lobbed insults at the prosecutor, Michael Chertoff. "It will become obvious that they were insane to bring this case in the first place," he declared. "And we are going to send Mr. Chertoff back to preparing wills. Maybe I can find him a job driving a sanitation truck in Jersey City."

I covered the trial in Trenton every day, usually poking fun at McCann in print. Each morning I had to face his parents, who sat in the front row of the courtroom looking worried and sad. I would have felt better had they yelled at me. But they looked like such kind, God-fearing people. How had they raised such a shyster? Whenever I felt a pang of guilt about the scathing stories I wrote about their son, I would convince myself that McCann had gotten himself into this mess. It wasn't my fault he was a criminal.

Once he got on the witness stand, I felt a little less guilty. His testimony contradicted the testimony of his own accountant, and he often talked right over the arguments of his own attorney. He admitted that when he doctored his tax returns, he scratched a message to the IRS in the margin: "Come and visit me."

Chertoff used McCann's arrogance to paint a vivid, convincing portrait of 1980s greed. McCann was a liar, a con artist, and a thief, who used hundreds of thousands of dollars that were not his to purchase a Mercedes-Benz, rabbit furs, rare coins, stamps, and $7,000 in tickets to sporting events. He attended football games with the likes of Donald Trump and Roy Cohn.

Even when testimony got bogged down with tax and banking jargon, the trial would be brightened by the spectators who watched from beyond the red velvet rope separating them from the accused. The courtroom was always filled with a character or two, including one old lady who took McCann's side—and a one-hundred-dollar cab ride down to the courthouse to support him. She was one of the legions of Jersey City mumblers and wackos, openly voicing her opinions in court. She reminded me of the old woman who would yell at the statues at OLC Church. One afternoon, after Chertoff danced all over McCann in his cross-examination, she yelled out, "He doesn't even look like a lawyer. He looks like a shrimp." The judge pounded his gavel and demanded order in the court, but by then everyone was laughing.

It was Hudson County theater at its best.

The afternoon the verdict was announced, McCann stood silently, his face as red as his leather chair. The jury foreman stood as well, then calmly said, "Guilty," repeating the word fourteen more times, once after each of the charges. Each time the foreman said the word, McCann's face grew a little redder, until it looked as if it might pop like a big blister, right off his shoulders. McCann was convicted of fifteen counts of fraud, including swindling the S&L out of $300,000, evading income taxes, and covering up his crimes with lies. He was acquitted of one count of mail fraud.

When it was all over, his poor mother sobbed quietly into a tissue. McCann's bodyguard—the former *Jersey Journal* police reporter, whom I had replaced—ran interference, knocking reporters out of the way as the mayor made his way from the courthouse. When he got to the front steps, McCann made no cracks about sanitation trucks, no excuses about the Bush family. His only words were a testy "Where's the car?"

The prosecutor got one last shot in, though. "All of Mr. McCann's insults and offers of jobs driving garbage trucks don't really count for much now," said Chertoff. He would go on to bigger and better things—pursuing President Clinton on his Whitewater dealings.

Clinton got off. But McCann went to jail.

Even after he got out, McCann tried to run for mayor again. And had a large group of supporters. I figured Jersey City deserved him. Luckily, a judge ruled that McCann couldn't hold office. My mother was in the courtroom that day as part of her job. She did a small, celebratory jig.

Since my mother worked in the prosecutor's office, I avoided covering most court cases. The only other trial I covered while at *The Jersey Journal* was a Mafia case that was tried at the federal courthouse in Newark. I looked forward to taking the PATH train there every day. Newark had a cool, 1930s-era subway system, with WPA art on the walls. There was a towering Gothic cathedral, and blooming cherry trees in its sprawling park, fresh pink and green amid the urban decay. I realized just how sad Jersey City was when Newark was a noticeable step up.

The city's razor-wire fences and graffiti were balanced by its abandoned, but still grand Art Deco buildings. It was tired and worn, but I got a sense that something great had once happened there. It even had a real skyline. Jersey City, with the slogan "Everything for Industry," had only the decaying Medical Center, abandoned factories, and contaminated playgrounds as reminders of the good old days.

Going to Newark for the Mafia trial was also a chance to get away from disturbing personal subject matter: no chromium, Colgate development, Loew's Theatre fights, or Cold Storage memories.

My family was filled with criminals, but at least they weren't mobsters. Grandpa was once hauled in for questioning when gangster Frank Costello was called to testify in the 1950s. He got all dressed up for his "interview," feeling like a big shot, connected in the slightest way to a kingpin like Costello. But Grandpa didn't know anything. He wished he did. Every day after his interview, Grandpa sat glued to the television, watching the Costello Senate hearings.

The case I was assigned in Newark revolved around a Hudson County gang accused of racketeering. Their leader was charged with ordering the murder of a New York businessman, Irwin "the Fat Man" Schiff. He weighed over 350 pounds and had been shot gangland-style, twice in the head, while eating his banana flambé at Bravo Sergio, an Upper East Side restaurant. A mysterious blonde who had dined with him that night and had fled the scene showed up as a prosecution witness.

Attending the trial was like watching *The Godfather*. Except better. This was for real—and my family had nothing to do with it.

There was a petite brunette who fingered one of the mobsters in court as we all held our collective breath. The other reporters and I were seated in the first row, and we watched as she nervously testified that she made eye contact with the guy the night of Schiff's murder. He had been standing at the back door of the restaurant, keeping watch, to make sure the murder was carried out, when the brunette came down from her apartment to take out her garbage.

During a break in the testimony, the fingered man, Richard "Bocci" DiSciscio of Bayonne, turned his head to get a look at the clock at the back of the courtroom and accidentally made eye contact with me. His eyes, dark and empty, bore right through mine to the back of my skull. I hoped I never bumped into him in a dark alley while throwing out the trash. I found myself rooting for the prosecution.

Bocci wasn't the only one who made me nervous. The lead defendant was Bobby Manna, accused of being the head of the Hudson County mob and the consigliere, or number-three man, in the Genovese crime family. Manna was the guy who had been placed at

Kenny's disposal years ago, the guy whose father had shot Kenny in the ass. He was also the cousin of my high school boyfriend.

When my mother heard I was covering the trial, she got worried and said, "Don't think he doesn't know who you are. Those guys keep an eye on everybody." But Manna never said a word. He never even looked my way, not like Bocci had.

Manna, Bocci, and their boys—a restaurateur named Marty "Motts" Casella, from Secaucus, and former Hoboken cop Frank "Dipsy" Daniello—were also accused of plotting to murder John Gotti and his brother Gene. Their associate, union leader Rocco "Rocky" Napoli, was charged with conspiracy and labor bribery. The Statue of Liberty was even dragged into the indictment. Manna and his cohorts were accused of instigating a territorial battle with New York unions over control of the Liberty–Ellis Island restoration project.

The least of the charges had to do with illegal gambling. An FBI agent took the stand and explained some of the phrases the jury would be hearing in the gambling portion of the trial. *Runners,* he explained, were at the bottom of the pyramid and dealt with bettors on a day-to-day basis. They would run bets into the office where the numbers were turned in. Uncle Henry had been a runner. *Hit* meant a win, and *overlook* meant that a bookie reneged on a payment. I could have explained all that to the jury.

The best part of the trial were the secretly recorded conversations, taped at the Village Coffee Shop in downtown Jersey City and at Casella's in Hoboken, mostly in the restaurant's "Chariot Room" and the ladies' rest room—used as a private meeting place for the paranoid mobsters. It seemed that very few women frequented Casella's, though I recalled eating dinner there one Christmas Day years ago with my family. My father, tired of the King's Court and Top of the Meadows, had been on a new-restaurant kick and wanted to try Casella's steak. The day we went, the dining room was empty, which we attributed to the holiday. But Casella's was often empty, I learned. Now I knew why.

I wondered if our dinner there was secretly recorded, thrown on the pile of uninteresting, non-Mob-related conversation. Did they have my mother on tape complaining that the rigatoni was overcooked? My pregnant sister worrying aloud about the possibility of varicose veins?

Or my father complaining that the wait staff was rushing us out of there?

Nothing so boring was ever played in court. The dialogue from the tapes we heard was right out of a Martin Scorsese movie. We listened each day with big headphones and followed along with a government transcript. On one tape, a government witness named Vincent "the Fish" Cafaro was overheard telling his wife that he recently had lunch with his mother—who had been dead for the past eighteen years. The defense used that tape as evidence that Cafaro was out of his mind, and therefore an unreliable witness.

Between discussions of hits, the murderous and the gambling kind, the defendants joked on tape about their sexual conquests. Rocky boasted about wanting to give his "mozzarella" to one of his female co-conspirators. Everyone in the courtroom burst out laughing. The only one who kept a straight face—barely—was the judge, Maryann Trump Barry—the sister of Donald Trump. She looked like her brother in a wig and black robe.

In another conversation Rocky complained that he wanted a hot typewriter from a guy nicknamed Trolley Car. "You tell that skinny bastard Trolley Car I want my typewriter. You got two. Richie got two. The other guy got two. And where's mine? I want one." After Rocky got his typewriter, he complained the next day, "Okay. Tell him I need a VCR. Two of 'em."

The most controversial of Rocky's conversations was with Judge Zampella, the guy who had always been such a good friend to Grandpa, the one who brushed my mother off after Grandpa tried to shoot us. The same one who had gotten Grandpa the job in the library, and had let him go that Easter week after he broke all the furniture.

On the Manna tapes, Zampella could be heard saying, "You know, I stopped the investigation and that man has never said thank-you for what I did."

"Ungrateful kid," says Rocky.

In other tapes, Rocky could be overheard discussing how he was getting Zampella's help in expunging his criminal record. "I had Judge Zampella down here the other day," said Rocky. "I know what I'm doing."

He certainly did. In December 1987, Rocky was made an honorary deputy sheriff for Hudson County.

As a result of the tapes, Zampella was forced to step down. He was never charged with any crimes, but stopping investigations for your mobster friends and expunging their criminal records are not the activities a judge is expected to engage in, in his spare time. Not even a judge in Hudson County. My family saw Zampella's fall as karma, his payback for being rude to my mother and Aunt Mary Ann and for failing to keep Grandpa behind bars. He got his. That's what people said about Zampella.

All kinds of people were popping up in the government case: Hoboken policemen, Jersey City police officials, a Hudson County sheriff's officer, an investigator from the Hudson County prosecutor's office who was tipping off the mobsters during gambling raids. Just when I started to have some real fun at the trial, an all too familiar name appeared in the government transcripts. When I read the name, I held my breath and closed my eyes. I had to be seeing things.

I let my breath out, opened my eyes, and looked again. But there it was: cousin Mike's name.

In the August 23, 1987, recording, an unidentified male looking for a lawyer is overheard asking where Mike is. Nothing more. Nothing criminal.

Though Mike wasn't indicted, wasn't on the tapes himself, and wasn't a mobster, he had been a mayoral candidate and was therefore a public figure. I started to panic, right there in the courtroom, wondering if I was supposed to call the office and tell my editor that Mike's name was mentioned in the transcripts. Where was my allegiance?

I suffered a crisis of conscience trying to decide whether to be true to my editor or true to the family. Would I embarrass a relative, one that I actually liked? The mere fact that his name was mentioned, even though it was innocent, could be embarrassing. But it was also news. I thought about those afternoons in Aunt Katie's backyard and the long conversations I had had with Mike about his Norman Rockwell prints and books like *Lord of the Flies*. But that was a long time ago. Was it my responsibility to let the city editor—and the city— know that a former mayoral candidate's name was mentioned in the

Manna tapes? Or should I call Mike and let him know that his name was mentioned?

I did neither.

Instead, I did what Kunegunda did fifty years earlier. I kept my trap shut.

But it didn't matter. Another reporter covering the trial realized who Mike was and wrote a front-page story about Mike's name popping up in the transcripts. In the story, Mike denied any wrongdoing and said he often went to Casella's for dinner, that lots of people did. He even said he planned on calling the prosecutor to offer any help he could.

The Mike story blew over as quickly as it had blown up. No one paid much attention. But I couldn't wait for the Manna trial to be over. Neither could the jury. We were all relieved when Manna and his gang were found guilty. When the foreman delivered the verdict, jurors on either side of him held his legs so he wouldn't fall over.

With the verdict in and the trial finished, I figured I was safe. But Mike's name popped up again, in an AP story I read on the wire one afternoon. This time, Mike was disbarred for misappropriating client funds. Mike's name and picture wound up on the front page of the paper. So did Paula's long, Italian last name. The $20,000 used for the closing on our Summit Avenue house ten years earlier had been part of Mike's "misappropriated funds."

My sister and her husband had no idea that their money had been "misappropriated" and had no clue Mike was being investigated. According to Mike, the problem was discovered during an automatic audit on his account. His biggest crime was simply a matter of "commingling" of funds. In 1977, a law was passed that said lawyers couldn't mix clients' money with their personal money. With the $20,000 in trust, Mike had written checks from the same account.

"Whether you intend to rob them or not, even though no one loses a penny, it's automatic disbarment," Mike explained. "No ifs, ands, or buts."

In his defense, Mike told the Supreme Court of New Jersey he had been having personal problems. His house—the one where we had visited Aunt Katie and where Beansie had been reared—burned down. The rumor was that a bookie threw a Molotov cocktail at it because either Katie or Mike owed him money. Not long after, Mike suffered a broken arm. He had two coronary operations. Chubby killed himself. Uncle Al got cancer. Aunt Katie would go to the Mayo Clinic with him and entertain all the patients on his floor. Many a patient died with a smile on his face because of Aunt Katie—Uncle Al included. Aunt Katie suffered a stroke, but she survived. As if that wasn't enough hard luck, Mike also lost both legs to diabetes.

Mike "endured more grief within several years than many endure in a lifetime," the court found, but "his suffering did not prevent him from knowing what he was doing when he misused client funds."

When I went to visit Mike afterward at his house, the house rebuilt on the ashes of the fire, we chatted about his disbarment, about politics, and about Jersey City. He didn't seem to care that much about being disbarred. He said he hadn't practiced in years anyway, that he'd just done the house closing for Paula because she was a relative. What bothered him more was his inability to run for office because of his health problems. He knew he'd never be elected mayor, and had no plans of running again. But he still had tax-reform ideas that he hoped to share with the governor and other elected officials. Whenever friends and relatives dropped by or called, he tried to explain his complicated theories.

Every time the phone rang while I was there, Mike was very eager to answer it. But each time he rolled his wheelchair over to the phone, one of his prosthetic legs would fall off. I was a nervous wreck the whole afternoon.

"Want me to get that?" I exclaimed each time the phone rang, not sure if I meant the receiver or Mike's leg lying in the middle of the floor.

"No," he joked, bending over, his sense of humor still, miraculously, intact. "It's the only exercise I get."

It was getting harder and harder to decide what was newsworthy and what should be kept a family secret. My family popped up yet again in a story about Hudson County voter fraud. During the Secaucus City Council election, an especially scummy politician went a step beyond using the names of the dead to vote in his favor. Patients at Meadow-view Hospital were registered to vote by absentee ballot.

Some of the people at Meadowview didn't know who the president of the United States was. Some didn't even know their own name. Michael Lari, the council candidate who uncovered the scandal and tried to get the votes thrown out, had a list of fifty mentally and emotionally disturbed voters from Meadowview who were taken advantage of. The names weren't published. But *The Jersey Journal* had the list.

Political reporter Pete Weiss noticed a Stapinski name on that list and asked me if I was related. He handed it to me. When I saw Thomas Stapinski and realized what Pete was writing about, my face got hot. I had a vision of some Hudson County political operative conning my severely retarded uncle into scribbling his name and "voting preference" on a ballot. I swallowed hard, gulping down a strong urge to cry.

I hadn't seen Uncle Tommy in a few years, but I knew his condition hadn't improved. I could just picture his squinty eyes, like my father's, and that sad, retarded smile.

After I regained my composure, the Beansie temper rose higher than ever before. I wanted to drive my Buick Skylark to Secaucus and keep driving until I ran over the council candidate responsible for this. Then I'd put it in reverse, back up, and run over him again.

When I calmed down, I decided against the hit and run. The pen was mightier than the Buick Skylark. I decided to write a column about the voter fraud, how disgusting the whole thing was. I could describe Uncle Tommy and my visits to him as a child, how he had looked the last time I saw him, at Thanksgiving dinner at our house on Summit Avenue. There was no way Uncle Tommy could voluntarily cast a vote for someone. I would write a column about it, and write it with the venom that could only come from personal involvement.

But my family asked me not to. They were embarrassed.

Uncle Tommy had been a dirty family secret for decades, and they didn't want him trotted out, no matter how just the cause. What got me, though, wasn't my family's protests. I found out that this wasn't the only time Meadowview had been raided for Hudson County votes.

This had been going on for years. Uncle Tommy had probably been taken advantage of for decades. I just hadn't been in a position to notice. I suddenly felt helpless and very small in the face of all that corruption. I was a footnote, incapable of change in such a fucked-up place.

Heartsick and disgusted, I buckled under the weight of Jersey City and my family. Instead of writing a column about Uncle Tommy, I decided to leave *The Jersey Journal*.

As I searched for a reporting job in the tri-state area, I grew more and more bitter. What I really wanted was to get away from my family, and living in Connecticut or Long Island wouldn't accomplish that. But I didn't know where to go or how to get away for good.

I moved within a five-mile radius three times in less than three years, in a desperate attempt to make myself happy. From Weehawken, I moved back to Jersey City, to a duplex apartment downtown. I loved the place, but I hated one of my roommates, a vegetarian who yelled at me for cooking chicken in her stainless-steel pots. I finally decided to move out after she went to Nicaragua on a monthlong humanitarian mission and stuck me with her three-hundred-dollar phone bill.

Next, I moved to a Heights basement apartment, in a house that my sister had bought as an investment. Every time it rained, my kitchen flooded. But what finally made me move were the upstairs tenants, noisy postal workers who played Lynyrd Skynyrd when they returned from their graveyard shift each night. The Oriental rug in the vestibule and the pictures on the hallway walls vanished. I was afraid my stereo speakers would be next or, worse, that they'd shoot Wendell when he went up and asked them for the tenth time to turn down "Free Bird."

I considered moving in with Wendell, but I figured I'd just bring him down. I was so miserable, it was contagious. Instead, I moved to Manhattan, to a mouse- and roach-infested apartment at the mouth of the Holland Tunnel, and commuted every day to Journal Square.

While I searched for a new job, my weekly column became sharper, more biting, and increasingly controversial. I lambasted the planning board for eating lavish meals at the expensive Casa Dante Restaurant, Frank Sinatra for marketing his own inedible spaghetti sauce in a jar, and a local Italian parish for not welcoming black people to its annual feast.

The pastor of Mount Carmel, the parish I took to task, delivered sermons about me on Sundays and sponsored a petition drive to try to get me fired. The paper's only black columnist, Earl Morgan, and some white clergy members came to my defense. But things got ugly. In the mail, I got a dirty maxi-pad with my column wrapped around it. I got letters telling me I should shut up and get a proper woman's job, as a nurse or a secretary.

My family was forced to defend me week after week. While out with his in-laws at an Italian dinner-dance, Stanley almost choked on his antipasto when one of the guys at the table said, "So what about that Stapinski broad?" He was the pastor of Mount Carmel and was about to launch into a tirade against me, not knowing Stanley was my brother. Dolores, my sister-in-law, had to practically sit on top of Stanley so he wouldn't jump across the table and give the priest a black eye.

We laughed about it at the next family get-together, but it wasn't really funny. Not only was my family affecting my writing, but now my writing was affecting my family.

My sister got a job as a teacher at P.S. 27, which was named, ironically, the Zampella School, after one of the judge's relatives. In my column, I tried to stay away from the subject of education altogether for fear my sister would be fired. But it seemed that whatever I wrote about, there was some family connection.

Because of the attention my column was getting, Ma was transferred at work from the record room to central judicial processing court, where the bad guys were arraigned—and where there was less confidential information floating around. Working CJP was a much harder job for my sixty-year-old mother, and the prosecutor hoped that by transferring her down there, she would quit. He didn't know her very well. She would not be manipulated. Anyway, she had seen much worse at the DMV. Many of her former customers were now the bad guys being arraigned. They'd wave to Ma as they were led away in handcuffs. "Hey, Motor Vehicle Lady," they'd say. "What are you doing here?" Ma thrived at CJP, and became indispensable.

But her demotion was just another reason for me to get the hell out of Jersey City. If I left the paper, my mother's job would get easier. I was no longer helping her by sticking around. She wouldn't die if I moved away. Besides, her job at the courthouse was a conflict on so many different levels. Every week there was swag for sale in the courthouse hallways: clothes, fine china, knockoff designer watches, radios, electric razors. I wasn't sure if it was confiscated property from swag busts or if it was just plain swag that fell off the truck and directly into the courthouse hallways.

An investigator noticed my mother perusing some courthouse swag one afternoon and asked to talk to her. She was afraid that she was being caught buying swag, that the investigator was going to question her or, worse, have her arrested. Instead, he asked my mother to leave the bag of goodies under his desk for him to browse through so he could buy a few things for the wife and kids. He knew all about the swag. And so did I. So did everybody in the courthouse. Was I supposed to report this? My allegiance to my mother certainly outweighed any journalistic ethics.

I was struck by the irony. Just a couple of years earlier, I had yelled at a friend for voting for a candidate so his mother could get a city job. Now I was no better. Worse, really.

I told myself that journalistic ethics were for people more fortunate than I, for people without relatives in Hudson County. They were for people whose parents could afford them, whose families didn't have to rely on county jobs. I was rationalizing, but it beat ratting out my mother and her friends and the guy selling the swag.

The real reason I couldn't write about the courthouse swag was that I was wearing it. My mother had given me dozens of swag shirts, sweaters, and nightgowns from the courthouse hallways. The kids in our family played with swag toys and stuffed animals. My sister had swag china and a swag designer watch and smelled of swag perfume. There were knockoff handbags and gloves, underwear and slippers.

If I was to write about the courthouse swag, I would have to get rid of at least half my wardrobe. Then I would have to find Ma a new job, because she would be fired or, worse, ostracized from her circle of swag-buying friends.

Anyway, what was a little swag on the side? A cheap designer watch never hurt anyone, except the guy whose truck had been hijacked. I had grown up on swag. We all had.

Hadn't we?

There was only one way to solve the swag problem, only one way to help my mother get her job back in the file room, to avoid getting hit with the sadness that swirled around Mike and Uncle Tommy and to stop my brother from punching somebody in the mouth when I wrote my next column. I had to go.

At twenty-seven, I was getting gray hair from worrying so much about the conflicts of interest in my complicated little life. Vacations with Wendell weren't enough of a break. They only left me wanting more time away from Hudson County. I felt like the tired statue outside City Hall, so weary that I needed to sit things out for a while.

When Wendell left the paper and got a job at New York *Newsday,* I felt abandoned. I finally left *The Jersey Journal* and moved away. Not to Connecticut or Long Island or the Midwest or sunny California. In a moment of claustrophobic panic I moved far, far away, so far that no one—not even my mother—would visit me.

17

RESURRECTION

In a moment of insanity, I joined the Jesuit Volunteer Corps and took a job as a news director at a radio station in Nome.

Nome, Alaska, a few miles from Siberia. The station was called KNOM—*monk* spelled backward.

I had waited too long to leave. Far too long. It was as if I had been sitting on a springboard at *The Jersey Journal.* The longer I stayed and the more pressure I felt, the farther the spring was bent back. When the board finally let loose, in the summer of 1992, I was flung to the farthest reaches of the globe.

Nome seemed the opposite of Hudson County: no people, no decay, no corruption; just lots of snow and ice. Clean, cool, and empty. I went there sight unseen. I should have done a little research first.

There was crime and corruption in Nome. Since its population was only three thousand, there were fewer crimes, but per capita it probably worked out to be about the same as Hudson County. Alcoholism was rampant. Suicide was common. And worst of all, it was butt-ugly. It was the only place in Alaska that was as ugly as Jersey City.

There were rusted water tanks at the edge of town. And only three seasons: Snow, Mud, and Dust. The streets were not paved. There was a saloon on every corner. No mountain view. And there were no trees. It was so cold in Nome that there were no trees. I couldn't believe I had chosen a place that had less foliage than Jersey City. I didn't think such a place existed. But it did. And I was now a resident.

I tried to look on the bright side. When I first got there, I figured I'd be helping people through KNOM, maybe doing some kind of Christian outreach to try and make the world a better place. But the extent of our religious duty at the radio station was popping in a tape of the rosary at night, to lull the northern masses to sleep. It wasn't what I'd had in mind.

So I picked up where I had left off at *The Jersey Journal* and wrote stories about an Eskimo guy accused of stealing windows from a HUD-funded project and the state investigation into a local nursing home for native elders. There were reports of mutated walruses washing up on the shores of Eskimo villages because of the nuclear waste the Russians had dumped into the ocean. It was worse than the Jersey City chromium problem. Instead of the politics at city council meetings, I covered the politics at walrus-commission meetings.

After a few weeks of chasing stories like a madwoman, I looked around me and noticed everyone else was traveling about half my speed. Then I remembered why I was here. I had moved to Alaska to sit things out.

I put on my news blinders and decided to write only happy stories for a while, stories about sled-dog races and skating rink openings.

I tried to keep abreast of what was happening in the real world. While at KNOM, I read about the World Trade Center bombing on the AP wire. I remembered my old fear of the Twin Towers falling across the river and crushing my house. I couldn't believe it had almost happened. I was glad I wasn't there for it.

I was not surprised to learn that the bombers lived in Jersey City. I could picture them staring day after day across the river, hating those towering symbols of American capitalism, of progress, hating them enough to actually blow them up. One of the nation's biggest urban disasters was caused by a group of maniacs who felt they had something important to say but were powerless to say it—three guys from Jersey City. The place could drive you crazy if you didn't escape in time.

I was glad I did, as ugly as Nome was. I joined a bowling league, sang in a Christmas choir, and went on long walks along the town's beach, where gold prospectors still set up raggedy tents and panning equipment in summer. I wrote in a journal that cousin Gerri gave me as a going-away present and composed long letters to Wendell, who was now breaking stories about the World Trade Center bombing. At night, I put on my fur ruff and watched the aurora borealis light up the Nome sky.

Whenever I could, whenever the weather permitted, I got out of town and headed to the country. Just a short drive outside ugly Nome, you could find yourself in the middle of nowhere. Cool, clean nowhere.

After an eleven-mile drive or bike ride, it was a three-mile hike to Tom's Cabin, an old miner's cabin. A former Jesuit volunteer named Tom had discovered it and fixed it up a few years earlier. We current volunteers helped maintain it on our hikes out, chopping wood, sweeping the crooked floor, and restocking the canned food and first-aid supplies. There was a dirt road that led to Tom's, though driving was pretty rough going. Most visitors to Tom's Cabin walked it or biked it or snowmachined it, depending on the season.

Most people would stay out for the day and then hike back in and hitch a ride to town. Some spent the night. But it was sometimes tricky. Just because it was a nice day on the hike out didn't necessarily mean it would be a nice day on the hike in. If there was a blizzard, you could be trapped at Tom's for several days. And in the spring and summer there were bears. Everyone in Nome had heard about the group of volunteers who hiked out to find a bloody, broken window at Tom's— from the bear who broke in to steal the Dinty Moore stew left inside.

My bowling partners, Eric and Johnny O—short for John O'Gorman—decided to hike out to the cabin Easter weekend. And Johnny O couldn't wait to tell me.

"We're going out to the cabin on Saturday," John said, poking me in the arm on Holy Thursday. Johnny O was a big guy, so when he poked you, it hurt.

I rolled my eyes and punched him back, but negative reinforcement never worked with Johnny O. He'd poke you again the next chance he got. Besides, he was such a sweet guy, I'd always feel a little guilty after hitting him. He wasn't even aware he was hurting me.

"You should come with us," he said, his voice cracking a little in his nervous excitement. It was hard to feel enthusiastic around Johnny O. Any excitement usually paled in comparison to his. But sometimes it was contagious, like the June day he decided we should jump into the Grand Central River in our underwear.

He stripped right there on the road, and seconds later I was sitting on the metal railing in my panties and long-johns top, counting down to the plunge. The water was about thirty feet below, turquoise blue, deep, and clear right to the bottom. It was June, but there was still ice on the edges of the river. We looked at each other and laughed. "On three," he said. Together we counted, "One, two, three." And slipped off into the unknowable as everyone around us cheered.

Most people have never felt water that cold on their bodies. There's the quick ice cube down the back of the shirt now and then from the practical joker friend. But the water in the Grand Central that day was as cold as water gets without freezing. It was like a tub filled with ice cubes. That was the Grand Central in summer.

As soon as I hit the ice-cold water, the only thing on my mind was that I had to get out as soon as I possibly could. I pushed my way up to the surface and swam faster than I'd ever swum, crunched over the ice with my bare feet and ran up the embankment to my dry, warm clothes. All in five seconds flat. I thought it was a stupid thing to have done. But as the day wore on, the sun not setting that long summer's day, I was glad Johnny O had been so contagious. My body tingled for the next twelve hours. I felt more alive that day, physically, than I'd ever felt. The jolt woke me up and permanently removed the twenty-seven years of crud that had settled on my brain while in Hudson County.

Johnny O, one of my many friends and saviors in Nome, was now convincing me to take the hike out to Tom's in the snow. I wasn't very enthusiastic about snowshoes, and I didn't think I could keep up with Eric's cross-country skiing. He'd been all the way to the edge of the Bering Sea ice in storm conditions.

"I'll just slow you down," I whined.

But Eric and Johnny O insisted I come along.

On the Saturday before Easter, I took a hike out to Tom's with them. The bears were still sleeping and spring breakup, the time of year the ice on the sea cracks and floats out to sea, was just a few weeks away. There wasn't much danger of a snowstorm or a bear attack. Eric skied, Johnny O snowshoed, and, because I weighed just under a hundred pounds, my lightest since high school, I walked. Very lightly.

Traveling with two men also guaranteed a light pack. Hanging out with boys still had its benefits. Eric carried most of the water; Johnny O, most of the food. Eric, a fellow Jesuit Volunteer from Colorado, was convinced the Nome water was contaminated with nuclear waste from the Russian Far East. Johnny O, a former Volunteer, liked food even more than we did, so he carried most of it.

I tried the snowshoes for a few minutes. But they were uncomfortable and almost impossible to walk in. I had to walk with my legs far apart but keep them pointing straight or else the wooden backs would cross each other and I would trip. I traveled about fifteen feet in them, then decided I'd take my chances walking without them and tied them on the back of my pack. Though it was warm, in the forties, the snow hadn't melted in most places yet. There was a layer of ice on top of about two feet of powder. The melted snow that had frozen over in a slippery coating formed a thin but resistant shell.

One hundred pounds was just about all it could bear. Every ten minutes or so, my boot would plunge through, the white crust sucking in my entire leg. I'd struggle up out of the small hole I'd made, then push myself up with my mittened hands. That first step after a fall would plunge me right back into the snow. Once I fell in, it was as if the ice knew I was wary of falling in again. I fell in again and again, until I finally got my footing. In some spots where ice had collapsed, I'd tiptoe. Or pretend I was a deer, scurrying across the tundra. I wished myself lighter, held my breath. Where the ice looked sturdy, I'd hurry across. Where it looked like it might give, I slid slowly forward. It was not an easy way to travel three miles, but it looked a lot easier than the snowshoes Johnny O was wearing.

Most of the day, I walked in Johnny O's path. The flattened snow left by his snowshoes was packed hard and wide. Johnny O wasn't following any path. In the summer, there was a marked trail that hikers could follow out to Tom's Cabin. But in winter, everything looked the same, and I was more than a little worried we wouldn't find the cabin and would wander off in the wrong direction. Eric, meanwhile, danced and swerved around us, made circles in our paths, and served as an annoying reminder that we should have brought cross-country skis. To punish him, I placed my Walkman at the top of his backpack and set up mini-speakers right below his shoulders. Eric was our home-away-from-home entertainment center. While we struggled along, he played tunes from his back. But after a while Eric yelled for me to remove the speakers. We could hear him loud and clear, but he had no idea what we were saying behind his back. The music was too loud.

Within the first hour of the trip, distant pops could be heard from the Nome firing range a few miles away. Because the willows were still covered in snow, there were no birds yet. So once we got out of earshot of the shooting range and turned off the Walkman and stood still, there was silence. Complete silence.

I had never known complete silence. There was always traffic, always an ambulance coming or going, someone screaming outside my window, a clock ticking, a baby crying, the heat rising in the radiator, muffled sounds of the next-door neighbor's home entertainment system, a family story being told. In Nome, there had been dogs howling, drunks singing, the station humming, and snow machines roaring. Silence was something completely new to my ears. Something that took getting used to.

I had once heard near silence on the side of a road on a trip with Wendell. During one of our vacations from work, we pulled off the side of the highway in Northern California to take a look at the Milky Way. It was the middle of the night, so there were no other cars. Just some crickets. It was so quiet that we were scared, scared of the immensity of the heavens, of the possibility of an ax murderer lurking in the redwoods.

Wendell and I were scared of the silence and what might fill that void suddenly, violently. We jumped back into the rent-a-car and turned the radio up loud. That night, with the crickets cricketing and the road lights buzzing, we hadn't even heard total silence. But it seemed to me that no one but the people here, the people living above the tree line, had ever heard total silence.

In the isolated spots in the Midwest, in the South, and in the rest of Alaska, there were birds singing, the wind blowing through leaves and branches. The wind rustling against something. Whistling through canyons. Past cows or moose. But out on the road to Tom's, there was nothing to rustle. Nothing to whistle past. Nothing to sing, unless we did the singing. Just smooth, aerodynamic, wind-resistant hills of ice and snow. The hard-packed white outlines cutting across the blue sky were silent for miles. White and blue, the colors of winter, didn't make a peep.

We knew we were close when we heard the sound of icicles dripping in the distance.

Eric was the first to reach the cabin, so he dug the piled-up snow from the doorway. On our fourth and last hour of hiking, I'd grown tired. But now I was charged by the sight of the one-room shack and the lengthened hours of sunlight still shining on us. Like children let out of school early on a snow day, we dropped our gear inside the wooden door, grabbed three garbage bags, and headed for the hills.

Sledding above the tree line was a special treat, since there's nothing to hit for hundreds of miles in each direction. I felt like Santa Claus riding on the electric razor in that television commercial, the one where he goes gliding up and down, up and down, into TV infinity. As we gained more confidence, we approached steeper and steeper hills, until Eric and Johnny O decided to try the kamikaze hill, the vertical drop. I just sat back on my garbage bag and watched and laughed as their bags left the surface and they entered free falls and then landed in the soft powder below.

While the boys frolicked, I climbed to the top of an adjacent hill and crawled into a narrow, ice-blue crevice, where a line of noisy icicles hung. I leaned my head out far enough to place my mouth beneath them and drink in the cold water dripping from their tips.

That night we dined on Dinty Moore stew and ramen-noodle soup cooked over the stove that warmed the cabin. Eric got the fire so dangerously hot that it glowed red through the black cast iron. For dessert we had popcorn, Gummi Bears, and an entire box of rosé wine. For shipping purposes, most of Nome's wine came in big boxes rather than in bottles. We smoked from Eric's pipe and danced until 2 A.M. to the music from the tiny Walkman speakers, which were now placed on a rickety wooden shelf. I joked that we should keep it down. The neighbors might complain.

We finally turned the music off and set up our sleeping bags. But before I climbed in, I decided to take a look outside.

I walked out into the dark, cool night. The blue sky was now ink-black. The only light came from the stars and moon, far above the cabin's tin roof. I felt small and very far away from anywhere—closer to the moon than to the rest of the world. There was a peacefulness here that I hadn't felt on the highway with Wendell, and surely had never felt in Hudson County. This time the vastness of the night sky and the silence didn't send me hurrying back to the safety inside. It was the cold, finally, that chased me back to Tom's Cabin.

We slept long and hard, rising on Easter Sunday to the silence. It was the most solemn religious holiday I'd ever experienced. More holy than a visit to St. Peter's. More beautiful than midnight mass at OLC. Instead of incense, we breathed in the smoke from the chimney. The white snow was purer than the Easter lilies I had been forced to carry each year in Holy Thursday procession. There were no lily pots for me this Holy Week. Just empty cans of Dinty Moore to carry back home. To Nome.

18

VALENTINE'S DAY

I considered staying in Nome. I lived there a year and watched the ice break up and move out toward Russia. When summer came 'round again, I picked blueberries from the tundra and went soaking in the hot springs nearby.

But after twelve months in the middle of nowhere, I felt it was time to go somewhere. I considered buying a one-way ticket around the world and traveling for a year. Then I almost moved to Chicago to take a job at the *Sun-Times*. I also wondered what it would be like to live in Southern California, the colors bright and the weather warm. But the truth was, I missed Wendell. And Wendell was in New York.

I decided to go back to the East Coast, but not back home. I'd never go back there, really. I would visit from time to time, but I couldn't live there again.

There were things I missed about home, though. While I was away, I realized that not everyone knew what a brownstone looked like. I missed their smooth faces and high stoops and the solid feeling they gave you. I realized that the ingredients I needed for the food I liked to eat were not easily found in most grocery stores in Alaska, or in most of

America. I couldn't even buy a pound of rigatoni. Elbow macaroni was as good as it got at the Nome supermarket. No matter how hard I tried, I couldn't put sauce on elbow macaroni. It was a sacrilege.

The pace I was used to was not the pace of most towns, or even most cities. I talked too fast for everybody I met, and they made fun of my accent. The weather I was accustomed to, the way it changed just when I was getting sick of it, was not the same everywhere. In other words I was homesick, as much as a person could be for a place as sick as Jersey City.

On my first visit back to Jersey City after Alaska, I took my mountain bike on the PATH train, then rode up the hill to the Heights. Later, when I wasn't looking, someone stole my bike from my brother's garage.

I was lucky that the details I loved about Jersey City could be found elsewhere, namely Brooklyn, and that Wendell lived there. When I moved back to the Lower 48, I moved in with him. I announced to my inquiring Polish aunts that I was living in sin, right across New York Harbor.

The Brooklyn sidewalks were just like the ones in Jersey City, except I hadn't memorized their cracks and pockmarks. I could buy fresh mozzarella and pierogi, but while waiting in line I didn't have to see exclassmates and politicians I had exposed in the pages of *The Jersey Journal*.

Brooklyn was like Jersey City worked over by a stretching machine: The bad neighborhoods were bigger, but so were the good neighborhoods. They spread out for miles, with their brownstones and flowering trees. Just when I tired of summer, autumn leaves fell.

Out of the many spots on the globe that I visited, Brooklyn was closest to home. The good parts of home.

Brooklyn was part of New York, and its people seemed less beaten down than people from Jersey City. It was hard to be intimidated by something you were a part of.

The buildings I had gazed at from the Hudson River's edge always looked like a crown of jewels at night, the green-copper crown of the Woolworth Building a glowing emerald, the World Trade Center two strips of diamonds, and the Empire State Building a sapphire, ruby, or amethyst, depending on the holiday. The tops of the buildings were jewels sitting silently on the head of a sleeping king, riches that Jersey City residents coveted but couldn't steal.

The skyline seemed different from the other side. The people in Brooklyn didn't act like the world owed them something. They were proud, not arrogant; civic-minded, but never small-town. Though they ate the same food, had the same accent, and walked on sidewalks made from the same blue stone as people from Jersey City, they seemed more happy. Or maybe it was just that I was happy.

My relatives were still close by, but we were separated by two rivers. They were afraid to drive over to Brooklyn for fear they'd get lost in a borough so big. I could see them whenever I wanted, not whenever they wanted. I was a freelancer, and could write about all kinds of subjects that had nothing to do with me. Or them. I could cast off those family stories.

But I should have known better. You could choose your friends, my mother said, but not your family. They chose you, ages ago, centuries before you were born. And there was really no escape.

If anything, the family stories grew closer. They entered my generation and touched my family in ways we'd never seen, pissing on the hallowed ground of Gammontown. They showed that you couldn't run away from your relatives, and that no matter how far you ran, history would catch up with you and fix you good.

While I was still climbing mountains and mushing dog teams on the frozen tundra, one of the cousins I had left behind was establishing a career as a criminal. When I found out, it was no surprise. It's just that I had forgotten all about George, the kid with the light in his brown eyes, who had seen his father hanging in the doorway. I hadn't seen George in years.

In Jersey City, George never stood a chance. I always wondered whether if he'd grown up somewhere else, George may have turned out all right. Maybe he would have been a cop in an alternate universe. Or a famous bank robber. Or a mad scientist, his thick Barney Google glasses crooked above his crooked smile.

By the time he was eighteen, George had been convicted of aggravated assault and sentenced to seven years in prison. Four years later, let out early, George was convicted of robbery and burglary and sentenced to two and a half years. While I was away, George developed a heroin habit, like his father. He needed to support it, and in the fall of 1993, he was arrested in a chain-snatching but was let go when the victim refused to pursue the charges.

To get clean, George got a job at the Sewerage Authority, working with his mother's boyfriend, a former Colgate employee. But that didn't last. In the spring of the following year, he was arrested yet again for committing fifty-seven burglaries in a four-month-long crime spree. He complained that he'd been railroaded, that many of the crimes weren't his.

The police said that George had robbed neighbors' homes—mostly in the OLC neighborhood—on Colgate Street, Henderson Street, Morris Street, and Essex Street. One of the houses he hit was 171 Grand, right next door to where my Russian great-grandmother was killed by her husband years ago. They said he had burglarized six homes on Sussex Street, a few doors away from OLC, shattering the calm of Gammontown.

George also stole a blue Toyota van. He should have driven it to a faraway place. But he didn't. George stayed right in stinky old Jersey City. If he had to stay, he should have stayed close to home, within the safe confines of Gammontown.

In his criminal pursuits, George moved farther out of the neighborhood and into other areas of downtown, to more unknown territory. I think that the farther from home he went, the more risky his career became. Knowing your subject is essential, even in the world of crime. Knowing who owns what, who's a loudmouth, who's not, can help you stay out of jail. On Second Street, Fourth Street, Fifth Street, Eighth Street, and Pavonia Avenue, George got closer and closer to jail.

One of his most stupid crimes was count twenty-one: terroristic threats. George broke into a woman's house, and when she went to pick up the phone, he grabbed the receiver out of her hand, hung it up, and threatened to kill her if she tried anything more. It was one thing to commit crimes against property. It was another to threaten to kill the owners of that property.

But the biggest mistake George made was robbing the home of Nidia Colon, a downtown resident who also happened to be a Hudson County freeholder. George had no idea who Colon was. Which, of course, was the problem. Had he known she was a politician, George would never have burglarized her home. He just as easily could have robbed her next-door neighbor.

For George, the political became personal.

Before he was even convicted, George spent eighteen months behind bars, held on $50,000 cash-only bail. Eventually, he was given a 10 percent cash option and the family raised enough money to set him free. On November 6, 1995, George made the $5,000 bail. To stay off the streets and out of trouble, he worked Bingo at OLC to earn some pocket money. Maybe he should have hopped a train to another town, or a plane to Mexico.

Valentine's Day 1996—a day short of his father's anniversary in heaven—George pleaded guilty to twenty-nine of the fifty-seven burglaries. He could wind up serving ten years. His sentencing was a little over a month away, but the prosecutor argued he should be sentenced sooner, or kept in custody. He was worried that George might get into more trouble.

But George was allowed to leave the courthouse. Outside, his mother, Mary Ann, gave him six dollars to buy a Valentine's Day rose for his girlfriend.

George went home with his girlfriend to her apartment in the Heights, just a few blocks from our Summit Avenue house and down the street from Stanley's apartment. Tired from the depressing events of the day, and probably thinking of his father, George took a nap. Around 7:50 P.M., he woke up and asked his girlfriend to go out with him. He wanted to get some air. But she wanted to stay home. They argued. And George stormed out on his own, perhaps in search of somewhere to spend that six dollars, meant for Valentine's Day flowers.

That night, George's mother was home in Gammontown. Her Morris Street apartment faced where the Colgate factory used to be before it was closed and the fresh, soapy smell was swiped forever from the air.

Mary Ann was watching the soap opera awards when she and her boyfriend, Eddie, noticed cop cars speeding past the window. Eddie ran outside to see what was happening. Mary Ann followed, not even bothering to change her flimsy three-dollar canvas shoes. It was cold out, but she wouldn't be out for long.

A friend with a police scanner told Mary Ann that the cops were chasing a kid with a gun on the roof of 207 Warren Street. That was the street where Bromirski's Funeral Home was, where Daddy had been laid out. It was the street with the unobstructed view of the Statue of Liberty. During the statue's centennial celebration, people gathered early in the morning on Warren Street to get a view of the evening fireworks.

On February 14, 1996, there were no fireworks, of course. But a large crowd congregated there again, dozens of couples pulled away from the warm glow of their TV sets, huddling in the cold, their coats thrown over housedresses and pajamas, their necks craned in the hopes of getting a glimpse of some real-live police drama. Mary Ann joined the crowd.

In the frigid night, Mary Ann's feet kept freezing, forcing her to run back to her apartment. But she couldn't stay away from the scene of the crime: 207 Warren Street, which was right across from the house where George's father had died twenty-four years earlier.

It was at 204 Warren that Mary Ann and George had found him hanging in a doorway the night after Valentine's Day.

Mary Ann stood right in front of that house at 204 Warren in her cheap slip-on shoes, gazing up at 207, across the street, where the police chase was going down, the Statue of Liberty green and glowing, its back to her and the nosy crowd.

Cop cars were zooming past. Some policemen ran through the Italian restaurant on the corner, their guns drawn. Four plainclothes cops ran up the stairs of the brownstone.

Then Mary Ann heard the gunshots. One shot, followed by three in quick succession.

Boom.

Boom, boom, boom.

It wasn't clear who had been shot, if anyone, but with so many cops around it was a good bet the robber was down.

Mary Ann's first thought wasn't for the robber himself but for the robber's mother. Mary Ann, who knew the sorrow of having a troubled kid, thought no mother deserved the pain of losing a child, no matter what that child did.

The plainclothes cops, uninjured, ran back down to the street, got into their cars, and left. Meanwhile, more than two dozen uniformed cops arrived on the scene, their blue police cars parked in zigzags in the middle of Warren Street, their lights flashing.

When she got home, Mary Ann got a funny feeling, as if something had passed through her. She got goose bumps and wondered, for the first time, if maybe the robber was George.

"Eddie," she said. "There's something wrong, Eddie."

"Don't even think that," he said, changing the TV channel. He knew what she was thinking.

"You're thinking the same thing," she told him.

Eddie didn't answer.

The only hope Mary Ann clung to was that she knew George didn't own a gun.

She kept going back to the scene, where about thirty cops and, by now, a few reporters were gathered. There were TV reporters and the new police reporter from *The Jersey Journal*.

Mary Ann ran back and forth between Warren and Morris Streets seven times that night, her feet still freezing. In her panic, she hadn't thought to put on warmer shoes. On one of her last runs outside, a neighbor told her that the robber was a Puerto Rican. Mary Ann's heart pounded in her eardrums.

George's father had been Puerto Rican, so George was half–Puerto Rican.

One of the cops, the son of Ruthie, the crossing guard/lottery winner who had died of a heart attack, was on the scene. Mary Ann stood close and listened to what he was saying to his captain, to try and prove her worst fears wrong. She overheard him say that a second robber had gotten away.

Mary Ann went home one more time and turned on the Channel 9 news, which showed paramedics taking the robber out in a body bag. She couldn't see his face. But she was scared now, and told Eddie that if anyone knocked on the door, he shouldn't let them in. She went to the bedroom, got down on her knees, and started praying. *Please, God. Let him be the one that got away.*

There was a knock on the door. It was a homicide detective, and Eddie let him in. "There was just a tragic accident," said the detective. "A terrible mistake." He showed Eddie a picture of George. "Is this him?"

Mary Ann screamed that she wanted to see her son. But the detective told her she couldn't, that George was already gone. Not just in the way that Daddy was gone, but physically gone, too. George's body was on its way to Newark for an autopsy. Mary Ann prayed that there had been a mix-up, some kind of mistake.

Before she even saw her son's body, the police delivered an envelope to her house. Inside were George's thick glasses.

Mary Ann never really found out what had happened that night. She didn't believe the *Jersey Journal* version, that six hours after pleading guilty in court, minutes after leaving his girlfriend's house, George committed yet another robbery, this time at a fruit-and-vegetable store in the city's Greenville section—a neighborhood he'd never hit before. When a silent alarm was tripped, police arrived on the scene. But George pointed his gun at the cops and got away.

Leading police on a wild chase through the city, George finally crashed a stolen red Hyundai downtown in our peaceful parish neighborhood, got out, ran through several backyards, then climbed a fire escape to one of the tarred roofs. Police chased him on foot, jumping from roof to roof until George eluded them by breaking through a roof hatch, then kicking in the door of the second-floor apartment.

George chose the apartment carefully, knowing full well who lived there: a distant relative named Bob, the brother-in-law of my aunt Terri, my father's sister, the one who hit 057 straight the day I was born. Bob was an elderly bachelor and lived alone on Warren Street. When George popped in, Bob was asleep. But not for long. He came out in his pajamas, holding a searchlight.

George, holding a loaded .38, told Bob to keep quiet and not to worry, that he knew him, was related almost, and that he wouldn't hurt him. He was just trying to find a way out without the police seeing him. But George had trouble opening the kitchen window. He jimmied it and punched it but couldn't get it open in time.

The police busted through the door and told George to surrender. But George had no plans of going back to jail. He pointed the gun at his own head.

That's how I see him when I picture him now: frozen in time, with that gun to his head, which was filled with that awful memory of his father swinging in the doorway right across the street. It was like George's history was weighing heavy, as if cement shoes had been dragging him down for years and years. It was easier to just drown than to fight the sinking.

Maybe the memory of his father dying was like the vague memory of a bad dream you can't really recall but that flashes for a second when you get back under the covers the next night, weary and tired, all your defenses down. Maybe for that split second, with his gun to his head, George saw his father hanging there.

"I'm not going back to jail," George told the cops. "I'd rather die." The two police officers tried to talk George out of shooting himself but said he turned the gun on them. "If I'm gonna go, you're gonna go," they said he told them. The police opened fire. George was shot four times, in the hand, rib cage, leg, and—the fatal bullet—the Adam's apple.

He still had the six dollars in his pocket that his mother had given him for the flowers. But that part didn't make it into *The Jersey Journal*. It would have made him human, and there was no room for humanity in the police report. The picture the paper ran was an ugly mug shot of George, his hair cut in a fade, his chin covered in a goatee, his glasses as big and thick as when he was a kid. No crooked smile for the camera.

As George was carried out in the body bag, the cops were treated for trauma at a local hospital. Maybe they should have taken Bob with them. George's blood was splattered all over his apartment. Bob had been injured in the war while stationed in Casino, Italy. But this was too much to handle. He could barely cut his own meat anymore because of his handicap, never mind mop up this mess. Though the police sent a crew to clean most of it up, Aunt Terri wound up getting on her hands and knees and scrubbing Bob's kitchen floor.

Mary Ann didn't believe that George even had a gun. She thought that he was simply pulling his glasses out of his pocket when the cops burst into Bob's apartment, that they mistook the glasses for a gun and blew him away.

Even if he had a gun and they thought he was going to kill himself, why didn't they back off? she thought. Why didn't they come out into the crowd and get Mary Ann—his own mother—to talk him down?

There were conflicting reports about where George was shot. Was it the second floor or third floor? Was there a female eyewitness? Were there four shots or five shots? The cops told Mary Ann no one else was involved in the robbery, despite what Ruthie's son said that night. Mary Ann didn't believe George was the one who had robbed the store earlier that evening, that it must have been the other guy, the second assailant, who fled the scene, that George was just in the wrong place at the wrong time. In with the wrong crowd. Yet again. Mary Ann wondered who the cops would blame for their unsolved robberies now that George, their scapegoat, was gone.

She tried talking to the cops, tried having someone arrange a meeting with Bob, but no one would sit down with her. She wanted to ask Bob if George had suffered. "I wanted to go up there, to the place where he got shot, just to see it," she said. "He was a human being. He was my son."

Before the shooting, Mary Ann had never noticed Bob. But afterward, at the supermarket and at the Flamingo Diner in the neighborhood, Mary Ann would always see him. He'd be standing right next to her, waiting for his groceries to be bagged or for a cup of coffee, but he had no idea that she was George's mother. She wanted to poke him. But even if she could have, she would never have gotten up the nerve to talk to him, invite herself over to his house for coffee, ask him what had really happened that night.

George was laid out for two days at the Bromirski Funeral Home on Warren Street, on the same street where he was shot. The funeral director told Mary Ann to get a shirt with a high collar, to cover the bullet wound in George's throat.

I didn't go to the wake or the funeral. After Daddy died, I found it hard to go to wakes, especially those at Bromirski's. I only went when I really had to, like when Cioci Stella or Uncle Henry died. I hadn't been close to George, so I wimped out.

As often as she could, Mary Ann visited the cemetery where George was buried. It's the same cemetery where my father is buried, Holy Cross in North Arlington, the town where Aunt Terri lived, the town with all the sinkholes. My father was buried at the back, near the road and across from a bowling alley. George was at the other end, in an older grave, near the front gates.

Though his last name was different from mine, George's grave was marked STAPINSKI, the last name of Mary Ann's grandparents, who are both buried in that same plot. There was room for one more casket in the grave. And since Mary Ann was short on money, the family told her to bury George there, where his remains would mingle with the Stapinski ashes.

Mary Ann put George's picture on a shelf in her modest living room on Morris Street, not far from the Morris Canal basin on which barges once carried coal to New York, ignoring Jersey City altogether. Next to George's picture she placed a candle, which she would light every day, then blow out before going to sleep each night. She hoped that it would help push George's soul toward the light. She prayed each night that he was headed to a better place, far from Jersey City.

19

NO FILTERS

———

One afternoon, I got a call from my mother that my favorite cousin, Gerri, was "in trouble." I knew right away Ma didn't mean that Gerri was pregnant. I knew it was worse than that. Before I even heard what she'd done wrong, I was ready to defend her, write letters to her in prison or in rehab or wherever she was headed, to let her know that I'd be there for her. We were a forgiving family, after all, who had seen much worse. What with Grandpa, and Great-Grandpa Peter, Uncle Frankie, and Uncle Henry, Uncle Andrew, George, and all the crooked politicians.

Gerri wasn't even the first in her immediate family to get into trouble. In 1988, one of her sisters was indicted on charges of stealing money from the Hyundai dealership where she worked, but no one really paid much attention. It was just another blot on the family name. And besides, the charges were later dismissed.

But Gerri was different. Her trouble hit us hard, like a sock in the mouth you didn't see coming.

We all loved her. My father had loved her because she loved his hot roast beef sandwiches. My mother loved her like a godmother; my sister, like a Confirmation sponsor. I loved her because she always had time to play with me and never ignored me. She had the patience to teach me to ride a two-wheeler on the dead-end streets of North Bergen. Our birthdays were the same week. She had even given me that journal to take to Alaska. I thought maybe I could send her a journal so she could record her troubled thoughts. But I thought better of it. They were probably memories she'd much rather forget.

When Ma called to tell me about Gerri, I remembered last Christmas. Gerri had had her annual holiday gathering in her bachelorette pad, but the spread she put out seemed much more elaborate than usual. There was top-shelf liquor and shrimp—not the swag off-the-back-of-the-truck kind but expensive, store-bought shrimp. Since Daddy had died, shellfish was off our family menu. It cost too much.

Between stories of Grandpa throwing the Blessed Mother salesman down the stairs and Ma and Aunt Mary Ann dropping that big chunk of ice, Gerri showed us all the new furniture she had bought. Having recently suffered through the purchase of my first couch, I knew how expensive furniture could be. And this was nice stuff. Big. Real wood. Plus, there was a new bedroom set, with a fancy Christmas bedspread. There was Christmas china kept in a kitchen cabinet that my brother-in-law accidentally leaned on and almost knocked over. Gerri had a state-of-the-art CD player with multiple carts. I remember coveting it and the many Christmas CDs revolving around inside. Gerri had diamond earrings and a tennis bracelet. She drove a Lexus.

Even with a nice car like that, Gerri picked my mother and her father up at the airport in a limousine. Ma and Uncle Jerry had gone to Florida to visit Aunt Mary Ann, and there was Gerri at Newark Airport with a limo, a wet bar and all, ready to bring them home in luxury. My mother bragged about it, and it made me feel a little envious. Why couldn't I pick my mother up in a stretch limo? What kind of daughter was I anyway? Why didn't I get a real job that paid real money?

And then it occurred to me.

Gerri was up to something. I told my mother I suspected that Gerri was dealing drugs. I guess I was being catty, jealous that she had enough money to pick Ma up in style. But Ma didn't believe Gerri was running drugs. I didn't want to believe it myself. Doing drugs was your personal prerogative, but selling drugs was scummy. Gerri wasn't scummy. But something did seem strange.

Time passed, and I'd actually forgotten all about the limo episode and my drug theory until my mother called me long-distance to tell me about Gerri's trouble. She had been arrested. Not for drugs, Ma said, but for swindling her company out of $219,792.55. Nearly a quarter-million dollars. It wasn't just that she stole the money, but how she stole it that was the problem.

Gerri was the accounts-payable clerk at a laundry-supply company in Saddlebrook, New Jersey. It was her job to pay vendors. Instead of paying them, she placed the company checks in her own account, bit by bit, over a two-year period. No money laundering or elaborate schemes: Once a week or once every two weeks, she would take a company check, no matter who it was made out to, and deposit it into her account.

When the company discovered the missing money, they traced it to Gerri. They blamed the bank and held it liable for accepting checks that weren't even made out to Gerri. The big problem, what made Gerri's crime a problem for us all, was that the bank where she made the deposits was the same one where my brother-in-law, Basil, worked.

Basil was a bank vice-president. One terrible morning, he came across Gerri's name in a news flash that the bank had circulated about the crime. He almost fell off his ergonomic chair. Basil had worked all his life to rise above his Hudson County heritage. With my sister's help, he had bought a house, launched a respectable career, and had two exceptional children, one of whom went on to Harvard Law School, just like cousin Mike.

Basil and Paula had worked for years to separate themselves from the bad reputation of Hudson County and the criminals in our family. They even tried to get rid of their accents. They did everything to blend in with the yuppies who bought brownstones on either side of them. They stopped putting colored Christmas lights on the tree; only taste-ful tiny white lights would do. And the tree itself was no longer fake, but fresh and green. They stopped making sausage and meatballs for Sunday dinner and instead went out for brunch, toasting each other with mimosas.

They took Gerri's crime personally. And I couldn't blame them. The tellers in Basil's bank all knew Gerri as a familiar face, the vice-president's cousin, so they never asked any questions when she showed up at their windows with her deposit slips and her dirty laundry-company checks. Like us, they probably liked Gerri and trusted her fresh, open face and wide, white smile.

When Gerri's arrest report turned up on Basil's desk, he debated whether to keep quiet about being related to her or own up to it. If he stepped forward to face the heat voluntarily, maybe the boss would commend him for his honesty. He went to his boss and told him about the relation. Better that than let them discover it on their own and accuse him of being an accomplice.

Basil was investigated. But most of all, he was embarrassed. He had worked hard, trying to rise above his roots, his Hoboken days, and his long, difficult-to-pronounce last name. But he hadn't distanced himself from the family stories. He was now part of one. And so were we.

To prove his loyalty to the bank, and to punish her for what she did, Basil didn't defend Gerri. He showed no mercy. The bank went all the way with its prosecution.

At first Gerri pleaded not guilty, but then changed her mind and pleaded out to second-degree theft. She agreed to pay all the money back.

At her hearing, the judge asked if she had a family. Gerri said yes, meaning her parents, siblings, and us. But the judge wanted to know if Gerri had any children, because, he announced, she was going to prison. Second-degree theft carried a maximum of three years in jail.

Basil, meanwhile, got a promotion at an upscale suburban regional bank. His title was president. He'd started as a teller and was now making six figures, the hard way, the legal way, the non–Hudson County way. The white-collar way. But Gerri hadn't thought of that, I suppose. Or maybe she just didn't care. That was my sister's take on it, and the reason she couldn't forgive Gerri. It was one thing to screw people you didn't know. But it was another thing to screw your relatives.

I felt bad for Gerri and had a feeling she hadn't involved us on purpose. I secretly sent her a card once, no real message inside, just "Love,

Helene," to let her know I was thinking about her and was sorry for what was happening to her. But I felt guilty for weeks. My sister would have been pissed if she'd found out.

I figured that working so closely with all that money, day after day, the temptation to steal was just too great. That was Gerri's only excuse. But I tried to find others for her.

Aunt Millie had been sick, so maybe Gerri stole most of the money to help her pay her medical bills. Maybe she didn't realize how much money she had actually taken, since she stole it a little at a time.

Maybe growing up in North Bergen had done Gerri in: North Bergen High School, the White Castle, or running wild and being able to cook breakfast in the morning on her own. Maybe she went wrong because North Bergen was shaped like a gun, because it was filled with so many dead-end streets, or because it didn't get good television reception. Maybe it was because she didn't go to church every Sunday when she was little.

There were dozens of excuses. I could blame what happened to Gerri on local politics, on people like McCann and Mocco, who set bad examples for our generation just like Hague and Kenny had done years ago for Beansie's generation.

What I feared most was that Gerri was responding to a deep genetic pull passed on from Grandpa. She was, after all, named after him. Grandpa Jerry. And he did come and live with her longer than he had lived with us.

When it came down to it, maybe it was all just a matter of odds, like betting the number. With a grandfather like Beansie, one of us was bound to get into trouble. The criminal gene was just too strong and was sure to be passed down.

Maybe Gerri did what she did because she was there that night Grandpa tried to kill us. It was as if Grandpa had actually climbed those stairs back in 1970, past the dust bunnies and broken floor tiles, but had only one bullet in his gun. And Gerri got it. Point-blank.

She said she couldn't really remember that night, but the memory was back there, lingering like those antique bullets Frank shot into his head. Like George's forgotten memory of his father, invisible but potent, dragging him to an early death.

Stanley, Paula, and I remembered the night Grandpa tried to shoot us, and savored each unfiltered detail. Maybe it was the remembering—or not remembering—that made the difference.

Before she "went away," Gerri half-jokingly threatened to run Basil over in her car. Paula stood by her husband. And so did I. We weren't allowed to go anywhere near Gerri, especially Basil, who took extra care in looking both ways before he crossed the street.

Because of the bad blood between my sister and Gerri, we couldn't go to North Bergen and laugh about the family stories for fear that Gerri would come up in conversation or show up in the flesh, out on bail. As if she were waiting, revving her Lexus's engine.

Our other relatives didn't know about Gerri's crime or why my sister was mad. Ma was afraid of hurting her brother Jerry, so she kept quiet about the whole affair and suffered in silence. Our other cousins and aunts invited us all—including Gerri—to family engagements. We couldn't attend weddings or funerals, christenings or showers, since Gerri might be there. And we couldn't say why we weren't coming, since Uncle Jerry would have been devastated if everyone knew about Gerri. We loved Uncle Jerry too much to cause him such grief.

For seven years we stayed away and kept quiet. Our cousins thought we were just being snobby, that we didn't want to bother with them. The whole mess took its biggest toll on my mother and Uncle Jerry, who carried on their normal relationship for years, pretending not to know what the other one knew. They still traveled together to visit Aunt Mary Ann in Florida. Uncle Jerry came to my mother's house to do her taxes, and she repaid him with a big macaroni dinner. They pretended nothing was wrong. But without the family's comfort, and with that secret weighing him down, Uncle Jerry aged. And Ma grieved terribly for those lost family gatherings.

I was surprised I felt bad about missing the family functions. For years I had complained about all those baby showers where bows were taped onto paper plates and placed on the heads of my pregnant cousins as their friends oohed and ahhed. But now that the family gatherings were off-limits, I missed them. They left a strange vacuum in my life. My family was a pain in the ass, but they were my family and mine alone to complain about or avoid. I had thought they'd always be there to mock or cherish, depending on my mood.

It felt like a piece of furniture was missing from my living room. It was mostly crummy, secondhand furniture, but it was mine and had its particular place in the room. I couldn't get used to the brand-new hole it left when it was gone. And it seemed that every time I went out, there was something else missing when I got back.

During the family blackout, Aunt Katie died. My Brooklyn apartment was only a few miles from Jersey City and from the funeral parlor but two rivers, two tunnels, and one family fight removed. I was close enough to Jersey City that from my living room window I could tell the time on the red, glowing Colgate clock. I could see the stepped buildings of the Medical Center and the railroad terminal that Irene and Vita had passed through over a century ago.

From that same window I could see the Statue of Liberty—not the back view like the one on Warren Street or the tired version outside City Hall Park, but the real thing, her face, green and glowing, staring straight at me, daring me to cross New York Harbor for Aunt Katie's wake.

Feeling sad and homesick, I got up the courage and went.

The first thing I noticed was that Aunt Katie had on a pink dress that matched the drapes behind her. I imagined her getting up and joking about it, making a reference to Scarlett O'Hara sewing her outfit from the curtains.

Aunt Katie had always looked all wrong in a dress, too formal and ladylike. Now she looked especially wrong. I wondered if she had her strange-looking partial dentures in, too, for this special occasion. The last of Aunt Katie's special occasions. I tried to get close enough to see, but stopped short of sticking a finger into her mouth. It wouldn't have gone over well, even in my family.

As I knelt before the casket I pretended to pray, but instead, I just gazed at Aunt Katie. Her body looked especially small in its coffin, shrunken almost, and so awkward in that dress.

Great-Aunt Katie. She had seemed so much taller in life. She was so wise, with her advice on how to stop a mad dog and how to get your husband to stop drinking. But she was never full of herself. Aunt Katie was flawed, and was always the first to admit it.

I remembered her reciting a poem when I was a kid. She said she wrote it, but knowing Aunt Katie, it was probably plagiarized. It was about getting a chance to live your life over again. And it all came back to me now in the funeral home. In metered verse, Aunt Katie said she would be more careful the next time around, tell her sons that she loved them, take more long walks. I remember her stopping and choking back tears before she was done. We likely didn't get our lives to live over, she said, "but knowing me, I'd make the same damn mistakes again."

They weren't such bad mistakes, especially in the context of our family. There were worse things you could do.

Hardly anyone came to Aunt Katie's funeral. When I looked around and saw all those empty seats, I winced. Had the family been on speaking terms, there would have been more people there. But I wondered where all those men and women were that Aunt Katie had helped during four decades as a committeewoman. It was time for all those favors to be repaid. All those potholes she got filled, the broken traffic lights she got repaired, all the people she helped move in to the neighborhood, all those she helped get jobs and food baskets, the couples she counseled through family fights, the pastors whose raffles she sold. Where were they now, the ungrateful bastards?

But then I realized where they were. All those people were dead, of course, their souls joining the long parade of barely missed Jersey Citizens, marching on with the sad subjects of all those feature obituaries toward permanent oblivion.

At eighty-six, Aunt Katie had outlived them. I smiled my half smile, blessed myself, and got up from the kneeler, no longer so upset about the empty seats behind me. I sat in one of them and stared at Aunt Katie some more.

She had talked for years about how one shot of Canadian Club a day would keep her going. And she was right. Maybe Aunt Katie was even right about those Lucky Strikes.

It was the filters that killed you.

20

BORN AGAIN

Gerri was sentenced a month after her thirty-sixth birthday, and served seven hard months in a women's penitentiary, let out early for good behavior. While behind bars, she found God and was born again. She sent Paula a long, penitent letter, apologizing to her. In the letter, Gerri told Paula she hadn't meant to hurt her.

Because of the letter and because Gerri did her penance, my sister finally forgave her for her sins. Seven years was long enough. At a family party, complete with a cheesy karaoke machine, she and Paula got up together and sang the Sister Sledge anthem "We Are Family." It was a corny but poignant moment. Gerri practically cried, the prodigal daughter so happy to be back in the fold.

Paula and Gerri made up at my cousin Jamie's wedding, at a big restaurant on the Jersey shore. It was the first time the whole family had been together in seven years. We all excitedly posed for a group photo on the restaurant's giant, echoing porch, the unfamiliar sea air sticky and damp as we linked arms and held hands. If you looked closely at the picture, you could see that my cousin Susan and I—the babies in our families—were both pregnant with babies of our own. It was a new beginning, in a way. The beginning of an era. Or the end of a bad one. Life had come full circle in the blunt, poetic way it usually does.

Susan had a son with a sense of humor so sharp he made his grandfather—Uncle Jerry—sound like a mortician. Amid the family turmoil, the comedy gene not only survived but thrived. I was glad the fighting was over, that I was able to get to know little Alan and see what a pisser he was.

Optimist that I was, I naturally started worrying about negative traits that might get passed down from the family, like cancerous cells incubating year after year, waiting to cluster into a tumor and wreak havoc. A good sense of humor was a wonderful family trait. But what about a desire to kill? A penchant to steal? To run numbers? I was afraid to research the topic of criminal genetics, scared of what I might find. And, besides, what was the point?

There was little I could do, other than choose a good husband. It was no accident that Wendell's grandfather was a judge—the upstanding, righteous kind, not the nickel-pork-chop variety that usually got assigned in Jersey City.

"We have a lot in common," I told Wendell on one of our first dates at Boulevard Drinks. "Your grandfather's a judge and mine was a criminal." I figured the judge genes might outweigh the criminal genes if we ever decided to get married and have kids.

Maybe there were other measures I could take to guard my offspring from the evil genes. Though I'm not a believer in Original Sin, I planned to have my baby baptized. I figured that in my family, with all those sins floating around, it didn't hurt to get spritzed with a little holy water. Just in case there was such a thing as a soul, heaven, hell, and limbo, my baby would be protected.

Most days, I was still too sophisticated to believe there were such things. But once I became pregnant, I started to wonder. At night, when all was quiet and my mind let down its defenses, I thought about the drawings Sister Isabelle had made us sketch in third grade in anticipation of the coming end of the world, our own versions of heaven and hell—angels on downy wings and devils with pitchforks. Then my mind wandered to places like the Sistine Chapel and the museums hung with Bosch paintings, the Cold Storage, the piles of dead rats, and the emergency room into which Daddy disappeared, and I worried that maybe there was a heaven and hell after all. That there were souls that needed to be saved and prayed for, and souls that floated into the heavens on their own lightness.

With the baby fluttering inside me, I felt a sudden panic and a helplessness. Now that I was contributing to the family line, I was connected to something huge, to eternity or a continuum that would make my life a mere star in a Milky Way of lives that came before me and would stretch on after me. Long after me. I was part of it but so, so small. The thought made me feel lost and scared, like I had that night I got out of the car with Wendell on the California highway.

If there was such thing as a soul, were there billions of them circling the heavens or were they recycled? My family members were firm believers in reincarnation. It was really just another version of genetics, with a religious spin to give it all a sense of mystery. The rule was that the newborn baby inherited the soul of the dead person who had just exited the planet or was on his deathbed. The death and birth, or rebirth, usually occurred within months, weeks, or days of each other, although the difference could stretch as long as a few years.

Uncle John was convinced my mother was Great-Grandma Irene reincarnated, with her face, her wit, her straight black hair, and her love of dancing.

When my brother was born, Dziadzia was on his deathbed, which explained why my brother's name was Stanley. Dziadzia's real name had been Stanislaw. My father begged my mother to name my brother after him. Then, in an extra cosmic twist, Stanley was coincidentally born on St. Stanislaw's feast day. Ma had no choice. Stanley it was, even though Stanley never really looked like a Stanley.

Right after Babci died, I was born, and came out looking just like her, squinty eyes, big nose, thick, dark hair.

When Stanley had a son, just a couple of years after Daddy died, Alex came out looking exactly like Daddy. He even acted like him, quiet but observant, coming out with a great one-liner every now and then. I had wondered where Daddy had gone off to in that emergency room. And now I knew. Alex was Daddy all over again. It was as if someone had boiled Daddy down to his essence and then poured him into a much smaller mold. I could just picture this kid years from now, broiling a few lobster tails just like his grandfather.

I was all for reincarnation: Take a soul to give a soul. It seemed like a resourceful, environmentally correct way to run a universe. As long as my kid was recycled from someone I liked, someone good.

But in my family it was slim pickin's.

I wondered whose soul—if anyone's—my baby would inherit. I wondered if cross-gender reincarnation was possible. My mother was a good soul, but I didn't want her dying anytime soon. So her soul was off-limits. Maybe Aunt Katie would come back in my kid. Short, squat, smoking Lucky Strikes, throwing back shots of Canadian Club.

I had a boy and we named him Dean, after no one in the family. We simply liked the name. Fresh and new. It was an added bonus that Dean Street was not far from my Brooklyn apartment, the street where Grandma came to live with her brother right before she met Grandpa. Dean Street was where Grandma had nearly escaped.

When I took Dean home from the hospital, I stared hard at his face and searched for clues in his features. With each twist, his face would completely change, like a kaleidoscope, leaving little trace of the last pattern I viewed. Daddy was in there. But so was Ma, with Wendell's lips curled into my smirk. And he hadn't even been to Jersey City yet. Aunt Katie was nowhere to be found.

Mornings he looked like Stanley, and evenings, like Paula. He had my sister-in-law's toes, my father-in-law's piercing stare, and my mother-in-law's round head. But he seemed to have my attitude, thoroughly unimpressed with everyone around him.

Sometimes he was like one of those Stapinski smorgasbords, with all my Polish relatives bringing something different to the table. When he frowned, my baby was Daddy. When he was sad, Uncle Tommy. When he cried, Uncle Eddie. When he scowled, he was Cioci Stella. And when he lifted a toy too close to his face and his eyes crossed, Uncle Henry.

But when he smiled, my baby was Grandpa. The first time I noticed, it scared the shit out of me.

I asked my mother if I was seeing things, and she shook her head.

It's Beansie, all right. He only appeared in charismatic flashes. But there he was, Grandpa, smiling up at me, more often than I liked to admit. Grandpa the charmer. Grandpa the handsome guy who Grandma fell in love with seventy years ago.

I hadn't seen Grandpa smile much in my lifetime, but I recognized the grin from family photos he hadn't gotten around to destroying. It wasn't so much the smile itself. That was more like Wendell's and my own. It was more in the cheeks and around the eyes that Beansie came out to play.

My cousin Jamie—on a roll from the family reunion that occurred at her wedding—dug up some old family movies and had them transferred to videotape. I saw Grandpa in motion for the first time since childhood. Eyes blinking, lips moving, bald head nodding. The movies were from my mother's wedding: Grandpa in a white tuxedo jacket, looking slightly demented, walking my skinny mother up the St. Mary's Church steps. I watched the film several times, and each time I rewound and watched Grandpa ascend those stone steps, the less I hated him. The ice-truck dent on the left side of his head was clear as could be. I had always thought that was just an excuse. But there it was.

There was also a sad, vacant stare in his eyes that most snapshots couldn't capture, and a timid smile, a remnant of the charming one I knew from those pictures and from my baby's face.

Grandpa was pathetic, not scary. Now, when I looked at his picture, I felt an unfamiliar ache, one I associated with seeing Uncle Tommy at Meadowview. It was sorrow. Maybe it was because of motherhood, but for the first time in my life, I actually felt sorry for Grandpa. I preferred anger over sorrow. It hurt much less.

For years, my mother had said she believed that Grandpa had been in purgatory and that she should pray for him, to try and move him along. I had always assumed Grandpa had gone straight to hell.

When I asked my mother why she prayed for her father, she said she felt he had done his penance on earth and that he didn't deserve the fires of hell.

After we kicked him out back in 1970, Grandpa went to live with Gerri and her family. But he drove Aunt Millie and Uncle Jerry crazy, yelling all the time that the television was too loud. Once, when they went out, they left Grandpa to baby-sit. He screamed at my cousins all night, scaring the memory deep into them. My cousin Susan remembers him accidentally stepping on her Barbie Dream House and crushing it. He promised to buy her a new one for Christmas.

Because he was impossible to live with, Grandpa wound up alone again, wandering the streets by himself until he had a heart attack and wound up in the Medical Center.

My mother took mercy on him one more time and visited him there with Uncle Jerry. When they got there, Grandpa cursed and yelled and scared them away for the last time. The exasperated doctors sent him to the Trenton State Hospital psychiatric ward for over a year. While there, he wrote a letter to one of his sisters—his handwriting still impeccable and sane—begging her to take him out, to save him. He told her in the letter that he didn't belong there.

I imagined what that was like and how much worse it was than being like Uncle Tommy, retarded and unaware of what was happening around you. I imagined being trapped in a psychiatric ward, knowing that you're simply mean, not crazy.

Six months later, Grandpa wound up in John F. Kennedy Hospital in Edison, New Jersey. That's where he died, alone, Christmas morning.

The hospital was a half mile from my uncle Robby's new house, and when he heard that Grandpa had died there, he thought that Grandpa had been stalking him and his family. But it was just another one of life's little coincidences. Grandpa didn't even know that Uncle Robby had recently moved there. His son lived less than a mile away and Grandpa didn't even know it.

Now that I had a son of my own, I understood why my mother prayed for Grandpa. He had suffered in the worst way, alone. Though he deserved to be left all alone, it was still sad. And besides, family was family. If they didn't pray for your soul, who would?

No matter whose soul my son inherited, he would turn out just fine if I raised him right. But how did you raise a child right? Would I send him to Catholic school, to try and instill a sense of morality? Would I let him run wild, or watch his every move? Make him eat organic vegetables, or let him eat hot dogs from Boulevard Drinks? Should we stay in the city, or move to the country?

I decided I would hold him close but not too tight. I would sing to him and brush his hair and find trees for him to climb. I would protect him from oncoming traffic and head injuries, and would avoid putting him in a crib for as long as possible, so he wouldn't have to stare at the world through a set of bars those first few months of life. When he got a little older, I would teach him right from wrong. I wasn't sure how to go about it, exactly, but I figured it would come to me. I would take him to church on Sundays to give him some grounding and something to rebel against in life besides me and Wendell. He would know who was good and who was bad and how to tell the difference, and that sometimes there really was no difference. That most people were angel and devil, Beansie and Grandma rolled up in a complicated mess.

He would know about Vita's card game, about Peter beating Irene, about Grandma and Aunt Helen and their brothers, Uncle Sam and Uncle John and their brownstone on Grand Street and the books on their shelves. He would know about Dziadzia's bootlegging and Babci's accident, epileptic Uncle Tommy and Meadowview, Kunegunda and Uncle Andrew and the Polish revolution that never was, Uncle Henry the bookie, and Uncle Eddie and the bull, about Hague and Kenny and my mother dancing with the mayor-to-be at Victory Hall. My son would get to know my mother, and know her well, learn about how she was so much like Aunt Katie in her old age. He would know about Aunt Katie's job as a committeewoman and as a riveter, about the night of cousin Mike's campaign party, the night I wore my first pair of glasses, about everyone hitting the number the day I was born, about the igloos Paula and Stanley built on Sussex Street, about how Grandma died on Ash Wednesday, about Daddy and the lobster tails and the trips to Bubbling Springs and the Loew's Theatre. I'd eventually tell him about Frank, Kelsey, and the backyard; the OLC nuns and priests; Aunt Julie and cousin Stephen and the day John was shot in Arizona; about the stolen Blessed Mother and the salesman that Grandpa threw down the stairs. He would hear stories of Grandpa from Uncle Jerry and Uncle Robby, the bad stories and the funny stories, like the one about the day Aunt Mary Ann and Ma carried that block of ice and then let it go, only to carry it up again in the next retelling, forever and ever. He'd know about the day Uncle Sonny died, and, once he was old enough to understand, why Grandma married Grandpa. About Carvel and the stolen ice cream, Venice and the Stanley Theatre, *The Jersey Journal* and the night Stanley almost punched the priest in the mouth, the Manna transcripts, Mayor McCann and cousin Mike running one more time, Uncle Tommy voting, and my running away from home finally. He would know about cousin George seeing his father dead and then dying right across the street, about Gerri teaching me to ride a bike and stealing all that money. I would point to Jersey City from the apartment window, to the railroad terminal and the new shiny buildings, and sometimes I would even take him to visit.

On an overcast day, Jersey City could still bring me down, with its aluminum siding, junkies, and crumbling highways. But on a good day, a sunny, clear day, Jersey City didn't look quite as bad as I remembered it. And it wasn't just the distance that softened me.

The New York skyline was even more spectacular with the Colgate factory buildings demolished, no longer obstructing the view. A new Colgate development was filling the hole left by the old factory, the pile drivers so loud that they broke the windows of George's mother's house on Morris Street. Development spread farther inland, to other neighborhoods besides the waterfront areas, and was rising at a furious pace.

Activist Colin Egan founded a farmer's market right in the shadow of the horrendously ugly PATH building, where sallow Jersey City residents, deprived for years of good, fresh produce, could finally buy a nice tomato. The farmer's market was a footnote in Colin's list of good deeds. He, Joe Duffy, and Ted Conrad, before he died, eventually convinced the planning board that the Loew's Theatre was worth saving. It was being rehabbed and was fully supported by the new mayor, Bret Schundler.

The first Republican in nearly a century, Schundler was elected the year I went to Alaska. He was an investment banker with money to burn, so corruption was no longer an issue. He didn't need to steal money. He had enough. Finally, a mayor of Jersey City who had enough.

Schundler was all right in my book, Republican or not. Some people disliked him because he wasn't Hudson County born and raised. The worst accusation they could dredge up was that he owned a house in Jersey City but lived most of the time out of town in a second home in the suburbs. They said the first chance he got, he'd leave Jersey City flat and follow his ambitions for higher office. But I didn't think that was so bad. It was better than taking kickbacks and stealing taxpayer money earmarked for new schools and nontoxic playgrounds. In an imperfect world, I would take a politically ambitious, conservative commuter over a born-and-raised corrupt swindler.

Schundler was one of the legions of yuppies who had moved to downtown Jersey City in the mid-1980s. When he pulled up in front of his apartment in a cab in those first few months in town, the driver noticed the address and gestured to the front door. "My brother was shot to death right on your stoop," he told him.

Less than a year later, the day before he closed on his brownstone, Schundler was walking in the neighborhood and watched as police cars zoomed past him and his wife. When they got to the house they were about to buy, they saw that the cop cars were parked out front. They had just arrested two kids who tried to rob the house. Schundler's house.

Schundler thought twice about closing. But he went ahead and made Jersey City his home. Vice and all.

He knew, firsthand, that the city could be a tough place. At the turn of the new century, crime was down 40 percent from the time he took office. But it still had a long way to go.

There were still chopped-up bodies and floaters pulled from the Hudson River each spring. But times were changing. There was the lesbian-rough-sex murder case in Bayonne, and the Internet case, in which a Jersey City guy was accused of luring a California girl online and then murdering her. In the autumn of 1999, a Hudson County real estate baron who had bought Mayor Hague's fourteen-room luxury

Kennedy Boulevard apartment was allegedly gunned down by his disgruntled doorman, a three-hundred-pound former Board of Ed worker known as Big Daddy. The only witness to the murder was an eight-year-old boy. Bad news didn't get much more colorful than that.

The crime story that fascinated me the most, though, happened the summer before. A time capsule placed under the Christopher Columbus statue on Journal Square was missing when the statue was moved for construction. The time capsule, including photos, newspapers, and other mementos, had been sealed at the base of the statue in October 1950 by Judge Zampella and Hudson's other well-connected Italians.

The oblong copper box was supposed to be opened in the year 2000 and resealed until 2050. But when workers moved the bronze explorer from his perch on a hot August afternoon in 1998, to make way for a $7.5-million Journal Square face-lift, the box was nowhere to be found. The construction crew searched the base and dug through the construction rubble, but it was gone. Who could be low enough to steal a time capsule? It was almost as bad as stealing the Blessed Mother.

Jersey City was so corrupt it couldn't even hold on to its history.

But then again, neither could I.

As a freelance reporter, I stole other people's hard-luck stories and wrote about them. It was my job to sneak into their lives and take notes. Five-finger discount. Secondhand. I wrote about crime victims and celebrities battling cancer, infertile couples and union workers phased out from jobs they'd held for fifty years, people losing their businesses and kids dying of drug overdoses. They weren't my stories. But I took them and put my byline on them. I made them my own.

My family's stories were different. For years, I felt a sense of entitlement to them, the way rich kids must feel about the family fortune. True tales about stolen encyclopedias, lobster tails, a statue of the Blessed Mother, a hospital bed, rare coins, a quarter of a million dollars. They were my only inheritance—save for a few stolen objects that I got to keep along the way.

But I had been away too long, had missed too many family gatherings. Maybe it was that seven-year hiatus. Even the old stories were told less and less frequently, an eerie foreshadowing to what was happening to people like George and Gerri. The crime stories, funny at first, grew closer and closer to home, eating their way to the heart of the family, until they almost devoured us altogether. Gerri's crime had nearly wrecked us. And no one wanted to talk about it. It wasn't a funny story, and it wasn't mine to tell, really.

I wondered if any of the stories were mine to take with me wherever I went, like the books from Aunt Mary Ann and the stolen dictionary that went with me whenever I moved. Now that I was gone, I felt like I had to steal the family stories back, bit by bit, phone call by phone call, like a thief in the night, my relatives rightfully suspicious of my motives.

I wanted my son to know those stories, to show him where his mother grew up, to see it, taste it, smell it. But the smells I smelled at his age, both good and bad, were all gone. No more coffee or chocolate, soap or blubber. The factories had moved out long ago. The restaurants Daddy took us to were gone, too. Lobster tails, I discovered, were very expensive and difficult to cook. Daddy, like a champion figure skater, had only made it look easy.

I wanted Dean to meet the good people of Jersey City, the few I encountered throughout my lifetime. Though many Jersey Citizens were not worth meeting, there were some who'd surprise you with their no-bullshit attitude and willingness to do you a favor.

I wanted him to know that Jersey City had prepared me for the world—a harsh place, filled with jerks and criminals, no matter how far you traveled. In Manhattan, I once tripped and fell and watched people step over me at the curb. In Brooklyn, my apartment was broken into three times. In San Francisco, a big fat guy stole my wallet on a bus, then treated all his friends to the movies on my credit card. In Hong Kong, people pushed me out of the way to get a seat on the ferry. And in Cairo, a guy tried to grab my butt as I walked past him. I punched him hard in the chest and told him to go paw his wife like that. He had no idea what I was saying. But he heard the tone in my voice, and looked apologetic.

Because Jersey City had been so tough, I was always prepared for what might come my way.

I wanted my son to know that Jersey City was the world in high relief, stark black and white, with no punches pulled. The bad was especially bad, so the good stood out. When you met a good person—a truly good person—in a place as ugly and as awful as that, it could choke you up and make you want to cry.

I wanted my kid to know that, to know the characters I knew, to show him where his mother played, the wall on which I slammed a handball at age five, the pole I climbed, the door to my building, where the junkies came to hide, the door to the Majestic Tavern that I had pushed open with hands as tiny as his. But the Majestic was replaced by a Pakistani restaurant. And those doors opened the way for stories that were barely mine anymore, told in an accent that was slowly, surely fading.

ACKNOWLEDGMENTS

Thanks to Jennifer Rudolph Walsh and Ann Godoff; Tony Petrosino for his Web searches and for the poster of Journal Square; Jamie Vena Gottschall for her family research; Bob and Joseph Vena, Robert Vena, Jill Worthington, Susan Yenni, Edward and Elaine Stapinski, Michael Bell, Julie and Stephen Nowatkowski, Terri Gradowski, Mary Ann Koch, Mary Ann DelGreco, Eddie Meehan, Paula Muia, Colin Egan, Bret Schundler, Frank Culloo, Marcos Navas, Gene Scanlon, Anthony Cucci, Jaime Vasquez, Angie Wendolowski, Marybeth McGovern, Guy Catrillo, Bill Miller, William Rashbaum, Bob Leach, and Fred Friesendorf for their memories and expertise; to Pete Weiss, John Petrick, Olga Torres, Margaret Schmidt, Judy Locoriere, and the staff of *The Jersey Journal*; to Bessie Jamieson, Tom Boyle, Maria Schembari, Doug Roy, Brenda Tyson, Peg Latham, and the Millay Colony for the Arts, for giving me the space, both physical and mental; Sara Eckel, Laura Kriska, Jerome Gentes, Russell West, Kurt Jaskowiak, Andrew King, Luc Sante, Le Anne Schreiber, Kim Rich, Jodi Honeycutt, Jim DeRogatis, Deirdre Fretz, and Lauren and Paul Spagnoletti, for their encouragement; Ken French, Bruce Brandt, Charlie Markey, and John Norton in the New Jersey Room, Paula Spagnoletti, Stanley Stapinski, and Kathy and Walter Jamieson, for the answers to my many questions; my mother, Irene Stapinski, for her astounding memory and her nurturing skills; Dean Jamieson, for the luck and love he brought; and most of all, to my husband, Wendell Jamieson, for his countless edits, his boundless faith, and his incredible patience.

BIBLIOGRAPHY

Several books provided background and historical information. The most comprehensive was Thomas F. X. Smith's *Powerticians* (Lyle Stuart, 1982). Dayton David McKean's *The Boss: The Hague Machine in Action* (Houghton Mifflin, 1940); Richard J. Connors's *A Cycle of Power* (The Scarecrow Press, 1971); George C. Rapport's *The Statesman and the Boss* (Vantage Press, 1961); J. Owen Grundy's *The History of Jersey City* (Jersey City Chamber of Commerce, 1976); and John M. Kelly, Rita M. Murphy, and William J. Roehrenbeck's *Jersey City Tercentenary 1660–1960* (1960) were also essential. Other important sources included Bob Leach's *Saloon Stories,* his piece on Frank Hague, "To Touch His Garment," his story on Newsboy Moriarty, as well as his *Hague Picture Book* (Jersey City Historical Project, 1998); Joan Doherty Lovero's *Hudson County: The Left Bank* (American Historical Press, 1999); Kenneth T. Jackson's *Encyclopedia of New York City* (Yale University Press, 1995), Carlo Levi's *Christ Stopped at Eboli* (Farrar, Straus and Company, 1947), Helen E. Sheehan and Richard P. Wedeen's *Toxic Circles* (Rutgers University Press, 1993). Also helpful were Randall Gabrielan's *Jersey City in Vintage Postcards* (Arcadia Publishing, 1999); Robert R. Goller's *The Morris Canal, Across New Jersey by Water and Rail* (1999), and Patrick B. Shalhoub's *Jersey City* (1995), both from the Images of America series (Arcadia Publishing).

Several magazine and news articles were used as sources, including Thomas J. Fleming's "I Am the Law," from *American Heritage,* June 1969; William F. Longgood's "Jersey City Is Hard to Be Believed," from *The Saturday Evening Post,* April 3, 1954; an article on Hague from *Life* magazine, February 7, 1938; Brent Cunningham's "The Newhouse Way," from *Columbia Journalism Review,* January/February 2000; Frank Gallagher and Debra Kindervatter's story on the Central Railroad terminal, *N.J. Outdoors,* September/October 1989; Joan Cook's February 26, 1979, *New York Times* obituary on Newsboy Moriarty; Ronald Sullivan's December 2, 1970, story in the *Times* on the Mosquito Commission trial; and Frederika Randall's September 3, 2000, *Times* story on Matera; the *Hudson Dispatch*'s June/July 1934 coverage of Uncle Andrew's death; and Kevin M. Meyer's December 31, 1989, corruption roundup in the *Jersey City Reporter*.

A legion of anonymous *Jersey Journal* reporters and editors provided me with a rough draft of Hudson County's history: articles on the murder of Frank Kenny, from April 1916; the Black Tom explosion, from July and August 1916; Great-Grandma Irene's death, from November 3, 1922; the Majestic heist, from October 1923; Uncle Andrew's death, from June/July 1934; Grandpa's crimes from April 1, June 14, and September 6, 1935, October 18, 1943, July 25, 1948, September 19, 1951, and August 5, 1970; the death of Uncle Sonny on August 10, 1944 (once I tracked it down); Kenny's rally from May 6, 1949, his election, and Kenny's own article, "Cork Row, a Bit of Heaven in Downtown"; the closing of the Stanley Theatre, from October 1953; and Frank's DMV shooting, from September 1972 and July 1976.

A long list of bylined *Jersey Journal* reporters deserve credit as well. For information, I mined Peter Weiss's incredible body of work, including, but not limited to, his February 12, 1999, story on the Medical Center; his and Patricia Ford's coverage of the City Hall fire, from September 14, 1979; William Worrell's "race riot" story from August 3, 1964; Patricia Scott's jail coverage; Dan Rosenfeld's September 9, 1991, story on contamination at Liberty State Park, among dozens of other articles on toxic waste; Bernie Rosenberg's column on the Newark Bay Bridge accident; Joseph Albright's October 5, 1991, article and Nat Berg's March 29, 1965, story on cousin Mike; John Petrick's, Earl Morgan's, Emily Smith's, Bill Campbell's, and Peter Weiss's coverage of the Manna trial; John Petrick's October 19, 1991, story on his Medical Center tour; Deborah Yaffe's November 18, 1991, story on Aunt Katie; Michael Finnegan's, John Oswald's, John Petrick's, Peter Weiss's, and Bill Campbell's 1991 coverage of Mayor McCann's indictment, trial, and conviction; Elaine Pofeldt's, Kristen Danis's, and John Petrick's coverage of the Union Terminal odor stories; Agustin Torres's, James Efstathiou's, and Peter Weiss's stories on the Secaucus Council election; Agustin Torres's December 4, 1998, coverage of the Columbus monument; Stan Eason and Gilbert Martinez's February 1996 stories on cousin George; Greg Wilson's Secaucus election coverage; and Christina Joseph's and Melody Tanti's September 1999 stories on Barry Segall.

Helene Stapinski began her career at her hometown newspaper, *The Jersey Journal,* and since then has written for *The New York Times, New York* magazine, and *People,* among other publications. She received her B.A. in journalism from New York University in 1987 and her MFA from Columbia in 1995. She lives in Brooklyn with her husband and son.

DEATH

OF A

NIGHTINGALE

Also by Lene Kaaberbøl and Agnete Friis

The Boy in the Suitcase
Invisible Murder

DEATH

— OF A —

NIGHTINGALE

LENE KAABERBØL

AND

AGNETE FRIIS

Translated from the Danish by Elisabeth Dyssegaard

Published by

Soho Press, Inc.

853 Broadway

New York, NY 10003

Library of Congress Cataloging-in-Publication Data

Kaaberbøl, Lene.

[Nattergalens Doed. English]

Death of a nightingale / Lene Kaaberbøl & Agnete Friis ;

Translated from

the Danish by Elisabeth Dyssegaard.

p cm

Originally published as Nattergalens Doed, in Danish.

HC ISBN 978-1-61695-304-1

International PB ISBN 978-1-61695-440-6

eISBN 978-1-61695-305-8

I. Friis, Agnete, author. II. Dyssegaard, Elisabeth Kallick, translator.

III. Title.

PT8177.21.A24N3713 2013

2013016761

Printed in the United States of America

10 9 8 7 6 5 4 3 2 1

"Go on," says a man's voice.

"I'm tired," an older woman answers, clearly uncomfortable and dismissive.

"But it's so exciting."

"Exciting?" There's a lash of bitterness in her reaction. "A bit of Saturday entertainment? Is that what this is for you?"

"No, I didn't mean it like that."

They are both speaking Ukrainian, he quickly and informally, she more hesitantly. In the background, occasional beeps from an electronic game can be heard.

"It's important for posterity."

The old woman laughs now, a hard and unhappy laughter. "Posterity," she says. "Do you mean the child? Isn't she better off not knowing?"

"If that's how you see it. We should be getting home anyway."

"No." The word is abrupt. "Not yet. Surely you can stay a little longer."

"You said you were tired," says the man.

"No. Not . . . that tired."

"I don't mean to press you."

"No, I know that. You just thought it was exciting."

"Forget I said that. It was stupid."

"No, no. Children like exciting stories. Fairy tales."

"I was thinking more along the lines of something real. Something you experienced yourself."

Another short pause. Then, "No, let me tell you a story," the old woman says suddenly. "A fairy tale. A little fairy tale from Stalin Land. A suitable bedtime story for the little one. Are you listening, my sweet?"

Beep, beep, beep-beep. Unclear mumbling from the child. Obviously, her attention is mostly on the game, but that doesn't stop the old woman.

"Once upon a time, there were two sisters," she begins clearly, as if reciting. "Two sisters who both sang so beautifully that the nightingale had to stop singing when it heard them. First one sister sang for the emperor himself, and thus was the undoing of a great many people. Then the other sister, in her resentment, began to sing too."

"Who are you talking about?" the man asks. "Is it you? Is it someone we know?"

The old woman ignores him. There's a harshness to her voice, as if she's using the story to punish him.

"When the emperor heard the other sister, his heart grew inflamed, and he had to own her," she continued. "'Come to me,' he begged. Oh, you can be sure he begged. 'Come to me, and be my nightingale. I'll give you gold and beautiful clothes and servants at your beck and call.'"

Here the old woman stops. It's as if she doesn't really feel like going on, and the man no longer pressures her. But the story has its own relentless logic, and she has to finish it.

"At first she refused. She rejected the emperor. But he persisted. 'What should I give you, then?' he asked, because he had learned that everything has a price. 'I will not come to you,' said the other sister, 'before you give me my evil sister's head on a platter.'"

In the background, the beeping sounds from the child's game have ceased. Now there is only an attentive silence.

"When the emperor saw that a heart as black as sin hid behind the beautiful song," the old woman continues, still using her fairy-tale voice, "he not only killed the first sister, but also the nightingale's father and mother and grandfather and grandmother and whole family. 'That's what you get for your jealousy,' he said and threw the other sister out."

The child utters a sound, a frightened squeak. The old woman doesn't seem to notice.

"Tell me," she whispers. "Which of them is me?"

"You're both alive," says the man. "So something in the story must be a lie."

"In Stalin Land, Stalin decides what is true and what is a lie," says the old woman. "And I said that it was a Stalin fairy tale."

"Daddy," says the child, "I want to go home now."

"**G**UM?"

Natasha started; she had been sitting silently, looking out the window of the patrol car as Copenhagen glided by in frozen shades of winter grey. Dirty house fronts, dirty snow and a low and dirty sky in which the sun had barely managed to rise above the rooftops in the course of the day. The car's tires hissed in the soap-like mixture of snow, ice and salt that covered the asphalt. None of it had anything to do with her, and she noted it all without really seeing it.

"You do speak Danish, don't you?"

The policeman in the passenger seat had turned toward her and offered her a little blue-white pack. She nodded and took a piece. Said thank you. He smiled at her and turned back into his seat.

This wasn't the "bus," as they called it—the usual transport from Vestre Prison to the court—that Natasha had been on before. It was an ordinary black-and-white; the police were ordinary Danish policemen. The youngest one, the one who had given her the gum, was thirty at the most. The other was old and fat and seemed nice enough too. Danish policemen had kind eyes. Even that time with Michael and the knife, they had spoken calmly and kindly to her as if she hadn't been a criminal they were arresting but rather a patient going to the hospital.

One day, before too long, two of these kind men would put

Katerina and her on a flight back to Ukraine, but that was not what was happening today. Not yet. It couldn't be. Her asylum case had not yet been decided, and Katerina was not with her. Besides, you didn't need to go through Copenhagen to get to the airport, that much she knew. This was the way to Central Police Headquarters.

Natasha placed her hands on her light blue jeans, rubbed them hard back and forth across the rough fabric, opened and closed them quickly. Finally, she made an effort to let her fists rest on her knees while she looked out at Copenhagen and tried to figure out if the trip into the city brought her closer to or farther from Katerina. During the last months, the walls and the physical distance that separated them had become an obsession. She was closer to her daughter when she ate in the cafeteria than when she was in her cell. The trip to the yard was also several meters in the wrong direction, but it still felt soothing because it was as if she were breathing the same air as Katerina. On the library computer Natasha had found Google Street View and dragged the flat little man to the parking lot in front of the prison, farther along Copenhagen's streets and up the entrance ramp to the highway leading through the woods that sprawled north of the city's outer reaches. It was as if she could walk next to him the whole way and see houses and storefronts and trees and cars, but when he reached the Coal-House Camp, he couldn't go any farther. Here she had to make do with the grubby satellite image of the camp's flat barrack roofs. She had stared at the pictures until she went nearly insane. She had imagined that one of the tiny dots was Katerina. Had dreamed of getting closer. From the prison, it was twenty-three kilometers to the Coal-House Camp. From the center of Copenhagen it was probably a few kilometers more, but on the other hand, there were neither walls nor barbed wire between the camp and her right now. There was only the thin steel shell of the police car, air and wind, kilometers of asphalt. And later, the fields and the wet forest floor.

She knew it wouldn't do any good, but she reached out to touch the young policeman's shoulder all the same. "You still don't know anything?" she asked in English.

His eyes met hers in the rearview mirror. His gaze was apologetic but basically indifferent. He shook his head. "We're just the chauffeurs," he said. "We aren't usually told stuff like that."

She leaned back in her seat and again began to rub her palms against her jeans. Opened and closed her hands. Neither of the two policemen knew why she was going to police headquarters. They had nothing for her except chewing gum.

The court case over the thing with Michael was long finished, so that probably wasn't what it was about, and her plea for asylum had never required interviews or interrogations anywhere but the Coal-House Camp.

Fear made her stomach contract, and she felt the urge to shit and pee at the same time. If only she could have had Katerina with her. If only they could have been together. At night in the prison, she had the most terrible nightmares about Katerina alone in the children's barrack, surrounded by flames.

Or Katerina making her way alone into the swamp behind the camp.

It was unnatural for a mother not to be able to reach out and touch her child. Natasha knew she was behaving exactly like cows after their calves were taken from them in the fall, when they stood, their shrill bellowing lasting for hours, without knowing which way to direct their sorrow. She had tried to relieve her restlessness with cold logic. They were not separated forever, she told herself. Katerina came to visit once in a while with Nina, the lady from the Coal-House Camp, who reassured Natasha every time that she would personally take care of Katerina. Rina, the Danes called her. They thought that was her name because that was what the papers said. But Rina wasn't even a name. It was what was left when an overpaid little forger in Lublin had done what he could to disguise the original text.

Maybe that was why she was here? Had they discovered what the man in Lublin had done?

Her dread of the future rose like the tide. Her jaw muscles tightened painfully, and when she crushed the compact piece of gum between her teeth, everything in her mouth felt sticky and metallic.

The policeman at the wheel slowed down, gave a low, triumphant whistle and slid the car in between two other cars in a perfect parking maneuver. Through the front window, Natasha could see the grey, fortress-like headquarters of the Danish police. Why were there thick bars in front of some of the windows? As far as she knew, it wasn't here by the entrance that they locked up thieves and murderers. It seemed as if the bars were just there as a signal—a warning about what awaited when the interrogations with the nice Danish policemen were over.

The fat cop opened the door for her. "This is as far as we go, young lady."

She climbed out of the car and buried her hands in the pockets of her down jacket. The cold hit her, biting at her nose and cheeks, and she realized that she had brought neither hat nor gloves. When you were in prison, the weather wasn't something that really mattered. She had barely registered the snow the day before.

The older policeman pulled a smoke out of his uniform jacket and lit it, gave an expectant cough. The young cop, who already had a hand on Natasha's arm, sighed impatiently.

"Just two minutes," said the heavyset one and leaned against the car. "We've got plenty of time."

The young one shrugged. "You really should stop that, pal. It's going to kill both you and me. I'm freezing my ass off here."

The old one laughed good-naturedly and drew smoke deep into his lungs. Natasha wasn't freezing, but her legs felt weak, and she noticed again that she needed to pee. Soon. But she didn't want to say anything, didn't want the policemen to rush. She looked up at the massive, squat building as if it could tell her why she was here. Relaxed uniformed and non-uniformed employees wandered in and out among the pillars in the wide entrance area. If they were planning to seal the fate of a young Ukrainian woman today, you couldn't tell, and for a moment, Natasha felt calmer.

This was Copenhagen, not Kiev.

Both she and Katerina were safe. She was still in Copenhagen. Still Copenhagen. Across the rooftops a bit farther away, she could see the frozen and silent amusement rides in Tivoli, closed for the season. The tower ride from which she and Michael and Katerina had let themselves fall, secure in their little seats, on a warm summer night almost two years ago.

The big guy stubbed out his cigarette against a stone island in the parking lot and nodded at Natasha. "Well, shall we?"

She began to move but then remained standing as if frozen in place. The sounds of the city reached her with a sudden violence. The rising and falling song of car motors and tires on the road, the weak vibration in the asphalt under her when a truck rumbled by, the voices and slamming car doors. She was searching for something definite in the babble. She focused her consciousness to its utmost and found it. Again.

"*Ni. Sohodni. Rozumiyete?*"

Natasha locked her gaze on two men who had parked their car some distance away—one of them wearing an impeccable black suit and overcoat, the other more casual in dark jeans and a light brown suede jacket.

"Did someone nail your feet to the pavement?" the young cop said, in a friendly enough fashion. "Let's keep moving." His hand pressed harder around her elbow, pushing her forward a little.

"I'm sorry," she said. She took one more step and another. Looked down at the slushy black asphalt and felt the fear rise in her in its purest and darkest form.

They worked their way sideways around a small row of dug-up parking spaces cordoned off with red-and-white construction tape. Long orange plastic tubes snaked their way up from the bottom of the deserted pit. Next to it was a small, neat pile of cobbles half covered by snow.

Natasha slowed down. Gently. Avoided any sudden movements.

The old guy looked back just as she bent down to pick up the top cobble. She smiled at him. Or tried to, at least.

"I'm just . . ."

He was two steps away, but the younger one was closer, and she hit *him*, hard and fast and without thinking. She felt the impact shoot up through the stone and into her hand and closed her eyes for an instant. She knew that the young cop fell in front of the old one, blocking his way, because she could hear them both curse and scrabble in the soap-like slush. But she didn't see it.

She just ran.

NINA WOKE SLOWLY, with some kind of murky nightmare rumbling at the bottom of her consciousness. There had been a refugee camp that looked like Dadaab, the flies and the heat and that smell you never completely escape from, the stench of atomized human misery. But the children lying before her on the ground with starved faces and protruding bellies were Anton and Ida.

She rolled over onto her side and tried to escape the dream. 9:02, announced the large digital wall clock that had been the first thing she hung on the wall when she moved in. An anemic February sun was streaming unimpeded through the window; the shades she had bought at IKEA on a rushed afternoon in August were still lying in their packaging on the radiator almost six months later. Luckily, there were no neighbors. Outside lay Grøndals Parkvej, and on the other side of it the park and the railroad embankment, the reason she had bought the apartment. Centrally located yet still a quiet neighborhood, the realtor had said, a really good parental buy— did she have a son or daughter starting college, perhaps? When he had realized that she was going to be living there herself, he had adjusted expectations noticeably. Divorced mothers were difficult clients, it seemed, confused and unrealistic and with no perspective on their own budget.

The cell phone rang. It must be what had woken her, even though she hadn't really registered it, since it wasn't her ringtone. She poked Magnus in the ribs.

"It's yours," she said.

A groggy sound emanated from the fallen Swedish giant. He lay on his stomach, his head buried so deep in the pillow, it was amazing that he could breathe. His broad, naked shoulders were covered with short golden hair, and he smelled of semidigested beer. She nudged him again.

Finally, he lifted his head.

"Oh, my God," he said in his distinct Swedish accent. "What time is it?"

"It's Saturday," she said, since that was more to the point.

He reached for the cell phone, which was lying on the floor next to the bed along with his wallet and keys. Neat little bedside tables, his and hers, were not part of the apartment's inventory. The only place where she had made an effort was in Anton's and Ida's rooms, and they still hadn't turned out right. Everything was too tidy. It lacked the clutter of toys and discarded clothing, the scratches on the wall from hockey sticks and lightsabers, the remnants of stickers that wouldn't quite come off, odd splotches from overturned soda cans and soap bubble experiments. Quite simply, it lacked *children*. She hadn't managed to make it more than a temporary refuge. Home was still the apartment in Fejøgade, and that was where they had their life.

She got up and headed for the bathroom. A small bathtub that permitted only sit-up baths, yellowing white tiles from the '50s, and if you insisted on having a washing machine in there, you had to accept that you were going to bang your knees against it every time you sat on the toilet. But to sit in a Laundromat at an ungodly hour to have clean clothes for the next day . . . No, thank you. "Been there, done that," as Ida would have said.

After peeing, Nina gargled with chlorhexidine. She was susceptible to thrush and other mouth infections after her attack of radiation illness the year before. All in all, her resistance was not what it had been, she noted dryly. Otherwise Magnus probably wouldn't be lying in her bed now. The doctor and the nurse. Damn. How much more clichéd could you get?

He had just been through a divorce. So had she. They were both consenting adults and all that. But she knew perfectly well that it wasn't because they were adults. It was because they were both so unbearably lonely that any kind of intimacy was better than nothing.

Through the bathroom door she could hear his voice change from Saturday grogginess to professional clarity, and a rush of alarm raced through her. She spat out the petroleum-blue mouthwash into the sink, plucked yesterday's T-shirt from the dirty laundry basket and pulled it on, then opened the door.

He was getting dressed, the cell phone still pressed to his ear.

"Okay," he said. "No, don't give her any more. I'm on my way."

"Is it Rina?" she asked with an odd kind of pseudomaternal instinct. There were around 200 females at the Coal-House Camp, yet Rina was the first one she thought of.

"They've given her several doses of Bricanyl," he said. "But they can still hear crackling on auscultation, and she's hyperventilating."

Sweet Jesus, it *was* Rina.

"What happened?"

"Everything," he said. "Come on."

NATASHA HAD ENDED up on the wrong side of the lake, and there was only one way to deal with that. She had to get hold of a car.

The realization had been gnawing at her since the previous evening, or rather the previous night, because at that point it had been almost 2 A.M., and even if she had dared take a train or bus, they weren't running any longer, at least not to where she was going.

She had been so tired that her bones hurt. In particular her knees and the small of her back ached from the many freezing kilometers, and she knew that she couldn't walk much farther without resting.

Most of the houses on the quiet street lay dark and closed behind the snowy hedges. But she could hear music and party noises and beery shouts, and when she got to the next street corner, she saw three young men peeing into a hedge outside a whitewashed house that was alight with boozy festivities. She stopped, half sheltered by the fence of the corner lot, leaning for a moment against the cold tar-black planks.

"Laa, la-laa, la-laa . . ." roared one of the peeing men, loudly and in no key known to man. "Laa, la-aa, la-laaa . . . Come on!"

The two others joined in, which didn't make it any more tuneful.

"We are the champions, my friend . . ."

She realized that they were celebrating some kind of sports victory.

Presumably basketball—she suddenly saw how alike they were physically: broad shouldered, yes, but primarily tall, and younger than she had thought at first; she had been fooled by their height.

Yet another young boy emerged from the house. He seemed more low-key than his peeing buddies, just as tall but a little skinnier, a little more awkward. His dark hair looked damp and spiky, and he wore glasses. A girl tottered after him in high heels she could barely manage, the strap of her pink blouse falling halfway off one shoulder.

"Robbie, don't go yet!" she shouted shrilly.

"I need to get home," he said.

"Why? Dammit, Robbie . . . You can't just . . . Robbie, come onnnn!"

One of the three at the hedge quickly zipped up and tried with similarly incoherent arguments to convince Robbie to stay, but he shook them off.

"I'll see you guys," he said and started walking with long, fairly controlled steps down the street in the direction of Natasha. The girl stood looking after him, her arms folded across her chest.

"Robbie," she wailed, but one of the guys by the hedge put an arm around her and pulled her along with him back into the house. Robbie continued down the sidewalk as if he hadn't heard her.

Natasha was about to back up so that he wouldn't notice her, but he didn't go all the way to her corner. Instead, he stopped at a dark blue car not far from her.

"Whoo-hoo," one of the remaining party boys commented. "Does Daddy know you're driving his Audi?"

"They're skiing," said Robbie. "They won't be home until Thursday."

He remained standing with the keys in his hand as if he didn't feel like getting in while they were looking on. Not until they had followed their friend and the girl into the house did he unlock the car.

He was so tall. There was no way she'd be able to hit him and get away with it, and she no longer had a cobble or any other weapon. But he had a car key. And a car.

Without a car, she couldn't reach Katerina. Without a car, they couldn't get away, and they had to. In her mind, she once again heard the voices from the parking lot outside police headquarters. There was nothing recognizable about them, and what they had said wasn't alarming in itself. "It has to be today. Understand?" Ordinary words, not threatening—but spoken in Ukrainian. She felt a fresh rush of panic just thinking about it.

She glided up behind the rangy young man and placed her hand on his, the hand in which he held the keys.

"Not good," she said in English. "Not good to drive after drink."

A good guess—the short delay in his reaction revealed that he had been drinking. Not as much as the others but probably still quite a bit. He stared at her as if he was trying to remember how they knew each other. She took the keys out of his hand, opened the door quickly and got in.

"Hey, wait . . ." He stuck his leg in so she couldn't close the door and quickly grabbed the wheel. "What are you doing?"

Driving, she told herself silently. Driving to Katerina. But clearly he wasn't planning to just let her do so.

"Robbie," she said again in English. "Bad for you to drive. Let me. I take you home."

He looked at her through slightly foggy glasses. Using his name had had an effect. He thought they knew each other even though he wasn't sure how. And he was drunk. More than it had appeared at first.

"Okay," he said slowly. "You drive, er . . ."

"Katerina," she said with her most dazzling smile. "Don't you remember? It's Katerina."

HE DIDN'T FALL asleep in the car as she had hoped. Instead he directed her through the suburban streets, closer to the lake that separated her from Katerina, and finally got her to turn into a drive and park in front of a garage and a yellow brick house with old ivy growing all the way to the roof. The branches from the large silver birch at the entrance were weighted so heavily with snow that they brushed across the car's roof. She turned off the engine and tried to leave the key in the ignition, but he was still too much on guard and pulled it out himself.

"Thank you," he said. And then apparently was struck by a thought beyond getting to his own front door. "What about you?" he asked. "How will you get home?"

She forced herself to look away from the car keys in his hand and into his eyes.

"Maybe you ask me to stay?" she said.

She felt anything but attractive. Her hair had been wet with snow several times, and the shirt under the down jacket was stiff and sticky with old sweat. She only had a little bit of mascara on, if it wasn't smeared under her eyes by now, and she knew she was very, very far from the beautiful Natasha that Pavel had once shown off to selective friends as "my lovely wife."

He sucked in air, making a sharp, startled sound. But somewhere a surprising degree of sophistication appeared from beneath the boyish awkwardness.

"You are very welcome," he said. "This way, madame."

"Katerina," she corrected him gently. "Or you make me feel like an old woman."

SHE WOKE UP abruptly many hours later with a feeling of panic racing through her veins. Her head hurt, and she was once again sticky with sweat. The clean comforter that lay so lightly across her naked body had never been anywhere near a prison laundry, but it wasn't Michael lying next to her; it couldn't be, not anymore. The panic subsided.

It had grown light outside. Grubby grey winter light fell on piles of clothing, basketball shoes, a desk that had almost disappeared under heaps of books and paper, a green carpet marked with white lines like a basketball court. She hadn't intended to fall asleep, but the velvety blackness of her own unexpected orgasm had swept her into unconsciousness.

She felt a sudden tenderness for the overgrown boy who lay snoring with his face deep in the pillow—even more lost to the world than she herself had been. To be touched by another person. A person who hadn't pulled on clear plastic gloves to examine her body. A person who wanted to bring her desire, not pain. When was the last time she had experienced that? Not since Pavel.

She hadn't needed to sleep with him. He had left the car keys on a little table in the foyer. There had been several chances, but she hadn't seized them. Instead she had drunk shots and beer with him, and they had kissed on the sofa with way too much tongue, as if she were a teenager again. As if she were seventeen and had just met Pavel. And now she lay here in his bed, staring up at a huge poster of a towering black American basketball player who apparently was called Magic. Recalled the pressure of his hip against her stomach, the slippery feeling of sweaty skin against sweaty skin, his eager, choppy rhythm, a little too sharp, a little too hard and fast, yet still enough to give her that surprising dark release that had carried her into sleep.

He didn't move when she wriggled free of him and slid out of the bed. She stood for a moment, naked and dizzy on the green carpet, and felt so exhausted that she wanted just to crawl back into the nothingness with a heavy, warm body at her side.

"That won't do, my girl," she whispered, and it wasn't her own voice she heard, but Anna's. Neighbor Anna, Katerina called her, even though they hadn't always been neighbors. "Sometimes you just have to go on. One foot in front of the other. Without thinking too much about it."

She listened, but Anna-in-her-head didn't have anything else to say this time. And the real Anna was probably sleeping safe at home in the yellow farmhouse next door to Michael's.

Natasha pulled on her jeans even though they were stiff with dried road salt all the way up to the knees. The shirt she couldn't bear. She bunched it up and stuffed it into the pocket of her jacket and instead stole a T-shirt and a grey hoodie from Robbie's closet. The sweatshirt sleeves were about a foot too long, but she rolled them up and put on her down jacket before they could unroll again.

There was a saucy drumroll from somewhere on the other side of the bed, and Natasha gave a start as Freddy Mercury's voice suddenly erupted into the same triumphant refrain she had heard the victory-drunk players bawl out at the party the night before. It was Robbie's cell phone. It was lying with his pants on the floor by the desk.

She picked it up and pressed the OFF button frantically. Robbie hadn't moved. Luckily, it would take more than that to wake the sleeping warrior. She stuffed the cell phone in her own pants pocket, wrote a message on a pad that was lying on the desk and placed it next to his pillow. Then she went downstairs.

The car keys were still lying on the foyer table. She took them. In the kitchen she opened the refrigerator and drank a pint of milk without taking the carton from her mouth. She quickly examined the shelves, nabbed a package of rye bread and a big box of chocolate wafers for sandwiches, stuffing four or five pieces in her mouth right away. The sweet explosion of melted milk chocolate went directly to her empty energy deposits. The rest she carefully wrapped in foil again for Katerina.

She glanced at the clock over the sink. It was after ten, and it was high time she got going. Katerina was waiting right on the other side of the lake. And now Natasha had a car.

She took a knife from the kitchen drawer before she left.

"DON'T TAKE THAT one. It isn't ripe."

Olga glowered at Oxana, who had followed her into the garden and now drew herself up in a wide-legged stance, with an annoyingly grown-up frown on her face. It was so typical of Oxana to interfere just when Olga had gotten permission to go pick a melon for tea, if she could find one that was ready. Olga was the one who had helped Mother dig and turn the earth and place the small brown seeds in the ground one by one. Shouldn't she also be the one who decided when the first melon was ripe? Oxana might be two years older, but that didn't make her any wiser. No way was this going to be her decision!

To prove that she was right, Olga quickly bent down and rapped hard with her knuckles on the biggest melon, just like Mother usually did. The sound was muffled and hollow, and Olga felt as if she could almost see the red fruit through the rind, heavy and sweet and juicy. Her mouth began to water.

"What about the other side?"

Oxana pushed Olga lightly and hit the melon on its yellow, dirt-covered bottom, making a flat, wooden crack.

"See for yourself," said Oxana seriously. "It won't be completely ripe for a few more days."

"I don't give a fart," Olga said sourly. "We can eat it today, and it'll be perfectly fine—and anyway, I'm the one who gets to decide."

Oxana frowned again. "Speak properly," she said. "You're starting to sound just like the boys. It's better to wait until that melon tastes right. It's only dogs and boys—little boys—who can't help eating whatever is in front of their noses. Anyone with half a brain waits to dig up the potatoes until they are big and leaves the apples on the tree while they are small and green and sour."

Olga shook her head and suddenly couldn't help thinking about Mashka, who had had a litter of puppies last year and had scrounged around the compost heap for food until October. Mother had once slapped Olga because she had snuck a piece of rye bread out to the dog, and after that Mashka had had to manage on her own with whatever mice and rats she could catch. Mashka hadn't had time to wait for the potatoes to get big, or for the mice to get fatter, for that matter. Right after Christmas both she and the puppies had disappeared from the back shed, and it wasn't hard to figure out who had taken her, because at that same time, a group of Former Human Beings had drifted down the village's main street, reaching out with their skeletal fingers for anything edible on their way. The bark had been peeled from the trees, sparrows shot out of the sky; they had even eaten dirt.

Olga shuddered.

Poor Mashka. She herself had looked like a dead dog in the end, so perhaps it had been for the best that she had been freed from her suffering. But still. It wasn't nice of Oxana to speak badly of dogs in that way. They just did what they had to do to survive. Just like everyone else.

Olga grabbed hold of the watermelon and twisted it defiantly so that it let go of the vine with a small, crunchy snap. "It's ripe."

Oxana sighed in the way that meant that Olga was so childish, and Oxana herself so much more grown-up. But she nonetheless quickly followed Olga around to the covered veranda, where Mother had already heated water in the samovar. Mother took the melon, split it in half on the cutting board with the largest knife they had and didn't say a word about it not being ripe.

Olga looked triumphantly at Oxana. But Oxana just laughed and gave Olga's braid a friendly tug. It was odd. Sometimes Oxana pretended to be grown-up even though she wasn't. Other times she was just Oxana, like now, when she lifted little Kolja up from the rough planks on the veranda and danced around with him in her arms, as if there were a balalajka orchestra in her head. Kolja twisted his skinny little four-year-old body to get loose. He was a serious boy; even when he laughed, he somehow looked serious, as if he didn't believe that anything could be all that funny. Oxana's smile, on the other hand, shone like a sun, and she was beautiful, Olga thought, even now when she had just lost a tooth in both sides of her lower jaw and the new ones were growing in a little bit crooked. She was ten years old and a hand's breadth taller than Olga, but her teeth still looked too big for her narrow face. Her eyes were as blue as cornflowers.

Mother pulled off Kolja's shirt and vest so he could eat the first piece of watermelon without smearing the juice all over his clothes. Olga got the next piece and was just about to take a bite when she realized something was wrong.

"Shouldn't we wait for Father?"

"If he's not home in time for tea, there's not much we can do about it," said Mother. Her mouth had gotten small even though she was still smiling. "He'll be here soon enough."

"But . . ." Oxana had also stopped now, one hand hovering about the platter. "I can run down to the office and get him."

"No, never mind," said Mother. She pulled her blouse out and fanned it back and forth to get a little air against her skin. "He'll probably be here soon."

This was wrong.

As long as Olga could remember, they had eaten the first

watermelon together—all of them. When they lived in town, it had been a day of celebration, when Father cut the pieces and said funny things when he handed them out. "To my most highborn princess" or "to the most beautiful flower in the field."

Olga shifted uneasily in her seat, but she didn't say anything. It was one of the hottest summer days so far. Clothes felt sticky and itchy on the body, rubbing at the lice bites that had kept Olga and little Kolja awake all night. Mother had changed the straw in the mattresses, boiled the sheets and rubbed petroleum on the sleeping shelf, but the lice still bit in the heat and darkness until Olga was about to go mad. For some reason they weren't as interested in Oxana.

Olga scratched her neck and looked uncertainly at her big sister. It would have been best if Father was there too, but the large, sweet watermelon pieces lay in front of her, and it was unbearable. Oxana was right about that. She was no good at waiting.

She reached across the platter and took a thick slice. It was so juicy that the water dripped from her fingers, and when she took the first bite, it was wonderfully sweet and immediately pushed away her bad conscience. Mother could keep her rye bread, pickles and thyme tea today, and Oxana could stare at her as sourly as she liked. Olga took another piece.

"You're such a baby," Oxana said, outraged. "I'm waiting for Father."

Olga stuck out her tongue and kicked at Oxana under the table, but for once Mother didn't say anything. She had taken a piece of melon herself, bending her head over the table and carefully spitting out the black, mature seeds onto a piece of newspaper to be dried and saved for next year's crop. Then she pushed the plate of pickles toward Oxana. "Eat."

Oxana shook her head and glanced up the road.

Something was wrong. Olga could feel it all the way in the pit of her stomach. A kind of dark energy shone out of Mother now. It was like the wind that suddenly arrived and stirred up the dust in the road before a thundershower. From the Pretrenkos' house on the other side of the cabbage patch, Olga could hear laughter and Vladimir shouting something or other at Jana. Other than that, everything was quiet in the oppressive afternoon heat.

"Do you want to spoil the food?" Mother asked. She was pale with anger now. "Eat, or I guarantee that you will go to bed without food. Your father is drinking his tea someplace else today."

Oxana looked frightened. Mother rarely got angry, but when she did, she sometimes struck them. Mother's hands were hard and dry as wood. Now she got up abruptly and began shoving the food off the table with angry gestures. Kolja reached out fast, grabbed two more pieces of melon and raced down to the bottom of the garden with his prize. Olga remained petrified, looking at her mother. A kind of hidden knowledge began to bubble up to the surface.

The arguments had woken her in the night several times in the first months of spring. When Mother and Father argued, they whispered instead of shouting, so that it sounded like an excited hissing in the dark. Mother had never hidden the fact that she would have preferred to stay in Kharkiv, where Father had been a factory manager and a highly respected member of the Party. Even in the great hunger year, they had had bread and also a little sugar, salt and vegetables. To return to the village was suicide, she had said, but even though she cried, Father insisted.

It was the Party that had asked him to take over the management of the collective because he was known in the village and had a bit of experience with farming from his boyhood. And the Party was greater than Mother's tears, that much Olga knew. Father loved his Party and his country and would do everything possible to ensure that everyone would be better off. He would build a better future with his own hands. Olga had been on Mother's side, but of course Oxana had been on Father's, as she always was. And he was the one who got what he wanted in the end. Mother had dried her eyes, packed their things in silence and had followed him to the village where they had both grown up.

They had arrived in Mykolayevka in the fall right after the harvest, and Olga had hated the place instantly. Half the village's houses stood empty, with rattling shutters and broken planks and beams. Most of the trees along the main street had been chopped down, and the few that were left had been stripped of their bark and were as dead as the houses around them. Just two poplars remained by the house of the village soviet, their silver leaves rustling in the wind. The few people in the street were thin and starved and dressed in layer upon layer of rags and coats full of holes. Even Father had looked frightened, Olga thought, but then he said that this year, the harvest was already safe. The horror stories of the great hunger year would soon be only that: stories. They would see; it would soon get better. Oxana believed him, but Olga's stomach hurt, and she tried to hide her face against Mother's chest.

The first winter had been just as terrible as Mother had feared. Even though Father was the foreman for the kolkhoz, and the harvest was better than the previous year, the bread rations were meager. Father would not take more for his family than the ordinary workers received, Oxana reported proudly. Just once, he had brought home a load of potatoes and a barrel of rancid salt pork that he had bought on the open market, and that had lasted a whole month.

It had not been enough. Not even the salt pork had staved off the hunger altogether and silenced the hollow ache under the ribs. And spring had been the worst. While everything bloomed around them, hunger had gnawed at their stomachs worse than ever.

It wasn't Father's fault, that much Olga understood. And it had gotten better in the course of the first warm summer months. But

Mother still cried and scolded all the time and was thin and tired and grey even though the sun was shining and they had been able to collect the first potatoes in the garden over a month ago. She had lost two teeth in her lower jaw, which now gaped as emptily as Oxana's.

But it occurred to Olga now that the whispered arguments in the night throughout the spring had not been just about Mother's longing for Kharkiv and her fear of cold and starvation.

Father drank his tea someplace else.

A picture of Father down by the sawmill in the company of a smiling, full-figured woman whirled through Olga's head, followed by the laughing mug of Sergej from school. Sergej had lice and stank, like the little pig he was.

"What do you think of the widow Svetlova?" he had asked.

"What do you mean?"

"Do you like her?"

Olga shrugged. She had no interest in talking with Sergej, who was seven and disgusting to look at, with large pox scars on his forehead.

"You father does," he said and pulled his index finger quickly back and forth through a circle he made of the index finger and thumb on his other hand. It was deeply disquieting even though Olga didn't understand what it meant.

The realization hit her now like a spurt of blood, burning her cheeks and her stomach.

The widow Svetlova had made it through the winter in a better state than Mother. She had no children and was younger. Much younger, with round cheeks and broad white teeth without a single gap.

Oxana sat with her head lowered and picked at the splinters in the table. She was probably pouting because she hadn't gotten any melon, but she didn't deserve any better.

"Now look what you've done," hissed Olga. "You've made Mother sad."

Oxana shrugged. She scowled, eyes full of tears.

"You're such a baby," was all she said. "You wouldn't be able to wait for anything if your life depended on it."

"**M**AGNUS, DAMN IT,**"** snapped Nina, but Magnus was driving twenty-five meters in front of her and couldn't hear her clenched exclamation. The winding forest road to the Coal-House Camp was not at the top of the municipality's list of priorities as far as plowing went, and with every snowfall the road got narrower and the snowbanks on both sides got higher. Magnus was driving close to the speed limit, with Volvo steadiness on authorized winter tires, while her middle-aged Nissan Micra skated around the turns as if it had never heard the word "traction."

The Micra was an emergency solution. It was almost fifteen years old, the door handle on the passenger side had broken off and the gearshift suffered from a reluctance to return to the middle position unless you gave it a sharp whack. Someone had painted green racing stripes on its curry-green door, most likely in a desperate attempt to give it a bit of personality. It was not the dream car; it was the "what I can afford?" car. She couldn't do without it. The public transportation's tenuous connection to the Coal-House Camp, more officially known as Red Cross Center Furesø, ceased completely at 9 P.M., and night shifts were an unavoidable part of the job of nurse.

The Micra's front wheels spun without effect on the black ice, and Nina had to fight a deep-seated urge to step on the brakes. The car sailed sideways into the curve and only fell into the track again seconds before it would have collided with the snow. She shifted down and waited for it to slow. Ahead of her, the back of Magnus's Volvo disappeared around the next turn. Perhaps she should have come in the Volvo with him. But then there was the problem of getting home again, and they hadn't exactly announced their . . . affair sounded completely wrong, relationship even worse—their mutual loneliness relief to the world. Maybe not arriving at the same time was a good move. But the adrenaline made her stomach burn, and the slow driving necessary on the slippery roads felt completely counterintuitive.

Natasha had escaped custody. As unbelievable as it sounded, it was true. The authorities had concluded that she might try to get hold of Rina and had therefore sent police out to the Coal-House Camp, which was, Nina thought, not something she could really object to, except that they had apparently managed to provoke one of the worst anxiety and asthma attacks Rina had experienced in all the time she'd been in the camp. Nina understood why Magnus was rushing and cursed the Micra's insufficiencies both mentally and out loud. "Damn it, damn it, damn it."

When she finally rolled into the parking lot in front of the camp's main entrance, she instantly spotted two almost identical dark blue Mondeo station cars. Two cars. Presumably at least four people. Apparently there was no lack of resources when the object was to catch single mothers with a foreign background found guilty of attempted murder, Nina thought dryly. It didn't say POLICE on the side, but it might as well have. Did they really think Natasha was stupid enough to wander into the camp as long as they were parked there? The police had errands at the camp fairly regularly, and Natasha knew just as well as the rest of the camp's current and former residents which car makes she should be on the lookout for.

On the other hand, it wasn't particularly intelligent to attack two policemen with a cobble. Nina had a hard time recognizing Natasha in the hurried description of events that Magnus had given her on their way to the cars. Of course, Natasha could be pushed to act violently; probably almost everyone could. But when she stabbed her fiancé with a hunting knife, it hadn't been because he had physically abused her for months; it wasn't until she caught him with his fingers in Rina's panties that she had counterattacked. During all the time she had spent in Vestre Prison, she had been almost alarmingly silent and passive.

Until now.

"What the hell were you thinking?" Nina muttered to herself as she made her way up the barely shoveled walkway in the direction of the camp's little clinic. Something or other had clearly brought this on, but what?

She stomped the snow off her boots on the grate by the clinic's main entrance. Weeks' worth of frosty slush was packed in the metal grid so that it had had become like trying to dry your feet on an enormous ice cube tray. As she opened the door, though, the heat hit her like a hammer. Magnus consistently ignored all energy-saving suggestions on that point. "The people who come here are sick, depressed and hurt," he had said when the chair of the camp's conservation committee had protested. "I'll be damned if I'm going to let them freeze as well!"

Rina was half sitting, half lying on a cot in one of the two examination rooms. In the corner between the closet and the wall sat an aggressively clean-shaven young man in a hoodie that on him looked more like workout clothes than weekend wear. He had placed himself in such a way that he couldn't be seen from the window, and Nina concluded that he had to be a member of the Mondeo brigade. There had been a moment of heightened alertness as she came in, but now he relaxed back into a waiting position, apparently convinced solely by her age and appearance that she posed no danger.

"Hello, sweetie," Nina said, squeezed Rina's hand, which was limp and a little too cool. "What are we going to do with you?"

There was something about the slight, eight-year-old body and the narrow face that reminded Nina of the eastern European little girl gymnasts of the 1970s—Olga Korbut, Nadia Comaneci and whatever they were called. Not the smiling medal photos, but the serious, too-old-for-their-age concentration before the routine, the shadows under their eyes, the contrast between the cheerful ponytails and the hollow-cheeked, pain-etched faces. Rina's hair was blond like her mother's, thick, straight dark blonde hair without even the suggestion of curl or wave. Right now that hair was pulled back with a light blue Alice band, but even though you could occasionally sense that Rina felt she had fallen through a rabbit hole to an alternate universe, there clearly wasn't much Wonderland about it. Her breathing was still terribly labored. Tiny pinpoint blood effusions around her half-closed eyes revealed how hard she had had to fight to get enough oxygen into her tormented bronchial tubes. Yet it wasn't Rina's physical condition that made Nina's own heart contract as if it were something more than a pumping muscle.

"Sweetie," she said, sitting down next to the child and pulling her close. Even on good days, anxiety lay like permafrost just beneath Rina's thin crust of childish trust. Now the trust was gone. There was no wish for contact in the slight body; she just let herself be moved with an arbitrary shift in her weight that had nothing to do with intimacy.

Having changed quickly, Magnus entered, stethoscope in hand. Pernille, who had had the night shift, followed on his heels.

"I had to give her oxygen a few times," said Pernille. "And her peak flow is still nothing to shout about. But . . . well, you can see for yourself."

Magnus nodded briefly. "Hello, Rina," he said. "I just need to listen to your lungs a little bit."

Rina didn't react except with a quick sideways glance. Nina had to turn her partway so that Magnus could examine her.

"Come on, Rina. You know the drill. Deeeep breath."

Rina continued to breathe in exactly the same tormented rhythm, but Magnus didn't try to correct her. He just praised her as if she had done what he had asked. "Very good. And now the other side."

There was still no reaction, no sign that Rina was participating in the examination with anything but limp passivity. Nina gently pulled her close so that Magnus could place the stethoscope against Rina's chest. Over Rina's blonde hair she caught Magnus's gaze.

"Well, I can hear that it's getting better," he said, just as much to Nina as to the child. "Do you want Pernille to get you some ice cream?"

Rina loved ice cream and could eat it year-round, and it had gradually become the ritual reward for various examinations, especially those that involved blood tests or other needle pricks. Rina lifted her head and considered the offer. But then she collapsed again with a single shake of her head.

"Did you eat breakfast, Rina?"

Again a tiny shake.

"She didn't want anything," said Pernille. "Not even ice cream."

Magnus sat down on a stool so he was more or less at eye level with Rina. "Listen, Rina. It's super hard for the body when you have trouble breathing. It's as hard as playing ten soccer games in row. Do you see? And then you have to be a little kind to your body and feed it properly, even if you might not feel like eating."

That didn't make any visible impression.

"Rina, if you don't eat anything, we'll have to keep you here in the clinic," said Nina. "Wouldn't you rather go back to your room?"

The policeman by the closet cleared his throat. "It's best for her to be where she usually is," he said.

Nina stared at him with anger smoldering in the pit of her stomach. "Best?" she said. "For whom?"

"So that the mother can find her more easily."

The anger burst into flame. Only concern for Rina made her control herself. Couldn't he see that this was a child, a sick and tormented child, not just convenient bait for their trap?

"That's a medical decision," said Magnus very, very sharply. "And I'm the doctor."

But Rina had lifted her head again and suddenly looked more present and alive than she had at any point since Nina got there. "I'd like an ice cream," she said.

Oh, Lord, thought Nina. So that the mother can find her more easily. That was the only thing Rina had heard and understood. What if Natasha really did show up? And the police arrested her in front of the child? Nina didn't want to think about what that would mean for Rina's delicate balance and her grasp of reality here in non-Wonderland. She could see that Magnus was thinking more or less the same thing. But they couldn't do anything—couldn't even discuss it here and now while Rina was listening.

"Strawberry or chocolate?" asked Nina.

TEN MINUTES LATER, as she escorted Rina across the icy asphalt lot that had once been the barracks' drill grounds, it was with two of the Mondeo brigade on her heels, though they maintained a certain discreet distance that presumably was supposed to make them look like civilian passersby. Rina held Nina's hand, something she had otherwise stopped doing, and in her other hand she clutched the strawberry ice cream, which she dutifully sucked on every fourth or fifth step. At least it didn't look as if her breathing was significantly more labored now that she was moving and even though the air was cold enough to sting Nina's more resistant lungs. Pernille had done all the right things, had administered Bricanyl and later prednisone, had measured the oxygen and attempted to calm the panic. Physically, the girl was improving. But right now Nina was much more concerned with what was happening in Rina's mind.

In the middle of the grounds, Rina suddenly stopped. She gave a little tug on Nina's hand.

"What is it, sweetie?"

"He's dead," said Rina.

It took Nina a moment before she managed to reply, quietly and calmly. "Who?"

"Poppa Mike."

Poppa Mike? Did she mean Michael Vestergaard?

"Why do you think that?"

"That's what they said. The police."

The wind raced across the open square. Pin-sharp flakes that were more ice than snow bit Nina's cheeks and forehead, and she suddenly felt as if she were standing in an arctic desert, icy and isolated, infinitely far from warmth, shelter and human contact. Rina stood next to her and stared with great concentration at the strawberry ice cream, as if conquering it were a task she had set herself. She wasn't crying—in fact, her face was devoid of expression—but Nina was not fooled. She quickly checked the time—12:31—and looked up at the slate-grey sky with the apparently irrelevant thought that the weather would make it difficult to fly. Only a few seconds later did she understand why flying conditions suddenly seemed to matter. Whenever the situation had escalated from desperate to hopeless in one of the hellholes and disaster areas of her misspent youth, the skies had been her only hope. It was from above that help might arrive.

Unless Rina had misunderstood something, Natasha's former fiancé was dead—the man Natasha had once tried to murder with a hunting knife. And it had happened while she was on the loose after having brained a policeman with a cobble.

"Rina . . ."

"They are both dead," said Rina and took a determined bite of the strawberry ice cream. "Poppa Mike and Daddy."

Jesus. Poppa Mike *and* Daddy?

Nina realized that she knew absolutely nothing about Rina's biological father. She had placed a single-mother-from-Ukraine label on Natasha without giving it a lot of thought. "Are you sure, sweetie?" she asked carefully.

"That's what they said." Rina's voice shrank, got smaller and thinner, not because of Nina's doubt, it turned out, but because the next thing was what had made her world shake. "They said Mama did it."

"Mama?"

"Yes, that Mama killed them. Both of them."

Suddenly the Mondeo brigade's size made more sense. They weren't hunting a woman found guilty of a single—relatively ineffective—homicide attempt. They thought that Natasha was a double murderer.

Nina was all at once extremely conscious of Rina's hand resting in her own. The girl's delicate fingers were trembling, not just from cold and fear, but because the asthma medicine was affecting her. Anton's hand was different, more solid and square and usually more dirty.

Anton was with Morten now, in the apartment in Fejøgade. Maybe they had made pancakes; Morten sometimes did that when he had the time and energy and was in a good mood. Maybe they were all three still sitting at the kitchen table while Morten lingered over an extra cup of coffee and talked about music with Ida, and the checkered oilcloth got more and more spotted by Anton's marmalade fingers. Only Nina was missing.

I'm not sure I can do this, she thought, without completely knowing what "this" was, just sensing that the war had started again, and she was too tired, too old and not suited to fight it. I wouldn't mind if someone came to rescue us right now.

Rina gave her hand a little tug, this time because she wanted to continue. "I'm cold," she said.

"No wonder," said Nina. "It's freezing out here. Let's get you inside."

Somewhere behind them, the two Mondeo men had halted. Now they started moving again. Was it one of them who had said that "Poppa Mike" was dead? And that Natasha had killed him? How could they say such things while Rina was listening? No hope of rescue from that quarter, that much was certain. But who else was there to turn to?

SØREN RECOGNIZED THE number right away even though he hadn't called it in over six months.

He stopped in his tracks, and another runner on the path had to swerve around him. His pulse was at 182 and his breathing so labored that he had to let the telephone ring several times before he took the call, but he didn't for a second consider not answering.

"Yes," he said.

"It's Nina. I don't know if you remember me. I was the one who—"

"Yes. I know who you are."

He saw her with crystal clarity in his mind's eye. The first time he had met her, she had been sick as a dog with radiation poisoning, frightened and furious. The hospital's patient uniform didn't fit her any better than it did anyone else; she was stick thin and smelled faintly of vomit, and her short, dark hair covered her scalp like a matt of shaggy and untended fur. Only her eyes had revealed that there was still life in the ruins—the intensity burned through clearly in spite of the fact that the rest of her had to be categorized as "more dead than alive."

She had been difficult, uncooperative and suspicious, and he had to threaten her with prison, a moment during the interrogation that he wasn't very proud of. She probably had no idea that he had later done his best to shield her—her and her pretty illegitimate network. In his eyes, people like Nina were perhaps a bit too trusting toward some of the illegal immigrants and other borderline cases they supported with medical aid, shelter and other emergency essentials. But damn it, people should not be prosecuted for basically doing a good deed.

Another runner trotted by him in the tense staccato style people tended to adopt when the going couldn't be trusted. Even on this disgustingly cold winter afternoon, there were lots of joggers on the path around Damhus Lake. The route was too short; he had circled the lake four times, which made him feel a bit like a hamster in an oversized wheel, and even though the council did clear the paths of snow, they were still slippery and greasy with a grey-brown mixture of gravel, slush, goose shit and salt. He would have preferred the woods of Hareskoven or some other, less crowded place, but the snow made the forest paths more or less impassable, and when he had tried to exchange his running shoes for cross-country skis a few weeks ago, his old knee injuries had protested so violently that he'd had to toss the skis back up on the carport rafters again.

The phone had gone quiet, long enough for his pulse to drop to around 140.

"What can I do for you?" he asked at last.

"Forget it," she said suddenly. "I shouldn't have called."

The background noise and the faint whistling disappeared. She had hung up.

He stood looking at the phone for a few seconds. There was a limit to how long he could stand still. He was already getting cold, and a harsh wind blew over the lake's frozen surface. An open hole in the ice was teeming with screaming, quacking, cackling waterfowl— mostly ducks and graylag geese, but there were also five or six swans and a raucously aggressive gang of black-headed gulls.

He pressed the DIAL button. She answered at once. "You must have had a reason for calling," he said.

She still hesitated. "It was mostly because . . . you're not an idiot."

An ironic "thank you" was about to slip out, but he stopped himself. Irony wasn't what was needed here. "What's happened?" he asked instead.

"You are the twenty-six-year-old mother of a little girl," she suddenly said, in a peculiarly rushed staccato tone. "You've escaped from Ukraine; you get engaged to a Danish man; he's a sadistic bastard, but you tolerate it because you are more afraid of being sent back than of what he does to you. Not until you catch him with his fingers in your little daughter's underwear do you snap. You buy a knife and stab him in the throat. He survives, but you are found guilty of attempted murder and sent to jail."

She stopped, but he just waited, his muscles getting stiffer, the cold creeping across his skin along with the sweat. He stood perfectly still. He sensed that if he as much as shifted his weight, she would fly away again.

"You spend sixteen months in Vestre Prison doing nothing but what they tell you to do. Passive. Easy to handle. And then you suddenly attack a policeman and escape. And this is where it gets really weird. You don't go to get your daughter. Instead you head directly for your ex-fiancé, and then you kill him."

He could hear her breathing now that his own was calmer. Hers was stressed and shallow. Forced.

"Does that make sense?" she said. "Is it logical?"

"I don't know," he said. "Too much of the picture is missing."

"But your first impression?"

"I can't say," he insisted. "It would be pure speculation."

"Okay. Forget I called."

"No, wait. I just said that I didn't know enough."

She sighed. "That's something. The police here think that they know everything. They are apparently convinced that Natasha murdered both the sadistic bastard and Rina's father."

Rina's father? Who the hell was that? Nina wasn't making it easy to follow her.

"Where are you?" Søren asked.

"The Coal-House Camp. Rina—that's Natasha's daughter—she . . . Damn it, she can't take this!" The anger rose in her voice. "They're using her as bait in their Natasha trap, and they don't give a shit if she's up to it or not."

He would probably have done the same thing—kept an eye on the girl with the assumption that the mother would contact her sooner or later. He didn't tell Nina that.

"What's Natasha's last name?" he asked.

There was a pause.

"I don't remember," she admitted. "Something . . . something Ukrainian. Wait. Dimitrenko or something like that. I don't remember how you spell it."

The computer was not particularly forgiving of alternative spellings, but on the other hand, how many Ukrainian women could there be who had just escaped from Vestre?

"I'll see what I can do," Søren promised recklessly. "I'll call you later."

"When?"

"It'll take awhile. At least a few hours."

"But you'll call?"

"Yes."

"Thank you."

The tension in Nina's breathing was gone. The relief made her voice younger and lighter, and he felt a prick of conscience. There probably wasn't anything he could do, and his only reason for trying was deeply unprofessional.

He wanted to see her again.

POLICE. OF COURSE, there would be police.

Natasha felt Katerina's proximity tug at her core. There she was, right on the other side of the fence, not in the family barrack where they had lived together before Michael, but in the rooms reserved for unaccompanied minors. She was there; she had to be there, even though Natasha couldn't see her.

But the police lurked like big, fat barn cats, just waiting for the stupid mice to scurry out of the hay.

"As long as it's light, you have no chance." She once again heard Anna's voice, a voice that calmly and sensibly forced her to listen even though Natasha wanted to run over and throw herself against the wire fence. She wasn't sure when she had stopped thinking of Anna as a real-world source of solace and good advice, and instead turned her into this odd inner fairy godmother who kept an eye on Natasha and made sure she didn't behave too stupidly. Perhaps it was since that night a year and a half ago when she had attempted to stab Michael in the throat with a knife. Was it then?

Natasha was glad Anna was there. It made her feel less alone.

She walked back through the deep snow, well over half a kilometer, to the little clearing where she had parked the dark blue Audi. She might as well try to sleep a little.

She brushed extra snow onto the car's license plate to be safe. She didn't think Robbie would report it stolen for the time being. He was probably still asleep, and when he woke up, he would find the note she had placed next to his pillow: *I'll be back.* ❤, *Katerina.*

Right now she wished she had called herself something else.

In the Audi's trunk she found a blanket and a thick tarp. She took them both into the backseat and cocooned herself inside. A sleeping bag would have been better, but she didn't have a sleeping bag.

THE BED IN the apartment in Kiev had been a revelation in several ways. Clean and white and delicious smelling, full of pillows, comforters and smooth, light sheets—Egyptian cotton, Pavel had said, and she just nodded. She had never before lain on a mattress that received the body in this way, firm and soft at the same time. At home in the room in Kurakhovo, you could feel the bed slats through the worn foam rubber.

And Pavel, Pavel, Pavel, Pavel.

He had driven into her life in a shiny red Alfa Romeo one day as she was trudging along the road between Dachne and Kurakhovo. She had missed the bus and would rather walk to the next stop than stand waiting in the cold. When he slowed down and asked if she wanted a lift, she had ignored him at first. She didn't want him to think she was one of those girls. But he had kept rolling along next to her, apparently indifferent to the trucks that roared by him honking and all the vulgar gestures and shouts from the passing drivers. He had spoken to her just as if they were walking along next to each other on the sidewalk, although they did, of course, have to shout more loudly. He was a journalist, he said, and was writing an article about safety in the coal mines. Did she know anyone who worked there? Or anyone who once had? "Everyone does," she said. There were practically no other places you *could* work in Kurakhovo; it was the mines or the power plant or unemployment. Her father had lost his job two years ago; her mother still worked in the plant cafeteria. "And what about you?" he had asked. It had gone on like that all the way to Kurakhovo, and finally when they had reached the outskirts of town, she had gotten into his car. Because by now her feet hurt and because she was getting hoarse from shouting, and because . . . because Pavel was Pavel.

She had insisted on a church wedding so that everyone could see that she had married well, to a husband who had both money and culture. An intellectual, as her father said, at once contemptuous and satisfied. Pavel didn't drink vodka. Not even at the wedding party, where he wore a dark Armani suit. Few of the guests could appreciate such details, but that wasn't important. Pavel looked like what he was. A success. At the same time, he had shown everyone else up for what *they* were and would always be. A bunch of drunken, shabby bumpkins with foolish grins and yawning gaps in their teeth. Uncles and aunts and cousins, and girlfriends from school who arrived on the back of their boyfriends' scooters.

None of them drove an Alfa Romeo. And none of them had an apartment in Kiev with a view of the National Museum.

The first night in Kiev, she had felt like the princess in a fairy tale.

"Come on. There's something I want to show you!"

Pavel smiled at Natasha, and she couldn't help smiling back. Genuine smiles that could be felt all the way to the heart, and she thought that it felt precisely like love in the movies and that she adored every detail of his face. The nose, which curved slightly, and the blond hair she knew he had inherited from his Galizien mother, who had been ethnic German. Pavel himself spoke fluent German and also English, and earlier in the evening, he had ordered in a restaurant with the same confidence as the men in the American movies.

"What is it?" she asked.

On purpose she let herself stumble clumsily into his arms. Her breasts under the new bra and the soft silk blouse grazed his chest, and she wanted to get closer, feel his weight and the strength of his arms. In fact, she thought, and felt shameful and happy at the same time, she would undress him all the way tonight and look at him before they did it. In the big white bed, on the sheets of crackling Egyptian cotton. She didn't know if it was normal to think like this, but she didn't care. The night sky turned above them, and she laughed lightly and giddily.

"Take it easy." Pavel gently pushed her away and dexterously placed his arm between them, so that their bodies were no longer touching. "Act like a lady, my sweet. We're in a public place."

The rejection smarted, but only for a moment. Then she let herself be led farther up the steep path toward the lookout in Maryinsky Park.

Pavel took her hand and drew her to an opening in the trees. They were at the park's highest point now, and above them stretched a gigantic shining arch, all the way across the square. The evening air was pleasantly warm against her skin.

"Arka Druzhbi Narodiv. The People's Friendship Arch," said Pavel and pointed at two stiff statues under the arch. "Those are the two brothers. A symbol of Russia and Ukraine. The statues are cast in bronze, and the bow is pure titanium. As strong as steel, but much lighter."

Natasha nodded but didn't know what to say. Or what he expected her to say. She was much more interested in a little enclosure with bumper cars and pounding techno music on the other side of the titanium rainbow.

"Can we?"

"You go ahead," he said. "I'll wait here."

Natasha pouted and deliberately put on a disappointed face. But he didn't budge. He just dug into his pockets and found a few bills that he placed in her hand.

"I'm too old for bumper cars, but you go ahead, sweetheart. Then I'll show you the view afterward."

Natasha had already changed her mind. It wasn't going to be fun. Not when Pavel stood there next to the ring like an adult waiting for a child. The little lecture about the statues had already made her feel like a schoolgirl on a class trip. But it was too late now. In her newly purchased high heels, Natasha tottered over to a neon-yellow car and got in, knees folded almost all the way to her chin. Pavel stood a few meters from the railing and lit a cigarette, a brand with a sweetish tobacco that left a wonderful taste on his soft lips. He'd buried his hands in the pockets of his long black pants. So much for the creases, but that was okay. She'd take care of that for him.

There were only three other cars in the ring. One was being shared by a young couple, and the other two were driven by two teenage boys, absolutely hammered, who were clearly intent on doing maximum damage to each other. Even before the power had come on, the two drunk boys were hanging out of their cars, laughing and cursing and insulting each other. Why on earth had she thought this would be a good idea?

The car in front of her whined and picked up speed, and she reluctantly stepped on the flat little pedal in the bottom of her car. It smelled of burnt rubber, and the heavy, monotonous bass from the techno music made her chest vibrate. A faint nausea came over her, totally different from the feelings of sexual excitement and expectation that had coursed through her only minutes ago. She turned the steering wheel and lost focus for a moment while the car rotated around on its own axis. Then she was hit hard from behind, and her knees slammed against the steering wheel. It hurt, but she still forced herself to laugh giddily and let her gaze seek Pavel's tall figure outside the enclosure. She wanted him to see that she was having a good time.

He wasn't standing there anymore. She caught sight of him farther away, in the shadows under the trees, together with another man. Natasha lifted her foot from the pedal and observed Pavel and the man, who at first looked as if he was having a laugh about something. He spread his arms, and you could see his teeth bared in an odd grin. A friend, Natasha thought. Pavel's friends were influential and important men, she knew—journalists and politicians and businessmen, some of them filthy rich. None of them had come to the wedding, though, because Kurakhovo wasn't the kind of place you invited people like that, Pavel explained.

Now Pavel was the one laughing and gesticulating, but there was something strangely stiff about the scene. As if the two men were performing a play in an open-air theater, with exaggeratedly caricatured gestures in honor of the people in the back rows.

Pavel stepped back and suddenly didn't look like the man who had called the waiter earlier in the evening and confidently left twenty percent on top of the already large bill. There was a touch of uncertainty in his body, as if he'd rather be somewhere else.

Then the other man hit him.

The blow came so fast and with such precision that Natasha only saw it because she was keeping a sharp eye on them both. Pavel's head snapped back and to the side, and his hands rushed to his face, but otherwise nothing happened. The man turned around and walked away, passing under the titanium arch that was as strong as steel but lighter. His steps were angry and smooth and almost synchronized with the noisy music from the bumper cars.

Natasha tumbled out of the car, though she was still in the middle of the black arena. She barely escaped being torpedoed by one of the teenage boys on her way to the exit.

Pavel stood leaning against a tree when she reached him, with two fingers pinching the bridge of his nose to stop a trickle of blood.

She wanted to ask him what had happened, but something in his gaze stopped her, and she just handed him a napkin from the new Dolce&Gabbana purse he had given her.

"It's nothing. You don't need to worry," Pavel said and smiled behind his hand. "The things I write are not popular everywhere in Kiev. Journalism is a risky business, you know."

She didn't know.

Yes, of course she had heard about journalists who were threatened and shot. Idealists. But for some reason she had never connected that with Pavel.

He must have seen the confusion in her face, because now he was laughing for real and lifted her chin so that her face was turned up toward his.

"No, of course you don't know anything about that, my beauty," he said. "But come on. I still haven't showed you what we came up here for."

"Let's go home," Natasha said, glancing in the direction where the man had disappeared. It was almost completely dark now, and the square was emptying out. Only a few small groups of young people still sat there, laughing and smoking in the warm evening.

Pavel shook his head and took her hand again. Pulled her with him. "A jerk like that is not going to ruin our evening," he said. "He's not worth it. Have a look . . ."

She turned obediently.

Beneath them Kiev's millions of lights glittered, reflected in the great black mirror of the Dnieper River.

"Our city, Natasha. Isn't it beautiful?"

He pulled her close, but the night's intoxication had receded, and the world had become more real again. She had a bad taste in her mouth, and a pile of garbage next to them gave off a sweet-and-sour smell.

"I love you," she said, hoping the magic words would banish the unpleasant grittiness of the reality around them.

"And I love you. Like mad. Like a total lunatic," said Pavel. And now it must've suddenly been all right even though they were in a public place, because he pulled her close, and she could feel his short, excited breath against her neck.

His kiss tasted sharply of beer and sweet tobacco, and a little bit of blood.

SHE WOKE UP in a forest far from Kiev, in an ice-cold car, and still with a bloody taste in her mouth. She had bitten her cheek while she slept.

Pavel was dead and had been so for a long time. And the thing that had killed him was now stretching its tentacles toward her and Katerina.

UKRAINE, 1935

"**W**HAT KIND OF person are you if you believe in God?"

Comrade Semienova rose from her desk and looked at the class with a mild, questioning gaze.

Olga squirmed on the bench. The question wasn't difficult, and she knew what she was supposed to answer if she was asked. People who believed in God were anti-Soviet and not quite right in the head, and like the kulaks, they wouldn't work and especially not on Sundays. The kulaks wanted to be fed by the proletariat, and the religious by their God, and their faith was so strong that they would rather starve and freeze to death in the street than acknowledge that they were wrong.

That was the truth.

But in a way there were more truths than that, and they rubbed strangely against one other in her head and made her uncomfortable as she sat on the hard school bench. Because Olga remembered that her grandmother had had a little gold crucifix hanging under her blouse that she sometimes pulled out and kissed with her big, wet lips, and that must mean that she believed in God, even if she worked with her hoe out in the turnip field until the midday heat forced her inside.

Her grandmother died three summers ago. She had been found out in the field lying next to her hoe. Father and Mother and Oxana and

Olga had taken the train from Kharkiv to be part of singing her out, and even though Olga was smaller then, she could still remember the stench in the tiny living room where Grandmother lay waiting for the burial party. It was because she had been lying there too long, Father said then. Much too long, out there in the field. Even now Olga hated to think about it—Grandmother in the field in the roasting afternoon sun. Even if Grandmother *had* believed in God.

Olga would have liked to ask Comrade Semienova if work in the turnip field didn't count as work for the Soviet state for some reason, because perhaps that was the explanation. But she didn't dare. If there were something wrong with Grandmother, it would be embarrassing for both Oxana and her. Comrade Semienova would definitely frown and might even get angry.

And that must not happen.

Comrade Semienova was the most beautiful thing Olga had ever seen, and she knew that Oxana felt the same way. Small and straight and with hair as fair and shiny as stalks of wheat. When someone answered correctly or when there was particularly good news from Uncle Stalin in Moscow, her glowing smile brought out two lovely dimples in her soft cheeks. She smoked cigarettes like a man, which somehow seemed incredible and wonderful.

She had come from Leningrad, arriving in the early spring to replace old Volodymyr Pavlenko, who had died of hunger-typhoid sometime during the winter.

The school had been closed until April because there wasn't wood or petroleum, and therefore no one knew how long old Pavlenko had lain dead and frozen solid in the house at the back of the school. Because he was frozen, he didn't smell like Grandmother had, but Olga couldn't help shuddering when she thought about it. Still, that was long ago, and now it was autumn.

"Fedir? How does the religious person think?"

Comrade Semienova let her gaze rest on Fedir, who sat all the way at the back of the class. He was thirteen and strong as an ox but also similarly slow.

"They are stupid." Fedir grasped for more words. "They want to steal from the people."

Jana, who sat next to Olga, groaned quietly and imitated Fedir's slightly out-of-focus gaze and open mouth. But Comrade Semienova was satisfied.

"Correct, Fedir," she said and lit up with her wonderful smile. "But you can also express it in a different way. Oxana?"

"They are counterrevolutionary parasites who do not wish to have a strong state."

Now it was Olga's turn to groan. Oxana was good at remembering all the long words. The best in the entire class, and that was probably why she also sometimes dared to stand next to Comrade Semienova's desk after class to speak with her at length. Oxana was neither shy nor afraid she might blush and stammer. It was annoying and disgusting to watch, Olga thought, because Oxana wasn't that much better than Olga and Jana. She just had no shame. But the worst thing was that Comrade Semienova couldn't see that Oxana was sucking up to her. On the contrary, it seemed as if she liked speaking with Oxana and in fact listened to what she said, even though Oxana was only ten and Comrade Semienova at least twenty. As if they were friends.

Now she nodded to Oxana with a confidentiality she didn't share with any of the other children. Then she raised her voice.

"Comrade Oxana is the best student in this school," she said, offering a slender hand in Oxana's direction. "Therefore, I have decided that she is to accompany me next week to a group meeting with Komsomol and the pioneer division in Kharkiv. I would like Oxana to sing the Internationale."

The class was completely silent. Even that little worm Sergej, who sat next to Jana, had for once stopped rolling boogers on the table and was keeping his arms and legs still at the same time.

Now Oxana was blushing. It was from pride, not shame, thought Olga.

"Oxana is talented," Semienova continued. "But you should know that we all, regardless of abilities, must strive to be better comrades, to work harder for Uncle Stalin's ideas about the dictatorship of the proletariat. Next time it could be one of you going along to Kharkiv if you work hard and improve yourselves."

Jana bent her head toward Olga and stuck her index and middle fingers into her mouth with a telling gagging gesture. Olga giggled deliberately. But inside something had begin to gnaw and rub, like the many truths she saw. Were you allowed to hate your own sister? She had a feeling that both Uncle Stalin and Semienova would disapprove of her thoughts if they knew of them, but it was hard enough to control her words and behavior. To control her thoughts was completely impossible. No matter how hard she tried, they often drifted into black areas and made her think that she might be a kulak, or on her way to becoming one. There were things she wished to have, even though no one was supposed to own anything. Bread and silk dresses and shiny headbands. And Semienova.

That was why she had begged and made a spectacle of herself—as Jana put it—until she had been included in one of the photographs taken when Oxana had been chosen as the school's model student in September. Semienova got the *Pioneer* magazine to come all the way to Mykolayevka. Of course, only the picture of Oxana made it into the newspaper, but Semienova had also asked to have the other developed and had placed it next to her bed in the room behind the schoolroom. Olga knew that she was included because Semienova had felt sorry for her, but the picture was a nice one all the same, with Olga and Oxana in the beautiful and almost identical traditional dresses Mother had sewn for them when they still lived in Kharkiv.

Olga wished that she was the one Semienova had chosen to sing at the pioneer meeting, and she wished that Oxana wasn't so beautiful, didn't have such blue eyes and didn't sing like the stupid, goddamn nightingale in the poplar tree down by the stream.

OXANA'S CHEEKS WERE still blushing when they passed the last house in the village and continued on the dirt road between the hills.

The trip to school was terribly long now, ever since they had moved out to Grandfather's farm, and every day when they passed by the old house, Olga cursed the widow Svetlova and her bloated cow tits. All Jana had to do was run along to the Petrenkos' house right next door, while Olga and Oxana had to trudge along the stream and over the rise. It was all right while it was summer and the road was dry and warm so that you could take off your socks and shoes and walk barefoot. But now it was September, and the rain had already transformed the road into two black muddy wheel tracks. Neither their bark shoes nor the extra socks could prevent the cold mud from getting all the way in between their toes as they walked. Disgusting.

In addition, on the road to Grandfather's, there were Former Human Beings who had dug themselves dirt hole shelters among the birch trees and sat staring at them with starving eyes as they passed by. Sometimes they whispered and hissed up there among the trunks, begging for bread—"*khleb, khleb*"—but mostly they just stared. The worst was the children wandering around with bloated bellies and sores on their arms and legs. Most of those children had disappeared during the winter. The ones who remained were more dead than alive, and Olga had more than once thought about giving them a piece of her bread.

But hunger gnawed at her too—every day, all the time. Through gruel and porridge and nettle soup. When she closed her eyes, she thought about all the things she had eaten when she was younger. Whole plates filled with potatoes roasted in oil. Salt pork and sausage and cheese and pierogi. It would all come back, Oxana said, and she also said that Olga had to be strong and save her bread for herself, because the children among the birches were already marked for death by scurvy and typhoid. No matter how much bread they ate now, they would die, crushed between the great millstones *golod* and *kholod*— hunger and cold. Olga could not ease their suffering with a single piece of bread. And Olga knew that Oxana was right. In the spring she had seen boys by the pond behind the house catching tadpoles and swallowing them live. That kind of hunger consumed everything and could not be satisfied by Olga's two half-eaten crusts, and every time she had the thought, she let her bread slip back into her pocket and felt how her stomach, which at first had protested in panic, grew calm again.

Once she had decided to keep the bread, she discovered that she actually hated the Former Human Beings. They had stolen from the peasants and now sat there begging bread from her, so terribly hungry herself, who had never stolen as much as a stalk of wheat. That truth warmed her all the way down into the pit of her stomach. But she was still angry at Father too, because it was his fault that they had to walk the long way through the birch grove every day.

It was Father's fault that they had had to move. Father and Svetlova's cow tits.

Jana had told her that Svetlova had moved into their old house with Father just two days after Grandfather had come with the horse and wagon to collect Mother, Oxana, Kolja and her, and that Svetlova on that very same day had used Mother's laundry bucket to rinse her dirty underwear and hang it up on the veranda so everyone could see it. Mother had cried when she heard, and after that no one spoke of Father any longer. It was forbidden.

"Just think," said Oxana dreamily. "A whole day in Kharkiv, and I'm going by train with Comrade Semienova."

"Hmmmm."

Only once in her life had Olga traveled by train, and that was when they had to attend Grandmother's funeral. Otherwise, she had only seen them at a distance in the railroad town of Sorokivka. You needed permission from the GPU for that kind of travel. And money. Something occurred to her.

"But who will pay for your ticket?" asked Olga. "It costs at least five rubles."

"It will be taken care of," said Oxana importantly. "I've already discussed it with Comrade Semienova. Oh, Olga, I wish that you could come too."

Olga shrugged and smiled faintly. It was hard to resist Oxana when she was happy. And Olga wished that she would be happy all the time because then she herself might escape from the gnawing and disconcerting worms inside.

"Maybe you could ask Comrade Semienova if I could come along. We can sing together. 'Zelene Zhyto'—'The green, green wheat.' We know it. We can do it in harmony."

Olga hummed the first soft notes of the song that Mother had taught them. A harvest song that everyone who had grown up in a village had heard in the fields when the wheat and oat were harvested. But Oxana just shook her head.

"I don't think so." There was genuine sympathy in her voice. "Only one student can be selected from each school in Kharkivka Oblast, and besides, you are still much too young to understand what a political meeting like that is about. That's not at all the kind of song you sing there."

She looked around and quickly handed Olga a piece of bread. They never ate in school. Oxana especially didn't like the hungry eyes of the others, and Mother had carefully instructed them never to show that they had bread. Instead, they crumbled the bread into little pieces and ate them quickly and discreetly on the way home. Preferably before they reached the birch trees.

Comrade Semienova said it was the dirt-hole people's own fault that they were starving, and that was another truth. Olga knew that it was true. Still, it was nasty that they were there, and she was happy when Oxana described how everyone would be fine as soon as the next five-year plan was put into action. Uncle Stalin would make the country so rich that even the Former Human Beings would acknowledge their mistakes and receive salt pork and butter on their bread every day. Oxana was certain because she knew it from Comrade Semienova, who told her things that were not said in class. Great things were on the way, she said and winked teasingly.

"Soon, little Olga, you'll be able to stuff yourself. You'll become so fat that Sergej will need longer arms if he is to reach all the way around you when you kiss."

Olga couldn't help laughing and swatted at Oxana, who broke into a clumsy gallop toward the house. Oxana's bark shoes sank into the mud with small, soft squelches, and she lifted her dress so you could see her thin, stockinged legs and large, bony knees.

For a brief moment, she turned her head and looked back at Olga. Her blue eyes glittered savagely and exuberantly above narrow rose-colored cheeks. Behind her, the chestnut's wine-red leaves and the yellowing birch trees shone vividly, and all at once Olga felt a choking fear shoot up, paralyzing her as she stood in the muddy wheel track. A sort of premonition.

"Oxana," she said, "don't go."

But Oxana didn't hear her.

SØREN FOUND HIS boss in the well-equipped exercise rooms under PET's headquarters in Søborg. The Danish Security and Intelligence Service believed in keeping its employees fit. Søren knew Torben didn't like to be disturbed in the middle of training, but they usually came to an understanding more easily in person than over the phone. Torben did put down his weights and listened with at least some patience while Søren sketched the circumstances surrounding Natasha's escape and the killing of her ex-fiancé. Then he leaned back on the bench and grabbed the weights again to complete another set before answering.

"Spot me?" he asked. "I'll try for twelve."

"Okay."

Søren positioned himself so he could help with the last repetitions if necessary. Lips pursed, Torben breathed in through his nose and out through his mouth, in time with the motion. The weights shot up in an explosive press. Then he lowered them slowly, very slowly, to the outer position. Then up again with something that sounded like a snort. The Adidas shirt was dark with sweat and could probably be wrung out. At the ninth repetition, his extended arms began to shake, but Torben didn't give in, and when Søren moved to put a hand under his elbows at twelve, he hissed an angry "no" and took it by himself.

He lay on the bench, hyperventilating for a few seconds, before he sat up and gave Søren a triumphant look. "Not bad, huh?"

Søren handed him the water bottle without commenting. He knew he should offer a friendly "Well done" or something like that, but he couldn't quite do it. It felt increasingly false, like a scratchy old record that should have been thrown out long ago. He no longer felt at home in that sweaty, towel-swiping changing room community but didn't know what to replace it with. Perhaps it was just that he didn't have much in the way of relationships outside of work. Maybe he had made a mistake all those years ago when he hadn't just agreed to have children with Susse. Maybe they would still have been together. Now she lived with her jazz musician husband in a bungalow with a white fence and cocker spaniels and pear trees in the yard, and her youngest had started high school. They were still friends—that much he had salvaged from the fire. And he wasn't exactly envious of the family idyll, just . . . a bit pseudonostalgic. That could have been me. But it couldn't have been, of course, because with him it would have been a different story.

He wrested his concentration back to the case, if it could be called that. Right now, there wasn't much PET meat on it, he knew.

"I've called police headquarters," he said. "They have a Ukrainian policeman sitting there who doesn't speak English. From GUBOZ, apparently." GUBOZ was the special division that dealt with organized crime in Ukraine. That was pretty much the only alibi Søren had for looking into the case. Fighting organized crime was, after all, a PET concern.

Torben considered him over the top of the water bottle with his cool steel-grey gaze. "That's right. You used to be a language officer," he said.

"Russian and Polish. Nineteen eighty-one and nineteen eighty-three." Possibly the most intensive schooling Søren had ever been subjected to—a bombardment of words that approached brainwashing, constant tests, an eternal rhythm of classes, homework, physical training, sleep—classes, homework, physical training, sleep . . .

"Yes, today they're learning Arabic and Afghani," said Torben and screwed the lid onto the bottle again.

"Pashto. Or Farsi, depending."

"Yes. Is your Russian still usable?"

"Pretty much."

Torben nodded and dried his face, neck and shaved head with an often-washed greyish-white towel.

"Okay. Go ahead and give them a hand, since you're so curious. And why is that, by the way?"

It was stupid to try to lie to Torben. As Søren's boss, he took that kind of thing very badly, and besides, they considered each other old friends. That Søren had begun to doubt whether constant physical competition really could be called a friendship didn't change the fact that they had known each other for over twenty-five years. "Natasha Dmytrenko's daughter apparently lives in the Coal-House Camp. And Nina Borg, you know, the nurse from . . ."

"Yes, I remember her."

". . . Nina called because she was worried about the girl. And about the mother too."

"What did she imagine you could do? Save mother and child from the cruel Danish police?"

Søren shrugged. "Something like that, I guess."

Torben shook his head. "Aren't you a little too old to be playing Don Quixote?"

"Don Quixote is old. Or at least middle-aged. That's the point."

Torben got up and returned the weights to the rack. "Thank you," he said. "If there are other literary niceties I need to have explained, I'll be sure to tell you. The point here, my friend, is that you are getting involved in something that most likely doesn't concern either you or us."

"I know. But the man is from GUBOZ, and that must mean—"

"That there is some suspicion of organized crime, yes, thanks, you don't need to spell it out. Okay. Talk to the Ukrainian if you absolutely have to get involved. And if there's something in it, it goes directly to our own OC boys. I want my group leader back on his counterterrorism perch by Monday at the latest. Understood?"

With PET's usual fondness for English terms, OC was the accepted abbreviation for the Center for Organized Crime.

Søren mentally clicked his heels and saluted. "Yes, sir."

Torben gave him a look but otherwise ignored the sarcasm. "Want to grab a brew later?"

That was Torben's way of dealing with the boss/friend issue. The beer invitations usually came when he had been most boss-like.

"Maybe. Or . . . There probably won't be time."

"Up to you. You can join us for dinner if you feel like it. Annelise is doing a roast."

"Thank you. But . . . maybe another time."

"Mmm. Okay." Torben had already turned around and was making his way over to the pull-down machine. Søren suddenly realized that Torben hadn't for one moment expected him to say yes.

"I NEED A WORD with you."

It sounded more like an order than a request, Nina realized, but she didn't care. The policeman was so young, he automatically started to obey. He was on his feet before it occurred to him that a nurse was not actually above him in the chain of command. But by then it was too late for him to sit down again without looking like an idiot. He was also young enough that not looking like an idiot was pretty high on his list of priorities.

"What about?" he asked.

"Let's go outside," she said.

Rina looked at them with the alertness of a wounded animal, and the policeman apparently realized—much, much too late in Nina's opinion—that there were certain things you didn't discuss while an eight-year-old was listening. He followed her into the hall. Rina's eyes trailed them the whole way. She sat on her bed with the Moomintroll-patterned comforter pulled all the way up to her chest. Nina had found her a Donald Duck comic, which she dutifully had looked at, but judging by the random page turning, she wasn't getting a lot out of the story.

"We'll be right outside, sweetie," said Nina, and she didn't know if that sounded like a comfort or a threat to the child. Her anger swelled another notch, and she closed the door carefully before letting loose on the policeman.

"I understand that Rina's stepfather is dead." She didn't like to give the bastard the legitimacy of having any kind of place in Rina's life even now, but Rina had called him "Poppa Mike." Whether Nina liked it or not, he was, in fact, a part of what Rina had lost after Natasha's ill-considered attempt at homicide.

"May I ask where you received that information?" asked the young policeman, possibly in an attempt to regain his authority.

"From Rina, who got it from you."

He actually blushed. The color rose along his neck and washed over his well-defined cheekbones. He couldn't maintain eye contact.

"Fuck," was all he said.

"Yes," Nina said and felt her attitude soften. He didn't try to explain it away or apologize, and that was something. "How could that happen?" she asked.

He shook his head. "We didn't think she spoke Danish," he said. "She didn't answer when we asked and didn't say anything at all to anyone. We were told that she was mute."

"Mute?" Nina's voice rose again.

"No, that probably wasn't the word. 'Speech issues' is what I think they said."

"That just means she has a hard time talking to strangers," said Nina. "And that she often can't speak in stressful situations. And no matter how little she says, she hasn't lost her hearing."

"No. I'm sorry."

"When was he killed? And how?"

He shook his head. "I'm not at liberty to discuss the case with . . . anyone."

"A little late for that, isn't it?"

He didn't answer.

"Did it happen after Natasha escaped?" asked Nina. "Is she a suspect?"

"I can't comment on that."

"And what about Rina's father? Is it true that he was murdered too?"

But if there had been an opening, it had closed again. He was once more annoyingly police-like and looked as if the word "fuck" had never crossed his lips.

"I'm sorry," he said. "I can't comment on that."

"Well, then comment on this," she said, irritated. "I don't want you in Rina's room. I don't want any of you in there. She's traumatized enough already, and as long as you are there, I don't have a snowball's chance in hell of talking with her about it or getting her to relax. We can easily make it an official medical order if that's necessary and outline precisely why your presence has already had a powerfully negative effect." The last part was pure coercion.

He squirmed. "I have to consult," he said.

"Consult all you want," she said. "As long as you do it out here and not in there."

She turned her back on him and went back into Rina's room.

The Donald Duck comic lay on the floor like a discarded prop. Rina sat with an old, broken cell phone, the only toy she had brought with her to the camp when she had arrived at the age of not-quite-six.

The psychologist had found it interesting, Nina remembered. "Does she ever speak into it?" he'd asked.

"She whispers," Nina had said. "Mostly she just presses the buttons and listens. But sometimes she whispers as well."

"Is there any pattern to when she does it?"

"I think it's mostly when she's feeling sad," said Nina. "Perhaps it distracts her."

"I think it's encouraging that she attempts to communicate her feelings," the psychologist had said. "Even if it's not with us. You should definitely let her keep it."

Now, more than two years later, Rina still had her phone and clearly needed it more than ever. Her bitten nails pressed the buttons with almost manic intent.

Nina picked up the Donald Duck comic and placed it on the little dresser next to the bed. "Would you like another ice cream?" she asked.

Rina looked up. She shook her head silently and finished dialing. She held the telephone up to her ear and listened.

It occurred to Nina that that was precisely what she was doing—listening. She wasn't pretending; this wasn't an act-like-the-grown-ups game. She was listening in earnest. For the first time, Nina wondered what it was Rina expected to hear.

She sat down on the desk chair and pretended to look out the window, but she was really keeping an eye on Rina's expression, and that was why she saw it.

Suddenly the girl's face opened, and she smiled. A completely open smile that, for some reason, gave Nina the chills. She felt like grabbing the phone out of the child's hands but held herself back. As the psychologist said, it was good for Rina to attempt to communicate with someone.

But what did you do if this "someone" began to answer?

There was no doubt in Nina's mind that Rina had indeed heard a reply, and it was highly unlikely to be because the defective phone had suddenly started working.

There was a quiet knock on the door. The young policeman stood outside.

"I've spoken with the chief," he said. "She says that it's okay for us to be in the room next door on the condition that you and your colleagues have someone with the girl at all times. Press this if you notice anything alarming."

He handed Nina a little black box with a red button. A personal attack alarm. Nina remembered that not long ago, they had discussed whether the night shift at the center should be equipped with them.

"Okay," she said. Not an insignificant victory. "Thank you."

Rina looked at the policeman with her animal gaze until Nina closed the door again. The cell phone had disappeared into her pink backpack. The psychologist would probably consider that a step backward, but Nina couldn't help feeling relieved.

T HE WALLS WERE a calming dove blue; the chairs and tables of light wood and lacquered steel all looked like something you might find at a high school from the '70s. But the fact that the tall patrician windows were covered with bulletproof glass cooled the atmosphere a bit, Søren noticed, and made it impossible to characterize the police headquarters's combined coffee-and-lineup room as cozy.

"He speaks almost no English," said the detective inspector, discreetly flipping his thumb in the direction of a young man who sat drumming his fingers impatiently on his jean-clad thigh. "And the other one, the one we could at least speak to, seems to have vanished into thin air."

"The other one?" asked Søren. Until now he had heard only about one man.

"Yes, there were two of them. They came to speak with the fugitive—well, at that point she wasn't a fugitive yet, but . . ."

"So you've lost both an inmate and a foreign police officer?" Søren spoke with a certain coolness. He knew that the safety involving the transport of inmates wasn't ironclad, at least not unless the so-called "negatively strong" inmates were involved. If one of the more peaceful ones got away, it was usually pretty anticlimactic. They often turned up on their own when they had taken care of whatever it was that was so important to them, or if not, you could collect them undramatically a little later in the day at the home of a much-missed girlfriend or at the birthday celebration of some family member. The system responded with an extra thirty days and the revoking of a few privileges, and that was that.

But this was different. Natasha Dmytrenko didn't miss her fiancé—she had done her best to kill him once before, and now he was dead. It also worried Søren considerably that a member of the not ill-reputed Ukrainian militia appeared to have given his hosts the slip.

The DI grew defensive. "We can't just lock our foreign colleagues in a cage," he said. "He got pretty upset when he heard that she had escaped, and suddenly he was gone as well."

Søren regarded the one Ukrainian policeman they still had under control. The man had short brown hair and a face broader than the average Scandinavian ones Søren was used to seeing. There was a restless, coiled energy in the drumming fingers and the tapping heel. A dark tie and a white shirt lent a bit of formality to the jeans getup and the '70s hippie suede jacket that hung over the chair back behind him. He must be around thirty, Søren estimated, young but no kid.

"What's his name?"

"Symon Babko, police lieutenant in some subdivision of the criminal police."

Søren just nodded and elected not to tell the young assistant criminal policeman that this "subdivision" could swallow the entire Danish police force more than once without even noticing.

Even though it wasn't said very loudly, the Ukrainian policeman must nonetheless have picked out his name through the ambient noise of chair scraping and cafeteria talk. He raised his head—what a chin, Søren thought; there was a warrior-like determination to that chin—and looked directly at Søren.

"*Dobry den,*" said Søren, holding out his hand and presenting himself. "Søren Kirkegard, PET."

"Hello," said Babko.

He had unusually large hands, Søren noticed. They looked out of proportion to his thin, knobby wrists. As if someone had attached an inadequately thin handle to a spade.

"I'm sorry. I speak only Russian, not Ukrainian," said Søren.

Babko laughed. It was an amazing volcano eruption of a laugh that started far down in his skinny middle, moved up through his entire body and made his shoulders shake before finally rolling out across the cafeteria landscape with such power that conversations around them ceased.

"My friend," he said, with laughter still in his voice, "when you have sat in a chair for almost twenty-four hours without being able to say anything but 'Hello,' 'Thank you,' and 'Where is the toilet?' there suddenly is not as much difference between Ukrainian and Russian as there usually is. We will no doubt understand each other."

THEY BORROWED AN office on the second floor with a view of the parking lot.

"It was down there," Symon Babko said, pointing. "Down there she got away."

"Natasha Dmytrenko?"

"Who is really called Natasha Doroshenko," said Babko. He pushed a worn file folder toward Søren. "She was questioned in two thousand and seven in connection with the killing of her husband, Pavel Doroshenko. Immediately afterward, she disappeared. There is, therefore, a request for detention."

Søren opened the folder. Natasha Doroshenko looked like a frightened teenager in the photo that was glued to the first page of the detention order, but that was the way she looked, he remembered, in most of the photos that accompanied the Danish case files he had had the chance to skim. He attempted to speed-read to get an overview but had to accept that his linguistic proficiency wasn't quite sufficient. The Ukrainian differences from the Russian he was used to teased his eyes, similar to the way Norwegian or Swedish forced him to read more slowly. It would take a while to digest the material, and right now it was more important to engage with the man who sat across from him.

"Tell me," he said instead.

"In Ukraine, she is still wanted in that connection. She hasn't been found guilty. Not yet. But she's wanted. So when we learned that she had been recognized in Denmark, we were naturally interested."

Søren nodded. "Are murder cases normally handled by GUBOZ?" he asked neutrally.

"At first it was a simple murder case under the jurisdiction of the criminal police. I wasn't attached until a week ago when the extradition case started." Babko looked closely at Søren. There was a subtext here, Søren sensed, but he wasn't sure that he could read it.

"So you have formally requested her extradition?" he asked.

"Yes. But even before the extradition got properly underway, Colonel Savchuk had successfully requested an interview. The Danish officials were apparently very forthcoming."

That searching gaze again. Søren was annoyed that he was clearly missing something, but he sensed that a direct question would be a mistake.

"I assume Savchuk is your English-speaking colleague?"

"That is correct. *Colonel* Jurij Savchuk."

Finally Søren understood. With his slight emphasis, Babko was making it clear that Savchuk had a higher rank than he did and that he therefore was in a pinch right now. He couldn't officially criticize a superior, though Savchuk had apparently left without being polite enough to tell his hosts where he was going or why.

"Where is Colonel Savchuk?" asked Søren.

"He is presumably investigating Natasha Doroshenko's disappearance," said Babko carefully.

"On Danish soil?"

"I assume he is doing so by agreement with the proper authorities." It was clear that if this was not the case, Babko wasn't at fault.

As far as Søren knew, there was no such agreement, and he strongly doubted that the "proper authorities" would take kindly to an unauthorized freelance effort from the Ukrainian police. But he let it pass. "The killing of Pavel Doroshenko," he said instead.

"Yes. On September twenty-third, two thousand and seven, Doroshenko was found in his car near Lake Didorovka. At that point he had been dead for a few days. It was at first assumed that he had been murdered, since he had some obvious lesions, mostly on the hands, but it later turned out that the cause of death was heart failure, presumably caused by pain and shock."

"He was beaten to death?"

"Yes and no. Four of the fingers on his left hand had been crushed—extremely painful, but under normal circumstances not lethal."

"Crushed how?"

"In the car door."

"And I assume it couldn't have been an accident?"

"Unlikely. The door was slammed shut across his fingers several times. Normally you put a cable or thin rope around the victim's wrist, and the hand is pulled toward the door while the victim sits bound in the car and already trapped by the seat belt. It's said that the best tactic is to stick your hand as far out of the car as possible, so that the door slams closed on the wrist instead of the fingers, but it is very difficult not to attempt to pull your hand toward you. That's the most natural reaction."

Søren listened to the cool and almost routine description of the torture. "In other words, that happens regularly? This type of violence?"

"Yes. It's a fairly common way of punishing people who, in one way or another, have had their fingers in the wrong pies."

Søren's eyes fell on the teenage-slim Natasha Doroshenko. "It doesn't seem likely that this is a . . . punishment . . . that his wife could administer."

"Not on her own, no. A petty criminal called Bohdan Pahlaniuk later took credit for providing the muscle. But he claimed to have been paid by the wife because she was upset that Doroshenko couldn't keep his hands off other ladies. Pahlaniuk said that the intention wasn't to kill him." Babko tapped the case file with a square index finger. "Page two."

Søren turned the page. Yes—page two was a confession signed by Bohdan Pahlaniuk and dated November 16, 2007.

"How was he caught?" he asked.

"Pahlaniuk was arrested and held for another assault a month or so after Pavel Doroshenko's death. The Doroshenko confession surfaced in connection with that. But a warrant was out for her just a few days after the killing."

"Why?"

"The most obvious reason, of course, was that she took off and left the country with her daughter a few hours after she had been questioned. But there were some other suspicious circumstances as well. Even though her husband had disappeared four days before he was found, she hadn't reported him missing."

"How long had they been married? How was their relationship?"

"They were married in two thousand. She was only seventeen. He was quite a bit older, in his mid-thirties."

"Twice her age?"

"Yes, it's not that uncommon. She's from a small town near Kura-khovo in Donetsk Oblast. It's not the greatest place in the world to live when you are a young girl wanting a bit of fun in life. Since the coal mine began shutting down production, everything has ground to a halt. There are whole neighborhoods that are practically ghost towns. He was a journalist, lived in Kiev in a fancy apartment—her ticket to the city and a completely different lifestyle."

"Do you know whether there were, in fact, 'other ladies'?"

"He had the reputation at least for being a bit of a *babolyub* before he married. Maybe the leopard hadn't changed his spots just because he signed a wedding license."

Søren considered the possibilities. There was apparently a certain amount of substance to the case against Nina's young widow, and yet . . . certain peculiarities jumped out.

"Am I correct in assuming that Colonel Savchuk is a man of a certain position?" he asked.

For the first time in the course of the conversation, Babko sat totally still. The bouncing heel stopped bouncing; the fingers ceased drumming against the coffee mug.

"That's correct," he said. "In SBU."

SBU was the Ukrainian secret police. Not exactly an organization with a spotless reputation.

"Not GUBOZ, then."

"No."

"What is his interest in this case?" asked Søren. "Wouldn't it normally be handled by someone at a lower level?"

Babko looked at him for a few seconds with a poker face. "Correct again," he said finally.

His replies became more and more minimal, Søren observed, the closer you got to Savchuk.

"Is he carrying his cell phone?"

"Presumably."

Now we're down to one word, thought Søren dryly. What would be next? Syllables?

"Do you have a number?" He deliberately shifted from the formal to the informal address to reduce the distance between them. *We are colleagues*, he tried to say. *Help me out here.*

Babko shook his head—a single abrupt gesture.

Silence filled the office. You could hear the traffic outside in Hambrosgade accompanied by the hissing of radial tires through slush.

"So you have no way of contacting him?"

"No."

Not only was Babko a man playing away from home, but his only teammate was apparently more of an opponent than a fellow player. Søren could almost pity him, but only almost. Because one thing was clear: Babko was by no means telling Søren everything that he knew.

The Ukrainian militia was no knitting circle. Every year Amnesty International registered countless instances of torture, misuse of power and corruption, and the country's own ombudsman in this area had had to note that up to three-quarters of those arrested were subjected to some form of abuse. In many instances the interrogation methods appeared not to have changed significantly since Soviet times when quick confessions were necessary if you were to solve the required 80 percent of your cases. Whether you had the correct guilty party was less important. It was all about closing the case in a hurry.

Was Babko one of the bully boys who routinely beat detainees with water-filled plastic bottles or kept them handcuffed for days? He didn't look like the type, but then, not many torturers did.

"**Y**OU'RE TO KEEP your mouth shut. Understand? What I do in my own house is none of your business or anyone else's."

Grandfather pounded the table so hard that the warm tea in his mug sloshed over the rim and soaked into the rough grain of the wood. Oxana started, but she didn't lower her eyes. On the contrary, she raised her chin in defiance, giving him a small, stubborn smile of the kind she normally offered Olga when she thought Olga had done something particularly childish.

But Grandfather wasn't a child. How did she dare? True, he was little and bent and moved with difficulty, but when he hit, he hit hard, fists to the face. He had gotten up, swaying and threatening, planting both his broad, lumpy hands on the table for support while he glared at Oxana. The smells of rank body and goatskin and vodka billowed in the air around him.

"But Russian vodka is the people's enemy," said Oxana. "We have to fight drunkenness, crime and religious sloth."

"Shut up."

Oxana collected herself. "But Grandfather," she said. She wasn't completely unaffected, because her voice had gotten a little bit shrill now. "You yourself have seen what vodka does to people. When men drink, they can't work. They fight and kill each other. It's the capitalists' weapon to anesthetize the masses."

Grandfather's eyes were half closed and swimming now. *"Kapital-istki, sotsialitski, kommunitski,"* he growled. He shoved the table so hard that all the mugs teetered, and one fell down and shattered on the floor. "That crazy teacher of yours means trouble. Stay away from her. You're smart, they say. It shouldn't be so hard to understand."

He stumbled around the table and fell toward Oxana, who had positioned herself by the brick oven, Grandfather's vodka bottle in one hand. She was furious. A bottle of vodka was not only hard to come by, it was also expensive, and the money could have served a more useful purpose. The standard bread rations from the kolk-hoz were only enough for bare survival, and bread and butter were expensive in the open market. Kolja needed the extra nourishment, as did Mother.

Grandfather raised his fist, and Olga instinctively ducked in her seat by the chimney. She expected any moment to hear the sound of Oxana's skull being split open by Grandfather's fists, but instead it was Mother's icy voice that broke the silence.

"Leave her alone."

Olga opened her eyes again and saw Mother standing in the door-way. The draft made her heavy skirt flutter faintly. It was cold outside now, with frost at night, and Mother's face and hands were red from the chill. Grandfather backed away from Oxana. He had wrenched the dirty vodka bottle out of her hand and was staring meanly from Mother to Oxana before he finally ambled out of the living room. He slammed the door hard behind him. Olga caught a glimpse of him through the dirty window. He looked like an angry wounded bear, thought Olga, crossing the little courtyard with short, lurching steps before he disap-peared down the road toward the village.

Mother signed deeply and sat down with little Kolja on her lap. The clay bowl that she had brought in from the barn was almost empty again today. Zorya's milk barely covered the bottom. The calf from the spring was long gone, and the cow was not a miracle machine that could produce milk from potato peels and straw. No matter how much you boxed her sunken udders, it was usually only possible to extract a few drops at a time. Now Mother brought the bowl up to Kolja's mouth.

"Drink, my boy," she hummed. "Milk from Zorya for you."

Kolja squirmed, wrinkled his little face and turned his head away.

"Drink, Kolja." Mother's voice was sharp now, and she pressed the bowl against Kolja's lips until he reluctantly emptied it in one swallow. Then he placed his face against Mother's throat and closed his eyes.

"Why doesn't he help us?" Oxana's voice flicked like a whip through the living room. "I've heard the widow doesn't lack for anything, and we are his children. You are his wife."

Mother didn't answer, just sat with half-closed eyes and stared straight into space. Olga didn't like it. Mother's neck, which used to be smooth and brown and smelled of herbs from the garden, had gotten wrinkled and stringy. Dirt caked her chest and breastbone darkly, and in a few places it had cracked and fallen off, the skin beneath showing a transparent pink. Olga knew that it had something to do with Father, even though she didn't completely understand why Mother had stopped washing from one day to the next. Just as it was clearly also Father's fault that they were living here instead of in the house in the village next to Jana.

It was Oxana who took care of bathing Kolja now, and Oxana who woke up Mother so that she made it to work in the morning, but the caked dirt on Mother's neck they couldn't do anything about, just as they couldn't get Father to love Mother again and ask them to move back into the house.

Oxana cursed quietly. "He's a shit," she hissed. "A no-good piece of shit." She spun around and began to put on her heavy coat.

Mother didn't move. In fact, it didn't even look as if she had noticed.

"Where are you going?" asked Olga.

"I'm meeting Comrade Semienova down at the school."

"But we just got home."

"Yes." Oxana smiled faintly. "But we are so busy, and Comrade Semienova has said that I, Leda and Jegor may sleep in the schoolroom when we've finished writing our article. We're going to have potatoes and salt pork and real tea that Comrade Semienova has had sent from Leningrad."

"But what if Grandfather—"

"Grandfather is an old drunk. He doesn't understand that these are new times."

Olga looked over at Mother and Kolja, who sat still as pillars of salt at the table. It was already getting dark, and when Grandfather came home, he would have emptied the rest of his vodka bottle and be tired and hungry and mean. "Can I come?"

Oxana looked at her in surprise over her shoulder. Then she laughed. "That wouldn't do, Olga. Remember that both Leda and Jegor are fourteen. You're only eight."

"So what?" protested Olga. "You're only ten."

"That's different," said Oxana, holding her head high. "Comrade Semienova says I have a very early understanding of the issues."

Olga felt an odd desperation creep up on her. A night without Oxana. She had never tried that before. Never. And especially now, when Grandfather would be angry and crazy, and Mother just sat there staring into empty space. "But did Mother say you could go?"

Oxana glanced quickly at the two unmoving shadows at the table. "Honestly, Olga," she said, lowering her voice, "Mother can't even take care of herself right now. I need to be the strong one. Do you understand what I mean?"

Olga didn't, but Oxana clearly wasn't planning to explain any further. She just tied her scarf under her chin and looked at Olga with a steady gaze. "Make sure to keep the fire in the oven lit, but don't light the lamp before it's necessary. We're almost out of petroleum, and what we have is rubbish anyway. It's better used on the lice."

Her hand touched Olga's shoulder lightly. "Trust me, Olga."

She opened the door and stepped out into the fall dusk. Olga looked after her as she tramped through the mud in the same direction that Grandfather had disappeared. Then Olga bent down and began picking up the shards.

"**Y**OU NEED TO speak to Heide," Søren was told. "And she's still out at the scene."

Michael Vestergaard had been found some hundred meters from his home in Hørsholm—in this weather at least a forty-minute drive from central Copenhagen. It wasn't that Søren minded the distance. If he was going to get involved in the investigation, he might as well do it properly. He was just a bit reluctant to drag Babko with him as long as he didn't know to whom the GUBOZ man reported. There was still no word of or from the missing Colonel Savchuk. On the other hand, the possible connection with the killing of Pavel Doroshenko was one of the things Søren needed to discuss with Mona Heide, and Babko was the best witness they had in this respect.

"Where are we going?" said the Ukrainian when Søren asked him to come along.

"To talk to one of my colleagues."

Babko looked as if he thought the answer was somewhat lacking, but he didn't say anything else—at least not until they reached the garage in Hambrosgade, and Søren unlocked the car door.

"Is this your car?" asked the Ukrainian.

"Yes," said Søren.

And then Babko's laughter exploded, loud and unreserved.

Søren considered the light blue Hyundai and didn't think it looked especially funny. "Is something wrong?" he asked.

Babko shook his head. "No, my friend. Nice little car. All is well."

Søren sighed. They might in theory speak the same language, or at least something closely related, but the cross-cultural understanding was still far from perfect.

"Get in," he said. "We're going to a place called Hørsholm."

THE COLD BEGAN to eat its way through the soldered seams of Søren's North Face jacket as soon as he got out of the car—so much for being "designed by mountain climbers and athletes." The sun, which had offered a certain illusion of warmth earlier in the day, had disappeared behind a dark grey, snow-heavy cloud cover, and an arctic wind blew across the hedges.

Tundra Lane. The name fit. Even Babko, who presumably was used to these kinds of temperatures, swore and shivered in his suede jacket. He took a small, round, knitted cap out of his pocket and pulled it down so that it covered the tops of his ears.

This wasn't the quiet residential street that Søren had imagined. True, there had been a suitable number of symmetrical housing estates just before the GPS directed them down a narrow side road. But this part of Tundra Lane was little more than a wheel track with snow-covered bogland and forest on one side and soft, hibernating golf course hills on the other. It was surprisingly isolated, considering that they were only about twenty miles from the center of Copenhagen.

Vestergaard's house turned out to be a big box of a McMansion, made of white brick with panorama balconies in the gables and wide, shiny squares of double glazing. Several police cars were parked out front, including the incident van. It looked more like a moving van than a police vehicle, thought Søren, in spite of the orange stripe with the POLICE label. He showed his ID to the frozen uniformed officer who stood by the police tape, then went over to knock on the door of the van.

"I have an appointment with Mona Heide," he said when a young guy in a black down jacket opened the door.

"She's still at the scene," said Down Jacket. "But you can wait in here."

Søren nodded. Even though he was curious, he had known ahead of time that the investigators were unlikely to let people they considered irrelevant stomp around the scene of the crime. He crawled up the ladder-like steps and introduced Babko in English.

"Pleased to meet you," said Down Jacket. "Asger Veng, North Zealand Police."

The inside of the van was somewhat reminiscent of a building site trailer, thought Søren. One end was set up as a kind of miniature cafeteria, with a dining table and minimal kitchen facilities; the other served as office and command center. Between the two sections there was an even more minimal toilet. The facilities were not particularly cutting-edge technology-wise, and the comfort was pretty limited, but at least it was warm, and an industrial-strength coffee machine stood gurgling by the sink.

"Coffee?" asked Veng, who'd noticed the direction of his gaze. "They have just concluded the on-site inquest, so it won't be long now."

"Where did they find him, exactly?" asked Søren.

"A few hundred meters into the bushes behind the golf course. He was sitting in his own Mercedes, wearing a seat belt and everything, but in the passenger seat."

"So he probably wasn't driving."

"No. And the only purpose of that drive must have been to get away from the house. It's not a real road, just a track for working vehicles—tractors, that kind of thing—almost impossible to navigate in this weather. Getting the car out of there again should be really interesting . . ."

"Who found him?"

"The neighbor. She was out walking her dog. Thank goodness for dog walkers. If not for them, any number of bodies would remain unfound." Veng poured coffee into white plastic mugs and waved a hand in the direction of a pair of black folding chairs at the dining table. "Have a seat."

They had barely had time to follow orders before there was the sound of steps in the snow outside.

"There she is," said Veng a bit unnecessarily. The door opened, and something that looked like a slender and athletic Teletubby swung into the van. Police commissioner Mona Heide pulled the protective suit's hood off with an impatient gesture and revealed a becoming short, ash-blonde hairdo and a pair of tasteful gold earrings.

"Heide," she said, offering her hand. No first name, no invitation to collegiality. She projected authority and professionalism that was in no way softened by the gold earrings or the confident, but not exactly subtle, makeup.

"Kirkegard," Søren said, instantly provoked into the same formality.

"It's nice of you to sacrifice your weekend." She didn't ask him why directly, but she was clearly wondering.

"No problem," he said, ignoring the unspoken question.

"We're happy to have the help in any case." She gave a short nod at Babko, who returned the nod politely but with a bit of reserve. He still didn't know why they were there.

"I understand that you can help us with the Ukrainian connection?" Heide continued.

"Probably," answered Søren. "I assume you already know that

Lieutenant Babko and his colleague Colonel Savchuk are here because of a death in Ukraine back in two thousand and seven?" He used their names on purpose so that Babko would know they were talking about him.

"Yes, Natasha Doroshenko's husband. We are, of course, interested in hearing more about the particular circumstances."

"Is she your chief suspect?"

"Let us say that we consider it likely that she is involved."

"More than one perpetrator?" he guessed.

She didn't answer at once. He could feel her reluctance to bring others into the confidence of her small, well-functioning group. She didn't want to discuss her murder theories with him. He waited without pushing.

"We believe he was killed where we found him," she said at last, "and that there were at least two people at the scene of the crime. A woman and a man." And as if this admission had resolved her internal debate, she offered him the rest freely. "Michael Vestergaard was found at a quarter past eight this morning by his neighbor, Anna Olesen, who was out walking her dog. She called us from the crime scene on her cell phone and stayed there until the police arrived. Pretty impressive for a lady of more than eighty, you have to admit. The coroner believes time of death was sometime between eight and eleven, but there's a significant factor of uncertainty because of the cold. It's hard to judge what is rigor mortis and what is just deep freeze."

"But the neighbor was sure that he was dead?"

"Yes. His throat was cut. That doesn't leave much room for doubt."

"Were there any other marks on him besides the cut throat?" asked Søren.

"Several blows to the face, some broken fingers—seven or eight. We won't know for sure until we get some X-rays taken."

Broken fingers . . . it sounded like the sort of coincidence that wasn't one. Still, Søren would like to make the link a certainty rather than a question mark.

"Are there any photos that Lieutenant Babko could have a look at?" he inquired.

"Not yet. Why?"

"Pavel Doroshenko had four broken fingers. It's apparently a common form of torture. It would be nice to know if Vestergaard's killer did it in the same way."

Another reflective pause. Then Heide abruptly got up and opened one of the steel cabinets that stood along one wall of the bus. She tossed two protective suits in crackling plastic onto the table.

"Here," she said. "You can look at him in the hearse. They'll be bringing him out in a little while."

WHEN YOU'RE GOING to see a dead person in a hearse, you expect them to be lying down. Michael Vestergaard wasn't.

"We couldn't get him out of the seat without damaging him too much," the coroner said apologetically to Heide. "It was easiest to cut the bolts and bring the lot."

Michael Vestergaard sat straight up in his car's front seat, which had been cut free and then secured inside the white Ford Transit. It had been sixteen degrees below zero the previous night, and the chill was immediately evident. Vestergaard's once-white Hugo Boss shirt now created a dark armor of ice and frozen reddish-brown blood across his chest. The head lolled backward and to one side, and the lower part of his cheek was stuck to his shoulder, frozen solid. His well-trimmed hair was white with frost.

"Isn't he unusually . . . frozen?" asked Søren. "Of course, blood freezes, but—"

"Blood, waste and other bodily secretions. But it also looks as if water was poured over him," said Heide. "Possibly to wake him from a faint or as a form of torture in itself. They weren't exactly gentle with him."

Søren suddenly had a flashback to a POW exercise in the distant days of his youth. The abrupt cooling, the short sensation of drowning when you inhaled water instead of air. It wasn't quite as cruel and systematic as waterboarding, but in the right—or perhaps the wrong—hands, a simple bucket was a pretty effective instrument of torture. With the current chill factor, it could also be a murder weapon, but Vestergaard had not lived long enough to die of cold.

"His hands?" said Søren. "Is it okay if Lieutenant Babko has a closer look at them?"

"Be my guest," said Heide in English.

Babko apparently understood the ironic English phrase, because he climbed into the hearse with Søren.

The frozen body curved in a way that somehow contradicted the backward-lolling head, as if two opposing forces had been at work at the moment of death. Automatically, Søren's mind began to replay the scene. He sensed the threat that made Vestergaard crouch forward, cradling his ruined hands against his stomach. Then the grabbing of his hair, the head that was wrenched backward, the knife slicing through tendons and arteries and throat cartilage. What Natasha had not managed a year and a half ago was now completed in one abrupt slash without hesitation or failed attempts.

"The hands," he said in Russian to Babko. "Is it the same sort of damage as to Pavel Doroshenko's?"

Both hands were swollen, blue-black and bloody, and on the left, especially, there were several obvious breaks. The cold and the stiffness of death had frozen the damaged fingers into a position that looked more like some marine life-form than a human hand—a meat-colored starfish, maybe, or a shattered coral formation. The outermost joints of the little and ring fingers were bent all the way back. On the middle finger, the tip was simply missing, and you could see the bone sticking out through the tissue.

With a careful, plastic-gloved finger, Babko bent the shirt's frozen cuff back to get a better look at Vestergaard's wrist. "There," he said. "You can see the mark."

There was a deep, dirty groove along the cuff edge. Thinner than a rope, thought Søren, perhaps a cable or a wire of some sort.

"Method is same," said Babko in English so Heide and the technicians could understand him. "Same, Doroshenko."

"Punishment or interrogation?" asked Søren, first in Russian and then in Danish.

Heide tilted her head a bit as she thought about it. "That hurt," she said. "If it was to make him talk, he was either very tough—or he couldn't give them what they wanted because he didn't know."

"Poor devil," said the technician.

Søren didn't say anything. Instead, he studied the shattered hands one last time. He had read the reports from the trial against Natasha, including the doctor's testimony that described in detail what Vestergaard had done to his then-fiancé. Maybe someone, somewhere, considered this fair retribution.

"**A**RE YOU OKAY?"

Magnus leaned against the doorframe with a coffee cup in one hand and a well-worn copy of *Car Magazine* in the other. The lines in his good-natured, dog-like face had begun to take on a permanent nature lately, thought Nina. Concern lines—was that a word? Like worry wrinkles, only more altruistic.

"Yes," she said, attempting to convince the machine to deliver a cup of instant coffee with powdered milk. "Rina has eaten a banana, and we are working on a cheese sandwich."

"What was that about her father?"

"She hasn't really said anything else, and I don't want to press her. But apparently it's true. I asked one of the guys from the Mondeo gang. He actually blushed and admitted that they had discussed it while Rina was listening. They didn't think she spoke Danish. What did they imagine? She has damn well lived here for more than two years."

"She doesn't say much," said Magnus. "It's easy to read her incorrectly. Those guys are actually pretty nice."

"That's what you think about everyone," Nina said.

"No," he said with a crooked smile. "Only about the ones who deserve it." He swatted at her with the magazine, looking almost frisky—like an overgrown foal with giant, knobby knees and a stubby tail. Where did all this awkward enthusiasm come from?

Sex, of course. What exactly was it that happened to men when they got a bit of not particularly fantastic sex? Now that it appeared Rina's physical crisis was over, Magnus exuded well-being. Why didn't Nina feel that way at all? Why the hell couldn't it be like that for her—as easy as taking a hot bath and feeling recharged afterward?

The phone vibrated in the pocket of her jeans. She answered it with a small, apologetic grimace in Magnus's direction.

It was Søren Kirkegard, the PET-man who wasn't an idiot. She felt a tug in the pit of her stomach. Why on earth had she called him? He was PET, damn it, not a lifeline in a quiz show. And not at all a friend.

"I wanted to update you," he said. "And ask you a couple of questions, if you don't mind?"

She couldn't really say no. After all, she had called him. "Yes. Okay."

"Good. How long have you known Natasha?"

"Since she came to the camp for the first time. It must have been . . . oh, I don't remember exactly. October or November, two thousand and seven."

"And how would you describe your relationship?"

Nina had to think about that. "It mostly centered on Rina," she said, stirring the liquid in her white plastic mug with her white plastic stirrer. For some reason the water in the coffee machine never got as hot as it was supposed to, and the powdered milk had a tendency to just float on top in small, yellowish lumps. "She had asthma even back then and . . . certain psychological problems. Nightmares. Anxiety attacks. It's of course not that unusual among the children here, but . . . well, anyway, we did our best for her."

"I understand that you were the one Natasha called after her attempt to kill Vestergaard?"

"How do you know that?" The words flew out of Nina, hostile, distrustful, before she had time to consider. He didn't answer her directly, but he didn't need to. He probably already had a whole pile of reports lying on his table. Why had she called him?

Because you needed help, she told herself.

She glanced at the clock above the serving hatch. Morten and the children were presumably eating dinner now. It wouldn't be pizza or some other kind of junk food—Morten was good at all that healthy stuff, always making sure they got enough vegetables and slow car-bohydrates. She closed her eyes a moment so she couldn't see the clock's digits. She knew that her time-checking was more than a bad habit. "OCD Lite," so to speak. Not quite on par with the poor people who scrubbed their hands bloody for fear of germs, but . . . she had to get it under control.

She saw the minute hand move down to 18:21. Tomorrow it was Fastelavn Sunday. Not content with merely importing American Halloween customs, Denmark still stuck stubbornly to her own homegrown equivalent as well, so now there were twice as many cos-tumes to be produced by long-suffering parents. Except this year, Nina wasn't long-suffering, she reminded herself; Morten would have seen to Anton's outfit for the school carnival. But she would still get to see Anton, and maybe even Ida too, if it wasn't beneath the dignity of a fourteen-year-old to participate.

"I'm just trying to get a clear picture," said Søren the PET-man on the phone. "You called emergency services, but you also went out there yourself?"

"Yes. I wasn't sure . . . sometimes people get flashbacks. Or halluci-nations. Natasha was pretty incoherent on the phone; I didn't know how serious the situation was."

"So you were, in fact, present just after the EMS got there?"

"Yes."

It came rushing back: the heat that felt more like August than Sep-tember, the dark hedges, the house with the front door wide open and all the lights on. The police hadn't come yet—just the ambulance. It was parked in the driveway, its back doors open. The EMS people were already rolling in the gurney, and she could hear the bastard shouting hoarsely.

"She stabbed me! She goddamned stabbed me!"

Natasha just sat in the middle of the lawn with her skinny bare legs pulled up toward her chest, gazing up at the moon as if the activity around her had nothing to do with her. She barely looked at Nina, even when Nina touched her shoulder and asked if she was okay.

"Take care of her," was all she said, and she didn't need to explain who she meant. "You take care of her."

"Where is she?"

"Neighbor. Neighbor Anna. Nice lady. She is safe there."

That was part of what had later been used against her at the trial—that she had carefully arranged for Rina not to be in the house that night. A premeditated, well-planned act, the prosecutor had said.

"Did you get any sense that there might have been other people present at the house? Besides Natasha and Michael Vestergaard?"

Nina had never been asked that question during the entire unbearably long police and court procedure afterward. "No. I'm pretty sure they were alone."

"And Michael Vestergaard hadn't suffered any injuries other than the cut in his throat?"

"No. What kind of injuries do you mean?"

"To his hands, for example."

"No. Why?"

"Sometimes people get defensive cuts," Søren said. "If they have time to try to fight off their assailant."

"I think it came as a complete surprise to him that she could turn on him like that," Nina said, with a sense that he knew very well there were no defensive cuts. That must be in the report, along with everything else. What was he getting at?

"But you knew Natasha well enough that you were the one she called," he said. "Why do you think she did that?"

"Because of Rina. She wanted me to take care of Rina."

"Did Natasha ever say anything about why she had fled from Ukraine?"

"No, we almost never talked about her past. She clammed up if you tried."

"I see."

"That's not very unusual," said Nina defensively. "I think that's true for at least seventy-five percent of the people here."

Her gaze wandered automatically around the half-empty passage in which she stood. Sometime back in the '90s, most of one wall in the barrack's passageways had been replaced with huge windows in a well-intentioned effort to transform the dim, nicotine-stinking smoking zone into lounge areas with green plants, lights, a view and a certain modernity. That just meant that many of the camp's inhabitants stopped using the rooms completely or huddled in the darkest corners where there was most cover. This was especially true of the people who had lived with the constant threat of snipers, in Kosova and elsewhere. The windows were still there, of course. They had been expensive.

"I'm aware of that," said the PET-man. "But did you get any sense of it?"

"Only that she was afraid. That she would do almost anything not to be sent back. I didn't even know that Rina's father was dead."

"No, I can imagine she didn't talk a lot about that."

"Did she really do it?" asked Nina. "And why? Was he a sick bastard like Vestergaard?"

"There's nothing to suggest that," said Søren. "I'll call again when

I know more. Take good care of the girl. There must still be police on the premises?"

"And how," said Nina.

"Good. We'll talk soon."

Nina stood for a few seconds with the silent cell phone in one hand and the coffee stirrer in the other. An update, he had called it. But the only one who had been updated was him. She had answered his questions without learning anything in return. Nonetheless, she felt a peculiar relief again, as she had when he had said he would "see what he could do." She threw the stirrer in the garbage next to the coffee machine, nodded briefly at Magnus and set off down the hall toward Rina's room.

She checked her watch. 18:27.

That must be it. For almost seven minutes, she had had the sensation of not being alone.

"THE NEIGHBOR WHO found him," said Søren. "Do you mind if I have a chat with her? She apparently knows Natasha Doroshenko pretty well."

Heide deliberated. "If you bring Veng with you," she said. "And a tape recorder. We've questioned her once, but of course we need to speak with her again. It's the yellow farmhouse, just on the other side of the hill."

Someone had cleared the road with a tractor, as evidenced by the broad, ribbed tire tracks. When you lived out here, you probably couldn't sit around and wait for the municipal snowplow to stop by. Babko slid into the passenger seat in the front and Veng into the backseat, and the Hyundai bravely struggled up the hill and down to "the yellow farmhouse."

It had probably once been quite a sizable farm, thought Søren. Four wings and various outbuildings washed in a traditional yellow ocher with shiny black wooden trim. The main house and one side wing had newly thatched roofs, golden and unweathered; the two remaining wings still needed a loving hand. Red tarp covered the most serious holes, and one gable looked as if it was mostly supported by chicken wire and rusty iron struts. A dog barked loudly from inside the house, and Søren saw one of the shades move.

Veng rang the doorbell. "It's us, Mrs. Olesen," he said. "DI Veng, remember me? And this is Inspector Kirkegard and a Ukrainian colleague, Police Lieutenant Babko."

The woman in the door considered them with a face devoid of expression. The dog, a classic Danish hunting breed, tried to work its way out of her grip on its collar, but apparently she was holding on tight. Her eyes moved from one to the other, a bit on her guard, thought Søren, but then, they did outnumber her—an invasive force.

"Come in," she said after a few seconds. "Is it okay if we sit in the kitchen? It's warmest there."

"Of course," said Søren.

"I just have to . . . Maxi, go to your basket!" She shooed the dog into the utility room, where it reluctantly lay down in a basket by the boiler. "It's this way."

Given the rural surroundings, Søren had unconsciously expected a kitchen like his parents' in Djursland—vinyl squares on the floor, scratched white-laminated cabinets from the mid-90s, mail-order pine furniture that had never quite been in fashion even when it was brand new. But this was, after all, Hørsholm, home of golf enthusiasts and would-be country squires.

The room was large and well lit—clearly several old rooms combined—with double glass doors leading out into the snow-covered garden, new floors of broad, rustic oak planks, white walls and a high-end, designer kitchen. A comfortable heat radiated from a massive brick wall oven that divided the kitchen area from the dining room.

"Ahhh," sighed DI Veng spontaneously and unbuttoned his down jacket. "Nice to come inside and thaw a bit."

Babko smiled as well. "We have this kind of oven in Ukraine," he said. "Out in the country. That's the only thing that works when it's really cold."

Anna Olesen looked at Babko. Her gaze remained cautious. "What is he saying?" she asked.

"That it's a good oven," Søren translated. "They have them in Ukraine too."

"This one is Finnish," she said. "The old oil-burning boiler is on its last legs, so it's not just for decoration."

Heide had said Anna was over eighty, but she moved like a much younger woman. Her hair had to be dyed, but it was done so skillfully, in a variety of golden-blonde shades, that the result looked completely natural. A pair of red reading glasses sat in her hair as if they were an intentional part of her styling, and the comfortable-looking oatmeal-colored mohair sweater hung loosely over a pair of neat grey wool pants. Søren also noted the high-heeled black shoes, the pink lipstick and the discreetly penciled eyebrows. In no way did she look like a shaken elderly citizen who had just found the body of her neighbor.

"I know you've already spoken with the police," said Søren. "But unfortunately, we'll probably need to inconvenience you several times."

"Yes," she said. "I understand that."

"Do you live here alone?"

"Since my husband died four years ago. The plan is for my daughter Kirsten and her family to move into one of the wings when we finish restoring it."

"But you were alone last night?"

She shook her head. "I wasn't here last night. I was having dinner at the house of some friends of mine and didn't get home until after midnight."

Søren didn't ask about the dinner—Heide's people would definitely check on that if they hadn't already. "Did you go past Michael Vestergaard's house on that occasion?" he asked instead.

"No. I came the other way, from Kokkedal."

"Did you meet anyone on the way?"

"No. As I told you, it was midnight, more or less. And this isn't exactly downtown during rush hour. But someone had been here. I could see car tracks in the new snow."

Søren looked quickly at Veng, but the detective inspector shook his head. "It had been cleared again before we got here," he said.

"Henrik does that," said Anna Olesen. "Henrik Rasmussen. He also takes care of the golf course. Groundskeeper. Or whatever it is they call it in golf-speak." A glint of humor lightened the guarded blue gaze.

"When was the last time you saw Michael Vestergaard?"

"Saw? I've seen his car a few times over the last couple days, but we didn't say hello."

"Was that unusual?"

"No. We used to be a bit more in touch, actually. He could be quite helpful on occasion."

"Did you see Natasha Doroshenko often when she was living in the house?"

Anna picked at a thread on her mohair sweater. "We met now and again. Her little girl liked to help feed the cats. We talked about her getting a kitten, but . . . Well, that never happened."

"What was your impression of her?"

"My impression? She was a nice young girl. Much too young for him, of course, but in her situation, security is probably not an insignificant attraction. I thought they were fine together until . . . well." She interrupted herself in the same way as before. "I had no idea things were that bad."

"I understand that you were out walking the dog when you found Vestergaard?"

The pink lips tightened. "It was more like the dog walking me. I had let her out when I got up, but she didn't come back in. That happens sometimes. She doesn't stray, not really, but she might take a little excursion if I haven't walked her enough. When my husband was alive, she would never have considered setting as much as a paw outside the garden without him. He used to take her hunting and had her trained to perfection, but now . . . Anyway, when she had been gone for an hour, I realized I would have to put on my rubber boots and go search. And then, of course, I heard her."

"She was barking?"

"Yes. She was sitting next to the car—that is, Michael's car—and barking as if he were a fox in a hole. And then I could see . . . Well. I called the police right away."

"And stayed there, I understand?"

"Isn't that what you're supposed to do?"

"Did you notice any traffic during that time?"

"No. It was Saturday morning, so the few commuters we do have weren't going anywhere."

There was a very faint lilt to her voice that somehow wasn't pure Hørsholm. It could be the remains of a regional dialect she had shed, from Fyn or Bornholm, maybe. He couldn't decide.

"Were you born here on the farm?" he asked.

Again the guarded glance. "No," she said. "It was Hans Henrik's childhood home. We didn't move here until nineteen eighty-two, when his mother and father really couldn't manage it anymore. Before that we lived in Lund for years."

"In Sweden."

"Yes. I taught at the university. Classic philology."

Not your typical housewife, in other words—and more than averagely intelligent, thought Søren. Something about her aroused his curiosity, and he felt a sudden urge to rummage through her belongings, though what, exactly, he would be looking for, he didn't know. He had no legal grounds for such a search. If anyone was to do so, it would have to be Heide, he thought, with a grudging pang of envy.

UKRAINE, 1934

"**N**O, NO."

The protest was so faint, it could barely be called a protest. More like a kind of moan. Nonetheless, the young, beautiful GPU police officer immediately hit Marchenko across the mouth so the blood began to seep from his lips and gums. Marchenko bent forward and let it drip on the newly fallen snow. For some reason that was where Olga's eyes focused.

The red color against the blindingly white virgin snow was so vivid that it seemed almost supernatural in the midst of the grubby chaos. Behind Marchenko, most of his family's former belongings were bundled together in a tall, ungainly load on what had previously been his cart. There were a butter churn and pickling troughs and blankets and clothing and sacks. At the back of the cart sat a few sheaves of straw and the bucket from the farm's well. All of it had been tied to the cart by a couple of men from the kolkhoz. The three horses hitched to it stomped their hooves impatiently in the frozen wheel tracks and whinnied so the steam enveloped their muzzles.

Olga stood so close, she would have been able to stroke one of the horses' flanks if she stuck out her hand. But she didn't. The horse didn't look nice, she thought. The lower lip hung down so you could see the long yellow teeth, and its coat was bristly, mud caking its flank. She was closer than she wanted to be and also close to the scarlet blood spot in the snow in front of the cart.

Olga didn't quite know why she kept standing there instead of going home. Marchenko was the idiot Fedir's father and a kulak, and everyone knew that he had been behind with his grain deliveries for a long time. He had said that he didn't have any, and the village soviet had until now chosen to ignore his negligence. But today Jana had reported at school that the GPU had ransacked the Marchenkos' property and found grain as well as potatoes stowed away in a dugout under the house's foundation. It was the fault of him and the likes of him that everyone was starving, Olga knew that well, but somehow none of them looked quite like the fat kulaks on the poster outside the village soviet's office—especially not Fedir's little sister, who hung on her mother's arm. Her face was narrow and her eyes large. She wasn't much older than Kolja, and every so often she opened her mouth and cried out, a long, thin scream like a hare in the claws of an eagle. The family had been sitting outside in the cold all day, waiting for their judgment, and the child was blue with cold and exhaustion.

The cries made Olga feel sick deep down in her stomach, but still she couldn't tear herself away.

"There are at least one hundred twenty funt," said Oxana, pointing at the six sacks of grain that were just then being carried out and placed on a separate cart. "Just think how many mouths that can feed."

Olga nodded. She couldn't remember ever seeing so much grain at once—and not just any grain, but wheat, supposedly. She had heard that from the talk among the gathered villagers. Most of them had come to say goodbye. Marchenko's brother was there, and several of his neighbors, noted Olga. The men were smoking and talking quietly while the women had pulled their shawls close around their shoulders and were glancing nervously at the four armed GPU officers.

A GPU officer shouted something, and now the driver from the collective climbed, huffing, onto the load. He swung the whip over the sharp backs of the horses. The animals leaned forward heavily in their harnesses, but for a long moment seemed stuck in place until the wheels finally scrunched along in the slippery tracks and the cart began to move.

For a moment Marchenko looked as if he was planning to follow it, but he remained standing next to the four bundles that the family had been allowed to keep. What he had now was an idiotic son, a wife and a small daughter, thought Olga. Because Fedir was definitely an idiot. Even though he was fourteen, he stood sobbing as loudly as his little sister, and it was almost unbearable to keep watching. And yet she couldn't stop.

One of the remaining GPUs apparently felt the same way, because now he poked Fedir in the side with his rifle and told him to start walking.

"Where to?" Fedir stared at him with his wild, cross-eyed gaze, and the GPUs laughed almost kindly.

"To the station in Sorokivka. You're going on a trip, comrade."

Fedir smiled back in confusion, hoisted two of the family's bundles on his back and, neck bent, began to make his way through the crowd of gathered neighbors. One woman tried to sneak him a piece of bread, but he saw it too late and dropped it awkwardly on the road. When he straightened up, he saw Olga and Oxana and froze in his tracks.

"Oxana," he said. A special light slid across his face. "I'll come visit you when I get back."

Oxana lowered her eyes and nodded briefly, and just then Olga noticed the silence around them. As if all sound had been sucked out of the world. For the longest time, people stood mutely, staring at Fedir and Oxana. Then Oxana pulled her scarf closer around her face, turned her back on Fedir and began to walk away. Olga hesitated.

The young, smiling GPU officer poked Fedir again and drove him in the opposite direction down the main street of the village along with the rest of the family. Marchenko was silent now and walked with heavy, stooped shoulders while behind him, his wife struggled to keep the child in her arms. Only Fedir turned back one more time and raised his arm in a farewell that was impatiently swatted down by the boyish GPU officer.

Oxana marched with quick steps toward the stream, and Olga began to run to catch up with her. At the same moment, she felt a sharp stab of pain in her shoulder blade. Something hard and pointy had hit her, but when she looked over her shoulder, she couldn't see anything but the frozen ground and the fine dusting of new snow behind her. She increased her speed but stumbled and fell in the stupid bark shoes on the stupid cloddy ground. "Oxana, wait."

Oxana turned. She backtracked two steps and offered her hand to Olga, who got to her feet, swaying, just as she was hit by an even harder smack. This time it was on her forehead, and she felt a warm trickle of blood run down over her cheekbone. She didn't understand at all, but apparently Oxana did. Oxana raised a fist toward the Marchenkos' house just as another stone whistled toward them.

Oxana's eyes threw off sparks. "Act like it's nothing," she said breathlessly, pulling Olga along toward the stream. 'It's just Sergej, that idiot."

Olga tried to walk as fast as Oxana but stumbled and fell again. She couldn't help looking back.

No more stones came.

HE INCIDENT VAN was still pretty empty, noted Søren. Some of Heide's people were searching the house in Tundra Lane. Others were going door to door in the adjacent housing estates in the hopes that someone had noticed a car or anything else of relevance. Michael Vestergaard had not been considerate enough to get himself murdered in a public place with frequent traffic and CCT cameras. On a pitch-black, ice-cold winter night out here in the no-man's-land between the golf course and the so-called urban development, they would be lucky to find even one pathetic jogger.

Veng poured coffee on automatic pilot, but before Søren had a chance to drink it, his cell phone rang. It was Susse.

"Are you busy?" she asked. Her voice was so stressed that it sounded like a stranger's.

"What's wrong?"

There was silence for a short moment. Then she began to cry. In the background he could hear unfamiliar sounds of steps in long corridors, mumbled voices, metallic clicks and a sort of hydraulic hissing.

"Susse . . . What's wrong?"

"Ben," she managed to say between muffled sobs. "Sorry. There's no reason to cry now. It's just . . . he felt ill. We're at Herlev Hospital. They say it's a little blood clot in the heart."

"Do you want me to come?"

"No, no. It's okay now. But . . . if you have time. The dogs."

"Of course I have time."

"Thea is on a ski trip with some kids from her class. And the neighbors are on Fuerteventura. They'll be home tomorrow, and Barbara is on her way home too, but she's stuck in the snow somewhere outside Fredericia. So . . . so you're the only one here who has a key."

Barbara, Susse's oldest, was at the School of Design in Kolding. A long trip when the snow made train travel irregular.

"Susse. Stop. Of course I have time. Are you okay?"

"I was okay until I heard your voice. Then it all came crashing back again. Sorry. I was so afraid. He was in such pain, and I could see in his eyes that he thought that . . . Damn it, Søren. He's fifty-three. He can't be turning into a heart patient."

Ben had lived the hard life of a touring musician and had smoked twenty cigarettes a day for most of his life, although now he had quit. In Søren's opinion, this placed him dead in the center of the target group for a heart attack, but there was no reason to say that out loud.

"I'll take care of the dogs," he said. "Call if there's anything else I can do. Any time."

"Thank you."

He stood for a moment, thinking. Babko's restless energy had worn off, and he was sitting in a slump.

I could get a patrol car to drive him back to headquarters, thought Søren. But on the other hand . . .

On the other hand, he was convinced that Babko could tell him more if he could just poke a hole in the Ukrainian's jovial but uninformative façade. Perhaps it would help to get away from the uniforms and the coffee-and-adrenaline atmosphere. "Do you feel like helping me feed my ex-wife's dogs?" he asked.

· · ·

THERE WAS A string of belated Christmas lights along the white fence. There were birdseed balls on branches of the pear tree and dog tracks in the snow. Susse's two cocker spaniels were barking eagerly, and even through the door you could hear the soft slaps of wagging tails hitting walls and furniture.

Søren unlocked the front door, and the dogs came leaping. They needed to pee so badly that they barely took the time to say hello.

"You meant it," said Babko.

"Yes, of course. What did you think?"

Babko just shook his head. "Your ex-wife?"

"Yes. Her husband ended up in the hospital with a heart attack." Common-law husband, actually, but Babko probably didn't need those kinds of nuances. "Come on in. We might as well have a decent meal. You must be getting tired of cafeteria food."

He could see that Babko was . . . shocked was probably too strong a word, but thrown off-balance, at least. This was unexpected for him. He looked around at the white hallway, the rows of shoes and coats, a couple of Barbara's watercolors, the old school photos of Thea and her that hung on the wall facing the living room. Ben's African-American genes revealed themselves in the form of dark, bright eyes and a warm skin tone. They were attractive children.

"They aren't yours?" said Babko and pointed.

"No," said Søren. "But I'm the godfather of the youngest one."

Søren saw that the information was received and stored in the Babko computer, but what the Ukrainian thought about it, he couldn't tell. Suddenly he himself grew uncertain about whether this was a good idea. Handcuffs and beatings with filled plastic water bottles. Fingers crushed in car doors. If Babko was one of the nasty boys, it wasn't a good idea to show him a vulnerable point. Susse and her family might not be Søren's family in a conventional way, but they were definitely a vulnerable point.

Trust. To earn it, you have to give it.

The dogs came racing in with snow pillows under their paws and snow in their fur. Søren gave them what he thought was a reasonable amount of dry food in the ceramic bowls in the kitchen. Then he opened the refrigerator. There was a pot with some kind of chicken stew, smelling of curry and onions—and a couple of good Belgian beers.

Might that not be enough to build a relationship of mutual trust?

BABKO PUSHED HIS empty plate away, stretched and yawned deeply and sincerely.

"Sorry," he said. "I didn't really get any sleep last night."

"Didn't they offer you a bed?"

"Yes, but . . . I hoped Colonel Savchuk would return."

It was the first time Babko had voluntarily mentioned the SBU colonel—a breakthrough for bicultural understanding? Søren decided to consider it a step forward.

"Why is it that both SBU and GUBOZ are so interested in the Doroshenko family?" he asked and took a modest sip of his beer.

Babko looked around the kitchen. Susse and Ben had combined the old kitchen with the dining room, so they sat at a large flea-market find of a table, surrounded by plants, IKEA shelves with books, records and CDs behind shiny glass doors and with a view of the bird feeder in the garden through a blue terrace door.

"It's nice here, " he said.

Søren didn't answer. He let the question stand.

Babko smiled crookedly. "You're a patient man," he said.

Søren continued to wait. Babko took a swallow of the Belgian beer. He sighed, an unusually deep sigh that would have seemed overly dramatic coming from a Dane. But it wasn't. The sigh came from the same place as the laugh—from the bottom of his chest and possibly also from the bottom of Babko's Ukrainian soul.

"Once," he said, "I must have been eight or nine years old, it was a few years before the Independence . . . once we were going on a school trip, and the bus that came to pick us up was so dirty, you could barely look out the windows. My teacher asked the driver if he could at least wash the windshield so he could see safely. The driver just pointed to a certificate that indicated that the bus had been washed that morning, less than an hour ago. It clearly hadn't been, but it didn't matter; the certificate, with signature and stamp and everything, said it was clean, and so it was clean. My friend, do you understand what I am saying?"

"I'm not sure." Søren was having a lot of trouble seeing the connection to Natasha Doroshenko, but he was willing to listen.

"The truth. The truth is what it says on the certificate. It's completely beside the point if the window is covered in dirt and crap, as long as you have the paper saying it's clean. That's the way it was in Ukraine. That's the way it still is, except that the people writing the certificates are replaced once in a while. And when you meet a man who actually looks at the window and not at the certificate, at the truth and not at the most convenient version of it—a man who wants to change Ukraine if he can—then you don't believe it at first. You look for the hidden motives. You look at the money and wonder where it comes from. You wonder how he has gotten so far if he is really so clean."

Søren sat completely still. He didn't fidget with his utensils; he didn't touch his beer. He didn't want to risk interrupting Babko's monologue. For the first time, he felt he was getting some insight into what went on behind the jovial mask.

"During the Orange Revolution, we thought there would be a new day," Babko continued with a sudden hand gesture as if he were cutting something away. "We thought that corruption and the misuse of power would disappear or at least shrink, but nothing happened.

There was just a new group of people writing the certificates. So you don't believe it. For a long, long time you don't believe it."

Søren waited, but this time it seemed as if Babko had come to a halt again. "But then you become convinced?" Søren attempted to prompt him, not too lightly, not too hard, just the right amount of pressure.

"Little by little," said Babko. "Little by little. When you have kept this man, this very clean man, under observation for more than two years on the orders of his opponents. After two years, you are convinced and deeply depressed."

"Why?"

"Because he doesn't stand a chance. We've been ordered to find something on him. We don't find anything. Suddenly there is nonetheless a file of well-documented accusations, of corruption, witness statements, confessions and an arrest order. Fabricated from beginning to end, but it doesn't matter. There are stamps and signatures and certificates, pages and pages of them."

"Is he arrested?"

"Not right away. The folder . . . is lost. But a new one quickly appears. And then he is arrested. Detained. And in Ukraine, that is . . . no fun."

"No. I know." Plastic bottles and handcuffs. But Babko wasn't one of the torturers. Søren believed that now. He was a person who longed for decency and integrity, the way a man longs for a woman he can't have.

"I thought, he's done for. That was that. They got him. But that's not how it goes. Suddenly he is released again. The prosecutor has to apologize and say that the evidence was flawed."

"It was."

"Yes, but that doesn't usually mean anything. It didn't mean anything this time either. That's not why. Someone made the accusation go away, as it so often happens, even in the cases where you've seen the proof yourself before it disappeared."

"So your clean man isn't so clean, after all?"

"That's the odd thing. I think he is. Why else would he want to investigate who made the accusations disappear?"

"And that's what he did?"

"Yes. Most people would have thanked their lucky stars for the unexpected justice and let it go at that. Not him. He discovered that I was the one who had made the original file disappear."

"Did you get an appropriate thank-you?" Søren couldn't quite keep the irony out of his voice.

Babko laughed—a somewhat quieter version of the volcano laughter that could make people turn around to look at him. "That depends on what you mean by 'appropriate.' He grilled me several times to find out if I knew anything about the prosecutor's sudden change of heart. That's gratitude for you . . ." But the thought seemed to cheer him up. Cheer him up immensely, in fact.

Søren thought about his own boss. A career man, true, fixated on competition, but basically decent. He backed up his people, he followed most of the written and unwritten rules, and it was absurd to imagine that he would consciously hang someone on trumped-up evidence. That was not how he played the game.

Babko came from a country where that pretty much *was* the game. Søren tried to imagine what it would be like never to know if you'd been bought or sold, who was the buyer and who was the seller, and what version of the "evidence" you were using any given week. Of course the Danish system had its flaws. There were omissions, excuses and lies; there were favors and nepotism, of course there were. It happened from time to time that loyalty to the team degenerated into cover-ups—yes, it happened, but it was the exception, not the rule. It was a rare Dane who believed he could avoid a ticket by adding a bill when he handed his driver's license to the officer. Søren didn't feel amazed gratitude for having a boss who had reached his position with his personal integrity more or less intact. He took it as a given.

Babko did not have that luxury.

"Who is he, then—your clean man?"

"Filipenko. Nikolaij Filipenko. Have you heard of him?"

Søren thought. "I don't think so," he had to admit.

"He was an amazing soccer player, had twenty-one games for the national team before he was injured. That's why almost everyone in Ukraine knows him. That's probably also why he was elected to Verkhovna Rada the first time, because people knew and liked him. Otherwise it can be expensive to run an election campaign in Ukraine. And though he has money, he doesn't have *that* much money."

"So he's a member of Parliament?" The way Babko had discussed Filipenko, Søren had gotten the impression that he was a superior within the police.

"Yes. For Ukrainska Justytsiya, a small centrist party. They probably didn't believe their own luck when he wanted to run on their platform; otherwise they would never have gotten a foot in the door. He's on the parliamentary committee for the Eradication of Organized Crime and Corruption. Many hope he'll be our next minister of the interior. And Colonel Savchuk is his brother."

At last. The connection.

"So you're saying that the man we have . . ." Søren was about to say "lost," but the colonel wasn't a missing wallet, after all. ". . . lost contact with . . . that he may be the brother of the future Ukrainian minister of the interior?"

"Half-brother. And not many people know. They didn't grow up together. Savchuk is twenty-six years older. An entirely different generation."

"Same father or same mother?"

"Mother. Tetjana Filipenko. She owns U-card." Babko must have seen that it didn't mean anything to Søren and explained briefly, "It's a Ukrainian credit card. Like Visa or American Express."

"It sounds as if she's fairly wealthy."

"Extremely. U-card let the average Ukrainian acquire all the consumer goods we felt we had to have after the old regime fell. *Who do you call when you need a bit of cash? U-card, U-card, U-card . . .*" The last was offered in a mellifluous falsetto that made both dogs lift their heads.

"So there's nothing odd about her son being able to afford to run a Ukrainian electoral campaign?"

"U-card has supported the campaign with exactly 30,000 hryvnia. No more, no less. They've made a big deal out of that, and it's true. I've spent over two years checking. Nikolaij Filipenko is not a man who built his career on his mother's money."

"He sounds . . . remarkable."

"He is."

"And you still haven't answered my question. Why are you here? You and Savchuk? Why the two of you specifically?"

Babko closed his eyes for a brief moment, as if there were something written on the inside of his eyelids that he needed to read. "My friend," he then said, "be happy that you drive a small car."

"Why?" Søren recalled Babko's volcanic eruption of laughter at the sight of it.

"Because if you drove a big one, I'd never tell you this."

Søren forced himself to be patient. "What?" he asked.

"No one in GUBOZ or the regular criminal police knew that Natasha Doroshenko was in prison in Denmark until Savchuk appeared and requested an extradition order. Maybe SBU knew. Maybe it was something Savchuk had found out on his own."

"Okay."

"I was added on at the last minute."

"Why? Why you?"

"Because someone has asked me to start an investigation of Savchuk's circumstances."

"You're his guard dog."

"Yes."

"And what do you expect to find?"

"My friend, I have no idea. I have a suspicion that it was Colonel Savchuk who made the accusation against Nikolaij Filipenko go away back then. But to disprove false evidence is not a crime—at the worst, it is a declaration of war against those who have fabricated it."

"And you still don't know why he's interested in Natasha and Pavel Doroshenko?"

"No. I've poked around in the case a bit, as much as I had time for. The permission to interview Natasha came through unusually quickly."

Søren couldn't decode the questioning tone in the last statement. "What do you mean?" he asked.

Babko shrugged. "Perhaps the Danes are just efficient at that kind of thing. What do I know? But in Ukraine, if you need to speed up the paperwork . . ." He let the sentence dangle there unfinished.

"Did you think that Savchuk had bribed someone?"

A shrug. "As I said, my friend, it's good that you drive a small car. Honest cop car."

Søren finally understood Babko's appreciation for his practical little Hyundai. Ukrainian police with well-paying clients in the corruption shop apparently didn't drive Korean dwarf cars.

"What kind of car does Savchuk have?" he asked.

Babko laughed. "A huge BMW. But maybe his mother gave it to him." He rolled his shoulders a little. "In fact, he's got it with him."

"I thought you flew."

"*I* flew. He was already here. He was kind enough to pick me up at the airport, but that might have been because I had the extradition order."

"You don't by any chance have the registration number?"

A quieter version of the volcano laughter. "My friend, I just happen to." Babko pulled a small notebook out of his pocket and wrote it down. He knew it by heart, Søren noted. Then Babko tore out the page and handed it across the table. Søren received it with the appropriate gratitude.

Darkness had long since fallen outside among the pear trees. Babko yawned again, and even in the soft light from the Tiffany lamp his face looked worn.

"Do you want me to drive you to a hotel?" asked Søren. "Or do you want to go back to headquarters?"

"Headquarters." Babko yawned again. "There's nothing wrong with the bed there. And if Savchuk checks in, it's best if I'm there."

"You don't like it—that he doesn't check in."

"No. It's not good. For him or for me."

Without a doubt that was why the little piece of paper with the registration number had been handed over.

"Can you give me what you have on the Doroshenko case?" asked Søren to see if the cooperation stretched even further.

"You have the case folder."

"Yes. I mean *everything* you have."

The quieter version of the laughter. "Okay, honest cop. But I need it back." Babko pulled a USB drive out of the inner pocket of his suede jacket and handed it to Søren.

AFTER GIVING THE dogs a final airing in the garden, they drove back to headquarters. Babko disappeared in the direction of the apparently entirely satisfactory bed in the basement, while Søren headed toward the Communication Center under the roof of what had once been the women's prison. The noise was muted but ongoing. Only one of the operators looked up when Søren entered, and her gaze immediately slid back to the screen in front of her.

At the back of the high-ceilinged room sat a nearly bald man with round, well-padded shoulders that filled his light blue uniform shirt to the bursting point. Søren raised a hand. "Hello, Carlo," he said.

Duty officer Peter Carlsen smiled broadly and stuck two fingers in the air, continuing to speak on the telephone without missing a beat. When he was done, he got up and patted Søren on the shoulder with a smack that could be heard even through the stream of reports.

"Sonny boy. What the hell are you doing here?"

"Playing interpreter, for the most part. You've got a Ukrainian in the house."

"Oh, him. Is he of interest to the PET?"

"We're just helping each other out," said Søren vaguely.

Back at the police academy, the girls had given Carlsen the nickname Don Carlo because of a certain relaxed Latin lover charm. The name had stuck long after the pitch-black hair had disappeared and a middle-aged spread had asserted itself.

"What can I do for you?"

"The Ukrainian has a colleague, a Colonel Savchuk, who is . . . well, somewhat Absent Without Leave. He drove off Friday afternoon and hasn't been in contact with anyone since. We'd like to find him, of course." Søren handed Carlo the paper with the registration number. "So if anyone sees this . . . it's a BMW with Ukrainian plates."

"Okay. Is it the PET or headquarters who wants to know?"

"Both. And I'd very much like a personal tip-off right away."

"That'll cost you a beer." Carlo gave him an exaggerated conspiratorial wink.

"You *are* aware that you look like a fawning headwaiter when you do that, right?"

"Deal or no deal?"

"Deal."

"Good. And really . . . don't be such a stranger, huh?"

Søren agreed and headed home to Hvidovre to dig into Babko's files. It wasn't the same as having live witnesses to work with, but right now it was his best chance to get to know Pavel Doroshenko.

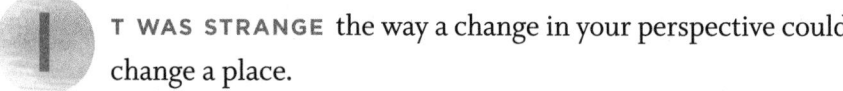

I T WAS STRANGE the way a change in your perspective could change a place.

The Coal-House Camp had been Natasha's home for many months, but from the edge of the woods, it looked foreign to her again. She was staring narrow-eyed down at the children's barrack from the little hiding place she had arranged under some low-hanging pine branches. It was dark now and had been for a long time. The evening had drifted into night while she'd sat hunched in her hiding place, but she felt no tiredness—just a background throb in her fingers and toes.

The camp's low barracks seemed stooped against the cold. The snow veiled the walkways, lawns and benches and made Natasha think of the cotton-ball snow landscape Katerina and she had been allowed to construct together in the prison's creative workshop last year. Katerina had arranged a cave for elves under a substantial piece of bark and placed other elves made of pipe cleaners outside the cave and on the little mirror that was supposed to look like a snow-covered pond.

"Should we add a troll too?" she had asked and had hesitantly run a hand through the box filled with wooden beads and pinecones.

"There are no trolls in elf-land," said Natasha.

"And not in real life either?"

Katerina's tone was different, and Natasha's trained ears instantly picked up a change in the rhythm of her breathing.

"Definitely not in real life," Natasha had said, as solidly and calmly as possible.

"But the camp isn't elf land." Natasha could hear Anna as clearly as if she had been standing next to her in the glittering snow. "The camp is a trap. You are the fox, and Katerina is the juicy piece of meat in the trap."

"I know," whispered Natasha. "I'll be careful."

The sense that Anna was with her evaporated as soon as she spoke out loud. No one was looking out for her now. The dark was dark, the cold was cold, and she was alone.

A thin but feminine shape moved behind the third window from the left. She assumed it was Nina. It was good that there was a woman with Katerina, but at the same time, it made things more complicated. Natasha opened and closed her hand around the knife handle in her pocket and attempted to hold back the racing panic that made her heart beat much too hard and fast. She took a deep breath and exhaled slowly, closed her eyes for a moment and concentrated on the weight of her body pressing against the earth, the cold air, the tree trunk's gnarly contours when she leaned back a little.

They had to get away, she and Katerina. Evil had come to Denmark now, and it was no longer safe here. But as long as Nina was awake and sat in Katerina's room with the lights on, Natasha had to wait. Anything else would be too risky. She would be seen. Nina would raise the alarm and call the police.

She tried to think about something else. About the very first days in the camp when Denmark had still looked like a safe haven. In the little leaflet she was given, it said that Denmark was a democracy, and that there were more pigs than people living here, as if the two were somehow connected. On the way here, she had seen the great refrigerated trucks with pictures of grinning porkers on the side, and for some reason it made all the horrors fade a little then. As if nothing wicked could reach her here in this ridiculous little, flat Bacon Land, where even the pigs smiled on their way to the slaughterhouse. Back then the fence had seemed a protection against the dangers she had run from. Even the most ordinary things—for example, the sight of the plastic chairs that were stacked every evening on the tables in the cafeteria with their legs up—brought tears to her eyes because it all seemed so ordered and calm. Even the fact that everything was so worn and nothing was clean for very long, even that was somehow reassuring—they weren't in Kiev anymore, in the apartment's traitorous luxury; it was more like Kurakhovo and the smell of her childhood. Katerina's sheets were patterned with nice little Scandinavian trolls, and Natasha had an odd feeling of being at summer camp with a lot of friendly people who were not out to kill her.

Later the despair set in. The grey fear of rejection cast a pall over the contours of the camp. As inhabitants disappeared, she knew she risked the same thing—knew the only thing she had won with her flight was a delay. She saw the fence for what it really was: a barrier to control the people inside, not a protection against the rest of the world. The greatest danger of all was let in through the main gate in the form of the apparently good-natured policemen who came to collect those who were being sent home. Even the Moomintrolls on Katerina's comforter began to look cruel, with devilish, taunting, superior smiles.

Then she had met Michael. It wasn't the way it had been with Pavel, not a dizzy falling in love, more a form of physical gratitude. Mixed with her desire for him and inseparable from it was the desire for permanent safety. She had loved him because he was a way out. So she had believed back then, and that belief made the camp fade away even while Katerina and she were still living there. It had become insignificant, a temporary refuge, no more. The sheets were weighted with neither hope or despair; they were just sheets.

The light went out in the third window from the left. A kind of electric shock raced through Natasha's body, as if the switch in Katerina's room were directly connected with her own nervous system. Now! Nina had either left the room or gone to sleep. Natasha believed she could overpower the nurse if necessary. Physically she was stronger than ever. It was easy if you had enough time. You stepped onto the edge of your bed and down again—first on your left leg, then on your right—a thousand times in the course of a day, every day. Then you lay down on the cell floor with your arms behind your neck and pulled your head up to your knees just as many times. Then came the push-ups. When she lay in her bed at night, she could feel her stomach muscles under the skin like steely ropes between her pubic bone and her lower ribs. The Barbie doll was no longer soft and smooth and obedient.

How long would it take the nurse to fall fast asleep? Natasha checked her watch. Ten minutes had passed since the light had gone out in Katerina's room, but a faint light still seeped out through the curtains in the room next door. It could be a night-light to calm a child who was afraid of the dark, but Natasha didn't believe it. That's where they were, the policemen.

She closed her hand around the knife in her jacket pocket again. Her fingers felt stiff and strange, as if they were no longer a part of her. But she could move them, and that was enough. Natasha measured the distance with her eyes. First five meters to the fence, and then about seventy meters across the snow-covered lawn. She had found pliers in the car's trunk, and she hoped they would be sufficient to cut a hole in the heavy mesh. Otherwise she'd have to climb across, but that would make it harder when she brought Katerina back with her.

Katerina. Now only minutes separated them, minutes and seventy-five meters. Natasha got up.

Then she heard it. The sound of a motor someplace in the forest behind her where there weren't supposed to be any cars. First a faint growl, then a shift to a lower gear and finally silence. There was no light to be seen through the trees. Only darkness and snow-laden branches. Natasha rubbed her nose with a numb red hand. Waited and listened. Then came the sound of car doors being opened and closed with careful, almost imperceptible clicks. A faint mumbling and the sound of heavy steps in the snow.

Silence again.

The desire to rush across the fence, shatter the window and drag Katerina with her out into the night was about to overpower her again. She was so close. Still, Natasha turned in the direction of the sound, got down on her knees and crept forward among the dark pines. Snow fell in cold showers from the branches onto her head and neck. Her unprotected hands hurt when they sank into the drifts, but she felt it only as a minor distraction. All her attention was focused on the sounds of the night, the whistling of the wind in the trees and the faint growl of trucks on the highway to Hillerød. How could the world make so much noise and at the same time be so still?

She crawled forward and through the next ruler-straight row of pines. The two narrow wheel tracks she herself had followed to the camp were only a few meters away now, and she could glimpse a faint light among the rippling black shadows of the trees.

A car was parked there, obscured by a storm of soft, whirling snowflakes. The headlights were off, but an interior light filled the car and created a faint orange-yellow aura against the black trees.

Natasha stopped in the shelter of a low, prickling pine and stuck her ice-cold hands inside her down jacket, confused. Someone had left the car and plowed a deep track among the trees to her right, but she couldn't see the person who had done it or hear anything but the freezing wind, which blew through the forest. She turned toward the car again.

The driver's seat was empty. But on the passenger seat sat a small, unmoving figure, staring straight ahead. The profile was sharply drawn, the nose aristocratically curved, and around the head was the silhouette of a huge, soft fur hat.

All at once the cold felt as if it came from inside as well as outside. It flowed from her chest through her abdomen and pooled in her arms and legs, making everything stiffen and hurt. Still she managed to move a little farther forward, close enough that she was afraid she would be seen if the woman in the car turned her head. Natasha knew the fear would kill her if it happened, but she had to be certain.

And then the woman did exactly that.

She turned her head slowly on a thin, wiry neck. Later Natasha remembered the movement as in slow motion: The huge gold earrings rocking slightly with the movement of the head, the bright red lips and the carefully powdered pale face. And finally the clear, pale blue eyes that stared into the dark without revealing any kind of emotion.

The Witch had found them again.

Natasha felt everything loosen in her body. She set off in the snow with a start like a hunted hare, stumbling through the trees without sensing the pine branches that whipped her in the face as she raced heedlessly back toward the camp and Katerina.

Seconds later a hollow bang sounded, and she knew she was too late.

DESPITE THE HOUR and the winter darkness, there was a pallid sheen on the walls of Rina's room.

It never got truly dark in the Coal-House Camp. There were lights along the walkways between the barracks, lamps above all the entrances and floodlights along the symbolic wire mesh fence that separated the camp's inhabitants from the rest of the world.

Nina gently stroked Rina's forehead, which was damp and cold with sweat. It was noticeably more quiet than usual in the barrack. Most of the children in the wing had a difficult relationship to men in uniforms and had for that reason been moved to empty rooms in the family wing while the watch over Rina continued. A faint scraping of chair legs and a low mumbling from the room next door was all that Nina could hear.

She found the book she had plucked from a shelf in one of the lounges earlier in the day—a paperback by some American author she had never heard of. She was forty pages into it but couldn't remember what it was about, and it occurred to her that if she was to read it now, she would have to turn on the ceiling light, which was equipped with an aggressive eco-bulb. She abandoned that particular project. Instead, she got up and stretched her legs, feeling the restless energy that always set in when she had nothing to do.

The room was small and claustrophobic, and the curtain-less

windows gave her an uncomfortable feeling of being watched. *Take good care of the girl*, PET-Søren had said, as if some other danger greater than Natasha lurked out there in the dark. It didn't exactly relieve her paranoia to see the personal attack alarm lying on the desk and staring at her with a glowing red eye in the gloom.

Nina took another look at Rina before she picked up her empty coffee mug and walked down to the coffee machine at the end of the hall. The machine hummed and sputtered and reluctantly sprayed the tepid coffee into the mug, and in the middle of a gurgling spray, she suddenly thought she heard something else. A low, flat bang, not a noise she recognized from the camp's usual nighttime soundtrack.

0:06. She stood for a few seconds with the plastic mug in her hand and listened while she gazed down the deserted grey corridor.

Silence. Then a soft bump and a faint scraping against the floor behind one of the doors. Silence again.

She realized that she had been dumb enough to leave the alarm in Rina's room. She swore softly, set the cup down and ran with silent steps toward the door to the room where the two police-men were sitting. She didn't waste time knocking. If anyone was in Rina's room, they needed to react instantly. Still, she was careful enough to let the door swing open without too much noise. A faint, sweet smell hit her.

The window was shattered. That was the first thing she saw. One officer was slumped across the table with his arms hanging heavily along his sides. She couldn't see his face but knew at once that he was either dead or unconscious. The same went for his colleague, who lay in a sprawling heap on the floor behind the table.

The shock propelled her back into the corridor, and she registered almost instantly that she was so dizzy, she had to support herself against the wall with one hand.

Gas. It was gas she could smell.

Without waiting to regain her balance, she tumbled the few meters to Rina's room. She didn't turn on the light but found the attack alarm on the table and pressed the button. Then she half-pulled, half-lifted Rina out of bed.

Rina hung dazedly in her arms but woke quickly enough that she could stumble along on her own two feet after Nina hauled her out into the corridor. They headed toward the coffee machine and the barrack's kitchen and dining hall. The dizziness was dissipating, but the walls were still trying to topple onto Nina, and the corridor stretched out ahead of her, elastic and unending, until she suddenly reached the door.

Behind them there was yet another hollow bang, and glass rained down over the linoleum floor. The big wall of windows in the lounge area had been shattered, and heavy feet stepped across the shards with a crunching sound. Nina jerked Rina along down the rows of tables and chairs and into the kitchen. She had seen the walk-in refrigerator clearly in her mind's eye even as she yanked Rina from her bed. It was the size of a broom closet, but it was airtight.

The heavy steel door was locked. Naturally. There were things that could be stolen in there, and this was a refugee center. Even the canned tomatoes were heavily guarded here. Nina fumbled with her passkey in the pallid light. The heavy lock clicked just as the door to the cafeteria was slammed open, and a broad, dark figure stepped into the dining hall behind them.

Nina pulled Rina into the narrow room with such force that the child whimpered as she hit the shelves of milk and cheese and juice. Nina had no time for consolations right now. She slammed the heavy steel door and heard the lock click once more.

She didn't know if he had had time to see them or to hear the slam and click from the lock. Her nausea closed in again; it was as if the gas's sweetish smell had coated her mouth and throat so that it was impossible to spit it out or cough it up. Next to her she could hear Rina's rapid, wheezing breaths in the dark. They stood so close together that they couldn't avoid touching. She put both arms around Rina's head, both to muffle the sound of that awful wheeze and also to remind Rina that she was still there.

Had he seen them? Did he know where they were? She strained her hearing to its utmost but couldn't hear anything but Rina. At least not until something hit the door to the walk-in with such force that the glasses on the shelf behind her clinked against one another.

She spontaneously tightened her grip on the girl's head, much too suddenly and tightly. But Rina didn't react. Said nothing, didn't gasp, didn't even alter the rhythm in her breathing. Not even when the second blow fell.

ATASHA DIDN'T EVEN make it to the fence. A broad, dark figure came running toward her, and the camp behind him was no longer a sleepy and deserted landscape—there were shouts, lights, people standing in the snow in various stages of undress, from overcoats to pajamas to vests and jockey shorts.

None of it mattered if he had killed Katerina.

The thought alone made her black and dead inside. She stood still because it was all she could do. Just breathing seemed a near-impossible task.

He ran past her, maybe forty of fifty meters away. Much, much too slowly she turned around, got her arms and legs to function, moved forward, a stumbling step and then another, until she was finally running, running as fast as she could, after the man who had perhaps murdered her daughter.

It was as if he could see in the dark. He didn't crash into the trees and branches as she did. And when an especially large branch hit her right in the throat, she collapsed and lay on her back gasping for a few seconds.

He stopped. Maybe he had heard her. He turned, and instead of a human face, she saw an insect-like creature with three protruding eyes that glinted faintly in the dark.

He can see me, she thought. Now he'll kill me. And if Katerina is dead, we'll meet in heaven. The thought did not offer any consolation.

From the camp there were more shouts and dogs barking, and just then a light blinked on right behind him. The Witch had opened the car door, and the interior light shone out onto the snow.

"Jurij?" she said. "Where is the child?"

"It didn't work," he said. "Some woman dragged her into a walk-in refrigerator."

"A walk-in . . ."

"Mm-hmm. I couldn't get the door open before the other guards showed up."

There was more barking. Natasha wasn't sure if it was from the handful of pets that lived in the camp or because the police had brought dog patrols. Possibly the man had similar doubts or else he hadn't spotted her, after all. At any rate, he quickly slid into the driver's seat and started the motor. The heavy car slid forward, headlights off, and within minutes the winter forest had swallowed car, man and evil Witch.

Natasha sat up. Katerina was alive. With those words everything existed again. An entire universe could be turned on or destroyed that quickly; that was how frail the world was.

THEY HAD BEEN living in Kiev for a few years when Natasha first discovered how easily everything could come apart. It began with a knocking on the door—loud, impatient raps, as if whoever was out there was irritated that the door hadn't opened at the first knock. Katerina was in her high chair eating pierogi, which Natasha had cut into bite-sized pieces for her. She dropped one of them on the floor in fright. "Whooo?" she asked.

"I don't know, sweetie. But now Mama will go look."

On the landing stood an older man in a suit, a brown case under his arm. He smelled of licorice and had a yellow-black licorice stain at one corner of his mouth.

"What is this?" he asked, waving a piece of paper in her face aggressively.

"I don't know," said Natasha, confused.

"The rent," he said. "You haven't paid the new rent."

"I don't know anything about that," she said. "My husband takes care of all that."

"Then you can tell your husband that he has to pay the same rent as everyone else in this house. It's been in effect since March. But he hasn't paid!"

"That must . . . be a mistake," she answered uncertainly. "I'll tell him when he gets home. He'll take care of it."

"I certainly hope so, little lady. If I have to come back, I won't be coming alone."

As soon as he had left, she called Pavel, but even though she tried for several hours, she didn't get hold of him. She felt as if the house had turned to glass. If anyone knocked on the door, it would all shatter and break. Natasha's magical castle, her beautiful rooms and all the beautiful things in them, the view of the National Museum, the trees outside, everything could disappear because of an old man who smelled of licorice.

Katerina sensed her anxiety and whimpered and fretted. Natasha attempted to calm them both.

Pavel will take care of it. Pavel will fix it, she told herself.

Finally Pavel did come home, exuberant and happy as usual. He kissed her on the mouth, deeply and hungrily, and lifted her up off the floor. This was when Natasha usually put her arms and legs around him, as if she were a child who needed to be carried. But not today.

"I tried to call," she said, and then the tears came rushing along with the rest of the story, even though she knew he hated crying. "A man came . . ."

"Stop. Dry your eyes, my love. You're scaring Katerina."

She sensed he was angry. She didn't know if it was at her, and she definitely didn't feel like making it worse, but she asked anyway.

"Pavel, is it true? Are we behind on the rent?"

"No," he said. "We pay exactly what we are supposed to."

"But why isn't it the same as what the others pay?"

"You don't need to worry about that, my love. I just need to make a call, then everything will be fine again."

And it was. Less than an hour later, there was another man at the door. He didn't smell of licorice but of expensive aftershave, and his cuff links were shiny and black, with a leaping golden jaguar.

Pavel did not invite him in even though it was terribly rude to leave him standing there in the doorway. "Natasha, this is Vasilij Ivanovitsj, who owns this beautiful house. Vasilij, this is my even more beautiful wife."

"It's a pleasure to meet you, Mrs. Doroshenko. And I regret that you were subjected to that unfortunate incident this morning. It was, of course, a mistake, and it will not happen again."

Natasha nodded silently. The man bowed gracefully, turned and left.

"You see," said Pavel and kissed her. "There's nothing to be worried about. Worrywart."

"I'm sorry," she said. "But I don't understand why we pay less than the others."

"Because Vasilij is a good friend," said Pavel. "That's all."

Natasha wanted so badly to believe it, and she almost succeeded. But if they were such good friends, then why hadn't Pavel invited him in? And why had Vasilij Ivanovitsj turned when he was halfway down the stairs and stared up at Pavel with eyes that were narrow and dark with hate?

THE DOGS BARKED. Natasha got up as quickly as she could. If she stayed here, she would be found. Katerina was once again out of reach, but at least she was alive.

SHE FELT AS if she had been beaten up. Nina's ears were buzzing, her entire body ached and there was a point at the back of her neck, at the meeting of spine and skull, where it felt as if a burning needle had been inserted.

She held Rina close despite her uneasy awareness that she was the one deriving comfort from the gesture, like a child holding a teddy bear. There was no reciprocity; Rina might as well *be* a stuffed animal. If it hadn't been for the loud, gasping wheezes that constituted the girl's breathing, Nina might have been tempted to check for signs of life.

Magnus and Pernille arrived with the oxygen. Magnus maneuvered Rina out of Nina's embrace with his usual calm authority. "Okay, Rina. Now we're going to make it easier for you to breathe."

Nina had to fight a spasmodic tension in her arms, forcing herself to let go. "She also needs salbutamol," she said before she could stop herself.

Magnus just nodded as if there were nothing odd in a nurse attempting to dictate a treatment he had undertaken hundreds of times.

It was 2:03. Forty-six minutes had passed since she had heard a key click unsuccessfully in the walk-in door.

"Nina, are you in there?"

It wasn't a voice she had immediately recognized. She was paranoid enough to hesitate for a second.

"Nina Borg? Police."

"Yes," she shouted. "We are here."

It had taken another fifteen minutes to get the door open. The lock had been damaged by the attacker's attempt to break it open, and in the end, they had to cut the hinges instead.

Outside there were people everywhere—or at least that was how it felt. There were probably only seven or eight, but the only one she knew was the camp's technical director, Henning Grønborg, who had apparently taken charge of the blowtorch himself. The rest was a whirl of yellow police vests, black SWAT uniforms and young policemen's faces wearing oddly nerdy protective glasses. Like well-behaved children at a New Year's party, thought Nina.

They tried to take Rina from her at that point, but she resisted. "Get Magnus," she had repeated, over and over again. "It has to be someone she knows."

Now she had finally let go. Her arms hurt just as much as the rest of her, in spite of the fact that she had only suffered a handful of bruises from furniture and doorways and whatever else she had bumped into on her confused, unsteady flight from Rina's room.

Pull yourself together. You are not exactly dying, she told herself.

A shiver went through her that had nothing to do with cold, though it felt that way. Right now she was deeply grateful for Magnus's insistence on heating the clinic to a temperature that would do credit to a steam bath.

2:11.

The children were sleeping now, she thought, Anton under his Spider-Man comforter and Ida presumably in sheets that were as pitch black as most of her wardrobe. For a while she had had Legolas from *The Lord of the Rings* on her pillow, but lately she had been talking about "the cynical abuse of Tolkien's work in merchandising," and Nina had had to quietly exchange a few Christmas presents before they reached the tree. The first post-divorce Christmas. Only Nina's first childhood Christmas without her father had been worse.

2:13.

Stop. She turned her watch so the face was on the inside of her wrist. It made it a little more difficult to check the time and normally helped her control her own personal mini-version of OCD. The improvement was relative—the compulsive checking of the time was replaced by involuntary movements in her lower arm every time she caught herself turning her wrist.

After her divorce, an exciting new development had occurred in the neurosis, she observed dryly. Now the checking of the time was often accompanied by an automatic picturing of what Anton and Ida were doing; she wasn't quite sure if that was better or worse.

"Nina Borg?"

She looked up. Yet another unfamiliar face, this time a younger man in civilian clothes.

"Detective Inspector Asger Veng, North Zealand Police," he introduced himself.

"Yes," she said tiredly. She couldn't even manage a politely encouraging question mark in her tone.

"May we take a few moments of your time? We have a couple of questions."

Yes, of course they did. If he had asked her to crawl naked through icy mud, her enthusiasm might have been at much the same level, but it was probably best to get it over with.

"WHAT HAPPENED?"

The shout sounded across the parade ground from a small group of freezing people who were huddled in the doorway of one of the family barracks. Nina recognized one of the camp's long-term inhabitants, a man from Eritrea, but she had to cast about for his name. Rezene, that's what he was called. He suffered from violent reflux attacks, so they saw him relatively often at the clinic.

Nina didn't know what to answer. When it came to the spreading of rumors among the camps' inhabitants, "wildfire" was an understatement, especially when the police were involved, and rumors were never harmless. They all lived with the threat of deportation as a constant stress factor. Even though Magnus did what he could to minimize it, there were a lot of sleeping pills and sedatives in circulation, and not so long ago, an Iraqi mother had shown up with three packs of nitrazepam that she had recovered from her sixteen-year-old son. When asked what he had been intending to use them for, he said that it was in case the police came to get them, because he would rather die in Denmark than in Iraq.

"It's okay," Nina shouted back in careful, simple English. "Someone tried to take a child. The police stopped them."

It was important to keep statements clear and uncomplicated.

"What child?" shouted Rezene.

"Rina. The little Ukrainian girl."

"Why ambulance?"

"Some policemen were hurt."

Detective Inspector Veng put a gentle hand on her elbow. It was presumably meant as a polite reminder of their real errand, but the touch irritated her.

"Yes, all right," she hissed. "It's hardly surprising if some of them want to know what the hell is going on."

"Your director *has* informed them," said Veng.

Nina had no doubt. Birgit Mariager had been the camp's director for almost five years now, and clear communication had quickly become one of her main concerns. But Nina also knew that even the clearest communication in the world couldn't prevent speculation, questions, rumors and doubt.

"Are they okay? Your two colleagues?"

"We don't know yet," he said. "They used a pretty nasty form of gas."

"There was only one person," Nina corrected him. "A man."

"Yes. I heard you said that."

They had asked even before they managed to open the walk-in. Nina understood that they needed to know who and how many people they were searching for and what kind of resistance they could expect to encounter if they found them, but it had seemed almost brutal to have to bellow her answers through the thick steel door when every shout made Rina's body start.

The ambulances were gone now, but the children's barrack was still closed off. Powerful projection lights made the snow glitter, and technicians were busy picking up glass shards and photographing footprints.

"We've got permission to use the director's office," said Veng. "Let's get you inside where it's nice and warm, all right?"

He was trying to be friendly, Nina told herself. It wasn't reasonable to hate him just because he was young, rested and professionally kind.

The two women who waited in the director's office were remarkably similar as far as height, weight, dress and hair color were concerned. Slender, blonde, well-dressed and well-groomed. In spite of what must have been a very rushed departure, Birgit had had time to put on both makeup and a freshly ironed white shirt. A fine gold chain ringed her still almost unwrinkled neck.

"Nina. Are you okay?"

Nina nodded. Birgit was actually okay. Most of the time.

"Please let me know if there's anything I can do."

The other woman, the Birgit clone, presented herself as Deputy Chief Inspector Mona Heide. At least *her* white shirt didn't look as if it had just come out of its cellophane wrapper. Her face didn't either. In spite of the careful makeup, the exhaustion was evident.

"I'll try to be brief," she said. "But it's important for us to find out as much as possible as quickly as possible."

"Okay."

"When did you first become aware that something was wrong?"

"I heard a crash. It must have been the gas grenade, or whatever it is they used, shattering the window."

"And when was that?"

"Six minutes past twelve."

Heide raised a well-plucked eyebrow. "You're very precise."

"I looked at my watch immediately after." Nina didn't think there was any reason to mention the OCD.

"Where were you?"

"By the coffee machine."

"Not in the girl's room?"

"No. But I had only been away for a few minutes."

"What happened then?"

Nina explained her quick look in on the policemen, hurrying to Rina's room, pressing the attack alarm, the clumsy flight to the walk-in.

"Why the walk-in?"

"It's airtight. I was pretty sure there was gas."

"And then?"

"And then he came in through the window in the lounge area."

"You're sure it was a man?"

"Yes." She recalled her brief but definitive glimpse. "He was big—both tall and broad. Completely black, including his face—he must have been wearing some kind of mask or hood."

"And it was just him?"

"Yes."

"You're sure?"

"Very sure. Listen, it wasn't Natasha. I know what you're thinking, but it wasn't her. She's a slight, slender girl. Smaller than I am—one meter sixty at the most, I would guess. And he was alone."

Heide eyed her calmly. "People often perceive events in a distorted way in situations like this. Everything happens fast, it's violent, you're afraid . . . few people ever describe an attacker as small."

"He *was* big."

"Precisely where and for how long did you see him?"

"It was only a glimpse; I was busy trying to open the door to the walk-in. He was entering the cafeteria."

The crunching of glass, Rina's breathing, the sweet-and-sour taste in the mouth that was a mixture of adrenaline and gas. The figure behind them, a faceless monster with three shiny eyes . . .

Three eyes?

"I think . . . it looked to me as if he had three eyes."

Veng and Heide exchanged a glance.

"Maybe he was using IR equipment," said Veng. "Combined with a gas mask?"

Heide nodded. Nina noted that they had finally begun to say "he" and not "they" or "her."

"Professionally done," said Heide dryly. "If you can say that about a failed mission."

"It wasn't Natasha," repeated Nina, just to make sure.

"I understand you've worked with the family for a few years?" said Veng.

Nina's mind tripped over the "family" part. In her world, an isolated and traumatized girl with a dead father and a mother who was in prison wasn't much of a family.

"Since they came here," she said.

"What has Natasha told you about her life in Ukraine?"

"Nothing. She never talked about her background."

"So you didn't know that she was wanted in a criminal investigation there?"

"Of course not. I didn't even know that she had a husband or that he was dead."

"Did she have any confidantes here? Among the other inhabitants of the camp or in Denmark in general?"

"Not that I know of. She did get engaged and moved in with . . . Vestergaard." At the last moment, she avoided calling him "that bastard" as she usually did. "The only other person I think she really spoke with was a neighbor. I don't remember her name."

"Anna Olesen?"

"Yes. That's right. Neighbor Anna. That's what Rina called her. I think she was kind to Rina while they lived there. At least I know that Rina liked her, and it usually takes her a long time to attach herself to a new person. I also got the impression that Anna was one of the few people Natasha trusted."

"And you don't know anyone else? Anyone from Ukraine, for example?"

"No." She thought about it. "We have had other Ukrainians here, but I think . . . I think Natasha avoided them on purpose. It's a little unusual; often they are very happy to have each other. Have the chance to speak their own language with someone who understands them."

"Letters? Emails? Telephone contact?"

"I don't know." Nina considered. "If she was in contact with anyone while she was serving her sentence, then Vestre Prison must know. While she was here . . . Of course, Natasha spoke on the phone now and then, but I think it was mostly with Michael Vestergaard or perhaps with Anna. In English, at least, and in the bit of broken Danish she knew."

"You haven't heard her speaking Ukrainian with anyone?"

"I don't think so. All I know is that she was terrified of being sent back. Most people here are, but with Natasha it was . . . unusually evident. And she was right to be afraid."

"What do you mean?"

"I think it's pretty obvious now. Someone is after Rina and her."

Heide gave a little, irritated shake of her head, causing her gold earrings to dance. "Not much is obvious about this," she said.

"We can at least agree that Rina is in danger," said Nina. "What are you planning to do to protect her?"

Heide looked at her coolly. "It wasn't the girl who was gassed," she said. "It was the people trying to protect her. It appears as if it is pretty risky to stand between Natasha and her daughter."

"Damn it. How many times do I need to say it? *It wasn't Natasha.*"

Easy, easy, Nina told herself. She knew that swearing and yelling would not make this calmly collected woman listen any better to her—on the contrary.

"I think we're done," said the deputy chief inspector. "At least for now. If you remember other contacts Natasha may have had, we'd very much like to know, and we will naturally need to ask for a formal statement at some point."

"So you're not planning to do anything?"

"We have two colleagues in the hospital right now," said Heide. "One of them is in critical condition. You may be sure that we are planning to 'do something.'"

Nina's stomach hurt. It was perfectly clear that Heide's priority was the hunt for the gas man and Natasha—not Rina's safety.

Veng had gotten up, a clear sign that Nina was supposed to do the same. He handed her a single sheet of paper. Nina glanced down at it automatically.

Victim support, she read. *If you have been the victim of violence, rape, a break-in, robbery, an accident, etc., it is natural and completely normal if you experience reactions such as feelings of unreality or loss of control, the inability to act, hyperactivity, emptiness, memory loss, fear of being alone, fear of recurrence, stomach pain, an elevated heart rate, difficulty sleeping, nightmares, guilt, despair.*

"They are very good," he said. "And you are welcome to contact them."

Nina snapped.

"What the hell makes you think," she said in her most glacial voice, "that I am anybody's *victim?*"

NATASHA HAD PARKED the car in the forest on the other side of the camp this time. The view of the children's barrack wasn't quite as good—the depot shacks were in the way—but there were still searching figures with lights and dogs in the woods around her former hideout. The snow had finally stopped falling. It covered the roadblocks and the cars and created an almost unbroken surface between the fence and the barracks, more orange than white because of the sodium vapor in the camp's streetlights. She couldn't see Katerina or Nina anywhere. Of course not. It had to be at least at least ten degrees below zero, and it was only 4:30 in the morning. She rubbed her tired eyes. It was useless. Even if she did see Katerina, what was she going to do? Freezing to death was about the only thing she could accomplish by remaining here, if someone didn't spot her and catch her first. It was unwise, but she couldn't help herself.

When she realized that the nurse had saved Katerina from the Witch, Natasha had felt a relief and a gratitude so powerful that the darkness around her spun dizzyingly as if she had drunk too many of Robbie's whiskey shots. The relief was still there, but the gratitude was receding. On the other side of the fence and the sodium lights and the police barricades, that skinny Danish woman was lying with her arms around Natasha's child, and although she knew that it was neither reasonable nor sensible, Natasha had never for a second been as jealous of the women in Pavel's life as she was of Nina right now.

YOU'RE TOO CLINGY with that child, Pavel had said. He had imagined that they would go on vacation together, just the two of them, maybe to Krim, or why not abroad? Why not Berlin? He spoke the language; there was so much he could show her. Or Paris or London if she preferred.

Seventeen-year-old Natasha would have been beyond thrilled. This was precisely the world she had hoped would be waiting out there once she had escaped from Kurakhovo. Nineteen-year-old Natasha, however, would rather sit on the grass in the park and stop Katerina when she tried to put ants or ladybugs in her soft little mouth. Kiev was enough. The apartment, Pavel, Katerina—why would she need anything else? Occasionally she had agreed to hire a babysitter so they could go to a restaurant, but she would be restless the whole time, constantly remembering something she had to call and tell the young sitter. It was someone Pavel knew. He said she was studying medicine and wanted to earn a little cash. Natasha would have worried less, she thought, if there had been a more grandparent-like person available, but Pavel's mother had died several years ago, and it was too far from Kurakhovo for her mother to come for a single evening.

Gradually he stopped asking. If that was how it was going to be, he said, then he wanted to hear no complaints if he went out on his own. That was when her jealousy had crept up on her. She sniffed him like a dog when he came home and tried to smell where he had been. She looked at his cell phone when he was in the bath and found a lot of unknown numbers and messages from people she had never heard of. Some of them were women, and she noted every female name. She turned out his pockets meticulously before she did the wash. And she couldn't help asking, "Who is the Anna you call so often?"

He looked astonished. "Anna? How do you know that?"

"Who is she?" she repeated.

"My God," he said and laughed. "Now you're being silly. It's my mother's old nanny. She's almost eighty, and she lives in Denmark. See for yourself." He showed her the number and then had to explain, and she was embarrassed and really did feel silly and stupid because she hadn't known that there was a difference between the numbers abroad and the ones in Ukraine. But how was she to know? She had never known anyone who lived abroad.

"Why did your mother have a nanny from Denmark?" she asked.

"It's a bit complicated," he said. "*Everything* was complicated then—Poles, Germans, Russians, Ukrainians, Galicia was one big mess, and nobody knew what would happen from one day to the next. Anna ended up in Copenhagen and got married there. But Mother never forgot Anna, and they kept on writing to each other for many years, even back when half their letters were snatched up by the censors. I've visited her several times, and, yes, I call her now and then to hear how she is doing. I care a great deal about her, in fact."

Nina put her arms around his neck. "That's okay," she said. "You are allowed to care for almost eighty-year-old ladies. Just as long as you love me the most."

"Silly thing," he said. He pulled her close, exactly hard enough that she knew he wanted to make love to her, and a powerful surge of heat exploded somewhere under her belly button, shot downward and then spread up to her breasts and neck. She gasped, and he laughed and let his hands slide down to cup her buttocks. They never made it to the bed.

IT WAS BECAUSE of Anna that she had chosen Denmark later, when all the bad things happened. When Pavel was dead, and Katerina and she could no longer be in Ukraine. Denmark was the only other country that Natasha had been to—Natasha, Pavel and Katerina had visited together twice—and Anna the only person she knew abroad. And when her caseworker began to look worried, and Natasha was terrified that it was her turn to be deported . . . then it was Anna who had made sure she got to meet Michael.

She felt a stinging pain in the pit of her stomach at the thought. She took out a piece of chocolate and let it melt on her tongue. Then, slowly and with difficulty, she chewed a slice of the dark Danish rye bread that looked just like the Ukrainian bread she was used to on the outside but that tasted completely different. To think that she had been so stupid. To think that she had been so happy. So happy that she would be allowed stay in Bacon Land forever, where everyone lived high off the hog, and no one needed to be afraid of anything.

ABOUT HALF AN hour later, Nina emerged from the children's barrack with Katerina. Natasha was out of the car before she knew it and had taken nine or ten steps toward the fence. Dangerous steps. A few more meters and she would have been completely visible from the camp.

She saw Nina speak with one of the officers who stood at the barricade around the barrack. The nurse pointed toward the clinic on the other side of the big, open grounds where the kids played soccer in the summer. The policeman lifted the striped plastic tape and let them through.

But Nina didn't go in through the clinic's front door. She and Katerina disappeared around the corner, then appeared again a bit later by the main entrance and the parking lot. The nurse took Katerina's backpack and made her get into an ugly little yellow car.

Natasha began to run. Just then she didn't care if all the policemen in the world saw her. She plowed a way through the high snow along the fence, but she was too far away. The little yellow car had started and was rolling out of the parking lot, slowly and carefully on the icy road, but still much too fast for Natasha to reach it.

Still she kept running, until her foot caught on a hidden tree root and she fell headfirst into the snow. And then she had to run all the way back again to the stolen Audi, which in her rush she couldn't figure out how to start.

When she finally got the cold motor going and made her way back to the road, the yellow car was gone.

Natasha pulled over to the side and bent forward over the steering wheel. Acid burned in her stomach; she could barely breathe. In all the time that she had been parted from Katerina, she had always known where her daughter was. The little man on the Google map could find her. Natasha could plan the route and calculate the distance; she knew what direction she needed to go.

The Google man couldn't find Nina.

Or wait. Could he?

"I know where you live," she whispered. She could feel the knowledge loosening her chest so she could breathe again. She had been there once, long ago, when she and Michael had just gotten engaged and it looked as if everything would be safe and all right again. When both she and Nina believed that Natasha's life could go on quietly in a house in Hørsholm, behind a hedge of flowering lilacs. In Bacon Land.

They had sat drinking coffee on Nina's sofa in her messy apartment full of books, children's clothing and rubber boots. Natasha wasn't sure what the street was called, but she remembered the house—an old red-brick building on a narrow side street off the same wide boulevard where, months later, Natasha had bought the knife she meant to stab Michael with. Jagtvejen. That's what it was called. The boulevard. Surely she would be able to find it. It wasn't a route she had practiced, the way she had practiced the way to the Coal-House Camp, over and over again. But the Audi had a very high-end GPS.

It might even be better this way. After all, there were no fences and no guards around Nina's house.

UKRAINE, 1934

O LGA KICKED HER way through the snow to the stable, where the cow lay waiting patiently in the dark. That was something cows were good at. Olga sometimes tried to imagine what it was like to be a cow and lie there on the cold earthen floor and wait for someone to appear with water and hay and potato peels and let light into the stable and shovel shit from the gutter and whatever else a cow needed to stay alive. Did Zorya even know that summer would return? And was she ever afraid of being forgotten?

If she was, she hid it well. Her large, glassy eyes rested calmly on Olga in the gloom. She lay on her side with the clumsy yellowish hooves pulled up against her stomach, which appeared unnaturally large and swollen in comparison to her flabby, shrunken udders.

Olga grabbed an armful of hay and loosened it carefully, trying not to get pricked by the many thistles. Then she threw it in front of the cow, who stuck her long blue tongue all the way out and pulled the hay toward her without getting up.

Frost covered the walls and straw like a fragile white spiderweb, and the water in the trough was frozen, but not so hard Olga couldn't make a hole in the ice with Grandfather's sickle for Zorya to drink from. Then she scraped the cow shit to the side and cautiously poked the cow to see if she wanted to get up. She didn't. Milk for Kolja would have to wait. If the cow stood up, Olga would also find some fresh pine boughs for her to lie on, because even though she had her usual thick winter coat, you could see her bones like thick branches under the skin. If the cow wasn't lying on something soft, those bones would gnaw through flesh and skin, and she would get sores and die.

Mother didn't take care of the cow.

She took care of the pigs in the kolkhoz and had the responsibility for all the squealing, hunchbacked beasts in Stable Number Two. Every morning she fought her way down there through the drifts to fatten up the swine. And that was fine with her. Or so she said. She might not be as strong as she used to be, but she was still a damn sight better than those two sluts from the Caucasus who were supposedly in charge of Stable Number One, but who, according to Mother, drank vodka and whored worse than the swine. Back when Father was still living with them, Mother wouldn't have said such things, but her speech had become coarse and rude now, especially when she talked about younger women.

"They can fuck, but I can work," she said, her laugh brief and hard, not at all like the way she used to laugh when they still lived in Kharkiv.

Olga stroked the broad, greasy bridge of the cow's nose and thought that it would have been nice to sit here with someone. Jana. But the mere thought of Jana gave her a clenching sensation in her stomach.

After Oxana's pioneer meeting, a number of children in the school fawned over her in a dog-like manner. Nadia and Vladimir and little Veronica, who was really a *niemcy*, an ethnic German, and had been forcibly relocated here from Galicia, but who still loved Comrade Semienova and the Party and all that meant in terms of khaki-colored uniform shirts and red banners. Her eyes were glued to Oxana in the schoolroom, and when Olga talked about the counterrevolutionary cells in the village that had to be crushed, little Veronica opened her tiny bright red mouth and sighed with devotion.

But not everyone looked at Oxana and Olga with such adoration. Some eyes were lowered when they turned around in the schoolroom. Whispering would suddenly cease when they walked by and later start up again behind their backs. Olga knew what they were whispering, even though no one had said it to her face. She had listened and picked it up piece by piece. They were whispering about Oxana and Fedir. They said that Fedir had been in love with Oxana, and that Oxana had gone for long walks with him down by the frozen stream. She had lured him into telling her about the wheat under the stable floor, and afterward she had reported it to the chief of the GPU in Sorokivka.

Everything had gotten worse after the letter arrived from the Marchenko family. Fedir's sister, the little girl with the hare-like scream, had never made it to their destination, which was so far north that you had to travel by train for a full fourteen days. She had stopped screaming on their third day in the cattle car. They had left her someplace along the tracks between Kharkiv and Novokuznetsk. No one knew exactly where.

Jana was one of the whisperers now. Fedir was her cousin, and even though Jana had made fun of him when he still sat in the back of the class, his disappearance had broken something between Jana and Olga, something that couldn't be put back together again.

That was the way things were, and there was nothing Olga could do about it.

She was not responsible for Fedir's banishment, but she was tied to Oxana by blood, just as Jana was tied to Fedir. Therefore they had to be enemies now, and it was a war that Jana threw herself into with a bloody rage.

Jana said that Olga was ugly and had body lice, and that she didn't want to sit next to her in school. Jana also said that she was just as dirty as her swine of a mother. Jana told the others in school how their old house sparkled now that Svetlova had taken over the house-keeping and that Svetlova was expecting a child who would soon replace Olga, Oxana and Kolja.

Outside the cow barn, Grandfather was making his way to the woodshed, coughing. Olga stood with her hand on the cow's neck and listened to the sound of the axe splitting wet birch wood until it hit the chopping block with a faint echo in the ice-cold air.

Then came the roar.

He was calling Mother, Olga could hear, and afterward he also called Grandmother, even though she had been dead for several years now. Olga felt a gust of terror blow through her. She wrenched open the door and raced across the yard to the woodshed.

Grandfather lay with the axe in his shin, cursing and shouting for vodka. Olga and Oxana had to hold down both him and his leg while Mother pulled the axe free from the bone. There was blood every-where. Even the bone bled, it seemed to Olga, and she knew bones couldn't bleed.

Mother sent Oxana off to get the barber, telling her to run as fast as she could. Olga got rags and blankets, and Mother tore a wide strip of linen from a sack and made a tourniquet right above the cut. She used the axe handle to tighten it and turned it around and around even though Grandfather screamed like an animal going to slaughter and cursed her to hell and back again.

"Would you rather die?" Mother just said when he stopped scream-ing for a moment out of sheer exhaustion.

Finally Oxana returned with the barber. He tied a piece of blu-ish-white sheep gut around the biggest of the pumping arteries and sewed the tear together with needle and thread. Only then could they help each carry Grandfather into the house.

Even after the barber was done, Grandfather didn't stop bleeding. Mother sat next to him and pressed one rag after another against the cut, her grip hard and frantic. Grandfather had drunk so much vodka that he could no longer speak, and spit and drool trickled from the corner of his mouth into his beard. There was a wet rattle in his chest. Olga wasn't sure if she was more afraid of him dying or of him waking up again. She was feeling sick and couldn't stop shaking, but Oxana was pale and calm and looked as if she were thinking of something else completely.

"If he dies, he is no good to us," she said gravely to Olga. "And even if he lives, he is no good to us. It is winter, and we have no man in the house."

Olga looked over at Grandfather. The darkness in the room was oppressive, and the glow from the oven illuminated it only enough that she could see the growing pile of soaked black rags on the floor next to him.

Olga knew that she shouldn't be thinking of herself, but still. Grandfather did more than just administer hard, unexpected slaps to the face and neck. Grandfather chopped wood and laid traps in the woods. The skins he sold were their only source of cash and goods like meat and sugar and tea and salt and petroleum; how would they do without?

The barber had cost rubles, Olga knew. Rubles and bread. And today there were no rations from the kolkhoz's communal kitchen because Mother had stayed home and left the pigs to the Caucasian whores.

LATER, WHEN GRANDFATHER was fast asleep, and dusk had fallen outside, Father suddenly appeared in the doorway.

Olga's heart gave a little jump for joy in the middle of all the sadness and nastiness. Father must have heard about the accident and had come to . . . to take Mother back. Now that he knew she was completely helpless in the world, he had realized what a big mistake he had made. The widow and the baby had to go, of course, but that would be okay. The baby would be small and could live in a smaller house. And in any case, that was Svetlova's problem, not theirs.

Father carefully stomped the snow off his boots before he stepped inside. His broad shoulders filled the whole room, thought Olga.

"*Tatko!*"

Without thinking she rushed over and threw her arms around him. She took in the familiar smell of sawdust and pine sap and noticed that it was now spiced with a very faint new scent of chamomile, which probably came from Svetlova's body. She didn't care. She burrowed her face into his open coat and pressed her nose and cheek against his woolen shirtfront.

He pushed her away.

His eyes were swimming a little, and Olga realized that nothing was exactly as it should be. He had been drinking, she could see, and behind him Oxana now stomped into the room and shot Olga a cranky look.

"You wanted to speak with me?" Father said to Mother, his expression foreign and hostile.

Mother got up on uncertain legs, nodding to Father as she smoothed her hair. Olga could see that she was attempting to hide the gaping holes in her rows of teeth when she spoke. "We need money, Andreij. Or at least some of your rations from the kolkhoz."

"Sell something," said Father. "The old man still has a cow, and that's more than most people. That it was allowed to survive last winter was a miracle in itself. Fat and pregnant as it was. If I were you, I'd eat it now before it is collected for the kolkhoz. That's the best advice I can give you."

Mother lowered her head but went on. "But your children," she said. "Will you let them starve because of this new bastard of yours? What kind of man are you?"

Grandfather stirred uneasily in the gloom behind her. He made a drawn-out, whimpering noise that sounded more like an animal than a human. He lay with his eyes closed, his breathing labored.

Father had narrowed his eyes to slits, and the rage and vodka made his face ruddy in the light from the oven. Olga was afraid now. It seemed like an eternity since he had sat on the veranda outside the house in Kharkiv and called Olga his "most highborn princess" and Mother "the most beautiful flower in the field."

Now he was a person she didn't know at all, and she realized that there was also more than one truth about her father. The man who loves and smiles one day can hate the next. Turn your back for a moment, and feelings will change and flow in new directions.

"*Tatko*," she whispered and grabbed hold of his hand. But he didn't notice her.

"I have been man enough for you," he hissed. "Now I am man for another woman, and I cannot support two families. It's hard enough with one."

Mother's face distorted in a terrible grimace. "You're lying," she said. "I know how much you have put aside over time. Jewelry from your mother. My silk shawls from town and my sewing machine. At least give me those things, Andreij, so I can take care of your children."

Father stepped forward and raised his hand. Even though he lowered it without striking, Olga knew that Jana had been right. He had chosen the widow and the new child, and she and Kolja and Oxana were nothing to him.

WHEN HE HAD left, they sat for a long time in the silent gloom. Then Oxana finally got up and began to get ready to go out again.

"Where are you going?" Mother's voice was flat and low, as if she were speaking from the bottom of a grave.

"To school," said Oxana. "There's something I have to discuss with Comrade Semienova."

THE DOORBELL'S SYNTHETIC ding-ding hammered at Søren's eardrum. He had a confused sense that it wasn't the first ring but perhaps even the fifth or sixth. He had been going through Babko's case files, both the official ones and the unofficial USB-key, until almost one o'clock, when he had had to admit that he couldn't think straight any longer.

He tumbled out of bed, still with a heavy sensation of sleep and unreality weighing down his body, and lifted the shade a bit so he could see who it was ringing his bell at whatever hour it was in the night.

An adult and a child. They were both bundled up in down jackets and scarves, and it was probably more a sense of inevitability than actual recognition that made him conclude that it had to be Nina Borg and the girl. What was her name? Katerina?

He looked down at himself. Bare, middle-aged legs and boxer shorts. Where was that robe Susse had given him for Christmas? He grabbed a pair of sweatpants instead and pulled them on over his hairy legs.

He turned on the light in the hall and the entranceway. Through the flecked glass of his front door the figures were just vague silhouettes, but he had been right. It was Nina holding the hand of a skinny blonde girl. The girl was clutching a pink backpack.

"You were in the phone book," said Nina. "Your address and everything. I didn't think that was allowed when you were in the PET."

"It doesn't say than I *am* in the PET," he said, feeling stupid with sleep and thoroughly unprepared. But despite the untimely invasion, he was glad to see her. "Come in."

"They don't know I'm here," she said.

"Who?"

"The police." She looked at him and corrected herself. "That is, the other police."

"What happened?"

"He tried to kidnap Rina."

"He?"

She gestured impatiently with her hand. "Someone. Not Natasha. Someone who uses gas grenades and infrared goggles."

He took a deep breath. "What happened to the guards?" he asked.

"They . . . one was taken away in an ambulance. Because of the gas. A very young man. They say it's critical, that he might die. He stopped breathing. He is under observation for brain damage. I took Rina and locked us into the walk-in refrigerator. Otherwise they would have taken her. Or rather, he would have. I didn't see more than one person."

Her eyes were huge. She was speaking calmly even though her sentences weren't quite coherent. She looked peculiarly happy, like someone who has said all along that it would end badly and finally has been proven right.

"They still think it's just Natasha," she said; this time she apparently meant the police. "They don't understand that Rina is in danger. But . . . you do. Am I right?"

"Maybe," he said. He wouldn't give her too much.

"You have to help me protect her," she said. "Will you?"

The words came out all edgy and awkward. He sensed that she didn't often ask for help.

"At least come in and have some breakfast," he said. "I have to call my boss. You understand that, right?"

A cop killing. If the young policeman died, it would be a cop killing. No one would condone Nina's disappearing act then. But when he looked at the little Ukrainian girl, about to collapse and breathing like a leaky balloon, he couldn't quite blame her.

"Is he . . . not an idiot either?" she asked.

He wasn't quite sure if Torben, with his adherence to rules and career focus, would be able to live up to her definition of non-idiocy. "He usually knows what's what," he said. "And he's super smart."

"Okay," she said, as if he needed her permission.

To be woken up in the middle of the night—or in this case, at a quarter to five on Sunday morning—was of course a part of the job for a man like Torben, but that didn't necessarily mean he liked it.

"What is it now?" he said shortly.

"Everything has gone pear-shaped," said Søren quickly. "Someone tried to kidnap the daughter from the Coal-House Camp, and one of the men from the guard detail is in intensive care. They say his life is in danger."

There was silence for a few seconds.

"Could it be the girl's mother?" asked Torben.

"It was a man. Of course you can't exclude the possibility that it was at the mother's request. But I'm calling because the girl is sitting in my kitchen right now with Nina Borg. And no one else knows."

"For fuck's sake, Søren. Why?"

"Because Nina is convinced that the girl would be in imminent danger if she stayed in the camp."

"That woman is hostile to authority and borderline paranoid," said

Torben. "How on earth did she manage to walk off with the kid without anyone noticing?"

"I haven't asked yet. But I would like you to contact our colleagues and explain to them that we are planning to provide Katerina Doroshenko with the necessary personal protection."

"Søren, I can't do that. Especially not if they have a dead colleague on their hands!"

"Maybe precisely for that reason. The girl's safety is not their priority. They just want to get hold of the perpetrator and Natasha Doroshenko—and that's not necessarily the same thing."

"Do you know something? Or are you just guessing?"

"The original Ukrainian case against Natasha Doroshenko, that is, the killing of her husband, is based primarily on two circumstantials: the fact that she fled the country, and a confession from a violent criminal who claims that she paid him to attack Doroshenko."

"That latter is perhaps more than circumstantial."

"Torben. It's Ukraine. You can extract confessions like that in so many ways."

"Okay. I hear what you are saying. But who is 'you' in this case, and why would 'you' do so?"

Søren tried to structure his argument before answering. "The Ukrainian policemen who originally came up here to interrogate Natasha are from two different services—as you know, Lieutenant Babko is from GUBOZ. His colleague, a Colonel Savchuk, is from SBU."

"Hold on," said Torben. There was a creaking, followed by footsteps and the sound of a door being closed carefully. Torben had left the bedroom, Søren guessed, in order not to wake Annelise and to be able to speak freely.

"GUBOZ *and* SBU," said his boss thoughtfully. "You have to ask yourself why they are interested in Natasha Doroshenko."

"Precisely. Especially when one of them disappears without a word to anyone, apparently blindsiding his GUBOZ colleague completely. A colleague who was sent up here specifically to keep an eye on him."

"What do you mean?"

As briefly as possible, Søren told Torben about Babko's admissions and about the connection between Savchuk and Nikolaij Filipenko, Babko's "clean man." "Unfortunately, I think Nina Borg's concern for the girl's safety is well justified."

"Because of Savchuk?"

"I have no grounds for claiming that. Not at the moment. One might equally well argue that Savchuk is missing because during his search for Natasha Doroshenko, he got in the way of the person or persons who attacked the Coal-House Camp."

"But you don't believe that?"

"Right now I don't believe anything. The closest I can come to a theory is that everything is connected to the killing of Pavel Doroshenko."

"Mmm." Torben had the habit of humming inarticulately when he was thinking something he wasn't saying. "Go on."

"It's speculation."

"Go on anyway."

"Doroshenko was a journalist."

"Yes."

"I've looked through his articles. He published a good deal of controversial material with sensitive personal content."

"Okay."

"Presumably you remember the Gongadze case?"

"The journalist. The headless corpse, which they at first tried to avoid identifying. When they couldn't get away with that any longer, it came out that the murder was committed on the orders of the interior minister, what was his name . . ."

"Kravchenko."

"Yes. Him. He got the journalist eliminated because he wrote critically about the administration's abuse of freedom of speech and civil rights, wasn't that the way it was?"

"More or less. Four officers from the SBU were sentenced for the murder, and the investigation of who gave the order stopped with the death of Kravchenko. He was found with two bullet holes in the head a few hours before he was to due to be interrogated by the public prosecutor, and Oleksandr Turchinov, Savchuk's boss in the SBU, closed the case with a declaration that Kravchenko had committed suicide."

"Very convenient."

"Yes. Of course, it *is* theoretically possible the first wound wasn't fatal and the suicide candidate was very determined, but . . ."

"It's pretty rare for people to shoot themselves in the head twice," said Torben dryly.

"Precisely. I'm not saying that Pavel Doroshenko is another Gongadze; I don't have any proof of that. But what if . . . what if he was killed by someone in the system either because they were hired to do so or because they were protecting one of their own? Then you can't really find fault with Natasha's decision to leave the country in a hurry."

"And where in this speculative scenario do you place Colonel Savchuk and his brother the politician?"

"Half brother. I don't know. I have no idea whether Savchuk is a hero or a villain in this." Among Doroshenko's articles there had been nothing about Nikolaij Filipenko, his half brother or their mother. Nothing that tied Savchuk to the case. "It's hard to get a sense of the relationship between the two brothers. There's such a great distance between them age-wise and . . . historically. Savchuk was born in the postwar years with a supposedly 'unknown' father, an army brat who himself made a career of the military. From what little I've been able to dig up on him, it seems he was with the Russians in nineteen seventy-nine when they moved into Afghanistan. Later he joined the KGB and just continued on to the SBU after the Independence. A bit of a Cold War dinosaur, it looks like, but there are a surprising number of those in that part of the world, and a wise man doesn't turn his back on them. Filipenko, on the other hand, was born in nineteen seventy-two. A completely different life—glasnost, perestrojka, independence. And it looks like a completely different personal life as well—the mother had at that point married a man who was somewhat younger than her, an engineer who later became a diplomat under Gorbachev. There are a number of foreign postings, two years of boarding school in England, engineering studies because he apparently wanted to follow in his father's footsteps, then soccer hero status, which he begins to turn into a political career in the late nineties. Apparently Filipenko is a humane, well-intentioned, decent man who wishes to get to the bottom of corruption in his country. What Savchuk is . . . That's more of an open question. And until now there was no other connection to Pavel Doroshenko than his energetic efforts to get the widow extradited to Ukraine."

"What does your friend Babko say?"

"He doesn't know either. He has given me a lot of material that I am trying to understand. Among other things I have a sense there is a pattern to the articles Doroshenko published, but I can't quite make the pieces fit together. I would like to speak with Babko again. But first I want to solve the problem I have sitting in my kitchen."

A pause. He could hear the refrigerator door open and the sound of something being poured into a glass. Tomato juice, if he knew Torben. Once in a while the juice was accompanied by Tabasco, ice and vodka, but not now, not when there was work to be done.

"Are you really convinced that the girl is in danger, and it's not just her mother who has tried to get hold of her?" his boss asked.

"If that was your daughter, would you have used gas? A grown man almost died from it. Would you risk it with your daughter—when that daughter suffers from severe asthma attacks?"

There was a swallowing sound as Torben took a sip of his juice. "No," he said. "I wouldn't. I would go as far as to say that it certainly doesn't sound like the mother has had complete control over the person or persons responsible for the attack."

"Then you agree that the girl is in danger."

A sigh. "Yes. That would follow. But listen. You know exactly how Heide and her people will react if we just waltz in there and take things over."

Søren was well aware of the tensions between the PET and the other divisions of the police. It was not the PET's primary job to make sure that those who committed criminal acts were taken to court and sentenced, and there were times when a prosecution would directly interfere with the security concerns of the PET. Once, in 1988, that schism had even cost the life of a young policeman, and the wounds still ached.

He could understand Heide's resistance and her fear that the PET's involvement might make it more difficult to construct a case.

"I'll call Heide," said Torben. "But only to make your collaboration easier. You're going to have to work it out between you. We have to make her feel safe. Make her understand that we want to help, not obstruct."

"And can personal protection of Katerina Doroshenko be a part of that help?"

"What level were you thinking of?"

"First, that the girl doesn't have to go back to the Coal-House Camp or any other place where she is easy to find."

"Okay. I think I can sell that—on the condition that they have access to both Borg and the girl when they are needed for questioning. But are you imagining an actual safe house?"

"If that's possible. Wouldn't that also make Heide feel safer, knowing Natasha Doroshenko would have a very hard time getting hold of the girl? She's unlikely to try to leave the country as long as the girl is here."

Torben snorted. "I can try. Okay. You stay where you are for the time being. I'll call when I have something for you. And keep a close eye on that paranoid nurse of yours, okay? We don't want her to give us the slip."

THE PARANOID NURSE sat at the little table in the kitchen with her head against the wall. Her eyes were closed, and Søren guessed she was close to nodding off if she wasn't asleep already, despite the hardness of the chair. She was still wearing her coat, and a little pool of water was spreading around her boots as the snow stuck in the treads melted.

The girl, on the other hand, was wide awake. She didn't look at him directly, but there was a guarded glitter from behind her lowered eyelashes.

He squatted down in front of her. "Are you hungry?" he asked her in Russian.

He saw Nina jolt and open her eyes. The child just shook her head. "Sleepy?"

A single nod.

"*Proshoo,*" she whispered then. "*De tut tualet?*"

"It's right out here in the hall," he said, still in Russian. "Do you want me to show you?"

She got up, still holding the backpack tightly. He didn't try to get her to put it down. Nina sat completely still and observed them with a carefully neutral expression. She didn't interfere with his attempts to make contact.

He showed the slight girl to the bathroom and turned on the light for her. Built-in halogen spots threw shiny reflections back from shiny black granite tiles and lacquered white cabinets. There were no calming bath toys and happy frogs on the shower curtain or anything else that might make a child feel at home, but at least it had just been cleaned, so hopefully it smelled more of Vim than of urine.

"Thank you," Rina said politely. She was clearly waiting for him to leave.

He closed the door but remained outside for a moment, listening. She didn't lock it, he was happy to note. He had no desire to deal with a child who had barricaded herself in his bathroom, either on purpose or accidentally—his six-year-old nephew had once gone into a panic when he couldn't unlock the door.

She stayed in there for a while. He let her be and went back to the kitchen to offer Nina a cup of coffee.

"That's unusual," she said.

"That I offer coffee?"

"No, that Rina speaks to someone she doesn't know."

"Maybe it was because I spoke Russian."

"Yes. Maybe. What did your boss say?"

"He's going to call me back. But we're trying to get you a safe house. Do you know what that entails?"

"Kind of . . . well, not really."

"Milk?"

"No, thank you."

"It can be more or less institutional, with more or less in the way of surveillance and guards, depending on how we evaluate the level of threat. The most important thing for Rina's safety right now, in my opinion, is that we make her hard to find. That's the best protection we can give her."

Nina put both her hands around the mug of instant coffee that he handed her. She sniffed the scent as if it were perfume. "So she's not going back to the camp?"

"No. Not if we can help it."

"I knew you weren't an idiot," she said and flashed him something that was more of a relieved grimace than a real smile.

"A few ground rules," he said. "If you haven't done so already, you need to turn off your cell phone. You can't use it. In fact, I'd prefer if you gave it to me." Søren didn't know what resources his adversary could draw on—if the adversary was Colonel Savchuk, with his rank and standing in the GPU, it was probably a considerable amount. Tracking a cell phone was not, these days, a PET monopoly, more was the pity.

"Okay." She must have figured out why, because she didn't ask any questions. She just fished her phone out of her pocket and handed it to him, meek as a lamb. Would wonders never cease?

"Does Rina have a telephone?"

"No."

"Good. Where is your car?"

"I parked it a few streets away. It's pretty recognizable."

"Good thinking. Do you have any sense of whether you were seen when you left the camp?"

"It's hard to say. Everything was still pretty chaotic. But if the deputy chief and her troops had seen me, I guess they would have stopped me."

She cleared perceived the police as the enemy. Again, Søren experienced that odd, don't-let-her-fly-away sensation mixed with a dose of wonder that she was sitting here. That she trusted him at least that far.

"Until we have the opportunity to move you to a more secure location, this is your safe house," he said. "That means that neither you nor Rina may leave the house—not even to go outside to smoke or anything like that."

"I don't smoke."

He considered the situation. The house was neither more nor less secure against break-ins than any other suburban house—or secure against escape, for that matter. It was easy for Torben to tell him not to let Nina wander off, but in reality there wasn't a whole lot he could do if she really wanted to leave. Not without restraining her physically—and wouldn't that be a fine thing for the fragile trust he hoped they were establishing?

"Would Rina understand if we tell her she has to stay here? That it's dangerous to go out?"

Nina hesitated. "Rina has lived in the Coal-House Camp for a long time now," she said. "She understands about rules. But . . ."

"But?"

"She really just wants to be with her mother. So if Natasha finds us, Rina is gone. You can bet on that."

"Do you think that Natasha would recognize your car?"

"It's not the same one that I had when she was in the camp. No, I don't think so."

At least Nina had been smart enough not to park it in the driveway, but his own professional paranoia would have preferred it to be even farther away.

He got up and went into the hall. Listened at the bathroom door.

The girl was talking to someone.

He stopped breathing for a moment to listen better.

"Are you coming soon, *Tatko?*" Søren could just barely make out the soft, quiet child's voice through the door. "We miss you. And Mom is . . . Mom is in the kitchen making poppy seed cakes. Guests are coming. Anna is coming. And Great-Grandmother. Oh, it would be *so* nice if you could come too. You *are* coming? Oh, that's good. Three o'clock. Kiss, kiss. I love you!"

Tatko. He was fairly sure it meant "father," even though it wasn't something a Russian child would say.

He quietly opened the door. Rina was sitting on the toilet, but on the lid, holding a cell phone up to her ear.

"Who are you talking to?" he asked.

She stiffened. "No one," she whispered almost inaudibly.

"May I see your phone?"

She held it tightly against her chest for a few seconds. "It's mine."

"Yes. I just need to have a look at it."

Rina handed it over reluctantly. Her breathing abruptly became even worse, wheeze in, wheeze out, a labored and uneven rhythm.

The cell phone was turned off. Dead. It was an old model, at least five or six years old. The display had a thin black crack across the upper left-hand corner; the back cover was cracked too, and absolutely nothing happened when he tried to turn it on. Presumably it hadn't worked for a long time.

He handed it to the girl. "Thank you for letting me see it."

She quickly put it away in her backpack.

Dear God, he thought.

"Who gave it to you?" he asked.

She didn't answer. Just stared at him, blankly and fearfully, gnawing at her lower lip as if she were trying to eat it.

"Your Tatko?"

She nodded. An almost invisible nod.

"I can see why you treasure it," he said.

NINA SCRUTINIZED THE young man who sat in Søren's kitchen. He was tapping away with concentration on some kind of cell phone/computer hybrid. Not an iPad—she knew what they looked like, at least, because Ida wanted one. This was something more exotic. The man's powerful jaw worked ceaselessly, giving a little irritating click with every chew, and a pack of nicotine gum peeked out of his breast pocket. Nina didn't really think he looked like a PET-man. He certainly didn't look like Søren. And he *wasn't* Søren, a fact that irritated her even more than his constant cud chewing.

She had slept for a few hours in Søren's guest room with Rina nestled against her. The sleep had been amazingly dream free. Even though she had been so tired her whole body buzzed with exhaustion, Nina hadn't expected to fall asleep so quickly and so deeply. Søren had had to shake her shoulder lightly to wake her up.

"I didn't want to just leave you," he'd said. "This is Mikael Nielsen. He'll be on watch for the next six or seven hours."

Nina was taken aback. She hadn't expected Søren would personally hold her hand twenty-four/seven; of course he would have other things to do too, and it was pretty generous of him just to provide his house. But the cud-chewing young man didn't seem an especially committed or confidence-inspiring replacement, and all her defenses rose up anew. The few questions she had tried to ask him were answered monosyllabically without him raising his gaze from his electronic thing even once. It was hard to determine if he suffered from what the Coal-House psychologist called "communicative issues" or whether it was just professional distance. One thing was certain—Rina would not begin to chat cozily with *him*. Especially not after he had insisted on taking away her security blanket cell phone to be *completely* sure it didn't work.

Nina was still amazed that Rina had spoken to Søren. Yes, he had an advantage because he could speak Russian with her. But that wasn't all. There was something solid about him. Quiet but immovable. Apparently his Paul Newman–like aura also worked wonders on traumatized eight-year-old girls.

She went back to the living room, where Rina was now lying on the couch with a comforter around her, her face turned toward the television screen. Little Japanese figures, looking to Nina primitively drawn or at least very stylized, raced by in a melee of explosions. Rina's eyes were almost shut. Nina debated whether she could get away with turning off the television but decided not to. It would be good if Rina fell asleep again—she needed it.

9:26.

Still an hour and thirty-four minutes to go until she would get to see Anton. The school carnival began at 11:00.

Rina was still clutching her backpack. The by now somewhat grubby mini Diddl mouse attached to the zipper appeared to be staring at Nina with supersized eyes. Nina wanted to hug the girl, silly stuffed mouse backpack and all, but she knew it was her own need and not the child's.

9:28. Morten might already be helping Anton with his costume. This year Nina hadn't been the one left with the choice between spending a fortune at the toy store or spending a weekend creating a costume. Anton usually had firm opinions about what he wanted to be. She remembered the year he insisted on being a traffic light—in terms of costume construction one of the easier options—it could basically be produced from a cardboard box, a couple of mini flashlights and some silk paper. But he had had a ball running around and yelling, "Stop! Red light!" to innocent passersby.

This year she had been left completely out of the loop. Morten hadn't even told her when the carnival was; she had had to track down that information herself on the school's intranet page.

She went back into the kitchen, where she had a better view of the street outside. Magnus would be here soon. He had promised to stand in for her so that there would still be someone familiar there for Rina. When she entered the room, the cud-chewing ceased for a moment or two before the PET guy lowered his gaze and continued tapping on his not-quite-an-iPad.

There was a faint noise from the living room. It was barely audible through the sound effects from the cartoon, but still reached Nina's Rina radar. She listened to Rina's whispering voice. For more than two years, she had seen and heard Rina use the broken cell phone. Not until yesterday had she seriously begun to worry whether it was something other than a game—perhaps a somewhat obsessive game, but still a game. Never in all that time had she guessed that what Rina was really doing was talking to her dead father.

Blind. Deaf. Dumb. How could Nina *not* have seen it? It made her wonder how well she actually understood the traumatized people who surrounded her. Maybe she wasn't really any better at solving their problems than at handling her own.

The thought gave her a hollow feeling inside. Her entire adult life, she had seen herself as someone you could count on when the going got tough. Someone who "made a difference"—that worn phrase used about everything from people who sorted their garbage and once in a while took the bus to those who went on dangerous, potentially deadly peacekeeping missions. She knew that she *had* been party to saving lives, to improving them. The cost had been her own family.

Or not quite.

It wasn't quite that black and white, she did realize that. Morten would probably have been able to live with the fact that she had a job that consumed her, that sometimes demanded so much of her that there was too little left for him—and sometimes too little even for Ida and Anton. That wasn't why he had ended it.

It was because she always had to go right up to the edge—and then take one more step. Because she, in his words, had transformed her life into a war zone. It wasn't enough to take an extra shift at the Coal-House Camp and attempt to help the people shipwrecked there. She had promised not to go on missions abroad anymore, and she had kept that promise. Instead, she had committed herself to aiding people Danish society considered "illegals." The ones who couldn't go to the emergency room or see a doctor, the ones who couldn't go to the police when they were the victims of crimes. People like Natasha who had to accept squalor or abuse, either because they had no choice or because almost anything was better than being sent back where they came from.

She was *good* at it. In a crisis situation she was calmly efficient, perfectly able to act, to think, to do something. She missed that capable version of herself when things became too humdrum. For Christmas this year Ida had given her a T-shirt she had managed to get hold of from some ad campaign extolling the virtues of public transportation; it was bright green and had the words WORLD SAVIOR printed in big letters across the chest.

Nina wasn't stupid. She had done therapy, and she knew perfectly well where it came from, this compulsion to save the ones no one else wanted to bother with. She could say precisely, to the minute, when it had begun: the day she had run home from school during the lunch break and had found her father in the bathroom in the basement.

She forced herself to remember. Consciously, dispassionately. *Don't avoid it. Confront it.* Water on the floor. Blood on the floor. Blood in the water. Her father lying in the water with all his clothes on, turning his head slightly to look at her with eyes that resembled those of a fish. That far she could go.

It was the hour following that she couldn't account for. No matter how hard she tried, all she could remember was going next door to get help. Right away. *I went over there right away.* She had repeated it again and again to the police, to the therapists, to the doctors and all the other grown-ups, even though they all kept on telling her that it couldn't be true. She remembered how frustrated she was that they wouldn't believe her, that they tried to make her accept their correct, adult, superior understanding of time and place. And the ugly, world-swallowing vortex she found herself floundering in when she began to realize that they were right. Almost an hour *had* passed between the moment when she went down into the basement and the moment when she came up again. And during that hour, her father had died.

Morten knew, of course. For many years he had understood, condoned, shielded and protected when she would allow him to do so. He knew the gap was there and what it cost her not to fall into it. What he couldn't accept was that their children also had to live on the edge of that abyss.

She listened to Rina's whispering voice and did not interrupt. Let the girl speak with her father, she thought. Who am I to tell her that she's wrong, that the phone doesn't work, that her father can no longer hear her and is never coming back?

When Nina had the sense that Rina was saying goodbye, she stepped into the living room. And it was only then that she saw that the phone Rina was speaking into wasn't the broken cell phone but the landline on Søren's desk.

"Who were you speaking to?" she asked.

Rina started. "No one."

Who did Rina even know that she would think of calling? Someone at the Coal-House Camp? Natasha? Rina had been speaking Ukrainian, but how on earth could she have gotten a number that would connect her with her mother?

"Was it . . . your father?"

Rina shrugged and bowed her head. "It doesn't work anymore," she said.

"Why not?"

"It's broken. He said so. The policeman."

Nina went over to the phone and pressed REDIAL. The telephone rang five, six, seven times. Then a friendly man's voice said, "You've reached Anna and Hans Henrik Olesen. We can't come to the phone right now, but leave a message, and we'll call you back."

Hans Henrik Olesen? She had never heard of the man and she couldn't figure out how Rina knew him.

But maybe Rina didn't know him. Maybe she had pressed the numbers randomly or called one of the numbers in the phone's memory.

"Rina. It's important. Were you trying to call your father?"

Rina stood there for a moment, gasping with her mouth open, and Nina was sorry to have pushed her. The girl's narrow face puckered and distorted as if she was going to cry, but no tears came.

"I just want to talk to him," she said at last, and the air wheezed in and out of her lungs, worse and worse, it seemed to Nina. "I miss him so."

So do I, thought Nina. How could he do that to us?

She put her arms around the girl, this time not caring whose need she was responding to. Rina felt light as a bird in her arms, a small, damp burden weighing less than it ought.

The time was now 9:42.

THEY CAME FOR Father in the beginning of December, and he didn't have time to say goodbye to anyone besides Vladimir Petrenko and the widow.

It was Jana who was able to report it in school, and maybe she did feel a little sorry for Olga, after all, because she let Olga sit next to her on the steps while the children gathered around her during the break.

"He was yelling and screaming all the way down to the crossroads," said Jana. "And Svetlova, big as a house, came waddling after on bare feet and tried to hit one of the GPUs with a log. Like this."

Jana got up and ran with heavy, spread legs over the lumpy, frost-covered ground, screaming, "Oh, oh," holding her stomach with one hand and swinging an imaginary piece of firewood in the other. The others laughed, and Jana happily repeated the performance a few times before she tired of the applause and stopped, cheeks glowing and feet apart. Her breath emerged in a white cloud from her mouth.

"Did they hit him?"

Olga thought Jegor looked almost eager. Her stomach had tied itself into a hard knot, and the air she breathed into her lungs was so cold, it seemed to make her chest freeze solid.

Jana didn't answer right away but remained standing, scratching her hair thoughtfully. She had lice, Olga observed. Jana's mother had

had a fever and a cough for the last two weeks and had not had the strength to comb Jana and her little sister with the lice comb the way she usually did. Even at this distance Olga could see the big, fat creatures crawling around in Jana's pale hair and was secretly pleased. Maybe that would teach her to lie about Olga's body lice. But it still hurt all the way down into the pit of her stomach. In the old days, she would have offered to crack the lice for Jana during recess, but now Jana would just have to crack them herself, if she could catch them.

"I think they did hit him once with the rifle," said Jana then. "Across the back of the neck. Afterward, he did what they told him to, even though he kept screaming."

"Too bad."

The boys had hoped for more, Olga could see. They had played Capitalists and Communists all recess long, and the capitalists had been beaten as usual. It was clear, they said, that Andreij should have been beaten much more severely for his crimes. As head of the kolkhoz, he had not only protected the kulaks, who should have been deported long ago, he had also ignored several thefts from the state's grain stores, even though the thieves had been caught. Those kinds of thefts could be punished with deportation or even death, but Andreij had openly flouted the law and neglected to report the episode to the GPU. He had even accepted a young mother who had been classified as a Former Human Being into the collective farm and had fed her kulak children through all of last winter.

In his house he had hidden several things that made him a class enemy. The GPUs had dragged both Mother's sewing machine and a silver candelabra from the house, and the widow Svetlova had brazenly worn a zobel fur and had owned two big copper pots. Even one would have been a conspicuous luxury; two copper pots was a clear crime against the people, who had toiled in the mines to bring up precious metal for the industry.

The boys then tried to guess where Andreij would spend his time in deportation. Obdorsk, or Beresovo, or maybe Samarovo. The farther north it was, the worse it would be. People got gangrene and lost arms and legs in the Siberian cold, and that was true both for those who ended up in a prison camp and for the more fortunate ones who were deported but allowed to live as free men. Letters from Siberia were full of horrors.

For the widow, it was a different matter, or so Jegor claimed. True, she had been forced to depart in woolen socks and without either zobel fur or overcoat, thrown out on her ass and ordered to find a place to live outside the village. She had a bad record now, but she probably had an old mother someplace with whom she could seek shelter from the winter cold for her unborn child.

Olga sat stock-still, picking at her felt boots and trying not to think the incomprehensible. Her father wasn't a class enemy, and she didn't understand how it had come to be that he was one anyway. It wasn't easy either, to figure out why some of those who had been deported were to be pitied while others apparently were getting what they deserved. Every day offered new truths that grated against one another inside her head, as painfully as sharp stones under one's feet. The others seemed to have no problem understanding. Self-confident Jana, Jegor and Leda and Oxana, yes, even Sergej, that little shit, knew when you were supposed to smile proudly and when you had to duck your head in shame. Knew which truths you should grab on to and which ones you should let go.

Old truth: Olga's father is Andreij Trofimenko, a trusted man in the village, a loving father and a loyal husband.

New truth: Olga's father is Andreij Trofimenko, class enemy and traitor, deportee and Former Human Being, a lousy father and deceitful husband.

Unwelcome pictures began to swim past her inner eye, even

though she bit herself hard in the cheek and tried to think about the soy candy from Petrograd that Comrade Semienova had offered Oxana and her last week.

Her father living in a hole in the ground like the ones the Former Human Beings dug among the birch trees up in the hills. His hands that had split the year's first melon two summers ago in the garden of their little townhouse . . . in her imagination, those same hands were now black and stinking with gangrene, even as he held the sparkling red fruit between his fingers.

"Eat, my lovely," said Father and handed the melon to her while he smiled with a toothless mouth. His nose was as black as his fingers, and he smelled of rotting flesh and vodka.

"I feel sorry for the baby," Veronica said and shook her head sadly. In the battle against the kulaks and the capitalists, she had had a passionate skirmish with Sergej and had her kerchief pulled down over her shoulders. "That a mother would do that to her child."

"Save your pity," drawled Jegor. "The brat isn't even born yet, and maybe Svetlova still has time to go to a doctor in Kharkiv, and that's the end of that, and nothing will ever hurt it again."

"Shut up."

Olga knew she should keep her mouth shut, but the words shot out. Her voice broke, sounding stupid and babyish. She wished Oxana was here, but Oxana was in the kolkhoz, arranging yet another political meeting, and now Jana looked at her with a mixture of pity and glee.

"What's wrong? I thought you didn't like Svetlova."

Olga shrugged, got up and quickly brushed off her dress. Her fingers were red and numb because she had left her mittens in the schoolroom, and she had forgotten to hide her hands in her coat sleeves. Right now she couldn't feel them, but when she went inside, her fingers would hurt, and the skin would split and itch. To her amazement, Jana brought her face so close to Olga's that their foreheads almost touched, and Olga had time to think that now she would definitely get lice.

"You better watch out for yourself," whispered Jana. "Your father may be a class enemy, Olga, but your traitor sister has blood on her hands now. Her own family's blood. If I were you, I would watch my back around her."

NATASHA PULLED HER coat closer to her body and glanced at her watch. It was almost eleven, and she had been sitting on the steps here for an hour and a half already, but she didn't dare leave now. Not even to find a place to pee, though it was starting to feel pretty urgent. If she left . . . if she as much as looked away for a moment . . .

She had found the street; she was sure this was it. The little corner store, the miserable-looking birch trees along Jagtvejen's median strip. It was here. But the houses looked more alike than she had remembered. The same worn red-brick fronts, the same anonymous brown doors. There was no ugly yellow car parked on the street, and she had looked at all the intercoms without finding Nina's name. But sooner or later they had to come out, Nina or the husband or the children, and then she could ask. Then she would make them tell her where Katerina was.

She had pulled the hood of Robbie's grey sweatshirt over her head in order not to be recognized. It would have been better to sit in the Audi, but cars lined the street bumper to bumper, and she had had to park elsewhere. What would they think, the Danes inside their apartments, if they looked out their windows and saw her now? Would they think that she was homeless, like one of those people who periodically froze to death during Kiev's cold winters in a stairwell like the one she was huddling in now?

She had been surprised that there were also homeless people in Denmark. More, it seemed, than in Kiev. But maybe that was because there were fewer police. In Copenhagen there weren't two policemen on every other corner. Here people could camp out in peace and quiet with their bags and packs and cardboard to sit on. Was that what she looked like? She was beginning to smell that way, that was for sure.

BEAUTIFUL, BEAUTIFUL NATASHA.

That was her, and of course that was what Pavel had fallen for, even though he said back then that it was her eyes and her smile, quite simply *her* that he had fallen in love with.

He spoiled her and treated her like a lady. He brought her to the expensive stores in the mall under Independence Square and discussed what suited her best with the salespeople while Natasha stood there without saying anything, because if she opened her mouth, they would be able to tell that she wasn't from Kiev. The clothes were different from the ones she would have bought herself. Narrow skirts that reached her knees. Soft silk blouses and white shirts and glittering bracelets, wide belts and high-heeled shoes. Classic, he said, because Natasha was a "classic beauty." He said the same thing to the hairdresser, who apparently felt duty bound to tell her how much eyeliner and mascara it was appropriate to use in Kiev. What she was wearing was too much and too cheap, and had a tendency to clump on the lashes. And the lipstick should not be pink and glossy.

"You're not in Donetsk any longer, honey," the lady had said and told her about Dior and Elizabeth Arden and other companies she had never heard of. Then she had cut Natasha's hair shorter than she'd ever had it before, to her shoulders, and with new sharp angles and waves. The color was fine as it was—like a Ukrainian wheat field, with touches of brown and gold.

"From now on, you need to come see me every third week, honey. Or there'll be trouble. Hair like yours can look like a million dollars if you take care of it."

Pavel kissed the new hair and new color on her lips and said that she was completely perfect.

Only much later did she realize that he also loved her for her ignorance—all the things she didn't know about him, about the world. He loved her because she was beautiful and dumb, *because* she was seventeen and came from Kurakhovo. A woman from Kiev, a woman his own age, would have asked more questions. Natasha didn't question. She only loved. She loved him, she loved the apartment, she loved that he went to work every day and wrote in the newspapers about important topics and spoke with important people.

She kept the apartment so clean that everything shone. She changed the sheets every day, like in a hotel. And she cooked the way he wanted her to. Traditional, he called it. Beautiful braided paska bread for the holidays, borscht, cabbage rolls and little pancakes with fried farmers' cheese, honey and sour cream, jam or apple sauce. In return he took care of her. She didn't need to work in a dirty factory or stand in the unemployment line. Katerina was born in a private hospital with brilliant white towels in the bathroom; a drip of clear anesthesia was inserted into Natasha's spine and took away all pain and worries. To Natasha, that had been the final proof back then that her life really was a fairy tale, so far removed from those girls from Kurakhovo, who, in the coming years, would be lying on rusty hospital beds with dirty covers, bellowing like cows as they brought their children into the world in a flood of shit and blood and torn placenta.

Pavel held her hand through every single contraction, because that was what men did in Kiev, at least the educated ones. And when Katerina finally lay in her arms, Pavel looked at her with so much tenderness that it was almost more than she could bear.

Beautiful, beautiful, stupid Natasha.

She didn't know it then, but she had learned it now.

In this world, you were punished for your stupidity, and you were punished hard. That was just as true in Copenhagen as it was in Kiev.

IT WAS COLD sitting on the steps, but it still felt more natural than standing. She would have liked to have a smoke, a refugee habit she had picked up in the camp and which had intensified in prison. Cigarettes were fantastic props during life in captivity because they gave you the feeling that you were doing something other than just waiting. You pulled smoke into your lungs and blew it out again, and you turned the cigarette in your hand and looked at it while it got smaller and smaller.

A door opened, and for a brief moment, Natasha thought she saw Nina's slender figure step out onto the sidewalk. It was the same impatient toss of the head, the same quivering energy in the body, but it was still wrong. This was not a woman but a girl in skinny jeans, basketball sneakers and a heavy leather jacket. A boy followed in a baggy ski jacket and an eye-catching black mustache taped to his upper lip. And then finally a man that Natasha recognized with certainty as Nina's husband, even though he somehow had become thinner and older looking—dark eyes and a broad jaw under a black cap. He was dressed like a teenager in worn pale jeans and a yellow down jacket. He must be forty, thought Natasha, but Danish men dressed like boys, not men.

Michael had been an exception, of course. He preferred classic shirts and dark pants and expensive jackets that had to be dry-cleaned and pressed and steamed, and somehow she always managed to get it wrong so that he got angry or irritated. Maybe her life would have looked completely different if she had met a boy-man like Nina's husband instead. If someone like him had lived in the house next to

Anna's farm. Natasha doubted that Nina's husband had ever touched the nurse in a way she didn't like. If he had, Nina would probably have exited both the bedroom and the apartment and slammed the door behind her. That was a luxury Natasha had not been able to afford.

Nina's husband, son and daughter walked toward her without noticing her. The boy wore lurid electric-blue pants and a pair of ludicrously oversized shoes that would barely stay on. Still, he had that energy in his feet which she recognized from the boys at home. He kicked stones, balanced on the curb and made small, energetic jumps to smack a flat hand against the traffic signs.

She got up, went over to them. Attempted to smile.

"Is Nina home?" she asked in her best Danish. After more than two years, she understood most things, but Danish words still felt like slippery stones in her mouth—foreign objects that didn't belong.

"Why?" The man gave her a cool, measuring look.

Maybe Nina had asked him to be on guard. Maybe she had said he should keep his mouth shut and not reveal where Katerina was.

"Katerina," she said anyway and stood her ground, blocking their way on the sidewalk. "Tell me where my daughter is, please," she said in English.

The boy with the big black mustache stopped abruptly and looked questioningly at his father.

"What is she saying?" he said. "Dad, come on. We're going to be late."

Nina's husband definitely looked unfriendly now. He stepped into the road to get by her, with the boy and the scowling teenage girl right behind him.

"I don't know what you're talking about. Nina doesn't live here anymore, and I don't know where your daughter is."

They couldn't leave. She had waited for hours; they couldn't leave.

Natasha grabbed the boy's sleeve and held on. "Have you seen Katerina? My girl? Is she at your house?"

The boy attempted to pull away, but she had a good grip on the soft down jacket and held him back. Grabbed hold with her other hand as well, on the collar under the boy's chin. His skin felt burning hot against her stiff, cold fingers. His eyes were wide open in surprise.

Then Nina's husband shoved her hard, forcing her to take a step back. Natasha's eyes slid from the boy and back to the man. She could see he was surprised, but he was also angry now. His eyes were dark, narrow slits in his winter-pale face.

For a moment she was sure he would hit her. Punish her, like Michael would have done. Pavel had never touched her, of course he hadn't—he had been too busy constructing pink castles in the air where violence would have clashed with the stage sets. Michael had had different ideas, and maybe Nina's husband wasn't as unlike him as she had first thought.

Natasha let go of the boy's jacket and took a step backward. "Please, tell me. I need to see Nina. She know where is my daughter. I have to talk to her," she said in her best English.

Nina's husband was walking away, shielding the children from her with his body. "Welcome to the club," he said over his shoulder. "The rest of this family has tried to make contact with her for the last fifteen years. So good luck with that. I have no idea where she is, and I don't care."

Natasha touched the knife in her pocket. But he was already on his way with both children ahead of him as if they were chickens he was shooing into a henhouse. Only the girl looked back.

T HE GYM SMELLED of apple fritters and coffee and faintly of sour gym sneakers. Nina's gaze moved like a radar shadow across everything that was shorter than a four and a half feet: Spider-Men, musketeers, carrots with legs, Tiggers, pirates, a slightly dated Ninja Turtle, a pumpkin—recycled from Halloween?—and a couple of witches, a Darth Vader and a knight in a silver helmet and a home-made coat of chain mail. My God, Nina thought, how many hours had it taken to sew all those key rings onto the leather vest—and what did it weigh?

She had to check the knight and Vader twice, but then she was certain.

It was 11:02, and Anton wasn't there.

The noise was earsplitting. Excited children's voices climbed to a register that would make any soprano envious, and the parents' attempts at chatting had begun building in a slow but relentless crescendo in order to be heard above the children and themselves.

"Coffee?" yelled a mother from Anton's class and handed her a mug without waiting for an answer. "Where is Anton?"

"He's coming with Morten," Nina yelled back and saw the mother's expression change because she suddenly remembered the divorce.

"Oh, right," the mother said. "But how nice that you can do this together."

"Yes." Nina smiled mechanically. 11:06, and still no Anton. Morten was usually early for these kinds of things.

"There's Minna," said the mother and pointed. "She wanted to be a shower stall this year. Isn't it amazing how creative children can be?"

Minna. Yes, that was her name. A highly energetic and slightly trying little red-haired girl whose freckled face right now was sticking out of a box affixed with a flapping plastic curtain, real faucets, a soap dish and a little steel basket with shampoo and a sponge. The red hair was, of course, crammed into a flowered bathing cap.

"We got most of it for next to nothing at IKEA," said Minna's mother happily. "She even has a spray bottle, so she can squirt people if they want a real bath experience."

"Fantastic," said Nina. 11:14. The teachers had already begun to herd the children toward one end of the room, where they were lining up. Two barrels hung from the rafters on blue nylon ropes, waiting to be beaten to a pulp in time-honored Danish carnival tradition. At least there were no longer live cats inside them, thought Nina with an involuntary shudder, looking at the grinning black paper cats that adorned the outside of the barrels.

"Little ones to the right and bigger ones to the left," shouted one of the phys ed teachers, a tall man from southern Jutland called Niels, who was currently dressed in a Robin Hood cape and a green crepe paper hat with a pheasant feather.

"Am I little or big?" peeped a Tigger who was definitely no more than four.

"You are little."

"What about meee?" hollered a brawny nine-year-old, a Frankenstein's monster rubber mask his only nod to dressing up.

"What do you think, Marcus? Back in line you go. You were behind Selma."

There he was. There they were, all three of them, Morten and Ida and Anton. Ida had not stooped to fancy dress, but the fact that she was here at all was a major concession. Anton was wearing a pair of blue overalls with extra big yellow buttons sewed on, a red shirt, white gloves and a red cap with a white M on the front. His eyebrows had been drawn on with a thick makeup pencil so they looked like black slugs, and a bushy black mustache decorated his eight-year-old upper lip.

Nina's heart flickered in her chest.

"Mom," he yelled and came racing through the crowd. "Look! I'm Super Mario!"

"Yes, you definitely are," she said. She couldn't stop her hands, which, entirely following their own agenda, tugged at the blue suspenders, touched his warm cheek, rested against his soft neck under the pretext of straightening his cap. He didn't want a hug, she knew that, not here, not now, while all his friends were watching. But her hungry hands couldn't quite let him be.

She could tell by Morten's tight shoulders that something was wrong, but she didn't know if it was simply because she was here. Should she have asked? No, damn it. She had a right to come see her son hit the carnival barrel without asking him first.

"Hi, Mom," said Ida.

A year ago it had been "Nina." Now she was Mom again. Ida also looked a little less like a caricature than usual—not so much doomsday mascara and a T-shirt that wasn't actually black.

"Hi, sweetie. It was nice of you to come."

Ida shrugged. "I've promised to cheer for the little maggot if he gets to be the Cat King," she said, referring to the honor bestowed on the child whose blow finally cracked the barrel. "Plus I made the cap."

"He looks totally cool," said Nina and, to her horror, felt a burning flood of tears well up. She had to control herself! Ida would never forgive her if she suddenly started blubbering in front of most of the school.

Anton had already moved on, in a peculiar gait that was supposed to look like the way Super Mario moved in his favorite Nintendo game. Ida gave her a quick fist bump on the shoulder—the height of teenage affection—and waved at another big sister who stood at a careful distance from the noise and the barrels, contriving to look bored.

"Millie! Hi, Millie!"

As soon as Ida was out of hearing, the question jumped out of Nina's mouth without permission. "What's wrong?"

Morten didn't answer right away. "I didn't know you were coming," he said.

"Of course I was coming. I usually do."

"When you have time . . ."

"Morten, can't we . . ."

"I may need to move," he said.

Her chest felt wooden. "Where?" she croaked. "Why?"

"I don't know," he said. "Far enough to rescue the children from your war zone."

"*What?*"

"You promised to stop."

"I have stopped. The network doesn't exist anymore. Besides, a clinic is being established, a clinic where people can be treated anonymously . . ."

He didn't even look at her. She could see that his entire body was on high alert. He was repressing an anger so great that there was barely room for it inside him.

"What?" she asked. "What is it you think I've done?"

"She touched Anton. She grabbed him. Do you know how frightened he was?"

"Who?"

"I don't know. Some disturbed woman who said she was your friend. She was looking for her daughter."

Natasha. It couldn't be anyone else.

"Where did you see her?"

Now Morten gaped at her. "Oh, I knew it," he said. "You know what? It would almost be easier if you were an alcoholic. Then at least there'd be Antabus."

Bang. The first blow connected with the decorated barrels to general cheering and applause. Bang, bang.

Nina stared at Super Mario Anton, almost wishing that Morten *would* move away with the children, at least for a while. Until . . . until this was over. Natasha had grabbed Anton. What would have happened if Anton had been alone? Natasha was desperate. Exactly how desperate Nina could tell from her own irregular heartbeats. And she no longer had any idea where Natasha's limits lay. "A child for a child—give me my daughter, and you can have your son." Would she do that?

Nina had no idea.

NATASHA EASED THE knife blade between the door and the doorframe and forced it. The frame shattered, and with a few extra wriggles, the pawl broke loose from the lock.

There had been no answer when she had tried the buzzer downstairs or later when, after making it into the stairwell on the heels of someone's pizza delivery, she rang the bell at the nurse's front door. But she had to check. She had to know. She walked rapidly down the hall, throwing all the doors wide open.

No one was there.

In the kitchen there were still dirty dishes by the sink, and someone had left the milk out on the counter. The girl's room was surprisingly neat, almost neater than the rest of the apartment. The walls were dark purple; all the furniture was black. Small, powerfully scented candles stood in red and orange glasses. The boy's room was one big chaos of sheets, LEGO blocks, stuffed animals and small plastic figurines that it seemed he collected; most of them looked to be some kind of monster.

Nowhere did she see anything that could be Katerina's. And the double bed in the bedroom only had one pillow on it.

Nina's husband had told the truth. Nina didn't live here anymore. And this wasn't where she had gone with Katerina.

Natasha knew that she shouldn't stay here, that every second increased her risk of being discovered. But her bladder was about to burst. She found the little bathroom at the end of the hall, closed the door and peed so hard, it splashed in the bowl.

Her thoughts were leaping in all directions, like the grasshoppers in the long grass next to the railroad in Kurakhovo. Katerina wasn't here. Nina wasn't here. She had broken into someone's apartment for nothing.

Alarms. Were there alarms? She hadn't heard anything, but perhaps not all alarms rang as earsplittingly as the one Pavel had installed in the apartment in Kiev.

IT HAD BEEN of no use. During the last eighteen months they had lived there, they were burgled four times. The first time she had been at the doctor's with Katerina and came home to an open door and an apartment that had been searched.

"In the middle of the day," she had said to Pavel when she called him, with a childish sense that break-ins were supposed to happen after dark. "Should I call the police?"

"No," said Pavel. "I'll take care of it. Where are you now?"

"In the apartment," she sniffed. "Where else?"

"Take Katerina to the park," he said. "Or wherever it is you usually go. Do it now."

"But the door won't shut. And everything is a mess."

"Just do as I say. I'll come get you when everything has been taken care of."

And he did. Everything had been cleaned up, the door was repaired and there was a new lock. If it weren't for the smell of fresh wood and paint, you would think it had never happened. He had even bought shashlik, rice and salad from the Tatar restaurant in the square so she didn't need to think about dinner. And when she wanted to talk about it, to tell him how afraid she had been, to tell him about the open door that she at first thought she had forgotten to lock, about the sensation in her throat when she realized that someone had been there, someone had gone through their things and taken her new iPod and earrings and necklace . . . then he had hushed her.

"We'll forget this," he said. "You can't worry about things like that. Life is too short."

The second time, he had bought extra locks and a safety chain. The third time she had been home alone. She had fallen asleep on the couch and woke up to the sound of a screwdriver splintering the doorframe. She had stood in the hallway screaming hysterically—"I'll call the police, I'll call the police"—so loudly that Katerina had woken up and begun to cry.

"There's a lot of crime in Kiev," said Pavel. "There's no avoiding it."

The fourth time . . . she didn't want to think about the fourth time.

SHE WASHED HER hands and her stiff, cold face and dried them on one of Nina's towels. Nina's husband hadn't wanted to say where Nina lived now. But sooner or later she'd have to go to work. Sooner or later she would have to drive down the narrow, winding road to the camp in her ugly yellow car that was only half the size of Natasha's stolen Audi.

More waiting. But Natasha had become very good at waiting.

UKRAINE, 1934

THERE IS NOTHING greater, nothing worse than death.

Or maybe there was. Maybe hunger was worse. It hurt when fat and muscle shrank away from your bones. In hunger there was, beyond the pain, also the fear of death, and maybe it was really fear that trumped both hunger and death, Olga thought. Maybe fear was worst.

Olga turned over one more time—carefully, so as not to wake up Oxana and Kolja. She was in her old sleeping place in the house in the village, on the bed shelf above the huge brick oven. The wood shavings in the mattress were fresh, and for once the lice kept their distance. In a way everything was as it had been before, and yet nothing was the same. The house still smelled of Father and Svetlova and the life they had lived together, and Father's absence filled the whole house—on this night worse than ever. Butka, who worked down at the lumber mill, had come to see Mother today and had told her that Father had not been sent to Siberia, after all, as Olga had imagined. In her thoughts she had followed him in the cattle car to the endless snow-covered steppes. She had felt his thirst and hunger and had hoped . . . had even prayed to the nonexistent God to protect him and bring him home whole, with all his arms and legs and toes and fingers still there.

In reality, he had made it no farther than to the GPU's headquarters in Sorokivka, where he had been held in the cellars for a while before finally being tied to a pole and shot. That had happened yesterday. Butka was sure, he said, because he had seen it with his own eyes, even though it had been hard for him to recognize Father. He had been terribly thin after just three weeks in prison. But they had shouted his name, Andreij Trofimenko, counterrevolutionary and Former Human Being, and he had confessed to all the charges, they said.

Mother cried, and Butka stood awkwardly in the living room with his fur hat in his hands, but Olga refused to believe it.

"Prove it," she said softly. "Prove that it is Father who is dead."

It sounded so terrible when she said it. Real.

At first Butka looked a bit uncertain, but then he seemed to remember something, dug into his goatskin coat and pulled out Father's little red party book. He handed it to Mother with a solemn expression.

"They let me bring this to you," said Butka softly. He neglected to mention the widow. She was gone now, and it was as if she had never existed. "It was the only thing he thought to take with him when they came to get him."

Mother opened the book with shaking hands, then let it drop to the floor. It remained there until late in the evening when Olga had surreptitiously picked it up. Small, dark flecks of blood covered the book's cover like freckles. Inside was a picture of Father with his hair combed back and a steady gaze that looked as if it was focused on a finer, better future—the one he had once said he would build with his own hands.

Olga had hidden the party book under her pillow. She could feel it as she lay here now thinking about hunger, fear and death, and what had been the worst for Father as he hung there on the pole and waited for the bullets to drill through his body. She was too tired to cry anymore.

She turned over again in the dark and bumped into Oxana's knee under the blankets. Oxana moved a bit in her sleep, but her breathing was heavy and calm. The familiar sweet scent of her breath, skin and hair surrounded her, and suddenly made it difficult for Olga to breathe.

Oxana had cried today too; big, shiny tears had run from her cornflower-blue eyes. She was the one who had opened the door and received condolences from the few neighbors who had dared to come by in the course of the day. Jana's mother had arrived with vegetable soup and freshly baked bread, and Oxana had answered virtuously, had carried the soup to the table and offered tea from the samovar and had drip-drip-dripped her tears into the tea and across the floor.

Olga breathed carefully through her mouth and turned away from the spicy scent of thyme and garlic and warm girl-body. She tried not to touch Oxana, not to think about her. Not to think about Father and not to think about Grandfather, who had been lying there for three weeks after the accident with his leg, unable to either live or die. He had become feverish and had drunk a lot of vodka, and in his fever had staggered over to the barn to brain the cow so the Reds wouldn't get her. Poor Zorya had been hit with the sledgehammer first across one knee, which had collapsed, and then twice on her broad, quivering neck, until he had finally managed to aim at her forehead and finish her off. The farm and the tools had gone to the state, but they had eaten meat at Grandfather's funeral.

Don't think, she told herself.

She tried to just lie there, completely still, and listen to the wind that grabbed hold of the house and made the woodwork sing and creak under the sky, which Olga knew was black and cloudless and filled with stars.

"Don't be angry at Uncle Stalin," Oxana had said. "The Revolution demands sacrifices from us all."

"**I S SHE DIFFICULT?**" Mikael Nielsen had asked when Søren turned over the watch to him back at the house on Kløvermosevej.

"She has actually been pretty cooperative," Søren had assured him. Now he wondered whether he should have warned Nielsen about Nina's oddities anyway. Small talk and bedside manners were not Nielsen's forte, nor did his restless nature adapt particularly well to the long, dull hours of surveillance during which nothing happened. But he was Søren's man, and he was available and willing to sacrifice his Sunday, and thanks to all his gadgetry, he saw pretty much everything that moved, even though he might not look particularly alert. He had immediately distributed a number of small webcams both indoors and outside, and if Søren knew him at all, he was currently engaged in tracking them all simultaneously on his self-designed tablet computer, colloquially known as The Gizmo—possibly playing Battleship or indulging in a game of chess at the same time.

Søren would have preferred to be there himself. But he needed to talk with Babko, and in spite of the new era of bicultural trust and peace, he had no intention of letting the Ukrainian anywhere near Rina. Apart from Søren's own people, at this moment only Heide and Heide's boss knew where the girl was. He had promised to bring both Nina and Rina in for a more thorough interview Monday morning if the girl's health allowed.

Babko had shaved and generally looked fresher and sharper today—Søren was in no way sure that the same thing could be said about him.

"I managed to get through most of it," he said, poking the substantial pile of papers. The printer had been going for almost two hours; it wasn't among the fastest, but it had been easier than going to Søborg to use the one at the office. He was still better at reading things on paper, and when he was also faced with a linguistic challenge, he needed all the help he could get. His reading speed had definitely not been optimal.

"Did you find it interesting?" asked Babko.

"Much of it, yes."

Pavel Doroshenko had been born and had grown up in a little village south of Kiev. His father was a dairy worker, and his mother had been employed at the same dairy for most of her adult life. The most unusual thing about the family was the mother's background. She was originally from Galicia in eastern Ukraine, one of the local minority of ethnic Germans who had been blown hither and thither by various national and military storms around the time of the Second World War. First the area had been under Polish rule, then the Soviets came, then the Germans, with a short-lived attempt to create an independent Ukrainian state, and finally the area had again been absorbed by the Soviet Union. Galicia's history was more turbulent than most, and Søren wondered how it had shaped Pavel's mother.

"You wrote 'Mama's boy' in your notes," said Søren. "Why?"

"She died in nineteen ninety-seven, so it's an entirely secondhand impression. I spoke with the father; he is still alive but hadn't been in contact with Pavel for several years. The marriage wasn't exactly harmonious. It's a small town, everybody knows everybody's business, and if Pavel was a ladies' man, he didn't get it from strangers."

"But they didn't get divorced?"

"No. You're familiar with the *propiska* system?"

"Yes." During the Soviet era, one needed an internal passport, a propiska, to live in a certain place. The propiska simultaneously served as right of residence to a specific address. "Is that still in use in Ukraine?"

"It was officially judged to be unconstitutional in two thousnd and one, but not a lot changed. So with certain modifications, yes. The short answer is that even if Pavel's parents *had* divorced, they couldn't just split up. At least not without exchanging the propiska on their little house for two propiskas to much less desirable apartments. Pavel's mother defended her right to the house with tooth and claw, understandably so. The result was that they lived like a dog and a cat. Funnily enough, most of the villagers sided with the husband, perhaps because her Ukrainian was pretty poor. She'd grown up with German and Polish, of course. Pavel was called Niemcy, 'the German,' in school, or 'the Nazi brat' if they were being particularly cruel. And apparently they spoke German together, his mother and he. She called him Paul. So you could say he grew up strongly motivated to succeed. He was going to show them all."

"And he did, didn't he?" said Søren, thinking of a few pieces he had found on the Web. German television in particular had apparently used Pavel as a local expert a few times. "A career as a journalist, a good income, an apartment in Kiev and a young, beautiful wife . . . to them, he must have looked every inch the successful media star."

"At least to his mother he did, though she didn't get to see the final chapters."

"I've looked at everything you found on him," said Søren. "His stories are generally pretty black and white, aren't they?"

Pavel Doroshenko never seemed to just write about people. He wrote about villains or heroes. The heroes acted "without thought of personal gain" and "with great personal courage" and were "tireless," "selfless" and "determined," whether he was describing a fireman in Chernobyl, a local businessman, the director of an orphanage, a mayor who fought crime in his city or just a retiree who had defended himself against a pickpocket. The villains were similarly described as "calculating" and "greedy"; they were "caught in their own snares" and could often look forward to "many years behind bars"; people foolish enough to defend them were described as "collaborators" or "coconspirators" without it being clear what the conspiracy consisted of. Pavel fairly often cited family background or ethnicity, creating the impression that evil was genetic rather than personal. To Søren, the rhetoric seemed oddly old-fashioned and pretty tiresome.

"You think so?" said Babko. "A lot of people write like that. At least in Ukraine."

"I haven't been able to find anything that explains Savchuk's interest in his widow."

"No, me neither."

"Is he another Gongadze?" Søren said, although broken fingers and a heart attack did not quite seem to match the gruesomeness of the decapitation of that particular heroic journalist.

Babko shook his head. "I don't think so. The people he would attack were mostly nationalists. At the beginning of his career, he was more politically focused—accusing the early nationalists of being a collection of Kosak-romantics, bumpkins and anti-Semites. Later his attacks became more personal, though funnily enough, most of the people he attacked still belonged to the Orange faction. The Blues—that is, the more ethnic Russian- and Moscow-friendly wing—he never wrote much about them, although there would be no shortage of material if he had wanted to have a go at them."

"Are his personal beliefs a factor here?" asked Søren.

"Possibly. Or it might just have been to please his audience. For a time, he lived and worked in Donetsk, which is a predominantly

Russian-speaking area. His motives could also have been more narrowly financial. There was and still is a lot of money flowing out of Moscow to willing mouthpieces in the media world. How else did you think Yanukovytsj managed to get himself reelected a mere six years after the Orange Revolution threw him out?"

Was that the pattern Søren's tired brain had tried to decipher last night? No. He didn't have Babko's local knowledge and couldn't automatically recognize the party colors of the people Doroshenko had written about.

"I wonder about two things," he said. "First of all, I think his style changes. It becomes even more purple yet at the same time less precise, wallowing in phrases like 'could it be that . . .' or 'might not stand up to closer examination.' In his earlier articles, he is sharper and produces names and facts. Secondly, as his income grows, the apartment in Kiev and so on . . . he writes less and less, and for more local and smaller media. The year before he died, he published almost exclusively on some Web news site, what was it called . . ."

"*Velyka Tayemnitsya.* The Big Secret, in the English version."

"Yes. It seems paradoxical."

"That's because he is no longer a journalist in the true sense of the word. He was producing *kompromat.*"

Søren's inner dictionary managed to provide a definition a second before he had to ask. *Kompromat*—by now a fairly old Russian abbreviation for "compromising material." A tactic in the information war that had roots all the way back to Stalin and which, in all its simplicity, consisted of digging up, fabricating and throwing as much dirt as possible at the person or persons with whom you were at war. American election campaigns were like Sunday school sessions by comparison.

"It's still used a lot?" he asked.

"Oh, yes. Big Bizniz. Now also as a more private enterprise. And the richest *kompromat* producers are usually the ones who don't print what they write."

"Blackmail?"

"Yep. As a *kompromat* producer, you always have two potential customers—the person who has paid for the dirt and the person you're planning to throw it at. The latter usually pays more."

"And the vague articles that just make suggestions but don't name names . . ."

"Those are warning shots. They let the victim know what he can expect if he doesn't pay up."

Søren looked at the pile of articles with renewed interest. That meant that the "warning shots" offered up a number of people who had good reason for murdering Pavel Doroshenko and possibly also for pursuing his widow. That is, if Søren and Babko could figure out whom the warnings were directed at.

14:11. EXACTLY A minute had passed since she last checked. Not good.

The sky was so thunderously grey that it might as well have been evening. Nina knew that she checked her watch more frequently on days when the sun didn't give her a natural sense of the time, but this was more than that. She pulled over to the side of the road, and only then did she realize that she had subconsciously been headed for Fejøgade.

Fuck.

"You don't live there anymore," she told herself. She said it out loud because she wanted her subconscious to *listen* this time. Damn it. If Morten saw her, he would probably think she was stalking them. Like one of those rejected ex-husbands who went home and polished their army reserve rifle and put on their best clothes before blasting off the backs of their skulls. That is, if they didn't take out their whole family first. Contemptible shitheads.

She carefully placed her hands on the steering wheel again. 14:11. Fuck.

"I just want to take care of them."

And they said that too, the men with the army reserve rifles. I just wanted to take care of them. When they shot the children, it wasn't to *harm* them. Shitheads.

14:12.

But the thought that Natasha had been there. At her home. Well, okay, at Morten's and the children's home.

14:12. Fuck. Fuck. Fuck.

I just want to take care of them.

"Are you having a nervous breakdown?" she asked out loud in English.

Why she was speaking English to herself she didn't know. And then she actually did know. English was the language of crisis. In Dadaab and elsewhere. And flying conditions were lousy.

"Nina, damn it."

She breathed very consciously now. Long, deep breaths. "Allll the way down to the pit of your stomach," as an instructor had once said. Panic-reducing big breaths.

The black anxiety inside her paid no attention. Nina didn't get it. Natasha wasn't more dangerous than the Finnish psychopath who had kidnapped Ida last year. And in that situation she had been able to think and act; she had done what was necessary for Ida to be rescued. Natasha was no more dangerous. Definitely not. Natasha was just a poor Ukrainian girl who had landed in some bad shit.

A poor Ukrainian *mother*, Nina reminded herself. And you have taken her child.

14:13.

She knew that it wasn't always the obvious crises that made people crack. An Iranian man who had survived multiple arrests, torture and threats without breaking down had completely lost it and had tried to smash a radiator one evening in the Coal-House Camp's recreation room. Afterward he explained, crying and incoherent, that it was because the noise from a defective valve reminded him of machine-gun fire.

But you haven't been tortured, she reminded herself. So how about turning down the drama a notch or two?

Outside on Jagtvejen traffic glided by in its lazy Sunday rhythm. A mother passed her with two carnival-costumed children, one in a stroller, the other lagging a few feet behind on tired cat paws.

For the rest of the school carnival, Nina had barely been able to keep it together. She had smiled and clapped for Anton's sake. He had been so caught up in the barrel-smashing and apple-bobbing and all the other hullaballoo that he hadn't noticed anything. But Ida had immediately spotted that something was wrong.

"What have you done now?" she asked, lashing out at Nina with all the old hostility that had seemed to be receding.

"Ida!" said Morten. "Speak nicely to your mother."

Nina felt a surge of wobbly and yet more destabilizing gratitude to him for defending her, even if the defense did sound a bit tired and hollow because he basically agreed with Ida. As soon as the bottom had fallen out of Anton's barrel, releasing oranges in all directions, she had kissed Super Mario on his cap and raced out the door.

Would you take my child, Natasha?

And Natasha answered her, a whispering voice somewhere inside: Why not? You took mine.

"No," Nina protested. "You *asked* me to take care of her. That's what I've done. Just that." But it was a lie, a big, fat lie. When the gates to Fejøgade had been shut in her face, banishing her from what right now seemed a perfect Eden, though it hadn't been so at the time . . . in that moment of despair and rejection, it had been Rina she had clung to. There had been so many nights when she had slept next to Rina ostensibly "to keep an eye on that asthma," but really because her own bed in the new-divorcée apartment had been unbearably lonely and impossible to sleep in.

So no, she couldn't go to Fejøgade. But the thought of returning to Søren's tidy suburban home made her panic accelerate. Magnus was there, she thought. Magnus would have to manage a little longer. He had a caring but more professional relationship to Rina.

She could go get the asthma medicine. Yes, that's what she would do. They had already used more than they should have, and they couldn't afford to run out. The drive back and forth would consume over an hour of unruly, fundamentally un-checkable time, and by then she might have calmed down a bit.

She started the engine again and headed for the Coal-House Camp. The time was 14:19.

UKRAINE, 1935

STOMP, STOMP, STOMP.

Olga stared down at the frozen wheel tracks as she walked. It wasn't all that far from the school to their old house on the outskirts of the village, certainly not anywhere near as far as it had been to Grandfather's farm up in the hills. And yet it felt farther.

Her heart beat hard and fast under her coat, and she increased her tempo, forced herself to breathe slowly and deeply, forced herself not to run. The heavy white blanket of snow that had fallen in the night hushed all sound, but she still caught most of it. Oxana's steady, confident steps to her right. A door that opened and closed in the house next to the cooperative shop. A quiet conversation between two men over by the sawmill. She could hear the way they stomped their feet and clapped their hands hard together to stave off the cold. Their cigarette smoke hung in the ice-cold air like a faint bluish veil.

They walked quickly. Olga because she was afraid. Oxana more likely because she was angry.

COMRADE SEMIENOVA LOVED Oxana. Leda and Jegor loved Oxana, and Mother and Kolja loved her too. But that winter it was as if everyone else had begun to hate her.

It had begun with Sergej's stone, the day the GPU had come for Fedir and the rest of his family. And after that the hatred had grown.

Although Olga caught only a sort of echo of it, as if the hostility bounced off Oxana and hit her instead, she felt it as a resistance in her body that made it difficult to move and breathe. It showed in all the little gestures, she had discovered. Men stuck their hands in their pockets and turned away. Conversations ceased. Smiles faltered and eyes were averted when Oxana and she walked by. People didn't yell or call names anymore; the hatred was in the silence and in the air she breathed into her lungs. So it wasn't until she was inside, at home with Oxana and Kolja and Mother, that she could breathe freely.

Uncle Grachev's house had become a dangerous place to pass, because even though Father and he had often argued about who would provide bread and vodka for the old folk, they had had a lot in common and enjoyed drinking and playing cards in the evening. Uncle Grachev was Father's brother. He had a huge beard and an odd, hiccupping laughter, and he used to pinch Olga and Oxana much too hard on the cheek. Olga had also seen him pinch Mother's behind when he was really drunk and had lost both kopeks and rubles, but Mother had never paid much attention, and luckily Grachev had his own wife, who was named Vira and was big and strong as an ox and ruled over both Grachev and the three large cousins with a firm hand. Their house was also big enough that Grandfather and Grandmother Trofimenko could live there, and when Mother and Father and Olga and Oxana and Kolja had first come to Mykolayevka in the fall, Vira and Grachev had invited the whole family to celebrate the first harvest after the great hunger. They had had honey cakes and tea and had listened to Cousin Fyodor's stories about his time in the army in Afghanistan. To think that the Afghan women were dressed in tents and were only allowed to see the world through a mesh of horsehair, while the men sat around smoking water pipes! Unimaginable wonders like that were blissful when served with tea and cake.

Olga missed Vira and Fyodor and even Grachev, in spite of the cheek-pinching, but since Father's death their house had been closed to Olga as well as Oxana. Vira pursed her lips together when they met her in the street, and the two youngest cousins, Vitja and Pjotr, ran between the houses with Sergej and threw hard, little icy snowballs at Olga and Oxana and even at little Kolja when he came along. Once Vitja had pushed Oxana into the open gutter, so she had fallen on the layers of frozen shit from the Lihomanovs' house.

Olga and Oxana always walked by as quickly as they could, making sure not to expose themselves unnecessarily; they were especially careful with their throats, eyes and cheeks, which they covered as best they could by bending their heads, hunching their shoulders and pulling their kerchiefs close around their faces. It was no longer a good idea to stop and warm their hands or chat with the other girls. Even Leda and Elizaveta, who, like Oxana, were eager young pioneers, steered clear of them in the open street.

The worst thing was that Olga liked Vitja and Pjotr and Fyodor and Grachev and Jana. Even now, even when they were being so awful to her. Last summer, before all the trouble with Father and the widow, she and Pjotr had gone down to the river together to fish several times. Once in a while they caught one of the fat barbel, a fish that could get so big, it required all the strength and concentration an eleven-year-old boy could muster to drag it to shore. Other times they had to make do with small fry that Mother made into fish soup with the head, tail, eyes, guts and the lot.

But that was over now too.

STOMP, STOMP.

Olga knew that she would be able to see their house now if she raised her head. Once home, she and Oxana would be responsible for building a fire in the oven, collecting water at the well if it wasn't frozen over, or melting snow on the stove if it was. Mother wouldn't be home until the pigs were fed for the last time that day.

She placed one felt boot in front of the other and tried to calculate how many steps were left. Probably about a hundred steps to the Petrenkos' house and from there another twenty to their garden fence. She fought the desire to look up. And then it came anyway, the sound she had feared since Comrade Semienova had closed the school door behind them.

Running feet in the snow.

Coming from behind, from the shortcut by the shoemaker's house.

The next second Olga felt the first hard blow against her shoulder. Little Sergej had caught up to them and now ran right behind them, buzzing like a wasp around rotten plums. Olga tried to slap him, which made Sergej laugh hilariously.

"Oxana," he said, "you're so good in school, you must also know that Noah had three sons. What was it they were called, Oxana?"

Now Pjotr and Vitja had arrived and were blocking their path. Olga also saw Jana's big brother Vanja and felt a new prick of terror. Vanja was seventeen and as broad-shouldered as a grown man.

"Come on, Oxana. What were they called? Sing for us."

Sergej yanked Oxana's kerchief down around her shoulders so she stood with her head bared. A lock of blonde hair had been torn from the tight braid at her neck and flapped across her face. Her eyes flashed angrily at Sergej and the other boys. Her mouth was a narrow black line in her pale face.

"Leave us alone," she said and tried to push her way past Pjotr. "Or I'll report you to the GPU. You have no right to bother me and Olga."

Vitja hit Oxana so hard across the mouth that her lip split and blood dripped down into the snow. Olga halted as if paralyzed.

"What were Noah's sons called, Oxana? Answer!"

Oxana pressed her felt glove to her lip and glared furiously at Vitja.

"Every idiot knows that Noah's sons were called Sem, Kam and Jafet," she said finally.

Sergej's little pockmarked face contorted in a sneaky grimace that revolted Olga. If only he had died of pox or hunger typhus or something even worse. It seemed to her that cruelty almost radiated out from his small, skinny body.

"Then I must be an idiot," yelled Sergej triumphantly. "I thought Noah's sons were called Sem, Kam and *Judas*." He hit himself across the forehead. "But you know that better than I do, Oxana. Thank you."

Sergej's words seemed to hit harder than Vitja's fist, because now Oxana blushed, and for the first time, she lowered her eyes. The loose strands of wheaten hair blew in the wind. Vitja gave her a vicious shove, so that Oxana lost her balance and had to fight to remain standing.

"Leave us alone," screamed Olga. She was afraid now. This wasn't like the other times, when ice chunks and rocks had hit them from secret hiding places. This time they were standing in the middle of the street. Two workers from the kolkhoz walked by, and Olga knew who they were and wanted to turn to them for help, but it was as if they looked right through her. They were talking and smoking and continued on without stopping. Now she noticed cousin Fyodor and Uncle Grachev a bit farther up the road, standing with parted legs and folded arms.

"Shut up," screamed Petjr. "Just shut your mouth."

He brought his fist down on Olga, but she managed to turn away from him so he hit her shoulder instead of her face. Then he grabbed hold of both kerchief and hair and yanked her head back hard. She fell. Pjotr dragged her across the trampled, hard-packed snow of the road and didn't let her go until she lay in the frozen sewage gutter with her face pressed against the ice. She could hear the sound of blows against Oxana's body, some hushed by overcoat and mittens, others clearer as they hit her face and other exposed bits of skin, but Olga didn't dare look up. She just stayed where she was like a coward hunched in the snow until she heard Vitja swear faintly; he was out of breath.

"Damn. We better get out of here," he said.

Olga lifted her head in time to see little Sergej kick Oxana in the stomach one last time before he set off running down Shoemaker Alley with the others. Farther down the road she could see the reason for their sudden departure: two riders down by the sawmill wearing the easily recognizable uniforms of the GPU, rifles over their shoulders.

Olga got up. The snow had crept in under her jacket and kerchief and now ran in small, cold rivulets down her neck and chest. Oxana lay a little distance off. In her overcoat and thick felt boots, she looked like a lifeless pile of clothes in the middle of the road, but she finally moved, stuck a leg out to one side, steadied herself with her hands and raised herself into a sitting position. They hadn't killed her.

Oxana brushed the snow off her pummeled face. One of her eyebrows was bleeding, as was her nose, and her cheeks were as red as poppies from the cold and the many blows.

"What are you staring at?" she said. "Help me up."

THE AREA AROUND the children's barrack was still closed off, and plywood covered the place where the glass wall had been. That was just last night, thought Nina. Less than twelve hours ago.

She walked over to the policeman who stood at the barrier. "Excuse me," she said, "I just wanted to know . . . How is your colleague doing?"

He looked at her with a measured gaze. He was older than the plainclothes men from the Mondeo brigade, which she at first perceived as odd, perhaps from a vague impression that seniority was supposed to get you out of uniform at some point.

"I can't say," he said formally.

She'd have to ask Søren, then. Or even the cud-chewer with the iPad that wasn't an iPad.

She walked across the old parade ground to the clinic. Oddly, the door was locked. Officially, the clinic was closed on Sundays, it was true, but it was rarely possible to adhere to the scheduled hours. When 400 traumatized people were crowded together in sixteen barracks, there was almost always someone with a medical need. But apparently not right now.

She went in and unlocked the medicine cabinet, found the little blue plastic box labeled *Rina Dmytrenko* and put the Bricanyl and Spirocort in her pocket.

On the shelf below stood another little blue box with another name on the label. Nina knew it contained a ten-pill foil pack of Valium. And she knew the pack would not be used because the Somali woman for whom it was intended was no longer in the camp.

She closed her eyes for a moment. One small pale blue pill. Ten milligrams. That was all she needed to make her anxiety go away. And no one would notice that there was one pill missing from the packet next time the cabinet was put in order.

But she had to go back to Søren's house. She had to be able to drive. To function. After a traumatic night, and less than three hours of sleep . . . no. No pill.

She *was* a bit calmer now. She had only checked her watch three times in twenty minutes, which was close to normal. It had helped to move, as if driving eased certain ancient fight-or-flight instincts.

She locked up the clinic again. When she passed the guard in the gatehouse, little more than a shed, she waved casually. He nodded briefly and raised the barrier. He knew her and wasn't surprised to see her on a Sunday.

It had started to snow again. All that snow, all that ice. It would probably be late March before they saw the end of it. She drove slowly to give the Micra a chance to handle the curves. The wipers squeaked across the windshield, struggling to push the heavy flakes aside. She should probably have cleared the car of snow again before she started, but it hadn't had time to cool down completely while she collected the medicine, and the problem would be solved within a few minutes.

Suddenly there was a light among the trees in a place where it shouldn't have been. With a muted roar of acceleration, a car shot out in front of her into the middle of the road.

Where did he come from? Where the hell did he come from?

She took her foot off the gas, shifted gears and stomped the brake to the floor, knowing perfectly well that none of it would help. Desperately, she wrenched the steering wheel to the left and managed to turn the Micra part way around, but it still sailed forward into the collision. She hit the snowbank and the other car at the same time with a muffled bang, and was jerked forward against her seat belt and then thrown back as the airbag exploded in her face. There was the sound of shattering glass.

She couldn't move. The airbag's material stuck to her face, as if someone were trying to choke her with a pillow. Something had happened to her hand. The Micra's motor was still on, but the sound was a forced insect-like whine, and after a few seconds, it ceased. At that moment the front door was yanked open, and someone attempted to pull her out of the car. It didn't work; she was still wearing her seat belt. Nina herself groped for the release button. The belt sprang loose, and she slid sideways, upper body first, out of the damaged car.

Cold air, snow, grey sky over dark trees.

Was she missing time? Seconds, minutes? She tried to lift her left arm to check her watch but couldn't.

"Where is she? Katerina. Where?"

Nina was lifted up and thrown into the snow again. She still couldn't catch her breath.

It was Natasha. Natasha had driven into her car. Her brain couldn't quite comprehend it, but that must have been what had happened. The Ukrainian girl sat on top of her, a knee on either side of Nina's chest. Her hair hung in iced clumps, and the Barbie-beautiful face was merciless and set in stone. She let go of Nina with one hand, but only to bring up something made of bright, glittering steel. Nina felt a sharp jab under her chin, the coldness of metal against her neck.

"Tell me. Where?"

"The police," gasped Nina. "The police have her. I don't know where. In a safe place."

"*Brekhnya.* You're lying."

"No. Natasha, you're only making it worse for yourself. Go to the police, give yourself up. Otherwise, you will never get to see her again."

Natasha's eyes became totally black. Her hand jerked, and Nina felt the metal point pierce through her skin to her windpipe. She's going to kill you, Nina thought, coolly and clearly. It'll end now. You'll be found lying in the bloody snow, and Ida and Anton will cry at your grave. She suddenly saw it with excruciating clarity in her mind's eye, like an over-the-top sentimental scene in an American B movie. It was filmed from above. The camera zoomed down on the coffin and the open grave, people with black umbrellas, the freezing minister. Then a close-up of the two black-clad children, Ida holding Anton's hand and shouting, "You're a lousy mother! How could you do this?"

She didn't know what time it was.

Then the pressure disappeared from her neck. Natasha remained sitting on top of her a little while longer, and Nina could see that the murder weapon—the potential murder weapon—was an ordinary kitchen knife, the semi-Japanese kind with a triangular blade, especially efficient when cutting meat.

And windpipe cartilage, Nina said to herself. If Natasha had pushed it any farther in, you'd be dead now, or at least in a few minutes from now, choking on your own blood. Murdered with a kitchen tool by one of the so-called poor wretches you thought you could help.

"You must know," said Natasha in English. "I saw you. Katerina was in your car. I saw it! You know where she is, you must know, you must . . ."

"No," said Nina. "They keep that kind of thing secret. It has to be secret, or it's not safe."

"Safe," repeated Natasha.

"Yes. They'll keep her safe. I promise."

Natasha rose to her feet and disappeared from Nina's rather blurred field of vision. Nina heard seven or eight stumbling, uneven steps in the snow. She stayed completely still except for reflexive blinks when sharp snowflakes grazed her eyelashes. Listening.

The sound of a car door. A creaking, scratching sound of metal against metal, an uneven acceleration. She turned her head and felt a delayed snap in her neck, like a gear falling into place. From her unfamiliar frog's-eye perspective, she saw the back of the other car come closer, felt the spray of the snow thrown up by the rotating rear wheels. Then Natasha drove forward again, the back end of the car making a few slalom-like sweeps from side to side before the taillights disappeared behind the snowbanks at the next turn.

Nina lay unmoving. She didn't know if she was hurt. Right now all she could think was, She's gone, and I am still alive.

THERE WAS BLOOD on the knife. The nurse's blood. Natasha had cut her neck. Not as badly as she had done with Michael, nowhere near, but worse than she had meant to. Natasha felt a deep shiver spread from her core.

Blood.

Nina hadn't screamed, hadn't flailed her arms as Michael had done. She lay still in the snow, looking up at Natasha. Her voice was calm, as if it were a normal conversation and Natasha had just asked her a completely ordinary question.

"It has to be secret, or it's not safe."

Danes didn't lie as much as Ukrainians did. It was as if they believed the truth made them better human beings. A Dane would feel the need to tell a terminally ill patient the entire truth about the cancer that would choke him in the end. For his own good, of course. "I have to be honest," a Dane would say, and afterward he would be relieved, and the one who had received the truth would be crushed. Natasha preferred a considerate lie any day, but she hadn't encountered many of those either in or outside the Coal-House Camp.

Was the nurse lying now? Natasha narrowed her eyes, looking down at the sprawling figure she was straddling.

It has to be secret, or it's not safe.

"Safe," she said thoughtfully, trying to understand the word. Safe was to be in a place of safety, a place where no one could harm you. Where the Witch couldn't reach you. But the price was that it was secret, and no one could know where you were.

That was a calculation she understood completely. It was in her bones. It had been in the pounding, chilly pain in her crotch and abdomen, the smell of sweat and semen, the near-throttling pressure against her throat and in the silence that could not be broken, no matter what form his anger took. With Michael, *that* had been the price of safety. She had paid it for Katerina's sake.

You can endure anything, she had told herself, as long as Katerina is safe.

Could she also endure the thought that Katerina would be safe in a place where Natasha couldn't reach her? Could she stand it if safety meant she could never touch her daughter or see her again, not even on wrenchingly brief prison visits?

Some women gave their children up for adoption so they would have a better life. Natasha would rather die.

Nina was saying something. Natasha didn't catch it all, she just heard the repetition of the word "safe."

The crushing, unacceptable truth was penetrating her, jerk by jerk, even though she didn't want it inside her. The nurse didn't know anything—even bleeding, even with the knife against her throat, she couldn't tell Natasha anything.

With a sharp wrench of translucent pain, the last connection to Katerina was severed. The trail of bread crumbs through the forest was gone; the birds had eaten it. There was no longer a way home.

A HOLE IN time, a sudden shift.

She was in the car. She was driving the car. Headlights approached her in pairs. The snow was drifting across the windshield. She had no idea where she was, didn't remember how she had gotten there. The knife lay on the seat next to her, still with blood on the tip. Inside her there was no longer a goal, no longer any direction or any meaning at all. The temptation to head for a pair of the lights moving toward her was overwhelming.

Suicides did not go to Heaven.

"Don't fill the child's head with that superstitious foolishness," Pavel had said. "There is no Heaven."

It was the day that Natasha's grandmother was being buried. September, but still so warm that the air shimmered above the asphalt outside the airport in Donetsk.

"Why not?" asked Natasha. "You don't know what happens when we die either."

"I know that there won't be any angel choirs and harp music for me," he said.

Katerina had been five. She listened when the grown-ups talked. Not always obviously, but with a silent awareness that made it seem as if she was eavesdropping even when she sat right next to you, as now, in the back of the taxi.

"So Daddy won't go to Heaven?" she whispered to Natasha.

Pavel heard it even though he was helping the taxi driver put the bags in the trunk. He also saw the silent pleading in Natasha's eyes.

"Sweetie pie," he said and slid into the seat from the other side. "That's a long time from now. We don't need to think about it."

"But Great-Grandmother is dead," said Katerina. "Where is she going if there is no Heaven?"

It wasn't as if Katerina had seen her great-grandmother all that often. Still, the question was serious, as was Katerina's worried gaze.

"Are you sad that she is dead?" asked Pavel.

Katerina considered. "She made good poppy seed cakes," she said.

Pavel smiled. "Good," he said. "Then we agree that there is a Heaven and that Great-Grandmother is there now. She has just baked a poppy seed cake and made us tea, and we can visit her when we sleep so she doesn't get too lonely. I'll just have to try and see if I can stand the harping."

Katerina accepted this and looked relieved. Death without life-lines was hard for a five-year-old to take on board, and Natasha was happy that Pavel had been as accommodating as he had and that Katerina couldn't see the irony in his eyes.

Twelve months later Pavel was dead. And for some reason Natasha had a hard time imagining that he sat next to God looking down at them. He no longer took care of them; in fact, he never had. It had just seemed that way until the day the Witch arrived.

SUDDENLY NATASHA KNEW what she needed to do. The world fell into place around her, and there was meaning and order again. She could protect Katerina, even though she no longer knew where Katerina was. She could make sure that safe really meant safe.

Once she had wondered at the fact that murderers could get into Heaven when people who committed suicide couldn't. Wasn't it worse to kill someone else? Now she was glad that was the way it was. She listened, but Anna-in-her-head apparently had no opinion of her new plan. Still Natasha felt calm, cold and determined. If Katerina really was to be safe, there was only one thing to do.

The Witch had to die.

"**T**HIS ONE," SØREN said, pointing at one of Pavel Dorshenko's many articles. "Why do I have a special feeling about this one?"

Babko stretched and stuck out his hand for the now fairly grimy paper. "May I see?"

> *"Solovi, solovi, ne trevozhte soldat . . ."*
>
> *Nightingale, nightingale, do not wake the soldier, for he has such a short time to sleep. Which of us has not heard this sentimental but beautiful song, whether it was Evgeny Belyaev, who thrilled us with his fantastic tenor, or the Red Army's talented male choir or more modern soloists? But who was this nightingale really, and whom did she sing for?*

Babko took a sip of his lukewarm coffee.

"It doesn't seem quite like the stuff he usually writes," he said. "But I can't see any great potential for scandal. Most of this is generally known. Kalugin's Nightingale. The story was even turned into a *Carmen*-like musical a few years ago."

They had had to return the borrowed office to its owner and were now once again sitting in the headquarters's dove-blue coffee room.

A Sunday lull had descended; only a single uniformed policeman was reading the sports section from one of the tabloids as he consumed his breakfast roll. Søren scanned the text once more. He could grasp the general sense—that it had to do with the world war and the dog-fight over Galicia—but his knowledge of contemporary Ukrainian history wasn't sufficient for him to catch all the nuances.

"What does it mean?" he asked Babko. "The stuff about the Nightingale?"

"She was a kind of Ukrainian Marlene Dietrich," Babko said and tapped a specific paragraph with a broad index finger. "Oletchka Marasova, she was called. She sang for Bandera's nationalist troops. She kept up morale and that kind of thing. But it turned out that she sang in more ways than one. She informed on several of them to the KGB, to a Colonel Kalugin—hence the name."

"Dramatic," Søren observed. "I can see why someone thought it would make a great musical."

"It was terrible," said Babko dryly. "Plot holes you could drive a cart through and so overacted and tear-jerkingly sentimental that some of the audience began to giggle. Very unhistorical and slightly embarrassing."

Søren sensed that Babko had been one of the gigglers.

"Doroshenko's version is not much better," said the Ukrainian. "Some of it is taken directly from the musical, as far as I can see. Other parts are tall tales and myth; he doesn't distinguish. All that stuff about Kalugin discovering her at an orphanage concert, for example, is nonsense. She did come from an orphanage, true, but she didn't meet Kalugin until she was grown. And she probably doesn't have quite as many lives on her conscience as Kalugin claims. She was given credit for a good part of general informer activity. The national army was, to some extent, an underground army and therefore very vulnerable to that kind of traitor. Many were accused, arrested and executed. Bandera was murdered by the KGB as late as nineteen fifty-nine, in Munich, I believe. And he is still a divisive figure. Some see him as a Ukrainian freedom fighter, a hero; others accuse him of war crimes and point out that he allied himself with the Germans for a while. A Ukrainian battalion was created under the banner of the Wehrmacht, and do you know what they called it?"

"No," said Søren, a bit irritated. This wasn't a quiz show.

"The Nachtigall Battalion. Funny, don't you think?"

"Does it have anything to do with her? Kalugin's Nightingale?"

"Probably not. Or if it does, the connection may run in the other direction—it made the nickname even more appropriate."

Søren skimmed the article one more time. If you ignored the tragic background of the war, it was basically a banal honey-trap story. It had even been illustrated with photographs of scenes from the musical, he saw, and an apparently random picture of two little girls in some kind of national costume. There were no captions to explain why that was relevant.

"It doesn't include an accusation," he said. "None of those badly veiled suggestions that there is a 'basis for a closer investigation' and so on. And it all happened a long time ago. So why do I still keep coming back to it?"

"Perhaps because it was published on September eighteenth, two thousand and seven," said Babko suddenly.

It took a few seconds. Then Søren felt an abrupt desire to smack himself on the forehead. "The day before Pavel Doroshenko was killed," he concluded.

"**Y**OU'RE LIKE A dog. A little, stupid one."

Olga looked at Oxana across the narrow table but didn't have the energy to answer, just waited for the next attack. Oxana wasn't really angry, she knew that. There was something teasing in the blue gaze. An invitation to a game of the kind they had played when they were a little younger in Kharkiv and even in Mykolayevka before everything went wrong. But Olga didn't accept.

"A dog sticks its tail between its legs and hides because it doesn't know any better. What's your excuse?"

There was a smile but also a flicker of irritation in Oxana's voice now. Olga still chose to ignore it. They were having oatmeal today. Water softened the oats so they somehow filled you up more than millet porridge and bread, and if you ate very slowly, it worked even better.

Olga emptied her bowl at a steady rate. She inhaled its smell and felt warmth spread through her whole body.

Mother also sat silent with her own portion, which wasn't much bigger than those she had served the children. She gave them a little hunk of bread each. Olga broke hers in half, carefully cleaning the bowl with the soft side of the bread before stuffing it in her mouth. Afterward, they cleaned the pot together in the same way. Oxana poked at Olga's hand, ruffled her hair and nipped playfully at her ear, but Olga pulled away instinctively. That was just the way it had become. She could no longer stand to be touched by Oxana.

She got up abruptly and began to comb Kolja's hair for nits. Mother had had to cut it very short, because when Kolja was being looked after at the kolkhoz, he often played in the collective house, where whole families slept, cooked and ate on the floor. Lice and other bugs jumped on him even though Mother made sure to wash him every day and had somehow even acquired some bars of real soap. They managed, as Mother said. There were oats and cabbage and winter carrots, and the fist-sized bread ration that Mother brought home with her every day from the kolkhoz, a chunk for each. But hunger stayed with Olga like a toothache. When she got up, when she went to bed and now while she was rinsing the pots and checking Kolja's soft short hair for lice.

Olga kissed him carefully at the nape of his neck and spun him around once. Mother had made a new coat for him from the red wool dress she had brought from Kharkiv. "Here I'll never need such finery anyway," she had said. "The hogs don't care what I wear."

"How nice you look," said Olga and smiled. "A real little man."

Kolja nodded. "I'm going to show it to Viktor and Elena and Marusja," he said but then got a worried wrinkle in his forehead. "Should I be the father or the big brother when we play family?"

Olga considered for a moment. "You should be the father," she said. "You're a father who has just come back from Moscow after an important meeting with Uncle Stalin, and he has given you this fine coat as a thank-you for all that you have done for the Soviet Union."

Kolja stood up straight and gave Oxana a serious look. "Like you, Oxana. I am going to build a better future with my own hands."

Oxana was putting on her coat. She looked at Kolja and smiled crookedly, but she didn't say anything. Oxana had become quieter lately. She was thinking of the cause, she claimed, but her spontaneous speeches about the better times that awaited them had become less frequent, and they warmed neither soul nor stomach the way they had done in the past.

Olga felt sore and tired to the bone, which really wasn't very far if you thought about it. Her ribs were visible just beneath the skin, and her hipbones jutted out so far that it really hurt when she knocked into a table or a doorframe. And she did that often. Hunger made them all clumsy, and Kolja fretful and whiny, but they were still alive while others were dead—Father and Grandfather and Jana's mother too, who had succumbed to tuberculosis just a month ago. Olga had watched from the window when she was sung out of the Petrenko house. Jana walked behind the funeral procession with her shoulders pulled all the way up to her ears, scratching her hair once in a while. She and Olga no longer spoke.

Mother had tied on both shawl and kerchief and reached for Kolja with an impatient gesture. "We have to go now, Kolja," she said in a thin voice. "Otherwise Mama Hog will get impatient."

Mama Hog, the largest of the breeding sows, was Kolja's favorite, and for her sake he was usually willing to hurry, but today he pulled himself free of Mother's hand and stuck out his lower lip. "I have to bring my rifle."

Olga looked around and caught sight of the stick that he had whittled smooth and nice and free of bark, and which had now been designated a weapon in the Red Army. She handed it to Kolja, who stashed it under his coat with a satisfied expression.

"Now we'll go," he said.

"Yes, now we'll go."

Mother and Kolja opened the door, walked out to the road and turned in the direction of the kolkhoz. Oxana remained in the doorway, looking at Olga.

"Come with me," she then said. "It will be all right. They won't dare to do anything."

Olga shrugged, not meeting Oxana's eyes. They had had this conversation before, and she knew what Oxana was going to say. Olga ought to go to school both for her own sake and for Uncle Stalin. She and all other children were the future of the nation. Oxana had reported the beating to the village soviet, and no one would dare to attack them again. That's what Oxana would say, but it would be lies, most of it, and even Oxana knew it.

Why else would Oxana go to so much trouble to get to the school without being seen? Olga knew which way she went. Instead of taking the long main street through the village, she snuck out through the orchard and followed the narrow path to the river. From there you could walk among the closely spaced birch trees to the back of the cooperative store without anyone seeing you unless they were really close. If you went through the gap between the wagon maker's shop and one of the village's deserted houses, you could reach the school without meeting a living soul.

But Olga wasn't having any of it.

After what happened with Vitja and Pjotr, she left the house only reluctantly, and when she did, it was mostly to collect water or logs or to stop by the Arsenovs. They subscribed to the local newspaper for Kharkiva Oblast and let Mother read it in return for helping them with their washing.

Oxana thought Olga was scared, but it wasn't just that. It was an unclear sensation of shame, even though Olga didn't think she had done anything wrong. It was the thought that she had been lying there in that frozen sewage ditch in the middle of the main street, her cheek pressed against the grubby ice and the sound of the boys' excited and breathless laughter in her ears. And as for Uncle Stalin—Olga had begun to grimace in her head every time he came up—as for good old Uncle Stalin, Oxana could take him and stick him up the ass of a cow, if she could find one that was big enough.

She didn't want to go to school, where Jana would be staring at her and Sergej would stick his oily face close to hers to whisper ugly words. And she didn't want to walk beside Oxana. Ever again.

OXANA FINALLY LEFT. Olga closed the door behind her and was alone.

That was okay. Better than going to school, at least, but she had to keep herself constantly occupied in order not to think too much. Today she was going to put their blankets out on the veranda. It was still cold, and with a bit of luck, the frost would kill some of the lice.

Olga took the birch broom and swept the floor as best she could, but the work quickly made her dizzy and short of breath, and in spite of the heat from the brick oven, she felt the raw cold through her underwear, dress and shawl.

She lay down on the oven shelf and covered herself with the heavy blankets and goat hides. The warmth from the heated bricks immediately made her doze off and dream uneasy dreams. Father was tied to a pole with his hands behind his back, and next to him stood the widow Svetlova dressed in a zobel fur and with her great, round stomach exposed and vulnerable to the gun barrels that pointed at them both.

Olga tried to wrest herself free from the dream, but the pictures kept coming in a swiftly flowing stream no matter how hard she squeezed her eyes shut. And then the pole was suddenly gone, and she was back in their own house and Father was outside hammering on the door with huge, heavy fists and screaming that she was to let him in.

She was still dreaming. It had to be a dream. But the insane hammering continued.

"Where is she? Where is your devil of a sister?"

I'm not going to open up, she thought. Why can't they all just leave us alone? The living and the dead.

A POLICE CAR FOUND her. Nina had made it into sitting position but no farther, her back propped against one of the Micra's front wheels. She wondered if the patrol car would be able to stop in time or would just continue into the Micra.

Luckily, the police had begun to equip their vehicles with winter tires. The patrol car came to a controlled stop ten or twelve meters from her. One of the cops got out; the other remained seated behind the wheel.

"Do you need any help?" asked the one who had gotten out.

Help. Yes, she did. All kinds of help.

"What time is it?" she asked instead.

The police woman squatted next to Nina. "Could you look at me for a moment?" she said. "Can you tell me what happened?"

"She drove into me," said Nina. "She must have been parked between the trees. She was waiting for me to come, and then she drove right into me."

The policewoman smiled in a calming way, but there was a bit of skepticism in her very young, very pretty face. "I think we need an ambulance for you," she said.

Nina decided she had been sitting there long enough. "No," she said. "I'm okay. Pretty much."

She thought she could feel a fracture in her lower left arm, but that wasn't exactly life threatening. She got to her feet on the first attempt but then had to lean discreetly on the Micra to remain upright until the dizziness wore off.

The hood was cold, she noticed. Fuck. That meant time had passed, and she had no idea how much. Her usual loss-of-time panic set in, but it was a familiar panic; she could control it. As long as someone told her the time *soon*.

"My name is Nina Borg," she said. "I'm a nurse at the Coal-House Camp. I was on my way home when another car suddenly appeared. I don't have a concussion; I'm completely oriented in time and place"—well, place at least—"and my own data. All I need right now is a taxi. And maybe a mechanic for the car."

The other officer, also a woman but somewhat older, had left the car and approached. "As long as you're not actually bleeding to death, we'd better set up a few warning reflectors. We prefer to deal with one accident at a time. What about the other driver? Did she just take off?"

"Yes."

The accident had been no accident. Natasha had been parked and waiting for her on one of the tracks the forestry workers used when they were transporting lumber. That much Nina had pieced together in her head while she was sitting in the snow, trying to muster the energy to get up. Belatedly she realized how they were likely to react when—or if—she told them who the woman was. It felt wrong, even now, to give Natasha up like that, to make it easier for them to find her.

"The other . . ." she said.

"Yes?"

"It was Natasha Dmytrenko."

"The one who . . ."

"Yes."

The treachery was complete.

One of the policewomen was already speaking very quickly into her radio. "Which way did she go?" the other asked. "And what kind of car was she driving?"

"I didn't see it very well," Nina said. "I think it was black or dark blue. Big. A heavy car. Maybe a Mercedes or an Audi? She drove that way, back toward Værløse."

The other officer cursed into her radio. "No, damn it. We can't even give pursuit while that stupid little car is blocking the way. Can we get some help out here in a hurry?" She shot a quick question at Nina. "When did she take off?"

"I don't know exactly," said Nina. "Five or six minutes after three, I think."

The policewoman lifted her well-functioning arm and looked at her well-functioning watch. Nina was jealous.

"So you've been sitting there in the snow for almost forty minutes?"

Forty minutes. Fuck.

"I guess I must have been," Nina said.

THE TAXI LET her off on Kløverprisvej at what she considered a suitable distance from Søren's house. She was gradually managing to bend and stretch her arm better. She still couldn't rotate it, so something was wrong, presumably a minor fracture. It might have been the airbag explosion itself that caused the damage, but it was still a lot better than banging her head into the steering wheel.

It was the cud-chewing Mr. Nielsen who let her in.

"It's after four," he said. "The boss has called twice to ask where you were. Fifteen minutes more, and we'd have had to upgrade our coverage."

"I'm sorry," said Nina. "Something unforeseen happened."

He looked at her as if nothing unforeseen ever happened in his world. And maybe it didn't. He looked like a man who not only had a Plan B but also Plans C, D, E, F and all the way to the end of the alphabet.

Magnus stood in the kitchen door. "*I* was starting to worry too. How did it go? Did Anton get to be Cat King?"

"No, but he was Super Mario and super stylish. How is Rina doing?"

"She's sleeping."

She knew she should tell them about Natasha and the accident, but she didn't have the energy right now. She had already been grilled twice by two different sets of police. The Coal-House Camp and Michael Vestergaard's house in Hørsholm were under the jurisdiction of North Zealand Police, while it was Copenhagen's Prison and Probation Service that was officially responsible for following up on Natasha's escape and her physical assault on an officer on duty. Nina felt as if she had repeated her story endlessly. All she had received in return was the information that the young policeman from the gas attack was conscious and out of danger. It was a huge relief—at least the officers hunting Natasha no longer thought they might be tracking down a cop killer.

Nina no longer knew how she felt about Natasha; she no longer fitted into any of the usual boxes. Some of the time Nina still saw her as Rina's mother and therefore a persecuted victim to be helped and protected; then Natasha would suddenly shape-shift into something wild and unpredictable to be kept at bay, a threat to Anton, a car waiting among the trees, a knife against the throat. Nina collected a little spit in her dry mouth and swallowed. She tried to concentrate on the present.

"What did Søren want?"

Nielsen Cud-Chewer paused for a second, possibly to indicate that he didn't completely approve her casual use of Inspector Kirkegard's first name.

"He had some questions. You can call him from my phone."

"In a little while," she said. "I just want to check on Rina. Here . . ." She awkwardly reached across her body to take the Bricanyl from her left pocket. "I went to get the last of her medicine."

The Cud-Chewer—who had stopped chewing cud, she noticed— looked like he was considering forcing her to call right this minute, but instead just activated the phone himself.

"She's back," she heard him say as she headed for the living room.

"What's wrong with your arm?" asked Magnus.

"Nothing," she said. "Nothing important."

In the living room, the television was still on, playing an eternal loop of noisy cartoons. Rina's socks stuck out from under the comforter at one end, but her head had completely disappeared. Perhaps the noise from the television was disturbing her sleep. Nina turned it off and switched on one of the two lamps on the windowsill. Rina didn't like waking up in the dark.

Then she noticed two things simultaneously.

The terrace door was slightly ajar. And in the silence that set in when she turned off the cartoon inferno, she couldn't hear Rina's breathing.

NATASHA FELT COOL and clear-headed. It was as if she was better able to think and act now that half her brain was no longer occupied with keeping track of where Katerina was. She dumped the damaged Audi in a snowdrift by a small forest and hoped that the snow would soon cover it so it would be just as hard to recognize as the other snow-covered roadside wrecks. There were plenty of those on a day like today.

She had to walk for a few kilometers along the road before the solution to her acute transportation problem revealed itself in the form of a long, sprawling inn with wide-open doors and men in shirtsleeves who stood in the doorway smoking. From inside the inn she could hear the loud, homemade songs that were a part of most Danish family celebrations, with the addition of jovial bass line, electric piano and a slightly tinny drum machine.

She edged her way past the smokers into the outer hall and proceeded down into the cloakroom in the basement without anyone taking any particular notice of her. In one of the many heavy overcoats hanging from the rack, she found a key ring with a Suzuki logo. The parking lot was behind the inn, next to the main entrance, and when she pressed the key's remote control, a helpful blinking light guided her to the right car. It was a small, ugly blue one, but it started without protest, and she drove unchallenged down the road and farther into the anonymous drifting snow.

She had no idea how to go about killing someone like the Witch, but it couldn't be that hard. Not when you were bigger and stronger than the person who was to die. And Natasha certainly was, because the Witch was tiny and more fragile than an egg. She pictured the old woman as she seen her in the backseat of the car in the winter forest, and in spite of her determination, Natasha felt a jolt of fear that she immediately tried to suppress. Stop thinking like a mouse, she said to herself. Now you're the hunter, and *she* is the one who has reason to fear. The days of shivering in the dark are over.

IN COMPARISON WITH the fourth break-in, the three first had been amateurish and almost peaceable. Natasha was wrenched from sleep straight into terror. She couldn't breathe, couldn't see. An unidentified pain raced up through her stomach, and it was only in the seconds that followed that she realized someone had hit her, and that the reason she couldn't scream was because something moist and acidic had been pushed into her mouth. An apple. They had stuffed an apple into her mouth as if she were a cartoon pig about to be roasted. The juice ran into her throat, and she tried to cough it out but couldn't. A hand in her face forced her head back against the bed's headboard.

"Not a sound. Get it, bitch?"

She did not get it. She didn't understand anything. There were two men in their apartment, and Pavel was nowhere to be seen.

"If you scream, we'll kill the kid. Do you understand that?"

She nodded, her fear choking her.

"Where is he?"

She assumed they meant Pavel, but she just shook her head. She tried again to spit out the apple, and this time they let her.

"Don't know," she gasped. "He isn't . . . don't know . . . where . . ."

"Listen, you whore. If you don't do exactly as I say, we'll fuck you till you can't walk. And afterward we'll do the same to the kid."

The words hit her harder than the heavy, brutal hands. She felt them inside her head, blows you couldn't block or duck.

"I don't know," she moaned. "He isn't here. I don't know."

"You can tell him that if he writes another word, we'll be back."

"Yes," she said. "I'll tell him. I will."

Not until they had left did she remember that Pavel was in Denmark. With Anna. He wouldn't be home for several days. She crept along the wall of the bedroom, down the hall and into Katerina's little room. The light was on, but Katerina was asleep. She lay with warm red cheeks and the blanket half kicked off, but she was all right; nothing had happened to her. Natasha let herself sink to the floor and sat with her knees folded up against her chest for almost an hour before she felt strong enough to get up again, find the telephone and call Pavel.

It was as if he didn't understand what had happened. Even though she told him, *told* him what they had said, told him that they had been *there*, in the apartment, he still didn't understand.

"But didn't the alarm work?" he asked, as if that meant anything.

"They said they would . . . Pavel, you have to come home. Now. Do you hear me?"

"I'll come as quickly as I can," he said. "Can't you go stay with your mother and father? My love, I understand that you are frightened, but that's what they want. That's why they do it."

"You're not going to write anymore, are you?" she said. "You'll do as they ask, won't you?"

There was a pause on the other end.

"Did they say what it was I couldn't write?" he asked.

"No. Just that you should stop."

"But it's my work," he said. "What we live on. I can't just stop."

She cried so hard, the snot was about to choke her. "You can just write good things," she said. "Things everyone will like."

"You can't live on that," he said.

She couldn't go home to Kurakhovo until the morning, when the trains would be running again. Instead, she got a knife from the kitchen and began breaking open his desk drawers, the ones he kept locked and didn't want her to look in. There wasn't much there. She knew there used to be more—old photographs, newspaper clippings. He had bought a scanner after the first break-in and used it frequently, so maybe it wasn't necessary to keep so many paper pictures around. There were some bank payment statements, some empty envelopes, a Dictaphone. The new digital camera he had just bought. A pack of condoms, which under normal circumstances would have made her insanely jealous. Now she barely cared.

It took her a few minutes to figure out how to make the camera show pictures on the little display, and it was hard to see them properly. There were pictures of various people and places, nothing she recognized. She turned on the Dictaphone, but there were no recordings on it. It was no longer the one he used when he talked with people, she remembered. His cell phone recorded the conversations for him now and stored them on a little flat memory stick.

Finally she looked at the payments. They were from U-card, the credit card that Pavel used most frequently. She was surprised to see how much he owed. And why was it that nothing was ever paid in? She looked down the long row of numbers. Nothing but outgoing payments, no deposits. Even though she let Pavel manage their budget, she knew this wasn't normal. You couldn't have a credit card like that, with everything going out, thousands and thousands of it, and nothing ever being paid back in.

Maybe it was like the rent—Pavel didn't have to play by the same rules as everyone else.

All at once she realized there *was* a link to some of the pictures in the little camera. She wasn't sure what it meant, but there was a connection. Two pictures showed a little old lady. In one a large man in an overcoat was helping her out of an even larger car. In the other she stood smiling broadly up at another man, a man Natasha knew mostly because he had once been on the national soccer team. Nikolaij Filipenko. And the woman holding his face between her hands was his mother, Tetjana Filipenko. Who owned U-card.

"WHO DO YOU call when you need a bit of cash? U-card, U-card, U-card! You call: zero, eight hundred, four hundred and two hundred twentyyyy."

She sang the little jingle aloud to herself, as Pavel had done when he flashed his gold card in expensive clothing boutiques and good restaurants. Happy, greedy Pavel who had treated that U-card like a goose who shat golden eggs, golden eggs he never had to pay for.

Natasha turned off the country road she was on and pulled over to the side. She drew the numbers with a finger on the fogged-over car window so she wouldn't stumble: 0-800-400-220. Then she found Robbie's cell phone in her pocket and called.

"U-card customer service. How may we help you?" The voice was young and mild and could almost have belonged to one of the scantily clad girls from the commercial. In the background Natasha heard the faint clatter of hundreds of fingers on computer keyboards.

"I would like to speak with Tetjana Filipenko."

"I'm sorry?"

Natasha waited a moment. "Tell her that Natasha Doroshenko wants to speak with her. Tell her to call me at this number."

"I think you have the wrong number." The voice at the other end had developed a sharp edge. "You have called U-card's customer service. We can block your card if it has been stolen. We can make a transfer for you. We can assist you with your . . ."

"Do you want to die?"

Natasha's question stopped the girl's memorized service patter, and the phone became silent. She could still hear the faint clicking from all the other keyboards and the soft buzz of other young women's voices in the background. Natasha pictured the young woman, far away in Ukraine, looking around for help. Considering her options. But she was surrounded by young women like herself, and they were all busy blocking U-cards and sending money through cyberspace.

"Tell Tetjana Filipenko that I called, and she should call me at this number. Natasha Doroshenko. Tell her."

She hung up and remained sitting with the phone in her hand. Closed her eyes and waited. The Witch would call.

UKRAINE, 1935

NO ONE WAS allowed to see the dead.

Not even Mother, although she screamed and cried herself hoarse in front of the village soviet's office. Comrade Semienova put her arm around Mother's shoulders and cried too, but she was still the one who held Mother back and prevented her from storming into the building where the GPUs were busy still. She had to wait until they were done examining the bodies, said Semienova. Nothing was more important right now than finding out what exactly had happened.

Olga stood behind her mother and could not cry, even though a hard, sharp pain had lodged itself just below her breastbone, like it sometimes did when something heavy hit you in the stomach. She couldn't cry, and she could barely breathe.

They had killed Oxana. That was what Comrade Semienova had told them. Down by the stream, with knives. The attack had been so violent that the blood had sprayed out over the snow and the naked birch branches in an arc several meters wide. That last detail Olga knew from Leda and Jegor, who had gone out with Comrade Semienova to look for Oxana. The first thing they had seen was little Kolja lying on the ground, staring emptily at the sky. His toy rifle was nowhere to be seen. Olga didn't know why she asked about it at all, but for some reason it felt important. As if the rifle could have made a difference. But he didn't have anything in his hand, said Leda, and he was dead, she could see that at once because his throat gaped like a broad red extra mouth under his chin.

Oxana had been lying a little farther off.

I want to die too, thought Olga. I want to die and lie together with little Kolja and even with Oxana, because now they no longer feel anything, while I hurt everywhere.

But she didn't die, and she couldn't think of anything she might do right now to make death happen. She could only stand there behind Mother and listen to her hoarse screams and look at Comrade Semienova, who had red, swollen eyes. Today she wasn't showing her dimples or smoking cigarettes.

During the night Mother finally stopped screaming, which was both a relief and a source of new fear, because what if she died of sorrow? Olga knew it was possible, because her own soul felt like it was twisting inside her and attempting to escape her body. Olga had heard that there was no greater sorrow than the one a mother feels when her child dies. And Mother had lost two children at once, and maybe that was more than heart and lungs and intestines and all the other things inside the body could endure.

Olga curled up, listening for Mother's breath in the darkness. She finally caught the sound, the kind of small, hiccupping gasps that small children sometimes made when they had cried deeply and for a long time. It was impossible to tell if Mother was sleeping or if she was awake. But at least she wasn't dead. Not yet.

Oxana would never sing again, and Kolja was done playing family and fighting great battles for the Red Army. Now he lay dead in the headquarters of the GPU. Olga suddenly wondered if all the lice on his head would follow him into the ground. The thought nauseated her, but she couldn't stop herself. Pictures kept popping into her mind, pictures of Kolja with his throat cut and lice that crawled slowly across his cold, pale scalp; of Oxana's sparklingly happy blue eyes that day when she had learned that she would sing at the Pioneer meeting in Kharkiv.

"You shouldn't have gone, Oxana," Olga whispered into the mattress. "I told you not to go."

I N A FEW quick frames of the footage, Rina slid down from the couch and under the coffee table. It took less than six seconds. Another camera had caught her at the garage and a ways down the sidewalk, a sequence of twenty-one seconds. Both recordings were almost two hours old.

"She's alone," said the Cud-Chewer and searched on among the not-an-iPad's stored pictures. "It's not a kidnapping."

"I thought you were watching her," said Nina. "I thought you were fucking professionals. What good is all that equipment if you can't even keep track of one little girl? She's eight, damn it!"

"The camera is set so that it registers ordinary movement in the room. I wasn't expecting her to worm her way across the floor!"

"Did she see you place the camera?"

The Cud-Chewer was practically chewing his jaw off its hinges. "Maybe," he admitted. "I thought she was asleep."

"Why exactly is it that people think she is deaf, blind and dumb just because she doesn't say very much?" Nina snarled.

Mikael Nielsen didn't answer. He was making a call, presumably to his boss.

The trick of placing a couch pillow under the comforter so that it looked as if there were still a sleeping girl there—Rina might have picked that up from countless television films. The ruse with the stuffed socks was all her own—it had probably been easier for her than to make than something that looked like a head.

Nina stared blindly out the window at the snowflakes that glittered whitely in the light from the streetlamp. It was freezing out there. Pitch dark. And Rina was alone.

Mikael handed her the telephone. "He wants to speak with you."

She took the phone silently.

"You know Rina," said Søren. His voice sounded calm, almost as if the world hadn't exploded around them. "Where would she go? Where would she think of going?"

Nina thought desperately. "The Coal-House Camp, maybe. One of the policemen out there was kind enough to point out that it was where her mother would look for her first."

"Okay. How would she get out there? Does she know how to take the bus?"

"Maybe. She doesn't know her way around the city as such, but she knows the right bus number."

"Would she talk to strangers? Ask for help?"

"I don't think so. You've met her. She barely speaks to people she's known for years."

"Other places?"

Nina tried to imagine Rina's mental map of Denmark. Where had she actually been? Not a whole lot of places other than the camp.

"Vestre Prison. We visited her mother there. But she knows Natasha isn't there anymore. Michael Vestergaard's house, of course. Hørsholm. It's close to Hørsholm."

"I know. Other places?"

"Not a lot. Tivoli, that kind of place. The National Aquarium. I think they once did a project about fish with the Coal-House children. I don't know!"

"That's fine. That's a good start." She could hear the professional,

calming tone she herself had often used. Praise made people relax—
and it worked on her too, even though she knew perfectly well why
she was being praised.

"What will you do?" she asked.

"We'll check the places you have given us, and the routes there,
focusing primarily on the camp and Hørsholm. We'll send people out
to look in nearby areas too—garden sheds, tree houses, that kind of
thing. Does she have any money?"

"I think so. They get an allowance. Natasha has sent her a little as
well, and she doesn't really use it."

"And she doesn't have a cell phone other than the old broken one?"

"No."

"Too bad."

"Søren."

"Yes?"

"She used your telephone."

"Mine?"

"Yes, the one in the living room. I thought she was just dialing
randomly; she said the old one didn't work anymore. The policeman
had said it was broken. I don't know if it was you or . . . or your colleague she meant."

"Okay."

"I thought she just wanted to speak with her father, but what if that
wasn't what it was? What if she called someone? In real life, I mean."

"Let me talk to Nielsen," he said, and she handed the telephone
back to the Cud-Chewer.

Nina zipped up her jacket. Luckily, she could open and close it
with her left hand.

"Hello—where are you going?" asked the Cud-Chewer.

"I'm going to look for her in the neighborhood," she said through
clenched teeth. "She may not have been able to get very far."

"Wait." Magnus had followed her. "Wait a second, Nina. We can't just run around randomly."

"It's urgent," she said.

"Yes, but we need to be a bit systematic. You go this way"—he pointed toward Kløverprisvej—"and I'll go this way. We'll meet again at the corner in half an hour."

Nina nodded, desperate to get started. Rina had run away before; they had done this before. And we found her then, she told herself. We will this time too!

She had spoken to two neighbors and looked in three garages when the realization hit her. *You have reached Anna and Hans Henrik Olesen. We can't come to the phone now* . . . Because of the male voice she hadn't put two and two together. But the wife's name was Anna. Like Neighbor Anna. The Anna she had met, the Anna who had taken such loving care of Rina the night Natasha had decided to try to kill her fiancé.

"Olesen, that's what she was called," she said aloud to herself.

On the other side of the street, going in the direction of Hvidovrevej and Damhusdalen, was a taxi. The green FREE sign shone like a signal in the dusky gloom, and before she had time to think, she had leaped into the road with one arm in the air.

SOMETIMES WHEN YOU have to do a really hard thing, you can't let yourself think. No looking down and discovering how deep the drop is beneath your feet, and no looking ahead either. You balance on a wire, and it can be ten or a hundred meters long. It doesn't matter, because you can't run anyway, and you can't jump the last bit to make it across the abyss. You can't cheat. All you can do is place one foot in front of the other. One step at a time.

Natasha was kneeling in the snow between the dense bushes, gazing out at the parking lot. The afternoon darkness had turned the snow grey. The sky above her was dark blue with faint, glowing streaks of light in the west, and she could feel the temperature dropping in the air around her, burning her fingers and toes.

She hadn't made a real plan. She knew it, but the simplicity of her idea still gave her a kind of solace, because she only needed two minutes. Maybe less.

One hand rested lightly on the tire iron from the car's trunk. It was heavy enough. More than heavy enough, she thought. And the wait would soon be over.

A group of half-grown boys crossed the farthest end of the parking lot. They ducked in turns, shoveling little piles of frosty snow together with clumsy mittens and throwing loose handfuls of it at one another in fun. The snow was probably too powdery for real snowballs. The sound of their shouting and laughter cut through the clear air, but besides that there was no sound except the faint rush of cars on the distant main road. Kastrup Fort, with its old fortifications and dungeons, lay deserted and empty in the winter dusk.

She knew the place from her time with Michael. He liked to bring them here when the weather was good, her and Katerina. There was a playground at the bottom of the grounds and a few beat-up, green-painted toilets with lots of graffiti. A bit higher up lay the restaurant with the large green clover lawn and the view over the ramparts, where weeds grew dense and wide-leaved in the summer and smelled sharp and sweet at the same time.

Michael and Katerina had played hide-and-seek on the steep stairs and labyrinthine paths that wound through the thicket of whitethorn and bramble on their way to the top of the fort. Once there had been lookouts here, soldiers and cannons. Now only bare cement circles were left. Natasha knew that it would be a good place to meet your enemies, exactly as it had been in the past. There were only two real bridges over the moat, but today that didn't matter, because the moat was frozen and covered with snow, so she could theoretically disappear in any direction. Theoretically. Whether she got away or not was of little importance. One step at a time. One foot in front of the other.

THE CAR ROLLED into the parking lot ten minutes before the agreed-upon time. Natasha recognized it from the woods behind the Coal-House Camp, long and black and shiny, like a hearse. The license plates were no longer Ukrainian but Danish, she noticed. The Witch might be a queen in Kiev, but here in Bacon Land, her power was reduced, and she had to hide like the freak that she really was. Natasha felt a fleeting sense of cold triumph as she crouched even lower behind the cover of the bushes. She hoped that her tracks in the snow wouldn't be too visible in the dusk and that the man and woman in the car would not be too on their guard.

A broad, slightly hunched figure got out and remained standing for a long moment with his hands on the car roof, looking around. She knew exactly what he could see because she had paced the parking lot herself several times: On one side, naked trees and dense shrubbery sloping down to a snow-covered moat. On the other, the old dungeon which Michael had said once held ammunition for the fort's four cannons. The stairs up to the meeting place she had suggested were narrow and icy, and as the man took the first step, he slipped and had to grip the steel railing in order not to fall.

He returned to the car and opened the door for the woman in the backseat. It was too far for Natasha to see anything but a shadow moving behind the man's back and a glimpse of a pale, upturned face. He said something, and Natasha knew what it was. Or at least she thought she did.

"You can't come up there with me. The stairs are slippery, and you're old. I will go up to the top and meet her alone."

That was about what he said, because that was how she had planned it. The old woman would probably resist. She wanted to come, thought Natasha, because what she wanted from Natasha meant so much to her that she had dragged her old, rotting body all the way up here through half of Europe.

Natasha held her breath while the man bent down to the old woman. Gestured. Eventually, it seemed, the old lady accepted. She moved farther into the backseat with her hands pulled up to her fur collar to shield herself from the cold. The interior light hit the sharp features of her powdered face for a second. Then the man slammed the door, and the old woman became nothing more than a dark profile behind the car window.

The man looked at his watch. It was hard to determine his age at this distance, but he wasn't young, thought Natasha. It was the heft that she noticed, the width in his body that didn't belong to a young man. Nonetheless, he moved up the stairs with surprising speed. She would not have long to enact her plan, most likely not more than a few minutes. That would have to be enough.

When Natasha could no longer see him because of the thicket of thorn bushes, she carefully counted to thirty. He should be approaching the meeting place. He wouldn't turn around at once, he would think that she was on her way, that she would appear from the sheltering bushes up there any moment.

It was quiet around her now, and she closed her hand more tightly on the tire iron. It felt heavy and cold and right.

One foot in front of the other.

Springing to her feet, she sprinted across the parking lot. The distance to the car seemed to stretch elastically, and twice she almost stumbled on the packed ice under the new snow, but she stayed on her feet and tried to increase her speed. She ran with the tire iron hanging like a dead weight in her right hand. Not until she reached the car did she raise it and hit the car window with full force. A hard, flat thump resounded in the silence, and her fingers lost sensation from the blow. Still, there wasn't much to see other than a long, thin crack that ran across the side window. The Witch's face had turned toward her. The eyes were narrow black slits, the lips pulled back in a grimace that revealed long, crumbling teeth. Natasha imagined how thin the skull would feel under the soft fur hat and the thin, downy hair. What it would sound like on impact. Like a nut being cracked inside a fur bag.

She raised the tire iron again, and this time she used both hands to follow through. There was another odd, dead thump, and the pain in her hands raced all the way up to her wrists. The face behind the window was now partially obscured by a white cloud in the glass. But the window remained intact, and the woman in there stared directly at her, as if Natasha were an interesting natural phenomenon of the kind you can go to see in a safari park.

She sensed the abyss beneath her.

Then she grabbed the car door and pulled the handle, without luck. Of course.

She had been so unbelievably stupid. Of course the Witch was still untouchable. Of course she couldn't kill her.

Natasha hit the window again, hammering away, and with every blow, the face became harder to make out.

"Die." Natasha was winded now, and her words sounded just as dead and flat as the impact of the tire iron. "Please—just—die."

She closed her eyes and struck again, and this time there was a little hollow sound like when a hard-boiled egg hits a table, but it wasn't just the sound that made her look carefully at the window's cobweb pattern. She could feel in her fingers that something was finally yielding. And true enough, a little black hole gaped in all the whiteness, and she hit the window again with full force in precisely that place and felt the euphoric sensation of almost reaching the goal when the glass yielded even further. One foot in front of the other.

As she raised the tire iron once more, someone grabbed hold of it and jerked it back with such suddenness that she swayed and tumbled backward into the snow. Blows fell on her face, hard and precise and in a steady rhythm. She felt two of her molars shatter and cut into her tongue, already warm with blood.

"Natasha Doroshenko?"

She was too confused to answer. Just shook her head stupidly and tried to get up.

New blows. Fast and hard.

"Natasha Doroshenko?"

This time she managed to answer yes, but in the instant that followed, everything rushed away from her in whirls of grey and black and red. The wire under her feet broke, and she dropped and fell straight into the abyss below.

THE PARTY BURIED Oxana. And Kolja too, even though he was neither a hero nor a pioneer. For Mother's sake, as Semienova said. So Mother wouldn't have to think of anything but the heroic deed her daughter had done, and for which she had bravely paid with her life.

"Your daughter is an example to Soviet youth," said Semienova. She didn't have red eyes any longer and now seemed more angry than sad, and with the anger, some of her shining energy had returned. She had become beautiful again. "A visionary little girl who valued solidarity above all else, even her own family. A true pioneer."

Olga couldn't help wondering whether she would also have been buried by the Party if she had been murdered along with Kolja and Oxana. Would Semienova have made a beautiful speech about her?

Mother sat with her head hanging limply on its thin neck and didn't look as if she was really listening to anything Comrade Semienova was saying. She hadn't lit the oven, and she hadn't swept the floor or cooked the porridge or done the washing. The whole house smelled like a dung heap, thought Olga, and she was constantly freezing.

"But there should be a panachydy," Mother mumbled then. "There should be a singing. My children must be sung out with 'Vichnaya Pam'yat.' Forever remembered, forever loved. I have to call a priest."

Comrade Semienova shook her head. "Oxana was not religious, and she had a strong will. A priest at her funeral would be an insult to everything she stood for. The funeral should be in her spirit, and the Party Committee has already—"

"And Kolja?" Now Mother lifted her head and stared at Semienova with a look that frightened Olga. "Must little Kolja be shut out of Heaven too?"

Comrade Semienova just smiled a sad little smile and stroked Olga's hair before she left. Olga had hoped she would stay a little longer because it was not nice to be alone with Mother, who just sat staring into the blue. But it was as it had always been. Comrade Semienova was busy with Oxana, even now when her body lay cold and hard in a coffin somewhere, and she could neither sing nor engage in interesting political discussions in the classroom. Even now, Oxana was more interesting than Olga.

Olga knew that it was wrong to think this way. In fact, she should feel nothing but sorrow now that Oxana was dead and had been murdered by the kulaks, as it said in the newspaper, but it was as if she couldn't stop the forbidden thoughts no matter how hard she tried. In fact, it was as if they grew and swelled the more she tried to drive them off. Like the time when Jana and she had begun laughing in old Volodymyr Pavlenko's class and had just laughed louder and louder the more he scolded them. It was as if they had been hit by a kind of madness that wasn't cured until he slapped them both quite hard.

Please don't let Semienova see what I'm thinking, prayed Olga quietly. She must not see what I'm thinking about Oxana . . . but now Semienova was on her way out and only turned in the doorway to say goodbye to Mother.

Mother didn't look up, but suddenly some force inside her seemed to come alive again. "Damn you, Semienova. Damn you to hell—you and all your fine friends in the Party." She wasn't speaking very loudly. "They were my children, and now you won't even let me see them. Not even in death can I get them back."

Olga held her breath, and Semienova, who had been about to close the door behind her, hesitated. She opened it again, and an ice-cold blast of winter raced through the living room, even though Olga had thought it couldn't possibly get any colder.

"Watch what you say," said Semienova. She looked shaken and upset, and Olga understood her. Mother should not be scolding her like this, and Olga felt sorry for Semienova. "I like you and your daughter, but I can't protect you from everything. Your ex-husband's family has already been arrested and is on their way to Sorokivka. There will be a harsh reckoning with the kulaks and their anti-Soviet propaganda."

It was no use. Mother couldn't be stopped. Her eyes were black pieces of coal in her pale face. "None of this would have happened if it wasn't for you," she hissed. "You have blood on your hands, and it will never come off."

Mother made an effort to stay upright for the funeral. She did not brush her own hair or change her clothes, but she washed Olga's face and braided her hair, her touch gentle. Olga found her good dress, the one she had worn in the picture Semienova took; it was still pretty, although the sleeves were now too short. Oxana's dress would have fit her better, but Mother had given it to Semienova so Oxana could wear it in the coffin. A waste. Wouldn't it have been better for Olga to be dressed nicely for the funeral and for Oxana to be in the too-small dress rather than the other way around? The coffin was closed anyway.

Olga pictured Oxana lying there beneath the heavy lid with her hair spread out on the pillow. Kolja was to be buried in his new coat, although without his rifle. Even though Olga had searched and searched for it down by the stream, she hadn't been able to find it.

Then they were off. Down the main street, where the snow had started to melt and turn to mud. Spring would come without Father and Kolja and Oxana, even though Olga had not thought it would be possible.

IN THE GRAVEYARD, a brass band was playing, and the pioneer division from Sorokivka had come. Some of the older children must have met Oxana, because they stood with tears in their eyes when Comrade Semienova stepped forward to speak. She looked wonderful in pants and a man's jacket, her mouth painted red. She spoke of how Oxana had wished for freedom for the workers and the peasants, and how she had often talked about how unfair it was that the kulaks still had so much when others had so little. Too good for this world, Comrade Semienova concluded. The people's nightingale had fallen from the sky, but her song would still sound in everyone's hearts.

No one said anything about Kolja.

NATASHA WAS PRETTY sure that she was going to die.

Not because the man next to her had said anything particular to her or had been deliberately threatening. It was more the way that the woman in the backseat and he spoke to each other—so quiet and relaxed, as if Natasha had already been taken care of and never would be a threat again.

"Did you speak to Nikolaij?" asked the man.

"No. No, I'll wait to call until we get home again. He thinks I'm in Odessa. I couldn't say . . ."

"No, I guess you couldn't." The man's tone had become dry and distant.

"Jurij, you know it's different with him. He doesn't understand these things."

"I know. Forget it, Mamo. It'll work out. We can leave tonight if you want. Then we'll be home by Tuesday morning at the latest. I need some proper food; I'm about to throw up from all the hot dog buns." He laughed a brief, explosive laugh and slammed one hand flat against the steering wheel.

Even though he was probably the one who would be in charge of the actual execution, it was the old woman who made the hairs at the back of Natasha's neck stand up. She made Natasha intensely uncomfortable, and Natasha couldn't help turning her head every other second so she could at least see her out of the corner of her eye. The Witch noticed and sent her a brief, unreadable look before turning her head toward the side window.

"What are we looking for, Jurij?" she asked. Passing headlights and the white overhead flicker of the streetlamps illuminated her narrow face and made deep black shadows of the furrows around her mouth and eyes.

He shrugged. "A good place," he said.

Natasha sank a little deeper into the seat. The blood kept collecting in her mouth, and she was tired of swallowing it. She considered how he might react if she spat it out, either on the bottom of the car or in a dramatic red splatter on the side window. She caught sight of herself in the side-view mirror, her ghostlike reflection flashing back at her each time they passed another streetlight. Her face looked battered and distorted. One of her eyes had almost disappeared in a swelling that seemed to grow with every glimpse. Strands of hair had come loose from her ponytail and were matted against her forehead, nose and swollen eyelid, but she was unable to push them aside or scrub away the bloody tracks under her nose. The man, Jurij, had bound her hands behind her back with thin plastic strips of the kind normally used to organize cables or attach plastic toys to brightly colored cardboard backgrounds.

Like a Barbie in a cardboard box, she thought. The face in the mirror, which was no longer really hers, crumpled and emitted an odd, sobbing snort, neither laughing nor crying. Little flecks of blood hit the man's hand on the gearshift. He shot her an irritated look, reached across her and searched for something in the glove compartment. Finally he found a pack of wet wipes and wiped his hands, cursing softly, before once more turning his full attention to the road.

The traffic abruptly slowed down and then almost stopped. Up ahead Natasha could see blinking blue lights and men in yellow reflective vests. Some of them read POLICE.

She considered whether there was anything she could do. The nice Danish policemen probably wouldn't be quite as nice now that she had attacked one of their own, but they wouldn't kill her and bury her in "a good place." But it was hopeless. She could neither wave nor knock on the window, at least not unless she began pounding her head against it. Jurij glanced at her and pulled aside his overcoat in a relaxed way so she could see the butt of a black pistol.

"First I'll shoot you," he said. "Then I'll shoot them if necessary. But first you."

She sat passive, her head bowed, while they passed the police car and the tow truck that was in the process of pulling two cars apart.

WHEN THE POLICE came to say that Pavel was dead, she hadn't been surprised. That is what happens when you don't believe in the reality of wolves, she thought. Meanwhile, her body registered an inner breakdown, as if her spine had finally succumbed to some long-term pressure and collapsed. Her legs became numb, and she could no longer feel her face. Her hearing came and went, and she had to ask the policeman to repeat the message several times to catch it all. In a car. At Lake Didorovka. What had he been doing there?

"Did he come off the road?" she asked, because maybe there was still a chance to normalize his death into the comprehensible everyday universe. But no. Of course not. It was homicide. A "suspicious death," they called it. That didn't surprise her either.

What took her by surprise was that they wanted her to say she had done it.

They brought both her and Katerina to the station and placed Natasha in a little room with green walls and both bars and netting in front of the window. Katerina was not allowed to stay with her. Natasha could hear her crying in the next room. It was a terrible sound; it filled her so she couldn't think, it made her chest and stomach ache, and she tried to make the officers understand that she would listen if she could just comfort Katerina first.

They asked her why she had done it.

Done what? she asked.

And then they explained that it was usually wives who killed their husbands, and she had probably grown tired of him and wanted his money. He has no money, she said, while Katerina cried; he owes several hundred thousand. To whom? To U-Card.

That made them hesitate. They went out into the hall and spoke quietly. Then one of them disappeared. The other asked if she wanted tea. No, no tea. Just Katerina. Yes, of course. Something had changed, as if "U-Card" was a magic formula that opened locked doors. Suddenly she was allowed to see her daughter. After a little while, the second policeman left too. Only a secretary remained, sitting at a desk.

Natasha lifted Katerina up onto her hip and asked if she was charged with anything. "No," said the secretary. "They just want a statement from you."

"Then it'll have to be after I go to the doctor with my daughter," said Natasha, with a new authority. "Can't you hear how labored her breathing is?"

She left the station. All they had with them was Katerina's little backpack and what Natasha had in the pockets of her coat; she didn't even have her wallet. She had to go back to the apartment even though her instinct screamed that she had to get away while she could.

Instead of going up directly, she rang the downstairs neighbors' buzzer. They had an au pair, Baia, a young girl from Georgia who for some reason was always in a good mood. She and Natasha had taken the children to the playground together on a few occasions—the neighbors had twins, a boy and a girl—but Natasha had the feeling that Baia had been told not to associate with her. There was a certain glint in Baia's eyes, a secretiveness in her giggling, that made it seem as if they were two teenagers playing hooky from school to smoke cigarettes behind the bicycle shed.

Today Baia wasn't quite as upbeat as usual.

"I've heard," she said. "Terrible. And the police have been here, also SBU, and they asked a lot of questions and stomped around upstairs for several hours."

"Have they left?" Natasha asked.

"Yes, I think so. It's quiet now."

Katerina stayed with Baia and the twins while Natasha snuck up the stairs. The door was wide open, just like with the first break-in. It was quiet in there, but as Natasha ventured into the front hall, she heard a faint noise from the living room. She glided silently toward the door and looked in cautiously.

Everything had been worked over. Drawers pulled out and over-turned, books cleared from the shelves, pillows and cushions cut open so the filling lay like snow across the wreckage. And in the middle of everything, there she was. The Witch. A tiny, bent old woman with white hair and a coat that reached almost down to her ankles and her shiny, high-heeled red shoes. She stood half turned toward the window, and the light shone right through her thin white hair so you could see her scalp and the outline of her skull.

Baba Yaha, thought Natasha, the old witch who lives in a cottage in the woods, a cottage that has legs like a hen and can run around like a living creature.

She stood with a picture of Katerina. The newest one, which they had had enlarged and framed so it could stand on Pavel's desk. Katerina wore braids and smiled shyly, but there was a sparkle in her big, beautiful eyes. "She looks like someone who is up to mischief," Pavel had said and had kissed the picture, and then the live model, six or seven times right under the hair at the nape of the neck, until Katerina screeched and said it tickled.

Baba Yaha ate children who came and knocked on her door. The fence around the chicken-legged house was made from human bones.

The old woman suddenly slammed the picture against the side of the table so the glass shattered and shards spilled across the desk and floor with a shrill tinkling. With her thin fingers, she peeled the photograph out of the frame and stuck it in her coat pocket. Natasha only managed to pull back her head just in time as the old woman began to turn around.

There was no time to think. Natasha grabbed her bag from the coatrack in the front hallway and raced down the stairs to Baia. An hour later, she was on her way to the Polish border in a rented car with only the clothes she had on, but with Katerina in the seat next to her, so close that she could touch her once in a while, as if it was necessary to make sure she was still there.

THE BIG MAN, Jurij, had taken them off the main road and into a semi-deserted summerhouse area. The road was only partially cleared, and the small wooden cabins on both sides were dark and cold. Natasha thought she could glimpse the sea among the trees at the end of the dead-end road. Her every instinct told her that this was it, they were going no farther. This was the place where Jurij would do what he planned to do. When he finally slowed the car, there were no longer any houses around them, and the road had narrowed even further. The car's tires spun a few times in the snow, caught hold and then finally stopped completely when Jurij turned the key and shut off the motor.

For a moment they sat silently in the faint interior light, all three.

"We've been looking for you for a long time," said the big man. "But you know that. Of course you know that."

He turned in his seat and gazed attentively at her, as if he was searching for an answer in her exposed and battered face. He was old too, thought Natasha, sixty years or more, and he didn't look anything like the tiny woman he had called mother several times. His face was meaty, his lips broad and spotted by age and tobacco. Only in his brilliant blue eyes could you clearly see that mother and son were related. Even now, in the gloom, and with the eyes partially shaded under a pair of heavy, baggy eyelids. The Witch had given birth to a monster and had suckled it at her own breast. This was not the son the little woman appeared with in the papers. He wasn't the suit-wearing, beautiful, clean politician. This son was a man who used his hands and got things done. Not the kind who built things but the kind who demolished them.

She avoided his gaze, feeling the blood pooling around the teeth in her lower jaw once more. She didn't dare spit but instead bent forward and let the blood dribble over her down jacket.

"Your husband, Pavel, was a coward," Jurij continued, unaffected. "Many believed he was a hero, a journalist who wrote the truth because he was a man with honor and integrity. In reality he only wrote what he was paid to write. And it was almost always lies. The truth, on the other hand, he was well paid to keep hidden."

Natasha didn't answer. Her tongue kept getting cut by the jagged edges of her broken molars, and what he said was not news to her. She had known it for a long time. Pavel was no hero.

"The question is," said the man, and again she felt his searching gaze. "How well did he hide his secrets, and where did he get them? How much does his pretty wife know? And what about his daughter? Even little pitchers have big ears."

Natasha tried to control herself, but the mention of Katerina made her twitch. And she knew he saw it and would store her weakness somewhere in his memory.

"I know nothing," she said. The blood sloshed under her tongue and made it hard to speak clearly. "Pavel never told me anything."

He sighed. An old man's exhaustion. The big hands rested on the steering wheel.

"Nonetheless," he said, "I will give you a chance to try and remember something. Where did he hide his papers and pictures?"

Natasha shook her head. "There were only the things in the apartment," she said, slurring her words. "There wasn't anything else."

She sensed at once she'd made a mistake by acknowledging that she knew something. She could see it by the tiniest of twitches in the heavy eyelids. "The things in the apartment . . ." he repeated. "You know we were there. You know we searched it."

It was quiet between them for a long moment, during which Natasha heard nothing but the faint hiss of small, hard snowflakes against the car's windows. Then the man opened the car door with a quick, angry jerk and stomped through the snow to the trunk. The old woman behind her emitted a long sigh and leaned back in her seat. Natasha caught the scent of her perfume and the musky smell of her mummified old body.

"I know nothing." Natasha turned as far as she could and tried to catch the old woman's gaze. "I don't know what you are looking for. Please don't touch Katerina."

She would have said more, but it was as if her words hit an invisible glass wall. The old Witch just looked at her. Her narrow face looked almost childish under the dome of the fur hat.

Then the car door on Natasha's side was thrown open, and Jurij grabbed hold of what was left of her ponytail and pulled her forward until she sat with her face between her legs. He worked fast, cutting the plastic strips off her wrists and attaching her right hand to the seat belt's buckle with a new one. Then he made a loop around her left hand—a thin rope—no, not a rope, a wire, a plastic-covered wire of the kind used for pulling boats up on the shore.

At the police station, they had shown her pictures of Pavel. Of his shattered hands that looked as if someone had hit them with a hammer. They had asked her why she had done it. Not *if* she had done it, just why.

She looked up at the man with the heavy eyes and the heavy body and understood for one burning second what he was planning. She opened her mouth without wanting to and felt her ruined lip tighten over her broken teeth, but there was still nothing she could tell him. If she had known, if she had been able to give him what he wanted, she would have.

He tightened the wire and pulled her left arm across the empty driver's seat, then disappeared out of her field of vision. She could feel by the pull in the wire that he was fastening it to something, but she didn't know what. He looked over his handiwork, growled, made some adjustments. There was nothing she could do. The seat belt and the plastic strip immobilized her in the seat; she had just a few centimeters' leeway. The strain in the arm stretching across the seat was uncomfortable, but that wasn't the problem. The problem was that her hand was positioned precisely where it would get caught when he slammed the door a few moments from now.

"I know nothing," she repeated, without any hope that it would stop him.

Surprisingly, he nodded and bent down so that she could see his face better. "I believe you," he said. "But sometimes one remembers the most incredible things." He looked like a kindly teacher awaiting an answer from a fumbling student. "I have asked you a question now. And your brain, the computer you have that remembers and thinks, is already hard at work. A little man has been sent down to rummage through the files in the archives, and I'm sure he will come back to us with something. Don't you think?"

Natasha shook her head silently. The details in his heavy face were imprinting themselves indelibly in her—the drooping cheeks, the burst blood vessels at the point of the cheekbones, the chin covered with bristly stubble, the five or six long hairs from each eyebrow that hung down over his Santa Claus–like blue eyes. She would remember that face till she died.

Which wouldn't be long—less than half an hour, most likely. That knowledge hit her once again, like a fist under her ribs.

"Look," he said. He took a folded piece of paper from his coat pocket, smoothed it out and held it so the interior car light illuminated it clearly. It was a printed copy of a black-and-white photograph of two girls. It was old, and the girls were wearing traditional Ukrainian dresses, like the ones folk dancers still used. "Where did this come from?" asked Jurij. "Where did your husband get this picture?"

"I don't know," she whimpered. "I know nothing."

She could feel the icy edge and the mechanism of the lock with the back of her fingers. She tried instinctively to pull her hand back, but the wire didn't permit it. Jurij straightened up and reached for the car door.

If all my fingers break, I can't drive, thought Natasha. If my fingers break, I can't turn the key and shift gears, and I can't . . . It felt as if her heart stopped in her chest for a moment. I can't kill the Witch.

Then he slammed the door. Natasha screamed, but she no longer attempted to pull back. Instead, she pushed her hand as far out of the car as it would go, so the door hit the her wrist and the heel of her hand rather than the fingers. The pain was excruciating, but she could feel that the bone was intact. She wasn't incapacitated. Not yet.

Suddenly she thought of aspirins.

Why? Why aspirins?

Jurij had opened the door again and was looking at her.

"Yes, it hurts," he said, as if he were a doctor who was sorry that a necessary vaccination involved a needle prick. "What about the little man? Has he found anything in the archives?"

Little man? There were no small men in her brain. Her brain was a mouse at the bottom of a tin pail, a mouse that raced around, jumped for its life and scrabbled at the smooth surface to find a way out.

He stepped back behind the door, ready to slam it again.

"No," she said. "No . . ."

And then it came. An image of Anna's home. She and Pavel and Katerina are at the dining room table eating cake. It is summer. The first visit to Denmark, and Katerina's second year in the world. Pavel would have preferred to go alone, he said, because he had many meetings to take care of, and he thought Katerina was still too little to fly. But Natasha pleaded and begged, and at last he'd given in. So now she is here in Denmark with Pavel's mother's old nanny. Anna is stern and distant, thinks Natasha, except when it comes to Katerina. With her she chatters cozily in a steady stream of Danish and a few Ukrainian words Pavel must have taught her. "Dog." "Cake." "Thirsty." "Sleepy." Short children's words that Katerina understands. Anna stuffs her with chocolate cake and brightly colored chocolate drops. Natasha is tired and has a headache.

"You can take a couple of my pills from the drawer in the bedroom," says Anna, now in English, which is the language they speak when Natasha is there. Otherwise, Anna and Pavel mostly speak German. It is all a big mess, and it's so hard to talk to anybody, and maybe that is why Natasha's head hurts so much. She has the sense that Pavel and Anna share something, that they are keeping her in the dark by speaking a language she doesn't understand.

"Panodil, aspirin or codeine," says Anna. "I think I have all three."

Natasha gets up and goes up into the bedroom and pulls out the top drawer of the dresser. She finds a plastic bottle marked aspirin, unscrews the lid and tips two pills into her hand. A few other pill containers rattle around in there, and at the back, some yellowed photographs lie loosely piled on the flowered paper lining the drawer. One of them shows two girls. It is very old and faded. The girls are dressed in the finest and most festive of traditional styles, and they are both looking seriously into the camera. It isn't Danish, she can see that, both because of the clothes and because of the lettering that reads, "Mykolayevka. Two nightingales." It's a little odd that it's here, she thinks, but maybe Pavel gave it to Anna. He has his own drawers at home, always kept locked, and in them are many old photographs that he doesn't want her to tidy or "mess up," as he calls it. This was before the first break-in. Before he got the scanner.

Natasha leaves this picture alone too. What does she need the past for? The present is bright and happy, at least most of the time—Natasha has discovered that it is entirely possible to be jealous of old ladies, even ones who decidedly do not want to sleep with her husband. Why do they have to chat so intimately in German all the time? Then she scolds herself as he would have, stupid Natasha, silly Natasha, takes the aspirin and joins the others again. They revert to English when they hear her on the steps, and Anna asks if she is feeling better now.

"ANNA!"

Jurij had opened the car door wide, ready to slam it again when Natasha suddenly said the name. Now he hesitated.

"I know where it is," said Natasha. "The picture. I know who has it!"

Jurij let go of the door. She felt the relief flood her like soft, warm water. Could it really be that simple? Was that really all they wanted? A picture from Anna? Her wrist pounded, sore and painful, but she could still move her fingers and hands, and in a miraculous way she now had a new chance to save Katerina.

"Where?" asked Jurij, and Natasha felt the wire loosen around her aching wrist.

"It's here," she said. "In Denmark. I'll show you where it is."

"**W**E SENT A man over there," explained Heide with somewhat exaggerated patience. "They are packing up out there so they can get home before the roads close, but Veng fought his way through the snowdrifts, and there was no one home. No sign of the girl, and Anna Olesen only showed up while he was actually knocking on the door. She had apparently been out searching for that dog again. He went through everything, including the stables, and the girl wasn't there."

"That's the number Katerina phoned."

"Yes, I understand that. But she isn't there."

"Okay. Thank you for trying."

"We'd like to find her as well," said Heide, refraining—pretty generously, Søren thought—from commenting on the fact that he—and the PET—was the one who had managed to lose the child in the first place. "Has her description been circulated?"

"Yes." Søren stared out across Polititorvet without really seeing his surroundings. "Will you keep me posted if something happens at your end?"

Heide promised. He knew she had her hands full, not just with the investigation of the Vestergaard killing, but also with the coordination of the hunt for Rina's mother. Natasha had been observed close to the Coal-House Camp earlier in the day when, according to the first brief report he had received, she had hit another car and fled from the scene of the accident. In spite of the apparently fairly definite identification, they were having trouble locating the fugitive. The weather was so bad that there was no point in using helicopters. On the smaller roads, especially north of Copenhagen, the snow had started to make its own roadblocks—and snow made no exception for patrol cars.

He had so far declined to put out an appeal in the media for information regarding Rina's disappearance. There was no reason to let the bad guys know she was out there, vulnerable and alone, if they didn't know already.

His stomach rumbled sourly. Too much coffee and not enough proper food. He hadn't eaten anything except two dry breakfast rolls and a cheese sandwich from the cafeteria since Susse's chicken stew the previous evening.

Susse. Ben. He had totally lost track: Herlev, the heart attack, even Susse's tears on the phone. Damn it. He quickly dialed. She was still in the hospital, he could tell from the background noise, but she sounded less distraught.

"It's better now," she said. "He slept well last night, and we're out of intensive care now. He says to say hello. And thanks for taking care of the dogs . . ."

"Anytime. You know that."

Babko, who was by now starting to find his way around the police headquarters's labyrinthine corridors like a native, came in and placed a cup of coffee in front of him, this time accompanied by a pastry.

"You look like you need this."

"Thanks," Søren said, though his stomach didn't quite agree.

"And one of the Danes gave me this."

It was a yellow Post-it note with a scrawled message from Don Carlo in the Radio service.

Call me. Car spotted.

Søren looked at his cell again and noted that Carlo had tried to reach him several times. Before he'd called Susse and Heide, there had been a number of conversations about mobilizing the search for Rina as well as a lengthy telephone report to Torben. He dialed.

"Hi, Carlo."

"Sonny boy. You asked us to let you know if anyone saw a Beemer with Ukrainian plates."

"Yes."

"We haven't. But a colleague who was on duty at a road accident on Englandsvej saw a black BMW 5 with Danish plates. He noticed it because one side window was smashed. He didn't get the whole number, but the Register can't find any BMWs with the partial he noted."

"Stolen plates."

"Yes. Almost certainly."

"Put out an APB. And alert the airport just in case that's where he's going." It was, after all, right around the corner from the Englandsvej sighting.

"Done, my friend."

"Thanks."

"No prob."

There could, of course, be several reasons for a BMW to drive around with false plates, but it was the first possible trace of Savchuk they had had at all.

Søren quickly put Babko in the loop. "There wasn't anything wrong with the window in the BMW when you saw it, was there?" he asked.

"No. But that could have happened later."

Søren checked his other missed calls. Don Carlo wasn't the only one who had called in vain. Mikael Nielsen was on the list too. Søren called him back.

"Yes?"

"Mrs. Borg walked out."

"What?"

"She and the Swede went out to search in the immediate vicinity. The Swede has just returned. He hasn't found the girl, and now he can't find the nurse either."

What was the matter with this case and these people? Couldn't Søren turn his back for one second without someone else disappearing?

"Hang on a sec."

He put Nielsen on hold and called Nina's cell. A second later it rang cheerfully in his inner pocket. Damn. He had taken it from her himself. For safety reasons . . .

"How long ago?" he asked Nielsen.

"They went out to search forty-five minutes ago. They went in opposite directions and had apparently arranged to meet again after thirty minutes. The nurse didn't show up. The Swede is worried."

So am I, thought Søren.

THE WIND WAS picking up. A corner of the red tarp on the stable roof flapped wildly, and the snow blew like smoke from the ridge of the thatch, so that for one distorted second, Nina's eyes insisted on telling her that the roof was on fire.

The light was on in the main house and in the courtyard, but otherwise the sky was dark, the pitch black that was a winter night in the country.

She gave the driver her credit card and blindly signed the receipt he handed her. He hadn't been eager to come all the way out here, had cursed the weather and the driving conditions and the long trip back to town. But she had said something, she didn't even remember what, that had made him to shut up and drive pretty abruptly. Now he was so eager to get out of the yard again that his wheels started to spin by the gable, and he had to let the car roll back a length before he could clear the little rise that led to the road.

The light came on in the hall, and the front door opened.

"Can I help you?" A small, slender silhouette stood in the lit square of the doorway.

"Anna?" said Nina. "It's Nina Borg. I don't know if you remember me."

A moment passed. Then Anna Olesen took a step back so the light fell on her hair and face.

"The nurse," she said. "You were here the night when Natasha . . ."

"Yes."

"Come in."

THE FIRE GLOWED behind the glass doors of the big white brick oven between the kitchen and the living room. Anna placed a Bodum glass mug in front of Nina.

"It's tea," she said. "I can make coffee too. But that'll take a few minutes."

"Tea is fine."

Tea, coffee . . . Nina didn't care. Her gaze wandered across the neat dining room table, the stove with two bubbling pots, preparations for dinner. For one or for two?

No Rina, anyway. Not here.

"I came to ask if you had seen Rina."

Anna wrinkled her eyebrows. "Little Katerina? A man came to ask the same thing a little while ago. But why on earth would I have?"

"She has disappeared from . . . the camp." At the last minute Nina chose to simplify the explanation. "And our only clue to where she might have gone is that she called here."

"Here? When?"

"This morning. Between nine and ten." Between 9:40 and 9:42, to be exact, but Nina had learned that people usually looked at her oddly when she gave the time down to the minute.

"I was probably still out with the dog then."

"Who was the man? The one who asked for her?"

"One of the policemen searching Michael's house. A DI somebody or other, I don't recall his name. But why would Katerina call me? I haven't seen her in . . . well, since then."

"She's had a couple of hard days. Maybe she needed to talk with someone who would understand her." But that person couldn't have been Anna, Nina thought suddenly, because Rina had spoken in Ukrainian. "You haven't seen Natasha, have you?" she asked casually.

Anna pushed her reading glasses into her hair and smiled sarcastically. "My dear, I know that Natasha is wanted by every police authority in the entire country. If I was really hiding her in my leaky hayloft, do you think I would tell you? But you're welcome to look."

"No, no, it doesn't matter." If Natasha was here, it certainly wouldn't be in the hayloft. But Nina couldn't really believe that she would dare to come here. Michael Vestergaard's house lay just on the other side of the hill; it must have been swarming with police for the past twenty-four hours. No doubt Anna had been questioned as well, by people who were somewhat more professional at that kind of thing than Nina was.

"How long has Katerina been missing?"

"For almost four hours."

"If she was really on her way here, she should have been here long ago. Unless . . ."

"Unless what?"

"The bus doesn't go down Tundra Lane; its nearest stop is at Isterødvej. That's quite a walk. And in this weather . . ."

"Are you saying you think she might have gotten lost?"

"Henrik cleared the road with the tractor again just before you came. You and your taxi were lucky you didn't try an hour earlier."

"We have to look for her. Or . . ." She glanced at Anna and noticed, really for the first time, that she was, in fact, talking to a fairly senior citizen. "I have to, anyway."

"Wait," said Anna. "I'll come. I just need to put some proper clothes on."

Five minutes later they were on their way out into the blizzard, armed with two powerful flashlights and, in Anna's case, a handful of dog biscuits and a leash.

"If that stupid dog would only come when I call her, she could help us. She's actually a trained scent hound."

Nina had only the vaguest notion of what that meant. Something to do with finding animals hurt or killed in traffic. Or something.

Killed in traffic. She stared out into the darkness and wished those words hadn't popped into her head.

UKRAINE, 1935

THE COURTROOM WAS small and crammed with people Olga didn't know, and she felt as if just breathing was a difficult undertaking. She couldn't help thinking that it would have been better if she had been allowed to stay at home with the lice and the cockroaches, but there was no way around it, Semienova had said. Olga was a witness, and it was important that she repeated everything she had already told the GPU. Several times. About Uncle Grachev and Fyodor and Pjotr and Vitja. That they were kulaks, that they had attacked Oxana because she was pure of heart and fought for the Soviet state and had reported Father, who had always been a kulak and an enemy of the people. Kulaks could not tolerate that there were people like Oxana. Kulaks spread hunger and destruction so that they themselves could eat until they became fat, and Oxana had been a threat to them. She was pure of heart.

"Pure of heart, pure of heart."

Olga formed the words silently. She knew what she was supposed to say because she had said it many times already. The truth. Everything she now knew about her Uncle Grachev and Aunt Vira and Pjotr and Vitja and Fyodor and even Grandfather and Grandmother Trofimenko, who had been jailed three months ago along with the rest of the family. They had all been a part of planning the murder of Oxana and little Kolja. It was revenge for Father, and Oxana's punishment because she was pure of heart and the people's nightingale. That was what Grachev had not been able to stand, coward that he was, and the GPU police had nodded and smiled kindly at her every single time she repeated it, and now—today—she carried the truth with her like a small, well-polished pearl, waiting to be presented to the judge, who had come all the way from Leningrad. There was even a great author who insisted on attending the trial, and Olga thought she had seen him among the spectators, a little man in a dark suit with sharp, pale eyes.

Olga straightened her back and glanced at Mother, who sat unmoving next to her. If she was pleased that Oxana's murderers would soon be held accountable for their misdeeds, she didn't show it. Her face expressed neither happiness nor sorrow, and her eyes had begun to look odd, as if they had been painted on her face in black. Her flat and lifeless gaze moved slowly around the room and seemed to focus too long on things that no one else took serious notice of. One of the judge's boots, the heavy ceiling beams and the whitewashed wall behind the desks and judges, which was greyish and had cracks in it. Someone should have whitewashed it again, thought Olga, just as Mother whitewashed the walls at home with the straw whisk that she dipped in lime. Her hands would become red and cracked and sometimes started to bleed as she worked.

Here the picture of Uncle Stalin was allowed to hang on a shit-colored wall, and that was wrong, just like everything else. The angry mumbling from the listeners, the stiff GPU people and the author and the pioneers, who had pushed their way into one of the front rows of spectators and stared at Olga warmly and eagerly.

The truth.

It shouldn't be so hard, but Olga's stomach hurt, and she felt as if she was going to throw up when Uncle Grachev was led into the room, accompanied by a wave of excited talk and hushed comments.

He was wearing a clean shirt, and his dark beard was washed and trimmed, but he looked older than she remembered him, and it was as if he was squinting against a light that wasn't there. Grachev hid his hands in his shirtsleeves, which hung loose and flapping on his thin arms. He admitted that he had killed Oxana. And he admitted that he was a kulak. And he admitted that he had hated the girl deep in his cowardly kulak soul because she was clean, and because she sang so beautifully. He said that he had murdered Oxana, but that he had done it alone. His sons were innocent and so were his parents.

"You've always been full of lies, Grachev!" a man behind Olga shouted spitefully, and several others availed themselves of the opportunity to spit angrily on the floor. Olga recognized the first one as Uncle Grachev's neighbor and card-playing friend. Olga had often seen them sitting together by the samovar, smoking and drinking tea and vodka. The neighbor also used to borrow her uncle's cart when he had to bring in the hay or needed to go to Sorokivka.

The truth.

Grandmother and Grandfather Trofimenko were dragged in and placed together before the judge. Grandfather had trouble staying upright and had to lean on the GPU officer who had led them in. Grandmother, who was tiny, smaller than Olga and stooped, stood without help but couldn't seem to understand what the judge was asking her. She just cried.

Kulaks, like their sons. People spat again, and Olga stole a look over at Comrade Semienova, who stood against the wall almost next to the judge's desk. She looked at once strict and sorrowful, exactly as she did in school when someone answered an important question incorrectly or maybe even said something stupid about Uncle Stalin. When that happened, she frowned exactly as she was doing now and tilted her head as if she was trying to figure out how she could best show them all the beautiful pictures of the future that were in her head. She had never looked at Oxana in that way, but sometimes at Jana and Olga when they giggled in class, and it was such a sad expression that Olga always wanted to apologize because she had upset Semienova.

Today she wanted to show Semienova that she had understood everything. That she knew what was needed to fix everything that was wrong in the world. Both Grandmother and Grandfather Trofimenko were beyond redemption, that much she could see already, but she could still make Semienova proud.

"Uncle Grachev is a kulak," said Olga. Her eyes met Semienova's, and Semienova smiled encouragingly at her. "The day Oxana and Kolja were murdered, my cousin Fyodor and he came to look for Oxana. She was to die because she was a communist."

"And what did you do?"

Olga sat so close to the judge that she could smell the strange, spicy scent of his grey coat, but she didn't dare look up at him. He seemed so stern, and he had large, springy grey hairs that sprouted like brushes from his ears and even from his nostrils.

"I cried," said Olga. "I begged for her life, but they wouldn't listen to me. They wanted to kill the people's nightingale, they said."

Someone patted her on the shoulder when she sat down on the bench next to Mother. She pulled herself together to smile faintly, but she couldn't really feel anything anymore. She didn't know if she was a hero or a sinner, and she caught herself envying Oxana her fate.

Oxana was a hero. Of that there was no doubt.

The newspaper had written about her, and Semienova asked the party leadership in Moscow for money to erect a statue of Oxana in pioneer uniform in the square in Sorokivka. The people's nightingale.

Olga clenched her teeth and stared down at her hands, which lay like dead birds in her lap.

The truth had left a sharp, metallic taste on her tongue. Nothing else.

HE BUS STOP sign cleared the snowdrift by only about a meter and a half, and the wind still whipped more snow across the open fields. They had called and shouted all the way down here, without result. Nina searched her pocket for her cell phone but then remembered that she had given it to Søren. Her left arm ached steadily, a deep but not especially insistent note of pain, like a soft bass line somewhere beneath the main theme: the fear of what had happened to Rina.

"Do you have a cell phone I can borrow?" she asked. "This isn't going to work; we need dogs."

Anna shook her head. Here was a woman who understood how to dress for the weather, thought Nina. A bright red ski suit covered her from head to toe and made her look like an overgrown kindergarten child on an excursion.

"I have one somewhere, but I rarely use it. I don't even think it's charged. We'd better go back to the house. Then you can call from there."

Why aren't they already here? thought Nina. Chains of men with Alsatians, lights, search teams? Sending one policeman to look around couldn't exactly be called a search.

And she felt almost certain that this *was* the place they needed to search for Rina. There were probably just two places in Denmark that could have activated Rina's homing pigeon instinct. One was the Coal-House Camp, the other was here. And it wasn't the Coal-House Camp that Rina had tried to call.

They turned around and walked back toward the house. Anna moved at a steady clip, and in spite of legs that were somewhat longer and younger, Nina had to quicken her pace to keep up. At first it was nice to have the wind hit her other cheek for a change, but it wasn't long before that cheek was just as numb as the one that had been frozen on the way out. When they were almost all the way back to the farm, a large, brindled dog came running toward them.

"There you are!" said Anna sharply.

The dog didn't pay any attention to the cool greeting. It jumped around, shaking its head so its ears flopped, and wagging its entire rear. When Anna didn't pay it much attention, it thrust its pinkish-brown nose into Nina's hand, so that her glove was soon covered by a fine glaze of dog drool.

That was when she discovered that it had something in its mouth. At first she thought it was a mouse, and in a way it was—a stuffed toy mouse with oversized ears, eyes and feet.

It was the Diddl mouse that had been attached to the zipper on Rina's backpack.

"MY HUSBAND TRAINED her," said Anna. "She never really bothered to listen to me."

"We have to try," Nina insisted. "What is her name?"

"Maxi."

Maxi had exchanged the Diddl mouse for a dog biscuit, but Anna still didn't show any sign of encouraging the dog to search, and Nina's experience with that kind of thing was limited to having seen cadaver dogs work. She attached the leash to its collar and then held the drool-covered toy mouse in front of the dog's nose.

"Search," she said as authoritatively as she could. "Maxi, search!"

The dog looked up at her, and she thought it looked as if it was grinning foolishly.

Something occurred to her then. "We should be able to see where it came from. It must have found the toy somewhere."

"The snow is already covering the tracks," said Anna.

"Yes, we have to hurry." She remembered that she was, in fact, dealing with an elderly woman. "You don't need to come," she said. "If I can just borrow Maxi."

"You don't know your way around here," said Anna. "We can't have you getting lost too."

THEY HAD WALKED perhaps four to five hundred meters in the deep snow—about as exhausting as wading in seawater at mid-thigh height—when Maxi finally seemed to understand what the exercise was all about and set off with a tug that almost dislocated Nina's one functioning arm.

"She's got a scent!"

"Yes," said Anna. "Let her get on with it. Hold the leash tightly, but go with her as quickly as you can. Run if you can."

The flashlight's cone of light danced across the snow. Shrubbery and saplings were bent low under the heavy snow, and once in a while Nina's foot caught on a branch or a stone she couldn't see. A fence blocked the way on the left—that must be the edge of the golf course. This was neither woodlands nor a real field, but a scruffy sort of in-between-ness, like the meager plantings the municipality tried to establish on highway embankments and the like. Nina had to halt the dog for a moment while she climbed over a partially fallen barbed-wire fence, then on they went through the drifts. Her jeans were ridiculously unsuitable for this, and the snow worked its way up her pant legs and melted down into her socks and boots.

Suddenly Maxi gave a high-pitched, sharp bark and threw itself forward with so much power that the leash slid between Nina's gloved and frozen fingers. She managed to keep her flashlight on the dog long enough to see it disappear into one end of something that looked like a scrapped railroad car.

She ran as quickly as she could.

The first thing the light illuminated inside the car was a tea table.

A cardboard box covered in a flowered tablecloth, four unmatched cups and a teapot without a lid. Napkins had been set out, and three cookies were neatly arranged on each of the napkins. The cups had been filled with a red liquid that didn't quite look like tea. Juice, maybe. Only one cup appeared to have been drunk from.

"Rina?"

Nina listened anxiously. No one answered, but she could hear the familiar sound of Rina's asthmatic breathing. She moved the flashlight around and saw in dancing glimpses that the freight car's raw wooden walls were covered by cutouts from magazines, photographs, plastic flowers, pale green glow-in-the-dark stars and planets of the same kind that Ida had once been briefly infatuated with, posters of large-eyed animals and long-legged pop starlets, but most of all photographs and ads and newspaper cutouts with one thing in common: they all showed fathers with their children, fathers who pushed strollers, father who held the reins of ponies in amusement parks, fathers who pushed swings, played, built, swam or just smiled and laughed with happy daughters. A secret den, thought Nina. A Father Temple.

"Rina!"

She was lying curled up under a pile of old blankets and towels in the corner farthest from the heavy sliding door she probably had not had the strength to shut completely. Her eyes were closed, her lips pale and wax-like, and beneath her eyebrows was the reddish-brown pinpoint bruising her asthma attack had given her, dark freckles against the almost blue-white skin.

Maxi barked once more and then began to eat the cookies.

Nina pulled her gloves off and placed her fingers against Rina's neck. The difference between her own cold fingers and Rina's skin didn't feel as significant as she had feared it might.

"Rina! Rina, wake up. Look at me."

She pinched Rina's earlobe. No reaction whatsoever.

"Oh, the poor little thing." Anna had appeared in the door. "What's wrong with her? Is she very weak?"

"She is unconscious," Nina said but couldn't see why.

"It must be the cold."

"Possibly." There was no doubt that Rina was colder than was good for her, but there was no stiffness in the muscles, no sign of the confusion that sometimes made hypothermia victims act paradoxically by, for example, beginning to take off their clothes.

Then there was a sudden exclamation from Anna. "Oh, no. What has she done?"

"What?"

Anna held up a pill bottle in a red ski mitt that matched her suit. Nina shone her flashlight in her direction but couldn't see what it was.

"These are mine," said Anna. "How did she get a hold of them?"

"Give them to me!"

Anna handed them over. Nina grabbed them and finally was able to decipher the writing on the damp, half-dissolved label.

"Diazepam," she said. "How many were in the bottle?"

Anna's wide eyes glittered in the glow of the flashlight. "It was almost full," she said.

"**H**ERE?"

Jurij stopped the car at the turnoff and squinted down the narrow track that ran between the snow-covered fields.

Perhaps he hesitated because the road was so small. There were only four houses in all: Michael's, Anna's farm and then two smaller houses almost all the way down by Isterødvej. Not many cars came this way. In the summer the grass grew so tall in the middle that it brushed against the bottom of the car. In an odd way that was precisely what had made Natasha feel at home. Not in Michael's house, but on the road that led there. When she lived with Michael, she sometimes did stupid things when he wasn't home. Walked out of the house and across the pebble-covered front drive, crossed the gravel road on bare feet and continued into the wilderness of knee-high grass and wild oats and clover and elder trees. And then she sat down in the middle of it all, so that she couldn't see the brick house or the garage or the pebbles, and turned her face to the sun, breathing in the spicy scent of grass and feeling the tiny legs of insects as they crawled across her feet. Strangely enough, it was neither Pavel nor her luxurious life in Kiev that she missed when Michael and she moved in together, but the flowering verges of her childhood. The kind that lined the road when Father and she rode their bikes to Grandfather's and Grandmother's farmhouse, the kind she had sworn never to return to. Natasha moved a little in the seat to wake up her hands, which were now bound behind her back again. She let her tongue slide across her broken molars and split gums, which had finally, finally stopped bleeding.

Tonight there was no green anywhere. The snow blew into the wheel tracks, but the road had been cleared not long ago.

"It's not a one-way street. You can drive through to the big road," she said.

He didn't answer. Just turned off the lights and got out of the car. She saw his dark shape pace down to the first turn in the gravel road and disappear. The car quickly became cold now that the motor was turned off. The hole in the side window was already providing plenty of fresh air. Natasha pulled halfheartedly at the narrow plastic strips but quickly gave up. Her right arm and wrist ached, throbbing violently, and the jerky movements only made it worse.

The woman in the backseat shifted uneasily. Now that there was no longer a fresh supply of warm air circulating through the car, Natasha could sense the Witch's rotten breath. Baba Yaha who ate children.

Jurij returned and got behind the wheel, cursing. He maneuvered the car decisively in between the snowbanks, headlights still off. The snow was falling more heavily. The snowflakes were hard and grainy and rattled against the window like claws.

Jurij wanted to turn in at Michael's house, but Natasha stopped him.

"It's farther on," she said. "The next house." She saw with a certain relief that there was no sign of life in there. Michael wasn't home.

The she saw the yellow-and-black tape. POLICE, it said. Her chest constricted, and she couldn't tell if it was from fear or hope. Right now she'd like one of the nice Danish policemen to come save her from the Witch and her son. But there were no policemen at the barrier, which was disappearing into the snow.

What had happened at Michael's house? She guessed a part of the answer before she asked, and she had little doubt that Jurij, with his large and capably destructive hands, would be the right person to answer her, if he wanted to.

"What happened?" she said.

"We had to have a chat with your fiancé to find out where you and the girl were," said Jurij. "He didn't even know that you had run off, but at least he told us where we could find the little girl. We didn't think you'd run far if we had her."

"Did you kill him?"

Jurij didn't react. "Where are we going?"

Michael was dead. She recognized that in Jurij's indifference. For him Michael was just as irrelevant as Natasha, who would also be dead in a very short time and therefore had already been removed from his calculations.

"Farther along," she said flatly. "On the other side of the hill."

Jurij engaged the gears again and let the car eat its way up the rise and down the other side. Behind them, Michael's house disappeared from sight. He was gone. Everything he had been, everything he had done to her, was gone now. She felt nothing at the thought.

Jurij let the car roll into the drive that led to Anna's farm.

"I'm going to park it behind the stable over there." Jurij pointed at one of the farm's yellow outbuildings. "It's best if the car can't be seen from the road, so there'll be a little bit of walking, Mamo. Are you sure you want to come?"

Natasha sensed the old woman's movements in the backseat. A determined nod, she assumed, because Jurij sighed, resigned.

He parked behind the low half wall that had once encircled the farm's midden. They got out and walked along the sheltered side of the stable where the snow wasn't piled as high, Natasha in front, with her hands still bound behind her back. Then Jurij and the old woman, side by side, like an aging couple. The old woman kept up surprisingly well, noted Natasha, in spite of the fact that the snow was ankle deep here and in several places slippery and uneven in the deep tracks left by a tractor.

The light in the hall was on, but Jurij didn't waste any time knocking. He pushed at the door, and when it opened—as usual, Anna hadn't locked up—he shoved Natasha ahead of him onto the pale golden floor tiles. Anna's rubber boots and clogs were arranged along the wall on clean and dry newspapers. The heat from the large kitchen hit her, and the snow brought in by their shoes melted almost instantly, making small, dirty pools on the floor. Poor Anna would have to get out the mop, thought Natasha, and marveled at how ordinary the thought was.

The old woman had followed her son and now approached the huge oven in the middle of the room with outstretched hands. Heat emanated from it and made the air billow in waves around the bird-like figure.

I could kill her when he turns his back, thought Natasha. Maybe she wouldn't even need her hands. She pictured herself rushing toward the old woman, cracking her own head against that frail old skull. Would it be enough? Or a kick. Maybe she could knock her down and kick her in the head. That was probably better.

Jurij had promised that he would leave Katerina and her alone as soon as they had found the picture. Beautiful, stupid Natasha would have believed him. In fact, she wanted to believe it, just as she also wanted to believe his promise not to touch Anna. But she was no longer beautiful, stupid Natasha, and she had seen her future in his indifferent gaze.

"Call her," said Jurij quietly. He had already checked both the boiler room and the kitchen and had taken the safety off his gun, which he now directed at the door to the living room.

Natasha felt her fear return. "Is that really necessary?" She nodded at the gun.

Jurij shrugged but apparently saw no reason to put it away. "Call her."

Natasha called Anna, halfheartedly but still loud enough that Anna should have been able to hear her. Anna's hearing was fine, she knew. There was no answer, and she realized that she hadn't heard the usual clicking of dog paws across the floor. No barking and no wagging mutt, whacking its tail into cabinets and chair legs.

"The dog," said Natasha and nodded at the water bowl that sat on the floor near the door to the hallway. "She must be out with the dog."

"In this weather?"

Jurij looked skeptically out the window above the kitchen sink. Snow whirled among the rosebushes in the yellow glow from the patio lights. He slammed open the double doors leading to the living room, walked with long strides into the room and started to systematically open cabinets and drawers.

As the work progressed, he spread papers and folders in a thin layer across the floor. He picked up a few and threw them on the floor again. Lingered briefly over a small tape recorder, but let it go and continued with a row of cans decorated with flowers that stood on the shelf above the couch. He pulled off the lids and upended them so that the contents—buttons and sewing material—flew out in all directions and hit the floor with small, distinctive whacks.

"Where was it you found the picture?" he asked then. "Show us."

"Upstairs," she said. "In the bedroom."

He made her go up the stairs first. She could feel the light pressure of the gun barrel under her right shoulder blade and tried to calculate what the bullet would hit if the gun went off right now. Probably a lung. And her heart, depending on the angle. She had never been particularly interested in biology, but she had, after all, seen pigs slit open, with intestines and kidneys and liver hanging out of the body cavity. She knew where the organs were, and none of them were expendable.

"But he won't shoot you, right? Not yet." Natasha formed the words silently with her lips. Here in Anna's house, the voice that usually lived in her head had gone conspicuously silent. She forced herself to look at the staircase in front of her. One step at a time. The Witch was also on the stairs now, but Natasha was already up. Too late to let herself stumble backward and crush the bird skeleton in the fall.

Jurij turned on the light in the bedroom and ordered Natasha to lie on the floor, which was surprisingly difficult with her hands bound behind her back. She managed to get on her knees, and Jurij pushed her the rest of the way so that she fell forward and hit her shoulder and chin on the wooden floor.

Then he opened the dresser drawer and emptied its pill containers and papers out onto the bed. The picture of Anna and her husband on vacation with palm trees and a light blue pool in the background fluttered to the floor in front of Natasha's face. Then the tips of Jurij's shoes approached her forehead.

"You didn't lie, did you? Sometimes people lie because that's all they can remember how to do. Maybe you are like your husband."

He touched her very lightly with the tip of his shoe. The sole scratched the bridge of her nose. The shoes were still wet. She turned her face away and waited while he looked under the bed and behind the wardrobe's enormous mirrored doors. She could see that the Witch had entered the room now, her feet making their way around the bed. Then she stood still and looked at the wall Anna had covered with pictures of her daughter. Natasha knew the pictures well. The daughter was called Kirsten and in the first pictures had been photographed at age three while she held an old-fashioned red phone in her hand and smiled in a friendly way at the photographer.

Farther down was a row of more or less anonymous school photos in which the girl's hairdo varied between short and slightly longer. In two of the pictures, her teeth were covered by braces. Then came the graduation photo, pictures of Kirsten with Anna's grandchildren, pictures of Hans Henrik and Kirsten at an amusement park with the kids. Katerina loved the photos, and for some reason the Witch also remained standing in front of the portraits. Natasha could see that she was leaning forward. Her head moved in small, uneven, hen-like jerks. Then she turned to the nightstand and picked up Anna's and Hans Henrik's wedding picture.

The Witch's hands shook so much that the picture rattled between her fingers. How old was she? Eighty-five? Eighty-six? Too old to lay a fair claim to more years in this life, and yet she was winning and Natasha was in the process of losing.

"Who is that?"

The Witch held the framed photo out to Natasha. Natasha couldn't see it properly from her position on the floor, but she remembered it from the many times she had been lying in this room, on Anna's bed, while everything hurt and she had fled from Michael, and Anna was patting her hair and murmuring, "There, there, there," as she tried to console her. Anna had said that Michael was better than Ukraine, and that was true, at least most of the time.

Natasha had looked at it so often. The picture of a woman who had married a good man and had lived a long life with him in peace and safety in Bacon Land. Wedding Anna smiled a bit crookedly and had her eyes partially closed against the sun. Her hair was in thick, roller-induced '50s curls under the veil, and she was made up almost like a movie star. Hans Henrik was young and strong and kind, had shiny, brushed-back black hair and didn't look like the thin and aging man she had come to know on her first visits to Denmark those last years before he died.

"That's Anna," said Natasha tiredly.

The old woman in front of her looked as if someone had physically shoved her. She tottered in her impractical half-heeled boots. Even now, with death so close that the old biddy must be able to feel the cold gust of annihilation through all the layers of shiny sable fur, she insisted on dressing like a woman.

"That's a lie. You're lying."

Jurij, who had stopped in the middle of dresser drawer number three, turned around and stared silently at them, and Natasha shook her head. She couldn't do anything more than that because of her awkward position on the floor. She tested her strips again, but nothing yielded even slightly.

The old Witch leaned against the wall for a moment. Her breathing had become heavier, and she picked up the picture from the floor again, narrowing her eyes as she studied it.

"You don't need to search any further," she said to Jurij. "Finish here and come downstairs. We'll wait for her by the oven."

Jurij grabbed Natasha's armpit and hauled her to her feet, but the faint sound of a motor from outside stopped him mid-gesture.

"Shit!"

He released her and let her tumble to the floor so he could reach out for the light switch and turn off the light in the bedroom.

"Stay where you are," he said to his mother. "I'll take care of this."

He grabbed hold of Natasha and dragged her across the bedroom floor to the little bathroom Anna had had put in so she didn't need to go downstairs at night. He swore the whole way but didn't let go until he had thrown Natasha on the tiles by the bathroom door. This time, she fell flat on her face and chipped her front tooth. He kicked her the rest of the way in, took the key and locked the door behind him.

Natasha lay on the floor and felt her tears burn in the cuts on her cheek. She was dizzy and wanted to let herself fall into unconsciousness, the way she had sometimes done when Michael was at his worst. Anna wasn't there to help, neither in reality not in Natasha's head. And maybe she would never help again after what Natasha had done.

SØREN POSITIONED HIMSELF behind a snowplow on Isterød-vej and stayed there. The driving had been bad even on the main highway to Elsinore, and after the exit, it had gotten much worse. It did no good to push it, especially not in a flimsy little car like the Hyundai.

"We run the risk of not being able to get back to the city tonight," he said to Babko. Not so good when Torben had made it very clear that he wanted Søren back at his usual post on Monday morning.

"I think I've had about enough of your headquarters," said the Ukrainian. "Fancy though it is."

The message that the BMW with the shattered window had been spotted at the exit to Isterødvej had come in almost three-quarters of an hour ago and had set off a whole chorus of alarm bells in Søren's head. It was simply way too close to two of the central locations of the case: the scene of Michael Vestergaard's murder and Anna Olesen's house, which was the address Rina had telephoned a few hours before she disappeared. He had practically dragged Babko with him out to the car and on the few stretches where conditions had allowed it, the little Hyundai had had its not particularly impressive acceleration pushed to the utmost.

Tundra Lane. He almost missed it even though he had been there the day before. Snow and more snow. The visibility was terrible. But it looked as if the tractor had been by relatively recently, and it wasn't as impassable as he had feared. He stopped and got out of the car to look at the tire tracks, but the snow was blowing so strongly, he could only determine that one or more cars had driven this way not too long ago. Whether one of them was a BMW with a defective side window, he could not say.

They stopped at the barricade by Michael Vestergaard's house.

"You go one way around; I'll go the other?" he suggested to Babko. He wished he had taken the time to get the Ukrainian a radio. Søren had a "colleague in trouble" button, but Babko didn't. The only channel of communication between them was their cell phones.

Babko nodded. Out of old habit, he patted himself where at the moment there was neither radio nor service weapon nor bulletproof vest, and grimaced. "Sorry," he said. "I feel a little underdressed."

Søren just nodded. They ducked under the tape, which in any case was being quietly buried in a snowbank. Søren turned on the flashlight he did have and then turned it off again. He had no idea what to expect if they came upon Savchuk. It would depend on the situation, and he would like to have the option of observing before he was observed.

The wind moaned around the corner of the house, but otherwise he couldn't hear anything except his own footsteps. It didn't look as if a car had come through here. Behind the bungalow he met Babko, who had just as little to report.

"Let's go see the lady with the good oven," suggested the Ukrainian.

When they were still about a hundred meters from the yellow farmhouse, Søren stopped the Hyundai in the middle of the road.

"Same procedure?" asked Babko.

"Yep."

There was a light on in the yard, but the only car parked there was Anna Olesen's red Mazda. Babko headed down along one stable wing; Søren turned his attention to the farmhouse. There was no dog barking, but there was a light on in the hallway. He went along the gable and into the garden to get a discreet look through the kitchen windows.

Just then his cell phone vibrated in his pocket, a single buzz. A signal from Babko.

The car is here, the text message said.

"LIEUTENANT BABKO, I see you've been busy."

Søren stopped mid-step, on his way around the stable corner. He carefully set his foot down into the snow again. In front of him, a few steps away and with his back to Søren, stood a large, broad-shouldered man in a long, classic overcoat. Babko was facing Søren but carefully avoided looking in his direction.

"Colonel. You've been missed."

"Really. By whom, Mr. Lieutenant? Who has such a burning interest in what I do?"

Søren had absolutely no intention of interrupting this fascinating conversation. He took a slow, silent step backward in the direction of the half wall around the old midden.

"The Danish police do," said Babko. "It's an unfortunate situation. If you have news of Natasha Doroshenko, you should report it to the Danes."

"And why would you think I have such news?"

"Among other reasons . . . because you are here. So close to where her Danish fiancé was murdered."

"The Danes won't know I'm here—unless you tell them."

Søren slid behind the half wall and began to crouch down to be less visible. In the middle of the move, his bum knee, the one that he'd had surgery on, cracked loudly.

Savchuk spun around. His hand disappeared into his coat, but at the moment the gun came out, Babko hammered the edge of one of his large, bony hands against the Colonel's neck.

The blow didn't hit with true precision, partly because of the thick, woolly overcoat, but mostly because Savchuk was moving. The gun was free of its holster, but by this point, Søren had left his half-covered position to come to Babko's aid. He threw his flashlight as hard as he could in Savchuk's direction just as the first shot rang out.

Savchuk fell over in the snow with Babko partly under him. There was yet another shot, a second before Søren kicked Savchuk under his jaw with all the strength he could muster. He grabbed the bigger man by the arm and rolled him on his stomach. Søren didn't have handcuffs, but right now there wasn't any resistance in the arm he was holding. Savchuk was unconscious.

"Are you okay?" Søren asked. His sense was that both shots had been fired in his direction without hitting him.

It took awhile for Babko to answer. "Not quite," he said.

Søren whirled around. Babko sat in the snow with both hands pressed against one thigh. Blood was seeping through his fingers.

Søren let go of Savchuk. He pressed the ASSISTANCE NEEDED button on the radio with one hand. Where the hell was the gun? It must be lying somewhere in the snow.

"Where are you hit?"

"On the outside of the thigh."

Better than the inside, where a huge artery supplied blood to the entire leg.

"We have an alarm from you," came the dispassionate voice over the radio. "What is the emergency?"

Something hit Søren in the side with a whistling kick, and suddenly he didn't have the air to answer. The radio slipped from his hand. He stretched his hands out in front of him without quite knowing why, maybe to support himself so he wouldn't fall. He still ended up in the snow, with a growing worry about where his next breath was going to come from. The kick had completely knocked the air out of him.

By the stable wall stood the tiniest, most ancient woman he had ever seen. Her mouth shone red in a powdered beige face, and in front of her she held a pistol that looked grotesquely huge in her wrinkled hands. She took aim again.

It was only then that Søren realized that he hadn't been kicked.

Fuck, he thought. I've been shot by a little old lady. And in another second, she'll do it again.

I T TOOK FOREVER to get the plastic ties off.

Natasha found the light switch after some fumbling and pressed it with her elbow. Anna had a first-aid kit in her linen closet, she knew—Natasha had needed it several times when she lived with Michael. And in that kit were scissors.

She managed to open the closet and, with her chin and shoulder, maneuvered piles of towels, cleaning rags and toilet paper onto the tile floor until she found the red plastic pouch with the white cross. It landed on the floor too. With difficulty she got down on her knees and slid sideways onto her bottom like a clumsy mermaid. The flap on the case was closed with a button that took several more minutes of fumbling to open. She shook the contents onto the floor, found the scissors with her stiff hands and guided the two short, slender blades to the black plastic bands.

Snip.

Her arms fell forward and suddenly felt twice as heavy and sore, which made no sense. But there was still a locked door between the Witch and her. She pressed her shoulder against it, testing. Her weight didn't seem to make any impression on either the jamb or the door.

She pushed the small angled overhead window open instead. A whirlwind of snow hit her, pricking her skin like the metal spikes on a hairbrush. She could hear voices somewhere in the howling of the storm—voices speaking Ukrainian. She thought one was Jurij's but couldn't be sure.

Suddenly she saw dancing lights along the road. Someone on foot was coming around the bend where the fat electrician and his wife lived, and when they passed under the lamppost in his driveway, even at that distance she recognized the dog, Anna's red snow suit and . . .

And Nina Borg. With a child in her arms, a child wrapped in a blanket, but it could only be . . . It made no sense, but it had to be Katerina.

A lie. The Danish nurse had failed her own gospel of truth and had lied to her. Katerina was not with the police, and she was not, *not* at all "safe." Hatred and panic rose in Natasha with equal force. The Witch was here, downstairs in Anna's house, and the nurse was on her way to the Witch with Katerina. For a moment she thought the Witch had paid Nina Borg to lie and now was sitting in her chicken-legged house, waiting for Nina to bring her the child she was going to devour.

But the Witch didn't know everything. She could not have known that Natasha would lead them to Anna's house. There must be another explanation.

Then the next wave of emotion arrived, and this time it was pure, unarticulated panic.

Katerina. The Witch. Katerina.

Natasha planted her foot on one of the closet shelves and was now halfway through the narrow window without having thought about how she would get down from the roof. But it turned out to be easy. The snow lay in drifts around the rosebushes beneath her, and she just jumped, hung in the empty space, then hit a snow pillow and thick, bristling rose stems and finally the cold ground. Seconds. She only had seconds to get to them and stop them before they were within reach of the Witch.

She had turned one knee in the fall but still ran, slipping and limping, through the deep snow. Behind her came the sudden sound of two dry bangs in short succession. Shots. But who had shot whom?

The dog barked briefly and started to run as if it were expecting a couple of ducks to come drifting down from the sky for it to collect. The flashlight figures hesitated. Then Nina put her burden down in the snow and ran after the dog, toward the farmhouse and the yard, in the direction from which the shots had come.

How stupid was that?

Natasha ran in the opposite direction, toward Anna and Katerina.

Anna, squatting in the snow next to the child, looked up in surprise when Natasha came running. She said something or other, but Natasha wasn't listening. She pulled the blanket aside, and Katerina's face appeared, closed and pale like the faces of the dead saints Mother had hanging above the kitchen table.

But Katerina wasn't dead. She couldn't be. Natasha desperately attempted to quiet her own hectic breathing so she could hear Katerina's, pulling her onto her lap and hugging her tightly.

"What's wrong with her?" she asked. "What happened?"

Yet another shot, followed by a piercing howl from the dog.

Anna jumped. Instead of turning around, she walked past Natasha on stiff legs and toward the yard, stupid as a pig that wanders into the slaughter stall without noticing the blood on the floor, just because someone jangles the feed bucket. She had lived too long in Bacon Land.

When she got to the corner of the main house, she stopped. She only stood there for a moment before she took three quick steps backward and turned around, but the light from the lamps in the yard had hit her, and yet another flat slap sounded.

The pig is dead, thought Natasha, and in a moment it will fall over on the bloody floor. But Anna was still standing. Natasha felt

Katerina move, a slight scraping of one knee against her thigh, and she got up quickly with her daughter in her arms and stumbled away from the road, into the deep winter darkness. She sank down into the drifts behind the rose hedge, better hidden by the darkness than by the leafless stalks, but she knew it wasn't enough. If the Witch had a light, if she looked this way . . .

The car. Could she make it to the car? No, it was no good; the keys were in big Jurij's pocket. Natasha wished that she had listened more closely back when acne-covered Vasyl had tried to impress her by hot-wiring his father's ancient Lada. But she remembered something about hot-wiring not working on new cars anyway, so perhaps it made no difference.

She saw Anna back away from the corner of the house and down the road, her hands held out in front of her.

"Stop," the Witch commanded. "One more step, and I'll shoot."

THE DOG HOWLED as if possessed. Long, piercing screams, as only an animal in pain can scream. Nina ran in the direction of the sound. It was where the two first shots had come from too. She fumbled in her pocket for her cell phone and only a second later remembered yet again that she had given it to Søren that morning.

She found the dog first. It had been shot in the back and was attempting to crawl through the snow to the house, leaving a wide and scarlet track behind it. She forced herself not to meet its gaze.

Behind the stable a big black car was parked, half hidden by the old midden wall. There was an unreasonable amount of blood in the snow, and it wasn't all the dog's. A man lay on the ground with his face downward, unconscious but alive to judge by his labored breathing, and a few meters from him another man sat on the ground, half bent over a third man, who was Søren. Had they shot each other? She couldn't see a gun.

She had recognized Søren immediately even though she couldn't see his face, just his back and neck. She fell to her knees next to him.

"Help," said the man who was still sitting. It was not a plea for himself but more of a calm instruction. "Shot. Chest. Get help. Him."

The telegram style was clearly caused by linguistic difficulties, not panic, though she could see that he himself was bleeding pretty heavily from a wound in the thigh.

I can't see anything, she thought. How can I help him when I can't see anything?

Søren was breathing, but not well. There was a bubbling sound.

"Let me," she said. In Danish. Of course it didn't help. "I'm a nurse," she attempted in English. "Let me take a look."

She was able to turn him over partially so she could see his face. His eyes reacted when he saw her, but he was gasping too hard for air to be able to speak. Blue lips. Hypoxia. She suddenly realized that what looked like red and white snowflakes on his chest was down— from where the shot had torn a hole in his jacket. Entry wound and no exit wound. His back had not been bloody. Pneumothorax. The lung had been punctured and was in the process of collapsing. With every breath he took, he was dragging air through the hole, air that was caught between the lung membrane, compressing the lung further.

A syringe, she thought, where the hell am I going to find a syringe? The only place there was even the tiniest chance of finding something she could use was in the house.

"I'll be right back," she said to Søren's conscious gaze. She ran, trying to calculate how many minutes he had left.

THE GUN WAS so large that the Witch had to use both her ancient hands to hold it. Natasha shrank down with Katerina in her arms, much too close, and with only the snow, the darkness and the rose hedge for cover. She was terrified that the Witch would hear Katerina's breathing, but it seemed as if the old woman only had eyes for Anna. The light from the gable illuminated Anna's hair and face and made the red ski suit glow like a torch in the middle of the whirling whiteness of the blizzard. Natasha couldn't see the Witch's face. Only the fur and the boots with the too-high heels that sank into the packed snow with every step the old woman took, making deep, precise holes, like punctures.

An odd silence had fallen. It was as if even the snowflakes stopped in midair.

"Are you a ghost?" asked the old woman.

"No," said Anna. She took half a step toward the old woman and held her arms out like you do when you want to embrace someone. She wasn't planning to embrace the Witch, was she?

"Stand still."

Anna stopped. She understands Ukrainian, thought Natasha. She doesn't usually. But when Anna began to speak again, it was in Ukrainian.

"They thought I would die," she said. "But I survived. And that wasn't so good, because by then the trial was already over, and the murderers condemned."

"I think you *are* a ghost," said the Witch. "How otherwise could I have stood by your grave?"

"It wasn't my fault. Semienova . . . They couldn't admit that a mistake had been made. Semienova had me placed with a family in Galicia, with the brother of an aunt of hers. Pötsch, they were called. They were ethnic Germans. And later . . . later it was easier to pretend that I was German too, otherwise I would have been sent back to Stalin."

"And so what? You were a hero, right? The people's nightingale?" The Witch spat out the last two words as if they hurt her mouth.

Anna stood still. Her face had transformed as her language had changed. There was an expression now that Natasha had never seen on a Dane. The unmoving mouth, the eyes that slid to the side . . . No, you couldn't break it into parts. It was just Ukrainian. If Anna had ever looked at Natasha with that expression, Natasha would have known right away that she wasn't born in Bacon Land.

"A dead nightingale," she said. "A dead hero. Who was still alive. How long do you think it would have been before they corrected that mistake? They had shot Grachev and Grandfather and Grandmother Trofimenko and . . . all of them. For my murder. If you have a murder trial, you also need a corpse."

"Kolja was dead. But maybe he doesn't count? *He* didn't get a statue, you know."

"Olga . . ."

The Witch laughed. A laughter without much sound, just a series of short hisses. "Olga? It has certainly been a long time. Several names ago. They are used up so quickly, it seems to me."

She began to cock the gun with shaking but competent hands.

"Are you going to shoot me?" asked Anna.

"Why not?"

"Haven't we lost enough? Olga, we are the only ones, the only ones who are left."

"So perhaps that was why you thought you had the right to bleed me for money? You milked me like one milks a cow."

"That wasn't me. It was Pavel. I shouldn't have told him as much as I did."

"No, you probably shouldn't have. Sister."

The Witch completed her gesture. Natasha could hear the small click as yet another projectile shot forward in the gun's chamber. Katerina stirred in her arms and made a tiny, sleepy sound.

Natasha knew that she wouldn't have more than this one chance. She was barely able to make herself let go of Katerina. But she did it. She placed her little girl softly in the snow and silently promised that she would return very soon. As soon as she was done.

She actually didn't much care right now if the Witch shot Anna. Because now she knew that it was Anna who had brought the Witch into their lives. All that time when she thought it was just Pavel's stupidity, Pavel's greed . . . It was Anna's too. That much she had understood. Because she had also watched Anna become wealthier. Had seen how there was money for a new kitchen, for the newly thatched roof, not just on the main house but also in the wing where Kirsten was going to live. She crept closer to the spot where Anna had dropped her flashlight.

"Olga, don't do it!" said Anna. It was clear she hadn't spoken Ukrainian for a long, long time. She sounded like someone in an old film.

"It's not a crime to shoot someone who is already dead," said the Witch. And at that moment, Natasha struck and felt the blow hit home, in spite of the fur hat, all the way to the frail, old eggshell skull.

The Witch fell forward, almost disappearing into the snowdrift by the gable. Natasha kneeled beside her and raised the flashlight again just to make sure.

This time no Jurij came to stop her.

ANNA STOOD IN the middle of the yard with a peculiar look on her face. At her feet crouched the dog, which had finally stopped howling. Nina didn't know if it was because it was feeling better or worse, but it wasn't dead yet.

"A syringe," she said to Anna. "Do you have one?"

Anna stared at her as if she had fallen from another planet. "Why would I have that?" she asked.

"Because I need one!"

"I don't."

"Something else. Some kind of tube. A pen."

Anna Olesen just shook her head, and Nina gave up on getting anything useful out of her. She ran up the stairs and into the house. The boiler room. A toolbox? Not a lot of slender tubes in there. The kitchen . . . She needed a knife in any case. Maybe there was a pen too.

She opened cabinets and tore out drawers and barely registered that there was already a mess that hadn't been there when they had gone out to look for Rina. Knives. Yes. Sharp enough to pierce the wall of the chest, though that in itself would not create a passage. She chose a slender, very sharp fillet knife with a patterned hilt. The blade was twelve to thirteen centimeters long—that had to be enough. The next drawer was full of spice glasses and completely useless. The next drawer . . . baking paper, tinfoil, plastic containers . . . Wasn't there a damned pen anywhere?

She looked around wildly. The seconds were passing. Her well-trained sense of time could feel them like an extra pulse, tick, tick, tick.

On the refrigerator hung a pad with a magnet and a pen on a string. Nina tore it down and took it apart with quick, sure hands. Out with the tip and the cartridge—it was only the hollow plastic part that she needed. She had her tube and her knife.

HE WAS STILL breathing—much, much too fast, and his gaze was hazier than it had been.

"Hurry," said the man who had been shot in the thigh. As if that wasn't what Nina was already doing.

She tore open the jacket and the shirt beneath it, drew a mental line from the nipple to the armpit and jabbed the knife in between the fourth and the fifth rib. It required more strength than she had anticipated. The muscles lay like tough, flat cables across the chest, and she needed to get past them and to the lung membrane—six, maybe seven centimeters. Thank God it was on the right so she didn't need to worry about the heart.

The thigh-shot man exclaimed, most likely something to the tune of, "What the hell are you doing?" She ignored him. When she pulled out the knife, there was a groaning sound of air being let loose, but only momentarily. She forced the sharp end of the pen through the cut she had made and sent a prayer to gods she didn't believe in. *Let it work.*

If her hopelessly improvised procedure worked, the air that was now trapped between the lung membranes would be released. The lung would have room to expand again, and Søren would be able to breathe.

She hadn't looked at his face at all while she did it. She had sensed his reaction to the pain, but only distantly. It had been necessary to think of his body as something mechanical, a question of tissue, anatomy and function. That perspective collapsed more quickly than his lung had when she met his gaze. It was darker than usual but already less hazy. He still needed proper drainage, oxygen and so on, and somewhere inside him was a projectile that would need to be removed. Lying on the cold ground wasn't helping him either, but right now it was too risky to move him. She had bought time; that was what was most important. Enough time, she thought.

She felt a jab in her left lower arm, and only then did she realize that she had been using it without even feeling the fracture.

She turned to the guy with the thigh wound, but he quickly held up a hand in front of himself. "Okay," he said. "I'm okay." He obviously had no wish for a taste of the Borg version of first aid.

The snow crunched. When Nina turned, she saw Natasha standing by the black BMW. Her face was so damaged that Nina only recognized her because she had Rina in her arms.

Rina. The pills. Rina.

She started to get up.

"Don't try," said Natasha. "Don't try to stop me." She opened the back door and carefully set Rina down on the seat.

"Natasha, Rina needs to go to the hospital." Nina got up, took the first step. "She has had an overdose of diazepam. Valium. She needs to be under observation; you can't . . ."

Natasha turned around and hit her straight across the mouth, a blow that hammered Nina's lips against her teeth and made her neck snap back with a whiplash jerk.

"You said, 'I'll take care.' You said, 'like my own child.' But you don't even know her right name. KA-TE-RI-NA. And you didn't take care."

"She needs treatment," Nina said. She felt the blood run down her chin on the outside and pool behind her teeth on the inside of her mouth. "Natasha, you're risking her life. She needs to be in a hospital."

Natasha shook her head stubbornly. She shoved Nina aside and went over to the third man, the one who lay on his stomach in the snow and hadn't moved at any point, even though she could hear him breathing fairly normally. Natasha rolled him onto his back. Then she kicked him in the face hard. She stuck her hands into the pockets of his overcoat and fished out a set of car keys and a wallet. A pair of black cable strips followed, but those she threw aside in the snow. She sent Nina a furious black look.

"All the time, you think, poor little Natasha, she can do nothing, she is so stupid. Poor, stupid Natasha. Beautiful and stupid, and people do what they like with her. But I'm not stupid. Katerina is *my* child. *I'll* take care now. You lose your children, but you can't take mine."

She got behind the wheel of the big BMW and drove away.

NINA SANK TO the ground next to Søren. The blood from her split lip dripped into the snow, dot, dot, dot, like the first third of a Morse code emergency signal. She observed it without emotion.

So much for Nina Borg, World Savior, she said to herself. That was that. Soon there'd be nothing left but the T-shirt. If there was one thing Natasha had managed to knock into her head with that blow, it was that she hadn't saved anyone from anything, and that there was, in fact, no one right now who wished to be saved by her. Rina was gone. Katerina, she corrected herself. You are a shitty mother even to children who don't belong to you. And flying conditions are still lousy. No help from above would be forthcoming.

She felt a hand on her ankle. It was Søren.

"Are you . . . okay?" he asked. The pause was the result of not being able to finish a whole sentence in one breath.

She looked down at him. His color was better, the lips a little less blue. He still had a hole in his lung. It was at once laughable and unbelievably touching that he was asking if *she* was okay.

She placed her hand on top of his. A little too cold, she noted, still in mild shock.

"I'm a hell of a lot healthier than you are," she said.

UKRAINE, 1935

"**E**AT!"

The lady at the end of the barrack stood with her arms folded behind her back, her eyes raking down the bench rows, and even though Olga hadn't been in the dining hall before, she immediately knew what was expected of her, and what the consequences would be if she refused. She could see it in the other children's faces; they had odd, rigid eyes and didn't look up or to the side, and she knew it from the two other orphanages she had stayed in over the course of the late summer.

What was expected of her was obedience. Nothing else. The consequences if she refused would target her body first. There would be locked doors, darkness, heat, beatings, hunger or thirst. But they might also be accompanied by humiliation. The recitation of Father's crimes against the Soviet state, or even worse, the story of Father's death on the pole where he had "howled like a dog." All the children around her were orphans like her. Children of class enemies, of the deported or just of parents who had fallen victim to hunger in the great hunger year. Still, the shame burned in her cheeks when the orphanage lady talked about her father. As if the very way that he had died was more undignified than everything else. Up against a pole. Howling like a dog. Thin and bony and beaten and toothless.

Olga shrank down over her plate and stared into the whitish-yellow mass of overcooked potatoes. The soup was covered in flies, which moved only lazily and unwillingly when she pushed at the spoon. Some remained lying there belly-up on the sticky surface, legs kicking. Olga was hungry after the trip from the station to what was called Lenin's Orphanage Nr. 4. She was someplace near a town called Odessa, she knew, but the orphanage was a lonely and windswept building stuck in the middle of the steppe, and even though there was now a touch of fall in the air, the midday heat was indescribable.

"Eat."

A sharp elbow poked her in the side, and she glanced at the girl who sat on her right, shoveling down her soup, quickly but at the same time carefully so not a drop was lost between plate and mouth. A pair of buzzing flies that were trapped in the sticky mass went right down the hatch too without the girl taking any notice.

"Eat it or let me have it," she whispered, looking impatiently at Olga. "The food will be cleared away in five minutes."

Olga's stomach growled a warning, unwilling to accept her indecisiveness, and she breathed deeply. She scraped some of the wriggling flies off the soup and brushed them off the spoon with her index finger. The first spoonful was the worst, but afterward it went pretty well. She took a mouthful and let it glide down her throat in one rapid movement, so that she didn't have time to either taste or feel it in her throat. Her benchmate followed her spoon with hungry eyes, but when Olga had scraped her plate completely clean, the girl took the time to examine Olga.

"What's your name?" she whispered.

"Oletchka," said Olga. That's what it said in her papers now.

"Did you just arrive?"

Olga nodded but wasn't sure she felt like doing this. She had already met and said goodbye to lots of girls since they had come to take her away from home.

It was the day after they had driven off with Mother. Olga had slept alone in the summer darkness the last night and had lain listening to the grasshoppers and the crickets that chirped in the grass outside in the overgrown garden. Mother hadn't touched the vegetable plot since Oxana and Kolja died, and through all of July she had just sat on the crumbling clay bench under the porch roof in front of the house, staring into space. Sometimes, not very often, she cried. Other times she asked Olga to sing, and Olga sang quietly and softly, almost as if it were a lullaby, and if she sang long enough, Mother might make a faint grimace which looked like a smile and say that she sang almost as beautifully as Oxana. Her daughter and the people's nightingale.

Uncle Grachev and Grandmother and Grandfather Trofimenko had been shot in the square where the statue of Oxana was to be erected, but neither Mother nor Olga talked about that during the dark summer nights. In fact, they didn't speak at all. The neighbors took turns bringing them a little food. Mother didn't eat anything much, but Olga took what she could get. And waited for something to change. For Mother to either die or get up again so that life could go on. But neither one happened. They just came to get her one day and said she had to be in a hospital because she was ill, and the day after, they also picked up Olga and drove her to the first of the orphanages. She was there for ten days. She lived in the next home for almost a month, and now she was here. With a new lot of strange children. Olga lowered her head, but the girl next to her wasn't put off that easily.

"Were your parents enemies of the people, or are they just dead?"

"Both, I think. I don't really know. My sister was a hero."

The girl stared at her with renewed interest. "What do you mean?"

"My sister is the People's Nightingale. They've erected a statue of her in the square in Sorokivka."

The girls sitting around them turned toward her, and Olga felt small and miserable and much too visible at the long table.

"I've heard of her," said one of the girls, her eyes narrowed. "There's a song about her. She reported her father for stealing grain."

It got completely silent, and Olga followed the skinny little flies wandering across her underarm. Didn't know what more she should say.

"But if she was your sister . . ." said a girl, hesitating. She sat right across from Olga. She was a little older, maybe thirteen, with a broad face and black eyes. Probably a Tartar from the Crimea. Olga had seen them at the market back when they were still living in Kharkiv. "You're full of lies," the Tartar girl continued. "Because if your sister is the People's Nightingale, then why are you here?"

"I don't know," mumbled Olga and wished she was just as dead as the rest of the world from which she came. "But I can sing too. I can sing 'Zelene Zhyto'—about the green, green wheat."

"By heart?"

The girl's tone seemed to Olga a bit more friendly, and almost against her own will, Olga felt herself grasp at that kindness, cling to it.

"Yes," she said. "I know a lot of songs by heart."

T HE WORLD WAS so damned small when you thought about it. Where could you live in peace? Was there a place anywhere where you could hide forever? Not in Denmark, at least, thought Natasha, and especially not now.

She let a finger run across Katerina's soft white forehead. She had fallen asleep again, on the worn sofa in front of the stove. The warmth in the living room had loosened her shoulders, so that she now lay like an infant with her arms stretched above her head, hands open and unclenched. Her hair was still damp from the bath, and her cheeks and lips blushed in the heat, ruddy and full of life. Right now Natasha was the only one on guard.

She had stolen a new car before she crossed the bridge to Malmö in Sweden, and with Jurij's money she had bought two frozen bags of corned beef hash in the tiny supermarket they had passed on their way north. Katerina had thrown up twice but had otherwise slept most of the way. The Danish blizzard had not come this way, and after a few hours on fairly clear roads, Natasha had found a dark farm that sat abandoned and neglected under the black pines. It was not a vacation home of the kind the Danes bought and upgraded with heated floors and running water. Here, the old furniture was covered in dust sheets, and it smelled of pine and soot from the oven and of the old people who had lived here once but were now gone. On a gas burner in the tiny, claustrophobic kitchen, Natasha had heated water so she could wash both Katerina and herself, and when she let the water trickle down Katerina's forehead, she felt almost like she had that morning many years ago when she had stood next to Pavel watching the priest do the same.

They were together, and everything could begin again.

Tomorrow they needed to move on. Through Finland and across the enormous expanses of Russia until they found a corner that was remote enough. Heat billowed from the cast-iron stove in the small, overly furnished living room and made Natasha sleepy, but there were things she needed to do before she could lie down next to Katerina and close her eyes.

She stuck her hand into Katerina's pocket and fished out Pavel's old cell phone. With a broken fingernail, she carefully removed the plastic cover on one side and plucked out the memory stick from the derelict phone. She transferred it to Robbie's little Sony Ericsson and promised herself that this was the last time she was going to use it. Tomorrow she had to get a new one.

The display lit up, and she tapped her way through the menus to the pictures, texts and recordings that were saved on the stick.

With one hand on Katerina's arm, she listened carefully to the scratched recordings, the voices that rose and fell.

If you were going to be invisible and untouchable in the world, you needed money, she knew that now. But you couldn't allow yourself to get greedy or careless, like Pavel. He was the stupid one. Not beautiful Natasha.

The voices on the recording sang in her ears, telling stories people would prefer to forget, and as Natasha felt sleep moving in on her, she hung on to the little phone and reassurance it gave her: once again, she had a future.

They would make it, Katerina and she. They would want for nothing.

I T HAD TAKEN a long time for winter to loosen its grip, and it had also taken awhile before the hospital let him go. But now most of the snow had melted, and Søren was gradually beginning his rehabilitation.

There was a FOR SALE sign from one of North Zealand's fancy real estate agents at the entrance to Tundra Lane, but it wasn't Michael Vestergaard's house, it turned out. It was Anna Olesen's thatched yellow farm.

Søren parked the Hyundai next to Anna's red Mazda. There were pools of melted snow between the cobbles, and crocuses blooming along the house.

It's been two whole months, he said to himself. It's a completely different place now.

Still, he could feel his body's discomfort at being here. This is where you get hurt, it shouted. This is where the pain is!

The old woman who had shot him had been found in a snowdrift by the house's gable with extensive injuries after a series of hard blows to the temple and the back of the head. She had later been transferred to a hospital in Kiev with astounding haste. It was clear that her condition was so serious that it made no sense to prosecute her, but still the case had gone unusually smoothly, Søren observed dryly. You could not say the same for Jurij Savchuk's case. He was still stuck in Vestre Prison, awaiting his Danish trial, and no one in Ukraine had expressed any desire to get him back. Apparently not even his squeaky-clean half brother, Babko had reported. Søren and he had called each other a few times to exchange reports and health bulletins.

There was barking from the front hallway. The dog appeared to have survived.

Anna opened the door. She didn't look quite like herself. It took him a few minutes to realize that she wasn't wearing any makeup. The eyes were older and more tired, the hair less carefully arranged.

"Is it you?" she said without curiosity. "What do you want? More questions?"

"Not really," he said. "I came to tell you something."

She didn't move, clearly preferring for him not to come inside.

"We haven't been able to find either Natasha or Katerina," he said. "And so we haven't been able to ask Katerina what happened that Sunday. We don't know where they are. We don't know how they are doing. We have no idea whether they are still alive."

"That's sad."

"Yes, we are not happy about it. But we have found a witness that saw Katerina get into a red car not far from Damhus Lake." This was a bit of an exaggeration. The witness had seen "a child who could be Katerina" and the description of the car was equally vague—it was red.

Anna didn't move a muscle. She didn't even glance at the Mazda, which Søren had kind of hoped she would. It would have been a lovely, unconscious confirmation.

"Why are you telling me that?" she asked.

"Because I do believe that children can grieve. I do think an eight-year-old girl can miss her dead father terribly. She would probably also be able to buy the juice and cookies herself, in spite of the fact that we haven't been able to find a store with anyone who remembers seeing her. But there's one thing I don't believe. And that is that she would steal a bottle of Valium and try to kill herself."

Anna Olesen observed him for a long time. Then she closed the door. After a little while, she opened it again.

"I would appreciate it if you would get off my property," she said. "If there is anything else you feel you have to tell me, you can contact my lawyer."

Søren remained standing there for a little while, just to irritate her.

ON THE WAY home, he called Nina.

"Did she say anything?" Nina asked.

"Not a word. Not a useful word, at any rate."

"Do you still believe she did it?"

"Yes."

"Why? Why would she hurt the child? As far as we know, they had a good relationship."

"I don't know. I'm just sure that she did it. Maybe Katerina posed a threat to her—a connection between her and Pavel Doroshenko's dangerous blackmail. I've spoken to her daughter, Kirsten. She had 'no plans whatsoever to move into that wing Anna was restoring and had, in fact, asked her not to do it. She was afraid her mother's finances wouldn't be able to cover the expenses, but that doesn't appear to have been a problem. On the other hand, there aren't a lot of bills for the work that was done."

"Off the books?"

"A good way to place money if you can't really explain where it comes from."

"I still don't understand it. There's a long way from a bit of blackmail to . . . to an attempted child murder."

"Katerina called her. Anna came and picked her up in her red car.

Together they went out to Katerina's nest and had that peculiar tea party, with juice in the cups. Katerina's cup contained pulverized Valium. In Katerina's head, they were having a party with her father. Who knows? Maybe Anna was even able to make herself believe that it was for the best. That the child would be spared any more pain, and all that."

"They spoke Ukrainian together," said Nina suddenly. "On the telephone when Rina called Anna. Can that have been enough? Enough to make Rina dangerous for her, I mean?"

Søren considered Anna Olesen's almost perfect Hørsholm façade. She hadn't been able to help herself, he thought. She wanted so very badly to speak to the child, and in the beginning that would only have been possible in Ukrainian. In Anna's eyes, this exposure must have seemed terrifying when she realized that her past was catching up with her.

"I can see how it might look that way to her," he said.

Nina was quiet for a while. "It did seem to me . . ." she said, then broke off.

"What?"

"When we were searching for Rina. Katerina, I mean. In hindsight, I think Anna was trying to make sure I wouldn't find Katerina too soon. She made no effort to tell the dog to search, for instance."

Søren sighed. "Could you swear to that?"

"Not really. It was more of a vague impression."

"Not conclusive."

"No."

Another silence.

"Will you go out there again?" asked Nina.

"Yes," he admitted. "In a little while."

"Do you think she'll say something sooner or later?"

"Not really."

"Why do it, then?"

"Because she needs to know that someone is watching her."

He could almost see her shake her head. "You're not God."

He laughed. "No, unfortunately not."

There was another short pause. Ask her, he told himself.

She said goodbye. He cursed. She had saved his life—wasn't he allowed to ask the woman out to dinner in return? But he didn't do it. Maybe it was because he still remembered with crystal clarity the moment where his crappy middle-aged knee had cracked so loudly that both Babko and he had been shot as a result.

Maybe he needed to find someone his own age.

And maybe he needed a bigger car.

MAGNUS HAD MET someone else. Nina listened distractedly to his careful and considerate explanations, the great respect he had for her as a person and a colleague, how happy he had been that they had been able to help each other through a difficult time, and so on. The concern lines on his friendly dog's face were incredibly deep.

The window was open, and a scent of loam and rain and spring in the air drifted into the apartment's tiny kitchen. In the evening darkness, you could hear the protracted metallic noise from a freight train passing down on the tracks. Nina poked at the rice from the Thai food he had brought—chicken cashew—while she considered how long she needed to let him talk before she could decently interrupt him.

"I'm handing in my notice," she finally said, when the considerate explanations showed no sign of ceasing.

He was jolted, and in his confusion he pushed his glasses into his hair. They were crooked, she noticed, and made the blond Swedish locks stand straight up.

"You don't need to do that," he said. "I mean . . . I'm sure we can figure it out, and if we can't, then I'm the one who'll look for another job."

It took her a moment to realize he thought she was giving notice because of him.

She couldn't help laughing. That didn't make him any less confused, she could see.

"Magnus, damn it," she said. "We're not exactly Romeo and Juliet, are we? I'm not planning to keel over dead on your grave."

"*Jag förstår inte,*" he said, suddenly slipping into Swedish in his total perplexity. "I don't get it."

She spelled it out for him. "I've thought about it for more than a month," she said. "And I've made my decision, so all you need to do is say 'okay' and 'too bad' and then wish me luck in my new future."

"But why?"

She shook her head. "I'm not sure I can explain it. Partly it's because I've come to realize that I'm no longer the same person I was when I took the job. I can't keep defining myself as the one who has to save everyone else."

He took off his glasses and started to polish them with a corner of his shirt. He observed her for a long time, but it wasn't uncomfortable. Then he smiled.

"And here I sat explaining and explaining," he said. "Were you listening at all?"

"Some of the time."

"Okay. I'm . . . I'm going to miss you. In several ways. What do you want to do next?"

"I don't know yet."

"You're not applying for another of those hellhole missions you used to do, are you?"

She shook her head. "That would be a step in the wrong direction, don't you think?"

"Yes."

"Who is she, your new love?"

"Do you really want to know, or are you just being polite?"

She snorted and took a sip of her wine instead of answering.

He got up. "Do you have a date in mind?" he asked.

"May first. But I've done a lot of overtime, so it'll actually be in a couple of weeks."

He gave her a long hug on the way out the door. "Take care of yourself," he said.

"You too."

WHEN HE HAD left, she felt a relief so intense, it was almost as if she were weightless. As if her feet's contact with the kitchen floor was a completely voluntary condition. She went over to close the small window overlooking the railroad tracks, then remained standing, looking down at the lamps along the park path, where a lone jogger came running, slap, slap, slap, along the asphalt ribbon under the blooming trees. She took her cell phone out of her pocket and called Morten's number.

"I quit my job," she said without preamble.

It took awhile for him to answer. "What does that mean?"

"How hard is it to understand? I've given notice at the Coal-House Camp."

"Where are you going now?"

"Nowhere! I just thought . . . I could find something where there would be more time for the kids. Something less hectic."

There was a faint click. He had hung up.

She stared at the telephone. Didn't understand. She had thought he would be . . . maybe not exactly happy, but less cranky. Less annoyed with her.

The telephone rang. Now he was the one who didn't say hello.

"Why now?" he asked, and his voice was so angry, it shook. "Why not one of the approximately six hundred times when I asked you to? One of the times when it would have meant something?"

"I thought you would be . . ."

"Yes. Sorry." He sighed. The anger left his voice as quickly as it had arrived. "Nina, I know it's not your fault, or not just your fault. When I think about what happened with your dad, when I think about the fact that you were younger than Ida is now . . . I can't begin to imagine how someone could make it through something like that in one piece. You are as you are, and . . . and there are many good things about that. But I don't want to renegotiate our agreement and offer the kids the possibility of something more, just because you've suddenly had the idea that you want to be more of a mother to them. And besides . . ."

"Besides what?"

"No. We'd better talk about that another day, when I know more."

"Morten. You can't just say something like that and then leave it there."

The relief had abruptly disappeared. There was nothing weightless about her whatsoever. What was he going to say? Something about the kids? He had spoken of moving, she suddenly remembered. That terrible Sunday. *Far enough away to save the kids from your war zone.* Was that it?

"Are you moving?" she asked.

"I don't know. Nina, there's no reason to talk about it now. I shouldn't have brought it up."

"They are my kids too," she said and hated the meekness that had entered her voice. As if she wasn't sure it was true.

"Yes," he said. "I've been thinking a lot about that lately."

"Morten . . ."

"Good night, Nina. I didn't mean to worry you. Forget it."

SHE LAY IN her bed with the window open just a crack. The alarm clock's large numbers shone in the dark: 2:12.

Okay, she said to herself. So it isn't going to be as easy as you thought. So what? Aren't you supposed to be the great crisis queen?

The clock's digits changed with a barely audible click—2:13.

She rolled out of bed, slowly and deliberately, and padded barefoot into the hall, to the closet where the toolbox was. She chose the bigger and heavier of the two hammers and placed it on the kitchen table. The next step was to carry one of the kitchen chairs into the bedroom so she could take the clock down from the hook on the wall.

There was no reason to get glass all over the place, so she wrapped a kitchen towel around the clock before she placed it in the sink and calmly and methodically proceeded to smash it.

She didn't know how long it took. Nor did she know what time it was when she went back to bed awhile later and eventually fell asleep.

"**S**HE IS SO small," he says, and there's a frustrated tenderness in his voice. "So small that you think you can pick her up in one hand. But you can't."

The lights are low; the machines are humming quietly. This is not one of Kiev's overpopulated public hospitals. Here, nothing is lacking.

The doctor clears his throat. "She's not young," he says. "And the risk of operating yet again . . . I hope you understand how great it is. It's a minor miracle that she is still alive. But that's the way some people are—the heart just goes on and on."

"Do you think she can hear us?"

"You're welcome to try speaking to her. She is unconscious. We've recovered more than twenty skull fragments from her brain by now, and there is no doubt that certain areas have suffered permanent damage. I honestly don't know how much more we can do."

"You have to try." It's not a request; it is an order, and that is how the doctor hears it.

"Yes, sir," he says.

"You don't know my mother, you don't know how strong her will is. If anyone can survive this, she can. She's not afraid of battle or of pain."

"I can assure you, there is no pain, not now."

"But . . . she's still there, right? There are still thoughts and dreams and memories in there?"

The doctor places a gentle hand on his elbow. "Even if we manage to wake her up, you can't expect her to be the same. The damage is too extensive."

SHE SEES ALL of this from above. Looks down at Nikolaij, her beloved Kolja, as if she was standing in a tower. It is that tenderness. That admiration she cannot do without. She might have been willing to let the rest of the world think what it likes about both the past and the present, if not for him. He has to love her. For his sake, for the sake of that love, she will not let anybody drag her name through the mud. The lies, the secrets, those many, many songs of betrayal, Kalugin's bloody nightingale . . . all that must stay where it belongs, in the tangled, filthy darkness of the past. She will not let it touch him. Whatever the cost, he must not learn the truth.

Then she falls down. Not into her body, but in the darkness of memories, where old ghosts rise from the grave and will not let you be. She can't eat, speak, move; she has a tube in her mouth and another up her ass. Most of the time she can neither see nor hear. But in the darkness she remembers.

UKRAINE, 1934

"WHERE IS YOUR devil of a sister?"

Olga opened her eyes just as a huge hand hit her roughly on the side of the head. She attempted to roll away from the next blow and to sit up at the same time. Attempted to get free of sleep's clutches. It took a long moment before she realized that the man standing in front of her wasn't Father but a man that she had said hello to only a few times down by the cooperative shop. Sergej's father. Fedir's uncle. He wasn't a big man. A bit bent and scarred, like his son.

He looked angry but for some reason Olga was sure that he had just been crying. It was something about his eyes and voice, which was thick and soft as if he had coated his throat with oil.

She didn't dare say anything because the man clearly wasn't normal. Men didn't usually cry. Not in that way, in any case. Olga crept even closer to the wall and pulled the blanket all the way up to her chin, staring at him all the while.

"Fedir is dead," said the man. He seemed to be mostly telling himself. One tear had made it all the way to his frost-cracked lips and hung there for a moment like a small, clear pearl. Then he sniffed. "Tell me. Tell me where she is, that little bitch of an informer."

Fedir. She remembered the infatuated puppy eyes he had made at Oxana the day the GPU officers evicted them from the house and sent them off to Siberia in a freight car. Now he had died somewhere out there, like the little girl with the hare-like cry, and that's why Sergej's father was standing here, shaking her with red, wet hands.

Olga felt a watery fear in her stomach. A nauseating lurch that went both up and down at the same time, so that something loosened in her bowels. And yet there was, somewhere behind the fear, a sense of unholy scarlet glee. At last, Oxana would be punished. Punished for everything she had done.

"Oxana usually walks along the stream on her way home from school," she said quickly. "She's probably on her way home already."

Sergej's father let her go, without a word, without a look. He left the door open on its hinges when he walked out, and Olga lay motionless for a long time, watching as his tracks slowly filled with snow.

ACKNOWLEDGMENTS

IN THE COURSE of the creation of *Death of a Nightingale*, we have come across questions that we couldn't answer ourselves—just as we did with our other books. How do you handle a frozen corpse, what is the PET's department for the Prevention of Organized Crime in common parlance, and how do you say "Where is the toilet?" in Ukrainian? Luckily, we have once again had many, many kind, helpful and wise people to advise us along the way, and with their aid, we hope we've been saved from the worst mistakes. A special thank-you also to family and friends, who again have taken the time to read, encourage and take care of dogs and children when things got hectic.

Thank you:
Nina Gladkowa Johansen
Lone-emilie Rasmussen
Hans Jørgen Bonnichsen
Vladimir Stolba
Henrik Laier
Gustav Friis
Kirstine Friis
Else Rognan
Inger Møller
Marie Friis
Lars Ringhof
Anders and Louise Trolle
Esthi Kunz
Lisbeth Møller-Madsen
Eva Kaaberbøl
Anita Frank
Inga og Henrik Friis
Lotte Krarup

Bibs Carlsen

Inger Johanne and Jakob Ravn

Knud-Erik Kjær Madsen

Erling Kaaberbøl

Lasse Bork Schmidt and Martin Kjær Madsen of SustainAgri

—and thank you also to our Ukrainian friends who have wished to remain anonymous. You know who you are.